Grant Wins the War

Grant Wins the War

Decision at Vicksburg

James R. Arnold

John Wiley & Sons, Inc.

New York • Chichester • Weinheim • Brisbane • Singapore • Toronto

Copyright © 1997 by James R. Arnold.
Published by John Wiley & Sons, Inc.

Maps © 1997 by D. L. McElhannon

Library of Congress Cataloging-in-Publication Data

Arnold, James R.
    Grant wins the war : decision at Vicksburg / James R. Arnold.
       p. cm.
    Includes index.
    ISBN 0-471-15727-9 (cloth : alk. paper)
      1. Vicksburg (Miss.)—History—Siege, 1863. 2. Grant, Ulysses S. (Ulysses Simpson), 1822–1885. 3. Strategy. I. Title.
    E475.27.A75   1997
    973.7'344—dc21   96-53871

To my wife, Roberta

Contents

Maps

Acknowledgments

A WORD IS IN ORDER about language, and then a few more—although volumes are needed—about the people who contributed to this book.

The quotes contained in what follows are as the words originally appeared. I have avoided the term "Yankee" whenever describing something from the Union perspective. Grant's soldiers did not think of themselves as "Yankees"—it was a term they understood to apply to New Englanders—but rather as westerners. The Confederates, who wore the label "rebel" with pride, did not differentiate: their foes were Yankees one and all.

I gratefully wish to thank Mr. And Mrs. Robert C. Arnold for their work at Vicksburg; Jon Bigler for his help at the Virginia Historical Society; Gordon Cotton at the Old Court House Museum, Vicksburg; Pam Cheney, David Keogh, John Slonaker, and Richard Sommers at the Military History Institute, Carlisle, Pennsylvania; Jim Gullickson, who provided diligent copyediting; Grace McCrowell, who processed my interlibrary loan request at the Rockbridge Regional Library; David McElhannon for his cartographic work; Ralph Reinertsen, who helped research several complex issues; the librarians and helpful staff at the University of Virginia, Virginia Military Institute, and Washington and Lee University; Terry Winschel at Vicksburg National Military Park, who kindly opened his archives and answered many questions; Matt Bialer, my agent, whose diligence found a home for this book; Hana Lane, who had the confidence to initiate this project; and Roberta Wiener, my chief of staff, wife, and soul mate.

Prologue

THE TALL, GANGLY MAN stooped to point to the map. It was the war's second year, 1862, and the Federal commander in chief was beginning to realize that if the rebellion was to be suppressed, he needed to assume a more active role in devising grand strategy. "See what a lot of land these fellows hold," he said, "of which Vicksburg is the key. Here is Red River, which will supply the Confederates with cattle and corn to feed their armies. There are the Arkansas and White Rivers, which can supply cattle and hogs by the thousand. From Vicksburg these supplies can be distributed by rail all over the Confederacy."

The speaker warmed to his subject. During his youth he had passed through this country, and assured his audience that he knew of what he spoke. Vicksburg meant "hog and hominy without limit," fresh enemy soldiers from the territory west of the river, and a cotton country where the rebels could plant without disturbance. President Abraham Lincoln concluded, "Let us get Vicksburg and all that country is ours. The war can never be brought to a close until that key is in our pocket."[1]

More than a year later, a volunteer Union army of midwestern men and boys fought and won a battle that drove the Confederates into Vicksburg's fortifications and assured its inevitable surrender. After the battle, fought on May 16, 1863, at a place called Champion Hill, the South could no longer win the war through their own generals' initiative. There could be spectacular rebel exploits, but, as a Louisiana officer wrote at the time, in the final analysis even Robert E Lee's Gettysburg campaign was nothing more than "raids on a grand scale, having no decisive results."[2] Champion Hill reduced Confederate president Jefferson Davis to reliance upon Union bungling or Northern war weariness to confer Southern independence. If a decisive battle is defined as one in which a nation fatally wounds its foe, Champion Hill was indeed a decisive engagement.

At the time, military operations elsewhere obscured the battle's importance. Most significantly, the Vicksburg campaign coincided with the Chancellorsville-Gettysburg campaigns in the East. Those campaigns featured the war's most publicized armies. Since they took place in the corridor between the warring nations' rival capitals, political and newspaper attention concentrated on them. To those living along the Atlantic seaboard, what took place in distant Mississippi paled in comparison.

Major General Ulysses S. Grant captured Vicksburg on July 4, 1863. The Battle of Gettysburg had ended the previous day. Then and thereafter, Gettysburg overwhelmed Vicksburg in popular attention. Following the war, the veterans' memoirs of the great struggle in the East received national and international circulation via New York and Boston publishing houses. General Robert E. Lee became first a Southern and then a national icon as tales of his dauntless Army of Northern Virginia spread. Likewise, Lee's opponent, the Army of the Potomac, became a venerated institution. The myth grew that Virginia was the war's decisive theater, where American military professionalism shone most brilliantly, while, in contrast, the war in the West was a less important, decidedly amateur affair. The fact that far more West Point graduates served in the East than the West, and that their published accounts greatly outnumbered those of westerners, contributed to this view. With first the contemporary media's eastern focus and then the postwar articles and books, the basis for all subsequent history was set.

Today the American Civil War remains an amazingly popular subject. Yet even among Civil War buffs, few people know the name of the army Grant took to Vicksburg or have heard about the battle of Champion Hill. Almost no one would call it the war's decisive battle. As is often the case, perspective comes from outsiders. In 1929, a British officer named J. F. C. Fuller took a break from his musings on mechanized warfare—musings that some forward-thinking German officers honed into a blitzkrieg doctrine that later threatened to conquer a continent—to turn his attention to the American Civil War. Fuller concluded that "Vicksburg, and not Gettysburg, was the crisis of the Confederacy."[3]

Few subsequent historians have attended to Fuller's words. But his assertion merits serious consideration. Grant's victory at Champion Hill permanently separated Vicksburg's garrison from outside help. Once Grant invested Vicksburg, its surrender became merely a matter of time. The only other Confederate stronghold on the Mississippi River could not, and did not, stand once Vicksburg fell. Some 37,000 Confederates surrendered during that July summer along the Mississippi. After securing the river, the Union host turned east to campaign against the South's heartland. To defend it, the South, in the absence of the rich resources of the Trans-Mississippi—the "hog and hominy without limit" that Lincoln had described in 1862—had to rely upon a much attenuated logistical base. It proved inadequate. More importantly, the South fought with a people grown demoralized by the knowledge that the enemy had cut their country in half.

Only one more time after Champion Hill did a major Confederate army fight a successful offensive battle. Thereafter, Grant and Major General William Sherman—the heroes of Vicksburg—collaborated in a grand offensive to which the South had no answer. In 1864, the combination of logistics and Grant's unrelenting pressure kept Lee's Army of Northern Virginia from delivering an offensive rejoinder to the Army of the Potomac's implacable advance. Forced into a static position, Lee could only sit helplessly and watch while the war was lost elsewhere. The victors' drums at Champion Hill had sounded the death knell of the Confederacy.

Admiral George Dewey, the hero of Manila Bay in the war against Spain, and whose ship was sunk beneath him during the Vicksburg campaign, observed that "success always makes success seem easy."[4] Indeed, Grant's victory at Vicksburg was neither easy nor inevitable. He began his campaign at a time of deep Northern despondency, his own career hanging in the balance. In a contest of leadership and strategy pitting Lincoln, Grant, and two U.S. Navy officers versus Davis and his handpicked defenders of Vicksburg, Grant conceived one of the great campaigns in military history. It was one of only two Civil War campaigns worthy of comparison to those of Napoléon.

For more than one hundred years after Napoléon's death, men related military theory and practice to Napoléon's concepts of warmaking and measured ideas and performance against his standards. Thomas "Stonewall" Jackson's Shenandoah Valley campaign and Grant's Vicksburg campaign achieved the mark. Emulating Napoléon's belief that it was better to drive one's soldiers on long marches in order to spare lives once battle began, the Valley and Vicksburg campaigns featured rapid marching. The Virginia scene of Jackson, wearing an ill-fitting uniform and battered kepi, urging his hard-toiling soldiers to "Press on, men; press on," finds a lesser-known echo when Grant, wearing a simple, dust-stained uniform with an untidy slouch hat, is seen outside of Port Gibson, Mississippi, saying, "Men, push right along; close up fast, and hurry on."[5] Both Jackson and Grant employed forced marches to occupy a central position between wings of the opponent's army—Napoléon's cherished maneuver—and both then turned to lash out in one direction and then in another. They used concentrated force to deliver telling blows against a dispersed foe.

While comparison to Napoléon can only stand up for so long—Grant's genius never shone so brightly as during that fateful April and May of 1863, whereas Napoléon's martial genius dominated European battlefields for close to two decades—the Vicksburg campaign exhibited several other Napoleonic features. Grant undergirded his campaign with careful logistical preparation. When he massed for battle he brought every available soldier to the field, sublimating those secondary considerations that so often consumed the attention and resources of weaker generals. He assessed the capabilities of the opposing commanders when planning his campaign. Sensing weakness and indecision, Grant took even bolder risks. He accepted war's uncertainty by flexibly adjusting to new circumstances while maintaining a determined focus on the main chance. Lastly, much like Napoléon before his greatest victory, at Austerlitz, six days before Champion Hill Grant predicted that "many days cannot elapse before the battle will begin which is to decide the fate of Vicksburg."[6]

Grant's strategy brought two armies in collision atop Champion Hill. Many common soldiers, North and South, realized at the time what was at stake, that they were caught up in something bigger than themselves. They risked their lives' blood to resolve the battle for Vicksburg. This book honors their sacrifice.

Part 1

Father of Waters

1

Battles on the River

The forts can be passed, and we have done it, and can do it again as often as may be required . . . It will not, however, be an easy matter for us to do more . . . as long as the enemy has a large force behind the hills to prevent our landing and holding the place.

—Rear Admiral David Farragut, July 2, 1862
(quoted in *Battles and Leaders of the Civil War*, vol. 3)

THE SPRING MORNING OF MAY 10, 1862, found the United States ironclad *Cincinnati* tied to trees along the shore of the Mississippi River thirty-five miles upriver from Memphis. To date the campaign had been going well. During the preceding days, Federal mortar scows had been bombarding Fort Pillow. It seemed a mere matter of time before their thirteen-inch mortars fired enough two-hundred-pound shells to reduce the Confederate fortification to rubble. Then the Union navy could continue its downriver offensive and bring the rebel fleet to battle. Meanwhile, the *Cincinnati*, along with a squadron of six ironclads, would guard the mortar fleet should the rebels be foolish enough to appear.

For most of the past month, rival vessels had sighted one another and exchanged some inconclusive long-range fire. But the Union fleet included the Western Flotilla and its ironclad gunboats, while the Confederate force was a mere collection of Mississippi River steamers. Given such a mismatch, no Federal sailor took seriously reports from civilians warning that the rebels planned an attack. Aboard the *Cincinnati* sailors were busy holystoning her decks when, just after 6:30 A.M., someone noticed boats rounding the bend downriver and closing fast. It was the Confederate River Defense Fleet.

Leading the way was the side-wheel steamer *General Bragg*, a giant bow wave indicating that she was pushing hard. In spite of the fact that they were operating in the known presence of the enemy, no Union ironclad, including the flag-steamer, had sufficient steam up to maneuver. The *Cincinnati*'s crew unmoored the boat while her engineers frantically threw oil and anything else that could burn quickly into the furnaces. She was barely under way when the *General Bragg*, propelled at ten knots speed by her great walking-beam engine, rammed and tore a gaping hole in her shell room. As water flooded in, two more Confederate vessels rammed the stricken *Cincinnati*. The Union ironclad rolled one way, then the other, and sank.

The River Defense Fleet, minus two rams disabled by their first blows, continued upriver to encounter another ironclad steaming slowly to assist the *Cincinnati*. The rebel ram *General Van Dorn* struck her such a blow that she barely managed to run her bow onto shore before settling in the water. When more Union boats appeared and began to hit the unarmored steamers with their heavy guns, the Confederates withdrew. They took satisfaction from the knowledge that by sinking two enemy ironclads they had dealt their adversaries a telling blow. During the entire hour-and-ten-minute action only four of the seven woefully unprepared Federal ironclads managed to engage. For the Confederates it was an exhilarating success, but one not to be repeated.

Indeed, the Civil War showed that the Confederate navy, utilizing pluck and surprise, could damage or sink U.S. Navy ships during the first encounter.[1] However, once alerted, the Federals could bring superior force to bear. That such a force was available on the Mississippi River was due to the efforts of two supremely patriotic and farsighted men, James B. Eads and Charles Ellet.

Eads was a well-known riverman and civil engineer. When the war began, he traveled to Washington to tell the authorities how he could build gunboats that would take the Mississippi River from the Confederacy. The combination of the navy's focus on the blue-water campaign to blockade Southern ports and narrow-minded bureaucrats almost thwarted him, but finally Eads prevailed. Naval Constructor Samuel Pook designed giant ironclads, purposely built for riverine combat. The design was a radical departure from anything previously launched, featuring broad-beamed, flat-bottomed hulls atop which sat slanting casemates sheathed in iron. A center-wheel, twin-engine propulsion system drove the boats. Eads was low bidder on the contract to build them, and pledged to finish the job in sixty-three days or face stiff financial penalties.

The prewar implausibility that warships would ever be needed on the nation's inland waters meant that there were no existing warship-building facilities. Geographic isolation from the East also forced Eads to create and improvise. Eads contacted foundries, rolling mills, and machine shops from Pittsburgh to St. Louis to provide armor and engines. Thirteen sawmills in Missouri, Illinois, Kentucky, and Ohio worked exclusively cutting and shaping white oak to build the vessels' frameworks. Naval depots on the Great Lakes delivered more than seventy nine-inch Dahlgren smoothbore cannon along with assorted eight-inch and thirty-two-pounder ordnance. The army pledged thirty-five forty-two-pounder rifled cannon. The guns required special carriages of top-quality seasoned oak, a job undertaken by the Eagle Iron Works of Cincinnati. Eads himself coordinated the work via telegraph, chasing down special machine items while supervising a skilled labor force of more than eight hundred men who worked in shifts around the clock. Simultaneously, and in sharp contrast, along the rivers to the south, Confederate naval officers were struggling in makeshift drydocks to fasten unshaped railroad iron onto cut-down, leaky vessels powered by wheezy, unreliable engines.

When launched in October 1861—a tad late but an amazing performance nonetheless—Eads's ironclads collectively were dubbed "Pook Turtles" because of their unique design and slow speed. A Union sailor described them as belonging to "the Mudturtle school of architecture."[2] Experience would show that enemy shot glanced off their sides, but that plunging shot fired from guns sited on the river bluffs penetrated into their bowels. In addition to the Pook Turtles, Eads converted one of his salvage boats into the *Benton*, an enormous 200-by-75-foot, two-hulled ironclad with a huge paddle wheel that churned between the two hulls. Eads's boats were built well enough that the navy was able to salvage the two ironclads sunk by the Confederate rams near Fort Pillow. And, fortunately, reinforcements for the Western Flotilla were on the way in the form of an army officer and his personal fleet.

The soldier was Charles Ellet. An imaginative civil engineer, Ellet had spent his prewar years unsuccessfully contending with an indifferent bureaucracy in an effort to interest the navy in the practical implications of the mathematical equation that states force equals mass times velocity squared. Ellet believed in the superiority of rams as naval vessels, particularly on rivers where an enemy could not dodge. With civil war looming, Ellet sent a pamphlet explaining his theories to the War Department. Secretary of War Edwin Stanton summoned him to Washington, listened, made him an army colonel, and told him to build as many rams as were necessary to drive the rebels from the Mississippi. Ellet used his special commission to purchase some one dozen miscellaneous craft. He achieved his desired velocity by installing powerful engines capable of propelling the rams at a speed of fifteen knots. He achieved mass by packing their bows with lumber and running three one-foot-thick bulkheads the length of their hulls so as to deliver a blow with a whole rigid unit. The Ellet rams carried no artillery but instead relied exclusively upon high-speed shock action. For officers he chose men who shared one characteristic, the last name Ellet, including his nineteen-year-old son. He tried to crew his rams with handpicked, daredevil volunteers and set off to spearhead, literally, the naval advance down the Mississippi.

That the strengthened Union fleet overmatched its enemy was demonstrated on June 6, when the rival navies collided on the Memphis riverfront to determine who would control a long stretch of water from Memphis downstream. In contrast to the Federal buildup, the Confederate River Defense Fleet had received no reinforcements. One ironclad lay unfinished in a Memphis boatyard. A second, named the *Arkansas*, had been floated downstream so she could be completed in safety. Nonetheless, the Confederate rams sortied to challenge the oncoming Union vessels.

Having learned caution, flag officer Charles H. Davis slowly marshaled his ironclads and prepared to engage. Meanwhile, aboard his ram *Queen of the West*, Colonel Ellet heard the first gun and exclaimed to his brother aboard the *Monarch*, "It is a gun from the enemy! Round out and follow me! Now is our chance."[3] Racing past the ironclads, Ellet proceeded to give a practical demonstration of the relationship between force, mass, and velocity. The fleets steamed hard at one another while cheering spectators thronged the Memphis levee to witness the carnage. From the bridge of the *Queen*, Ellet saw two rebel steaming rams side by side in the middle of the river with a third slightly behind toward the Memphis shore. Ellet realized that if he rammed the rightmost target her consort would, in turn, ram him. Likewise, if he rammed the left one the third ram would take advantage of her flanking position to attack the *Queen*. As Ellet recalled, "My speed was high, time was short, and the forward vessel presented rather the fairer mark. I selected her."[4]

From the Confederate viewpoint, the good of the service demanded cooperation, perhaps to the point of self-sacrifice. But the Confederate commanders were Mississippi River captains and pilots, a notoriously feisty, independent lot. They had entered the service with the understanding that they would not be placed under the orders of naval officers. Indeed, the concept of subordination was wholly alien to them. An old navy officer sniffed that they had "too much 'steamboat' and too little of the 'man-of-war' to be very effective." They were judged "unable to govern themselves and unwilling to be governed by others."[5] People familiar with their habits predicted that once under way the captains would never cooperate.

Outside of Memphis, the prophesied lack of discipline became manifest. The Confederate captains did what came naturally, which was to act in their own best interests. They balked before impact with Ellet's ram and gave the orders to back water. The *General Lovell* ended up presenting a vulnerable side to the oncoming *Queen*. The *Queen* rammed into the *General Lovell*'s broadside and crushed her hull. Terrified crewmen leapt overboard. Her captain managed to swim to shore, but many others drowned. Meanwhile, the *Queen* was too deeply stuck to extricate herself quickly. She presented a sitting target for the Confederate ram *Beauregard*, which drove into the *Queen*'s starboard wheelhouse. The impact severed the *Queen*'s tiller rope and crushed her wheel and part of her hull, but it also broke the *Queen* free from the wreckage of the *General Lovell*. Ellet emerged from the pilothouse to appraise the damage and was struck in the leg by a pistol shot. Disabled, without rudder control, the *Queen* limped upriver to safety.

The second Ellet ram, the *Monarch*, appeared just after the *Beauregard* struck the *Queen* and maneuvered so nimbly between two enemy vessels that the *Beauregard* accidentally delivered a disabling blow to her sister ram, the *General Price*. The *Monarch* then rammed the *Beauregard*, striking with such violence that piles of debris dropped from the rebel boat onto the *Monarch*'s forecastle. The *Beauregard* quickly sank. The ironclads came up to finish off all but one of the remaining boats of the River Defense Fleet. During the battle, seven rebel rams were disabled or sunk. Four of them would be salvaged and become Union vessels. Ellet had the enormous satisfaction of seeing his theories vindicated, but it had come at a supreme price. His leg wound festered and his strength slowly failed. Fifteen days after the battle, in the presence of his wife and young daughter, Ellet died.

Ellet's invention had spearheaded an important victory. After the victory at Memphis, only one more Confederate strongpoint presented a significant obstacle to Union control of the Mississippi River. Its name was Vicksburg.

FROM THE WAR'S OUTSET, an integral part of the North's war strategy had been to control the Mississippi River. With the destruction of the rebel fleet at Memphis, by June 1862 this objective seemed easily obtainable. Indeed, the beginning of summer brought high promise to all Union-loyal people because the war appeared to be just about won. In the East, an overwhelming Federal army had closed in upon the rebel capital. Richmond's fall seemed imminent. In the West, Major General Henry Halleck, the ranking departmental commander, had completed a slow but inexorable advance on Corinth. The Confederates could not resist Halleck's overwhelming force and had retired from this key rail hub. Then Halleck seemed unable to decide what to do next. President Abraham Lincoln wanted to send one of his divisions to capture Vicksburg, but Halleck judged that the force could not be spared for this purpose.[6] Instead, he dispersed his 120,000-man host, sending one part east, one part west, and scattering the remainder in between to guard the railroads. Thus it was that the Federal fleet steamed downriver toward Vicksburg accompanied by a mere handful of infantry at a time when Federal infantry were plentifully available.

Simultaneously, from the south came another Union fleet under the command of Tennessee-born Admiral David Farragut. The sixty-year-old admiral had entered the navy at the age of nine. Before he turned thirteen he had commanded a prize ship and served as a midshipman aboard Captain David Porter's *Essex* in an exceptionally bloody, ship-to-ship battle that saw 61 percent of the *Essex*'s crew become casualties.[7] Farragut's capture of New Orleans in April 1862 had presented the United States with two profitable avenues of exploitation. The key port of Mobile lay virtually defenseless. Alternatively, the lower Mississippi River was open to a Federal naval thrust. Instead of concentrating on one or the other, Farragut's fleet tried to operate against both objectives. Consequently, just like the fleet advancing downriver, Farragut's fleet lacked adequate infantry support.[8]

The objective of the Union naval attack was a thriving river town founded in 1814. In that year, a North Carolina minister climbed the Walnut Hills overlooking a bend in the Mississippi River. Newet Vick appreciated the site's trade potential. He named the place Vicksburg; its original population was thirteen Vick children and assorted relatives. Because of the steamboat trade, Vicksburg grew rapidly. Large cotton plantations blossomed nearby in the rich alluvial soil. The construction of a rail line connecting the city with the state capital in Jackson and points east, and another across the river leading to the Louisiana interior, made Vicksburg the only rail and river junction between New Orleans and Memphis. The city

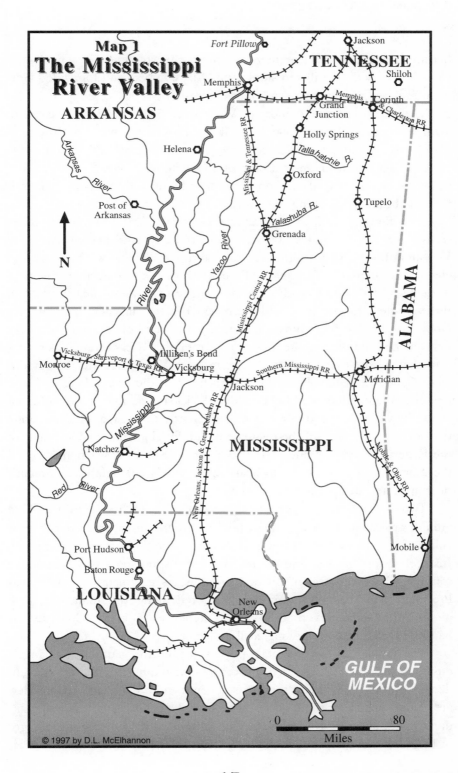

Map 1
The Mississippi River Valley

ARKANSAS

TENNESSEE

ALABAMA

MISSISSIPPI

LOUISIANA

GULF OF MEXICO

Fort Pillow
Jackson
Shiloh
Memphis
Corinth
Grand Junction
Memphis & Charleston RR
Holly Springs
Helena
Tallahatchie R.
Oxford
Tupelo
Post of Arkansas
Yalashuba R.
Grenada
N
Mississippi & Tennessee RR
Arkansas River
Mississippi Central RR
Yazoo River
Vicksburg
Milliken's Bend
Monroe
Vicksburg, Shreveport & Texas RR
Vicksburg
Jackson
Southern Mississippi RR
Meridian
Mississippi River
Natchez
New Orleans, Jackson & Great Northern RR
Mobile & Ohio RR
Red River
Mobile
Port Hudson
Baton Rouge
New Orleans

0   80
Miles

© 1997 by D.L. McElhannon

13

became a banking and commercial center; the splendid Warren County Courthouse, with its pillared sides topped by a cupola and four-sided German clock, was a towering symbol of its prosperity.

The year 1861 found most of Vicksburg's 5,000 inhabitants content. With an economy based upon trade, it is unsurprising that when the people of Mississippi had considered the question of secession, Vicksburg voters were against disunion at a ratio of about three to one. Still, when war came the city embraced the Southern cause by mustering troops and fortifying its bluffs overlooking the river.

After flowing south through alluvial bottomlands, the Mississippi River turns northeast five miles upstream from the city until encountering the Vicksburg bluffs. These bluffs cause an abrupt turn southwest, so that the channel parallels the first reach. From a bird's-eye perspective, the river formed an elongated U with a narrow tongue of lowland measuring from three-quarters to one mile wide between the two reaches. The highest ground, some 260 feet above the water, stood just below where the river first touched the bluffs. The high ground diminished in elevation as it continued along the eastern shore for two miles to Vicksburg, and then gradually receded from the shore. The sharp bend in the river, along with the height of the overlooking bluffs, rendered Vicksburg a most formidable position. Naval guns could not elevate sufficiently to engage batteries along the blufftops. Because of the poor command decisions that had left most of the Federal infantry behind, in the summer of 1862 naval weapons were all the Northerners could bring to bear when vessels belonging to Farragut's fleet appeared below the city on May 18, 1862.

Two heavy batteries anchored Vicksburg's defenses. On the high ground upstream of the city was a powerful four-gun battery. From here it could rake ships as they steamed downriver, made the turn, and continued. Just below the city was another heavy battery sited some fifty feet above water level. In this war of divided loyalties, its commanding officer was President Lincoln's brother-in-law. Scattered along the remaining high ground were some eleven other guns. Taken as a whole, the Confederates had prepared a three-mile-long artillery gauntlet.

The senior U.S. Navy captain present judged the gauntlet too dangerous to tackle. Instead, he tried bluster by demanding that the city surrender. Vicksburg's mayor and the garrison commander declined. A Confederate colonel spoke for them all when he issued a challenge: "Mississippians don't know, and refuse to learn, how to surrender. If Commodore Farragut or Brigadier General Butler can teach them, let them come and try."[9] Over the succeeding weeks the navy did try, but their shelling accomplished little beyond damaging some of the city's houses.

When Farragut himself reached Vicksburg on June 25, he learned that flag officer Charles H. Davis's squadron had arrived from Memphis and was above the city. Since Farragut had orders to link up with Davis, he resolved to run by Vicksburg's batteries. There was no particular advantage in doing this. His ships could do nothing above the city that they could not do below, but orders were orders.

At 2 A.M. on June 28, Farragut formed his ships in two columns and got under way. With a three-knot current running against them, Farragut's ships would be under fire for at least an hour. Farragut placed his three heavy vessels closest to the enemy, leaving intervals between them so that his eight lighter gunboats could still engage. Commodore David Porter, the son of Farragut's former captain, commanded a mortar flotilla that provided covering fire for the run. During the ensuing ship-to-shore duel, the fact that the Confederate artillery was positioned somewhat haphazardly made it difficult for the naval gunners to make out their exact location. For a loss of fifteen killed and thirty wounded, the fleet completed the run.[10] Farragut glumly reported to Washington that he had passed the forts and could do it again as often as required, but he could not conquer them. He concluded that nothing important could be accomplished without infantry.

On July 1 Davis joined Farragut above Vicksburg. At this time the Yazoo River presented an unguarded access to Vicksburg's undefended rear. A mere five thousand Confederate infantry occupied the city, but they outnumbered the infantry accompanying the fleet. So the navy marked time, hoping that Halleck would send more men. Meanwhile, Farragut attended to the business of investigating reports that the Confederates were finishing a powerful ironclad ram somewhere up the Yazoo River. The rumors were true, but only because of the tremendous exertion of Lieutenant Isaac Brown of the Confederate States Navy and his devoted crew.

The ironclad's name was the *Arkansas*, the vessel towed from Memphis before that city's fall. At the end of May, Isaac Brown had found his vessel a mere hull with disassembled engines, guns without carriages, and much of the railroad iron intended for her armor on the bottom of the Yazoo. For five weeks Brown drove his working parties hard to complete her. Fourteen nearby plantations lent their blacksmith forges. Around the clock, improvised drilling machines laboriously punched holes in the iron so the rails could be hung on the wooden framework. In contrast to the plentiful supplies of seasoned oak that Northern contractors used for their gun carriages, the *Arkansas*'s broadside guns sat on newly fashioned carriages built from freshly cut trees. The boat had many flaws. There had been no time to await the arrival of a machine to bend the iron around the boat's curves. Thin boilerplate iron covered her stern, giving the illusion of iron plating but very little actual protection. Although newly built in Memphis, her weak engines were prone to sudden stoppages. When only one stopped, she showed an alarming tendency to turn in circles despite the rudder. But her armored casemate contained ten powerful guns, and Brown was determined to use them to their best advantage.

In his mind, that could be obtained by remaining on the defensive and blocking Federal thrusts up the Yazoo River. But Brown deferred to Major General Earl Van Dorn, who thought that the ironclad could accomplish great things on the Mississippi River. So at dawn on July 15, the *Arkansas* steamed down the Yazoo looking for the enemy. Her decks had been sanded to prevent men from slipping in the expected blood. Surgeons handed out tourniquets to the division officers. Sailors filled buckets for drinking water and fire fighting. Many crewmen stripped to the waist and bound handkerchiefs round their heads, strapped on cutlasses and pistols, and placed loaded rifles with fixed bayonets near at hand. Having no experience in naval combat, they did not know whether the coming fight would involve boarding and hand-to-hand combat.

Around 7 A.M. the officer of the deck aboard the wooden gunboat *Tyler* reported the smoke of a steamer approaching. The *Tyler* was the scout boat for a three-vessel Federal group. Her captain, Lieutenant Commander William Gwin, ordered a shot fired across the steamer's bow to signal it to halt. The strange vessel ignored it and came nearer. As the mist lifted Gwin saw that this was no steamer. He had found what he had come looking for.

The *Tyler* rapidly cleared for action, her crew manning the guns without waiting for the boatswain's whistle. The rival guns engaged. One of the *Arkansas*'s first shells exploded above the *Tyler*'s deck, decapitating four men with the violence of its blast. The *Tyler*'s wooden sides could not endure prolonged punishment, while her own guns apparently could make little impression upon the *Arkansas*. One of the *Tyler*'s sailors recalled, "There are few circumstances more trying than to be exposed to a heavy fire and not be able to hit back."[11] Gwin prudently retired toward the other two vessels in the Union squadron. The commander of the ram *Queen of the West* chose to keep his distance. The captain of the ironclad *Carondelet* forged to the front to engage. Her commander, Henry Walke, had been Brown's friend and messmate in the prewar navy. Now Walke had a great opportunity. His ironclad had been purposely built to engage an enemy frontally. Her bow contained her heaviest armor and artillery. But after firing one wild shot, Walke inexplicably turned away from the *Arkansas* and thus presented the *Carondelet*'s thinly armored stern to hostile fire. As one of the *Arkansas*'s officers wrote, "We had an exceedingly good thing," and the Confederate gunners took full advantage.[12]

Zigzagging downriver to prevent the *Queen* from having an opportunity to ram, Brown chased the terrorized Union vessels as fast as the *Arkansas*'s overheated engines permitted. A shot from the *Tyler* penetrated the *Arkansas*'s pilothouse, mortally wounding her chief pilot and disabling her Yazoo pilot. A nerveless Missouri volunteer who knew nothing of these waters took the wheel and followed Brown's instructions to close on the enemy ironclad. The *Arkansas* gained on the battered *Carondelet* and Brown prepared to ram. Bravely the *Tyler* interceded. Her marksmen fired repeated volleys of small arms; one shot grazed Brown's temple, knocking him tumbling among the guns. Revived, Brown resumed his post to find the *Carondelet* plowing unsteadily through some willow reeds into the shallows. In fact, the *Arkansas* had shot away her foe's wheel ropes for the third time, causing her to steer wildly. But the *Arkansas* drew too much water to enter the shallows and ram. Accordingly, Brown ordered her port guns depressed and delivered a point blank broadside at twenty-foot range as the *Arkansas* steamed past. The *Carondelet* shuddered from the impact of the *Arkansas*'s one-hundred-pounder Columbiads and six-inch naval gun, heeling over and then rolling back deeply so that water poured over her forward deck shield. The *Carondelet* now lay disabled in a cloud of smoke with four killed, ten wounded, and two drowned when they jumped overboard to escape scalding steam. Hit effectively thirteen times, she would require a two and one-half month repair before returning to action.

The fight shifted to a duel between the *Arkansas* and the *Tyler*. Aboard the Tyler the situation, in the words of her acting master, "looked squally." The crew's last view of the *Carondelet* "was through a cloud of enveloping smoke with steam escaping from her ports . . . her men jumping overboard." Looking at their own boat, sailors saw blood "flowing freely . . . and the crash of timbers from time to time as the 'Arkansas' riddled us seemed to indicate that some vital part would be soon struck."[13] Lieutenant Commander Gwin shouted through his speaking trumpet to the commander of the *Queen*, ordering him to move up and ram the *Arkansas*. But the *Carondelet*'s defeat demoralized the ram captain, who conned his boat downstream away from the fight while Gwin, in frustrated fury, heaped invective around his ears. The running, unequal downriver fight continued. Fortunately for the *Tyler*, some of her shots had pierced the *Arkansas*'s smokestack, causing her to lose draft from her fires and slacken speed. Consequently, the Tyler drew clear. She had been hulled eleven times and suffered the most battle casualties of any Union vessel on this day.

A lull ensued as the *Arkansas* entered the Mississippi and steamed toward Vicksburg. It had been, in the words of a Missouri cavalry volunteer who served aboard her, "a pretty smart skirmish."[14] Ahead Brown spied a forest of masts and smokestacks. It was the combined Federal fleets, surprised at anchor in two columns formed along opposite shores—the fighting ships on the left and the transports and bomb vessels on the right.

Aboard the U.S. ships, officers identified the *Tyler* and saw her in company with a "long, low, dull, red, floating object."[15] Unconcerned, several officers thought it was the *Tyler*'s prize. Then the truth became apparent. Only one vessel, the former Confederate ram *General Bragg*, now in Union service, had its steam up, but her commander declined to attack. Reputedly, Farragut later remarked, "Every man has one chance, he has had his and lost it."[16] Brown, on the other hand, believed that his best chance was to hug close to Farragut's wooden vessels so that the Union rams would have no opportunity to strike. He ordered his pilot to "shave that line of men-of-war as close as you can."[17]

A tremendous cannonade ensued. Her own smoke cloaked the *Arkansas* so that her gunners could barely make out the Union vessels. They settled for aiming at the Federal gun flashes. Brown recalled, "As we advanced the line of fire seemed to grow into a circle constantly closing. The shock of missiles striking our sides was literally continuous."[18] Another Confederate officer likened the pummeling to the rapid blows of a sledgehammer. Twice cannon shot knocked Brown from his pilot's platform, breaking his telescope and temporarily stunning him. The call went out that the flag had been shot away. A young midshipman ran along the casemate roof through the barrage to knot the halyards and hoist up a new one. The Federal pounding reduced the *Arkansas*'s steam pressure by 90 percent and shot away the connection between the furnace and the smokestack, causing her internal temperature to rise to 120 degrees.

In battle, some men shirk and some rise to the occasion. Among the latter was a quartermaster aboard the *Arkansas* named Eaton. Eaton was an immense, strong man with a thick, unruly shock of red hair. He had the task of passing shells from the forward shell room while supervising the powder boys. An officer aboard the *Arkansas* recalls that as the battle intensified,

Eaton seemed to take charge, daring anyone to do less. To the shell passers: "Nine-inch shell, five-second fuse—here you are, my lad, with your rifle shell, take it and go back quick." To a gun crew having trouble pushing their weapon: "What's the matter that you can't get that gun out?" Like a cat, Eaton sprang from his place to throw his weight on the side tackle, and the gun lumbered into position. To a man faking an injury: "What are you doing here, wounded? Where are you hurt? Go back to your gun, or I'll murder you on the spot." To a wounded man trying to go below: "Mind, shipmate, the ladder is bloody, don't slip, let me help you."[19]

The concussion of a shot knocked over a sailor. Rubbing his sore hip, the sailor returned to his post, commenting that a second shot was hardly likely to strike in the same place. Almost immediately another shell entered the breach made by the first one and exploded. Nearby was Lieutenant George Gift: "I found myself standing in a dense, suffocating smoke, with my cap gone and hair and beard singed. The smoke soon cleared away, and I found one man left. Sixteen men were killed and wounded by that shell, and the ship set on fire." The executive officer seized a fire hose and extinguished the blaze.[20]

Aided by such stalwart warriors as Eaton, Brown conned his vessel through the entire Federal fleet. The Union ships fired full broadsides at ranges of thirty yards and less, but they seemed to have no effect. The ram *Lancaster* made a run at the rebel ironclad, only to receive a shot in her boiler. The release of scalding steam caused some of *Lancaster's* sailors to throw themselves into the water. The *Arkansas* approached a last Union ironclad, the *Benton*, and prepared to ram. But the *Benton* easily avoided the clumsy, cornfield-built Confederate ironclad. Brown confined himself to delivering a raking broadside as he passed, and with that the battle was over.

The *Arkansas* arrived at the Vicksburg wharf in full glory at 8:50 A.M. An Alabama soldier saw her hove into view: "It was a strange-looking water monster, apparently made out of railroad iron, and most of it beneath the edge of the water."[21] From the bluffs, citizens cheered her splendid run as if it were a horse race. Generals Earl Van Dorn and John C. Breckinridge, who had been watching from a perch high in the Warren County Courthouse, descended to meet the ironclad at the wharf. By this time the *Arkansas* steered so sluggishly that she had difficulty mooring, so Van Dorn and a staff officer rowed out in a skiff to congratulate Brown. From the outside it was apparent that the rebel ironclad had received a fearful battering, with her smokestack looking like an immense nutmeg grater, sides dented, ram broke, and hawsepipe destroyed. It was worse in her interior. The staff officer entered the "slaughterhouse"—the middle portion of the gun deck, so named because here, since the beginning of naval gunnery, an opponent concentrated his fire—to find that "the smoke was still rolling around, and mangled limbs of men were scattered about. I slipped on blood and flesh as I walked."[22]

Shortly thereafter, an artillery officer boarded the *Arkansas* and saw that "there was but one gun out of ten in working order . . . Their carriages were shattered, the embrasures, or portholes, were splintered, and some were nearly twice the original size; her broadside walls were shivered, and great slabs and splinters were strewn over the deck of her entire gunroom." He had to spread cinders to keep from slipping and looked about to see "walls . . . besmeared with brains and blood, as though it had been thrown by hand from a sausage mill."[23] From below came the groans of some three score wounded. Soldiers helped carry the injured to shore. The Missouri men who had volunteered to bring her to Vicksburg thankfully departed, and her remaining crew washed her decks and went to breakfast. She had fought two battles, but a third awaited. Moreover, since the Federal battering had loosened her armor, she was now vulnerable.

Upstream, Admiral Farragut could hardly stand the humiliation. He had predicted to Washington that the enemy vessel would not emerge from her lair. He wanted revenge and spent the afternoon preparing to destroy the *Arkansas*. From the port main yardarm of his flagship, the *Hartford*, sailors suspended the ship's heaviest anchor. Farragut intended to drop this atop the *Arkansas* should the two vessels again draw near to each other. That evening he led nine vessels downstream to destroy the *Arkansas*. The Vicksburg batteries opened fire and the heavens opened up as well. The torrents of rain reduced visibility, but some Union men had rigged a range light on the Louisiana shore opposite where the *Arkansas* was moored. Although Farragut's leading ship could not clearly mark the target, when it drew abreast the range light it delivered a full broadside.

But Brown had anticipated this and shifted position. Now he showed perhaps less judgment, because he could not resist the chance to return fire. By so doing the *Arkansas* revealed its new location. Still, all the advantages lay with the rebel ironclad. Union gunners could not see the rust-red *Arkansas* beneath the red clay bluffs. The *Arkansas*'s gunners, in turn, could clearly see each Federal vessel as it passed in succession. They were so close that Brown could hear his shots pass through their sides and the screams from wounded sailors. Although Farragut's ships were firing blindly, one of the *Hartford*'s eleven-inch guns sent a bolt that penetrated the *Arkansas*'s weakened armor and entered her engine room. It cut two crewmen in half and disabled her engine. Then, the current carried Farragut's fleet downstream and the battle was over.

When Farragut realized that he had failed, he proposed to Davis that they give it another go at high noon the following day. Davis could plainly see that this was a most difficult task, one that could destroy a man's reputation as well as his fleet. Referring to his experience above Memphis, he reputedly replied, "I have watched eight rams for a month, and now find it no hard task to watch one."[24] Five days later Davis relented, and allowed the ironclad *Essex* and the ram *Queen of the West* to attempt to sink the *Arkansas*.

The *Essex* was a converted St. Louis ferryboat whose iron sheathing weighed her deck down almost to water level. Unique for that time, the vessel's entire internal machinery was operated by steam. It was altogether appropriate that the Navy Department gave command of her to William Porter. Although his colorful brother David tended to overshadow him, William "Dirty Bill" Porter was a fine officer in his own right. Now in command of an ironclad named after his father's famous vessel, he had a chance to prove it. The plan called for the *Essex* to pin the *Arkansas* against the bank while the Ellet ram administered a lethal blow.

During the previous days, Brown had busily tried to get the *Arkansas* back into fighting trim. He appealed for volunteers to replace his losses. Initially, a good number came forward. However, upon examining the *Arkansas*'s interior, where the shot holes and splintered woodwork were easily apparent, and listening to the crew's tales of terrible carnage, most found a reason to seek other duty. Because of his balky engines and the fact that he had only enough men to serve two guns at a time, Brown kept the *Arkansas* moored with her bow facing upstream. When the *Essex* drew near, he nimbly slacked his bowline to present his iron prow to the blunt-nosed *Essex*. Porter could not accept a bow-to-bow collision and so swerved away from impact, raised the iron shutters on his gun ports, and exchanged a close-range broadside as he passed. Again the *Arkansas*'s inadequate iron hide failed. One of the *Essex*'s nine-inch solid shots struck near a forward gun port, crawled along the side and penetrated. It broke off the ends of the railroad bars, driving the iron fragments into the gun deck, killing seven and wounding six.

The *Essex* had no time to celebrate, for in swerving she had oversteered and run aground behind the *Arkansas*. For ten minutes she strained to free herself, all the while under fire from the batteries above. Two Confederate officers watching from the nearby shore saw an officer emerge from a trap-door in her turret. It was probably Porter. One of the rebel officers, a no-table hothead belonging to Van Dorn's staff, waved his sword and cried: "Come ashore, you d—— Yankee, and I will give you h——!"

"Go to h——, you d—— negro trader," came the reply.

"I had rather be a negro trader than a d—— negro thief," answered the enraged Confederate.[25]

It was that kind of war.

Finally, the *Essex* shook loose and continued downstream. Meanwhile, the *Queen* delivered a glancing butt, decided that duty had been done, and fled upstream. For the fourth time, Brown's seemingly invincible vessel, al-though reduced to a crew of twenty able-bodied men by battle's end, had withstood a superior force.

Two days later Farragut departed in disgust. The necessity of keeping up steam in case the rebel ironclad suddenly appeared consumed a prodi-gious amount of coal. Coal supplies dwindled dangerously. Mississippi fever had sunk its teeth into his crew with a vengeance. Likewise, only 800 of the 3,200 soldiers ashore remained fit for duty. Without an adequate in-fantry contingent there was little the navy could do. Lastly, Farragut wor-ried that his deep-draft ships would become stranded in the Mississippi once water levels fell. So Farragut withdrew, leaving the feeble infantry at Baton Rouge under the protection of the *Essex* and three gunboats while taking the balance of his fleet back to New Orleans. Upstream, Davis made a similar decision. Forty percent of his sailors were on the sick list, so he, too, pulled back from Vicksburg to rest and refit.

Machinists from nearby Jackson and distant Mobile rode the trains to Vicksburg to work at repairing the damaged *Arkansas*. Brown took advan-tage of the lull in operations to go on a short, well-deserved furlough. He fell gravely ill, probably with the same malarial fevers that were afflicting many of the *Arkansas*'s crew, including her chief engineer. Meanwhile, somehow no one would or could find competent engineers to replace the engineer. In his stead, men whose prior service was limited to much sim-pler riverboat engines took charge. Then, in the first week of August, the Confederates themselves did something to the *Arkansas* that the massed Union fleets had been unable to do.

It occurred because Generals Van Dorn and Breckinridge hatched a scheme for a combined army-navy assault against Baton Rouge. The *Arkansas*'s second in command, a mere lieutenant, could hardly decline. So he took the *Arkansas* down the Mississippi. Below Port Hudson, Louisiana, the engines stopped. The engineers conferred, but each had a different idea of what to do. Eventually, they managed to repair her machinery temporarily, so that at dawn the next day she continued. During the day, her ever-balky engines failed repeatedly. At last, unable to steer, she drove hard ashore with her unprotected stern facing downstream. Unfortunately for the *Arkansas*, the *Essex* appeared. Perhaps a resourceful officer like Brown could have done something, but he was absent sick and in his place the lieutenant in command judged the situation hopeless. He ordered the crew to abandon ship and set the ironclad afire. With colors still flying, the *Arkansas* exploded when the fire reached her magazine. So ended the twenty-three-day career of the most active vessel the South ever floated to defend the Mississippi, and thus the Union navy gained a measure of revenge, for without the presence of the *Essex* the *Arkansas* could have been pulled off the bar on which she had run aground and then repaired. Had she been safely repaired, or, better still from a Confederate perspective, had she never left Vicksburg, much of what was to come would have been far different.

Still, the Federal strike against Vicksburg in the summer of 1862 ended in failure. When the Union fleets retired they left the Confederates in control of both banks of the Mississippi for hundreds of miles. A lack of central direction, divided command, and army-navy rivalry had doomed the Union effort. Worse, it pointed out to the Confederates their areas of vulnerability. The Yazoo River was a back door to Vicksburg. The Confederates set about closing it. The city lacked any landward defenses. An engineer arrived to mark out a line of works to secure the city's eastern approaches. The Vicksburg artillery could not stop a passage by the Union fleet. More guns were sent. Because of the Confederate labors over the ensuing months, any second Union attack was certain to be resisted more effectively.

2

Fates Intermingled

A desperate stand will be made by the Rebels to hold this place. It is important to them to prevent the free navigation of the Mississippi; it is important to us that it should be unobstructed. They wish to have communication with Texas; we want to cut it off.

—Secretary of the Navy Gideon Welles,
January 9, 1863 (*Diary of Gideon Welles*, vol. 1)

In APRIL 1861, Winfield Scott, the United States general in chief, summoned Captain John C. Pemberton to his office. Pemberton had just submitted his resignation and Scott wanted to talk him out of it. Scott held high hopes because of Pemberton's Northern birth. Indeed, Captain Pemberton had recently learned that his two younger brothers had joined the Philadelphia City Troop in the U.S. Cavalry. His mother wondered why he did not return home and do the same. But the captain faced strong opposing pulls. He had received a letter from his Virginia-born wife: "My darling husband, why are you not with us? Why do you stay? Jeff Davis has a post ready for you."[1] So Pemberton weighed the wishes of Scott and his family versus his wife's pleas and his own sense of duty. He went south.

That Pemberton held a strong sense of duty would have surprised his former instructors at the U.S. Military Academy. While there the high-spirited lad skated on the edge of academic dismissal, showing a greater ability to accumulate demerits than to comprehend descriptive geometry. One too many drinking bouts almost led to his expulsion, but he managed to graduate twenty-seventh out of a class of fifty and thereby received a commission in the artillery. During the war against Mexico, the young officer

exhibited a surpassing respect for adhering to orders. Written orders specified that none of the junior officers should ride horses while accompanying
the troops on the march. Unaccustomed to walking, officers became footsore. Such was their discomfort that most everyone received verbal permits
to remount. One such officer who did so recalled that "Pemberton alone
said, no, he would walk, as the [written] order was still extant not to ride."[2]
Ulysses Grant, who provided this recollection of Pemberton to a newspaper
long after the war, then and thereafter concluded that John Pemberton was
a somewhat inflexible man.

When Pemberton decided to join the Confederacy, Brigadier General
Joseph E. Johnston quickly selected him to serve on his staff. Pemberton
supervised the artillery defense of some of Virginia's rivers against Union
gunboats. As was true with so many other West Point graduates from both
the North and the South, Pemberton received rapid promotion without having distinguished himself in any particular way. In the mind of the Richmond bureaucrats, his artillery training and Virginia experience qualified
him for service on the Carolina coast. Brigadier General Pemberton transferred to Charleston on November 29, 1861, where he served as a district
commander under Robert E. Lee. Having yet to encounter the enemy, on
February 13, 1862, he received a promotion to major general.

When Lee returned to Richmond in March, Pemberton became the
commander of the Department of South Carolina and Georgia. It was his
first independent command. A growing Federal naval presence alarmed
Pemberton. He resolved to evacuate key forts protecting Charleston harbor.
Only a "stand firm" order from Lee in Richmond dissuaded him from this
unwise course. Pemberton's leadership prompted South Carolina's governor
to complain to Richmond that Pemberton seemed "confused and uncertain
about everything."[3] In part this complaint was sheer prejudice. South Carolina's powerful politicians detested the idea that a Yankee was in charge of
their defense. What was important about the ensuing squabble was that
President Jefferson Davis found himself compelled to defend Pemberton's
appointment against all critics. Davis responded to South Carolina's irasci-
ble Governor F. W. Pickens by assuring him that Davis had such confidence
in Pemberton as to "be satisfied to have him in any position requiring the
presence of an able General."[4]

Eleven days later, Davis elaborated. During a long, personal interview,
Pemberton had provided the president with "a full exposition" on the subject of coastal defense. Davis admired a man who had mastery of detail,
seeing in such an officer a kindred spirit. Davis explained to Pickens that

the defense of the Carolina coast required an officer experienced in infantry and artillery service and acquainted with engineering. In Davis's view, Pemberton's education and service had given him the "requisite knowledge."[5]

As had been the case in Virginia, throughout his tenure in Charleston Pemberton did nothing to distinguish himself. During the one significant battle on the Atlantic coast, he preferred to remain in the rear, supervising the action indirectly. However, after Jeff Davis asserted that something was so, he was extremely unlikely to reverse himself. And so it was with Pemberton. Then and thereafter for the rest of his life, Davis found no important fault with John Pemberton. Davis particularly admired selfless patriotism. He believed that Pemberton had turned his back on a family fortune to come south, which was not really true, and that this was one more reason to trust his zeal. Still, Governor Pickens and South Carolina wanted the hero of Fort Sumter, General P. G. T. Beauregard, to defend Charleston. By late August 1862, Davis wanted Beauregard anywhere but in field command. So he appointed "Old Bory" to replace Pemberton.

In Davis's mind, Pemberton's successful defense of Charleston against a combined navy and army attack made him well suited to defend another Confederate bastion threatened by ships and infantry. So he sent the general to command the Department of Mississippi, Tennessee, and East Louisiana in the fall of 1862. Davis assured Mississippi's governor that Pemberton was "an officer of great merit."[6] To command effectively in Mississippi, Pemberton required seniority. Shortly thereafter, Davis nominated and the Senate confirmed Pemberton for the rank of lieutenant general.[7] Pemberton had indeed enjoyed a meteoric rise. During the war's early years other officers experienced similar ascents, but these usually came about after some field combat experience. In this war, Pemberton had neither directly commanded men in battle nor had he participated in a campaign. Now he held the mandate to defend all of Mississippi and Louisiana east of the Mississippi River.[8] He brought to his new command one characteristic that he shared with many other Confederate leaders: a domineering manner that tended to rub subordinates raw.

Not surprisingly, he was ill-received. One of Jeff Davis's Mississippi friends wrote that the army was in a deplorable state and that Pemberton had yet to make a positive impression on either the people or the army.[9] A Confederate sergeant observed, "I saw Pemberton and he is the most insignificant 'puke' I ever saw and will be very unpopular as soon as known. His head cannot contain sense enough to command a Regt. much less a

Corps. Oh what will our Country come to, when we are cursed with such worthless Commanders."[10]

Pemberton partially overcame such attitudes by dint of hard work. He inspected his troops, judged them ill-disciplined, and instituted a vigorous drill regimen to whip them into shape. He hurried along the completion of landward defenses to protect his district's two principal posts, Vicksburg and Port Hudson. The U.S. Navy's abortive strike at Vicksburg had shown the vulnerability of the Yazoo River as a backdoor approach to the city. The lieutenant general ordered Snyder's Bluff, high ground northeast of Vicksburg that dominated the Yazoo River, fortified. For good measure he had Warrenton, another blufftop position six miles south of the city, fortified as well. Pemberton made one other decision, overlooked at the time except by the harried officers charged with carrying it out. He ordered enough provisions stockpiled at Vicksburg to feed an army of 17,500 for five months.[11] This could mean only one thing: the lieutenant general wanted Vicksburg adequately provisioned for a long siege.

Although skeptical of a Northern-born general, some Mississippians warmed to Pemberton. Heretofore, many had wondered if the authorities in distant Richmond realized the importance of preserving the Mississippi Valley and the weight of the threats against it. Pemberton's energy, and the fact that the president, a native-born son, had handpicked him, convinced the Vicksburg press that the right man had arrived to defend the Hill City.

SOME 220 MILES NORTH of Pemberton's headquarters in Jackson, the Federal army prepared to advance on Vicksburg. The strategic problem Major General Grant confronted was one shared by all other major Federal commands. To win this war the North had to conquer a vast territory in which lived a people ready and able to wage effective guerrilla operations. Supporting this hostile population were large and capable field armies. In addition, experience had shown that invading armies required railroads or rivers to support their advance. Simple map study showed the defenders the possible avenues of Federal advance, and so it was easy for them to position their forces to block the attackers. There were only two ways for Grant's army to move against Vicksburg: parallel to and east of the Mississippi River, some 60 to 70 miles inland along the Mississippi Central Railroad; or by water down the great river itself.

To date, the Federal ability to clear the Mississippi River from Cairo to Memphis had been a consequence of the army's inland advance. When the

Union army marched south, parallel to the great river, the Confederates evacuated their posts on the river because they were outflanked and no longer tenable. To Grant, it seemed a good idea to continue with this approach. In addition, a secure line of communications was required to feed and supply his army. The Mississippi Central Railroad seemed to fill the bill. Grant decided to march south along the railroad, repairing this necessary lifeline as he went. If unopposed, he would eventually arrive in Jackson, Mississippi, forty-five miles east of Vicksburg. The advance began on November 2, 1862.

Grant's preparations for an advance did not go undetected. When Pemberton learned that Grant's army was stirring, he headed for the front in northern Mississippi. He spent six days there—his first real experience in the approximate presence of the enemy—decided the opposition was too strong, and ordered Holly Springs, a small rail depot on the Mississippi Central, evacuated and the army withdrawn behind the Tallahatchie River. Then he retired to his headquarters in Jackson. Pemberton would return for one more brief stint at the front, but clearly, as had been the case at Charleston, he was most comfortable directing the defense of his department from afar.

Grant eagerly followed in the Confederate wake. He snapped up Holly Springs, and there established his army's advanced supply depot. Continuing south, he nimbly outflanked the rebel army at the Tallahatchie and reached Oxford, Mississippi, in the first week of December. It had taken him more than a month to cover about sixty miles, but this could not be helped because he could move no faster than the pace at which the railroad could be repaired. From the Tennessee-Mississippi border south, the Federal army entered a territory made increasingly hostile by the Union soldiers' vandalism. A year and a half of war had hardened Grant's men, and now Mississippi felt the invader's scourge. An Illinois corporal explained: "A great many of the boys adopted a new style. Instead of asking now, they demanded, or went right in without saying a word. They would slaughter a man's hogs right before his eyes and if he made a fuss, cold steel would soon put a quietus on him."[12] If people fled from their homes or plantations and left them vacant, their property became fair game. Looting and burning were so common that Union soldiers marched past smoke-blackened chimneys and commented with deep approval that here was another "Mississippi headstone."[13] Stealing for the mere fun of the thing had become chronic, and "helpless women and children suffered much abuse."[14] Twenty-one-year-old Lieutenant Henry Kircher spoke for many when he wrote home that "the rebel must finally find out that waging war is no child's play but costs house and home and, yes, often lives."[15]

General Jacob Lauman issued a strict order forbidding foraging. In retaliation, soldiers assigned to his headquarters guard "stole him blind" one night.[16] A general who could not secure his own headquarters was not going to be able to protect Southern property. Naturally, the local inhabitants resorted to guerrilla warfare against the invaders. Consequently, every bridge, tunnel, and culvert required guards. Grant found his battle strength rapidly diminishing simply to secure the railroad against guerrillas. He issued stern orders against "gross acts of vandalism" and was ignored.[17] A veteran recalled that the men let their officers know "that they did not go down South to protect Confederate property."[18] Still, nothing the enemy had done so far had slowed Grant significantly and the future appeared promising. Then something his own government did upset everything.

Back in mid-November, to Grant's considerable surprise, General in Chief Halleck's support for a further advance became lukewarm. Halleck refused permission to rebuild the railroads south of Memphis and told Grant that the locomotives needed to haul necessary supplies were unavailable. Halleck concluded this puzzling telegram by announcing that "the enemy must be turned" by a movement down the Mississippi River "as soon as sufficient force can be collected."[19] At that time Grant failed to take the hint and continued with his advance along the railroad. Grant did not know that Halleck was ready to abandon the inland approach because politics had intruded, politics in the person of Grant's former subordinate John A. McClernand.

President Lincoln believed Major General McClernand to be a "natural-born general," a notion McClernand heartily shared.[20] Lincoln considered him brave and capable while recognizing that McClernand possessed an overdeveloped sense of independence. Nonetheless, McClernand had combined his lawyerly skills with his personal friendship for Lincoln to carve out a unique niche in the Federal high command. McClernand arranged with Lincoln to return to Illinois, where he would raise a volunteer force, and then go downriver and capture Vicksburg. By November McClernand was ready to begin and Halleck, unbeknownst to Grant, wanted to preempt him. Consequently, Halleck requested that Grant concentrate a force at Memphis for a direct strike against Vicksburg.[21]

Quickly Grant recast his plans. He had begun to doubt the wisdom of relying solely upon a single-tracked rail line that stretched two hundred miles through hostile territory. He described his position as extending "like a peninsula into the enemy's country."[22] His new plan called for the troops under his personal command to hold the attention of the bulk of the Confederate forces in northern Mississippi while Major General William T. Sherman slipped downriver with a powerful force and captured Vicksburg.[23] It would be impossible to coordinate closely the two commands, but Grant trusted that speed and surprise would triumph. So Sherman departed, and Grant relearned that surprise can work both for and against.

Already in this war, Nathan Bedford Forrest had displayed an ability to use cavalry boldly on the battlefield. Now he showed another talent. He took a ragtag group of men on a raid deep into Grant's rear around Jackson, Tennessee. What he lacked in horses and equipment Forrest planned on taking from the enemy. What he lacked in manpower he planned on recruiting in western Tennessee. He was successful in both; but, more importantly, his troopers did something that few cavalrymen showed an ability to do during this war: they thoroughly wrecked a railroad. Forrest's raid isolated Grant deep in enemy territory. Worse followed.

If in both his personal and professional life General Earl Van Dorn lacked judgment—his amorous activities would prompt an enraged husband to kill him the following May; the two battles he had directed to date had featured furious combat and bloody defeat—he was most decidedly a man of action. Rather than continuing to retreat before Grant's seemingly inexorable blue tide, Van Dorn resolved to carry the war to the enemy by capturing Grant's base at Holly Springs. Among the Confederate ranks were men who lived in and around the town. Working with them, Van Dorn devised a plan. He knew that the Union defenders composed three groups: an infantry encampment near the railroad depot on the town's outskirts; the balance of the infantry in the courthouse and adjacent buildings on the town square; and a portion of the Second Illinois Cavalry camped at the fairgrounds north of town. Van Dorn formed 3,500 cavalry troopers into three columns with one each assigned to a Union detachment. Then, on a warm, starlit December night, he led his cavalry toward Holly Springs.

They arrived at dawn. At the gallop, they approached a bend in the road where a federal picket post stood. The pickets sleepily peered through the gloom and realized too late what they faced. Van Dorn's cavalry rode them down and thundered on to the camp of the Sixty-second Illinois infantry. The hapless infantry numbered only about 200 effectives. They had no idea that the enemy was present until rebel troopers appeared at their tent flaps. A Confederate cavalier recalls, "The scene of a regiment, with night garments fluttering to the breeze, trying to dodge an avalanche of horsemen, was truly laughable."[24] Likewise, Van Dorn's cavalry managed to capture the infantry occupying the town square with little resistance. Apparently the garrison's senior officers had been drinking heavily the previous night and had then retired to comfortable beds in various houses scattered around town. Although the post commander, Colonel Robert Murphy, had received reports of the near presence of hostile cavalry, he had failed to share this intelligence with his subordinates. Murphy may well have still been in an alcoholic haze when the Confederates struck. His initial impression was that the enemy numbered no fewer than 6,000. He fled past the railroad depot only to be captured and taken to the rear, where he determined the enemy numbered "about 10,000 men."[25]

Only the Union cavalry at the fairgrounds put up any kind of fight. A group of them had been about to depart on a dawn patrol to look for lurking rebels. When the rebels came to them instead, they were at least mounted and ready to fight. A stiff skirmish ensued, but the attackers badly outnumbered the Union cavalry. Soon they too had either dispersed or surrendered. Until dusk Van Dorn's troopers engaged in the entirely agreeable task of looting the Federal depot. Here were complete sets of tack for their horses, crates of pistols and ammunition, and—better still—plentiful supplies of sugar, coffee, crackers, cheese, sardines, and canned oysters. A participant recalls that while boots and hats were the most popular loot, "it was amusing to see how tastes differed. Some men would pass by a dozen things which they really needed, and shouldering a bolt of calico, walk off apparently perfectly satisfied with their selection."[26] Setting torch to that which they could not carry, Van Dorn's men departed.

A chaplain who visited Grant the evening he learned the news of Van Dorn's raid found the general remarkably composed: "There was on his face no sign of disturbance that I could see, save a slight twitching of his mustache."[27] But if Grant were outwardly composed, inwardly he boiled. He had warned Colonel Murphy of Van Dorn's approach to no avail. Grant had been censured before by his superiors—most notably by Halleck—and by the press. Now he could look forward to more of the same. He could and did dismiss Murphy from the army, but he could not dismiss the impact of the Confederate cavalry raids. The destruction of Holly Springs meant that not only was his stockpile of supplies gone, but there was no way to replenish it because of Forrest's destruction of the railroad. For more than a week Grant was out of touch with the rest of the Union. More than two weeks would pass before his army received supplies from the North. Worst of all, he now had to give up his overland campaign. Three days after Van Dorn's raid, Grant decided to retreat.[28]

After the war, Grant told Sherman that if the army had then had the experience it later gained of maintaining itself without a regular base, he would have pressed on.[29] Such a bold move might have hastened Vicksburg's fall by six months. As it was, the loss of Holly Springs forced Grant to order his army to seek forage and food from farms and plantations within a fifteen-mile radius. To Grant's surprise, the army was able to live easily off the fat of the land. Grant later wrote, "This taught me a lesson."[30]

WHILE VAN DORN AND FORREST prepared their raids, General Sherman met with David Porter to arrange for the transportation of his infantry to Vicksburg. Porter had returned from the failed Vicksburg campaign of the summer of 1862 ill with Mississippi fever. Bedridden, he chafed at enforced inactivity, telling Assistant Navy Secretary Gustavus Fox, "I was much surprised getting two weeks' leave of absence. I did not expect more than ten days; two weeks is a great deal to lose in these times when a Rebel ought to be knocked in the head every five seconds."[31] Although Porter was keen to resume knocking rebel heads, Secretary of the Navy Gideon Welles was not certain that he was the man to command the Mississippi Squadron. He recognized Porter's qualities but feared the effects of his excessive ambition, boastfulness, and lack of respect for senior officers. For these and other reasons, many warned against promoting Porter. But Welles judged the squadron's current commander, Charles Davis, too intellectual, too kind and affable, and "not an energetic, driving, fighting officer, such as is wanted for rough work on the Mississippi," lacking Porter's "vim, dash" even "recklessness."[32] It took moral courage for Welles to make this appointment. He appreciated that Porter was a complex mix of good and bad traits. He knew that if Porter succeeded, the secretary of the navy would gain no credit. If Porter failed, the blame would be his.

When Acting Rear Admiral Porter raised his white starred, blue flag above the ironclad *Benton* in mid-October, he commanded a powerful fighting force. Its ironclads alone carried 114 pieces of heavy artillery, including 22 eight-inch, 5 nine-inch, and 1 ten-inch guns. Additional vessels were coming into service, including a class familiarly called tinclads—shallow-draught stern-wheelers drawing only forty-two inches, covered to a height of eleven feet with light armor that made them proof against musket shot. Highly maneuverable and capable of carrying up to two hundred riflemen, they were ideal for fighting on narrow rivers and overgrown bayous.[33] Five new ironclads were coming off the stocks and their design incorporated the war's lessons to date. But they also illustrated something else. Overall, a commendable frontier spirit of makeshift characterized the Western fleet. But there were a considerable number of design and construction errors, not all of which were honest mistakes.

It was becoming apparent that during this war there was a great deal of money for the keen and unscrupulous to make from a free-spending Federal government. The Civil War would popularize a new word, "shoddy." Porter found that the newly built ironclad *Indianola*'s combination of side-wheels and screw propellers left no space for bunking her crew. The *Chillicothe*'s turret gun ports had been cut five inches too high. The necessary patchwork jammed her steering wheel between her two forward guns so that the pilot and gun crews could not work simultaneously. So poorly and rottenly built were the North's wartime vessels that by 1880 the U.S. Navy featured ships built either before or after the war, but none built during the conflict.

Before he began active campaigning, Porter worked to integrate the army men of the Ellet fleet with his sailors. His insistence that subordinates care for their crews helped. "The comfort and health of the men" was to be an officer's foremost consideration, Porter demanded.[34] Porter's orders to inspect the crew twice daily to ensure that they were comfortably clad (and that they had their under flannels on!), the issue of fresh meat and vegetables three times a week, the provision of numerous stoves to dry the always dank belowdecks area, and a host of related measures molded the crews into an efficient force. If he enjoyed the privileges of rank—he wore magnificently tailored uniforms, maintained a fine table and bar, and brought on campaign his horse, comfortably stalled behind protective oaken timbers—he also worked very hard. Through three weeks of preparation Porter toiled from seven in the morning until ten or twelve at night, taking an hour off to exercise by riding his horse.

In the third week of December, Porter headed downriver. He encountered Lieutenant Commander Thomas Selfridge coming upstream. Born into a seafaring family, Selfridge had graduated at the top of his 1854 Naval Academy class. Porter had picked Selfridge as a comer, and given the young, aggressive officer command of the ironclad *Cairo*. Selfridge clambered aboard Porter's flagship to announce that he had lost his ironclad, sunk in the Yazoo River by a torpedo. Porter listened gravely. After completing his report, Selfridge asked if a court of inquiry should be convened. This was standard policy when an officer lost his command. "Court! I have no time to order courts," Porter exclaimed. "I can't blame an officer who seeks to place his ship close to the enemy."[35] He immediately gave Self-ridge a new command, but he also pondered the implications of what had taken place.

The sinking of the *Cairo* had come as a direct result of the North's naval superiority. While Midwest mills and foundries produced the material to build a large fleet, in the South a handful of ironclads sat on their stocks in various states of completion. The lack of both armor and engines kept them from being finished. Unable to match the North's naval construction program, the South turned to poor man's stopgaps. After the destruction of the *Arkansas*, Isaac Brown found himself toiling to guard the Yazoo River. Two men presented Brown with a newfangled scheme to help stop any Federal naval advance. Acting Masters Zere McDaniel and Francis Ewing described their experiments with naval mines, or torpedoes as the warriors of this period called them. Although Brown was somewhat hazy about the science involved, he was all for anything that might sink Yankee ships. With his blessing, McDaniel and Ewing procured five-gallon glass demijohns, filled them with black powder, and set an artillery friction primer into their necks. The friction primer was a short tube housing three elements: an explosive compound in the top; a roughened wire inserted into the compound and protruding out the top of the tube; and a small gunpowder charge in the bottom of the tube. A hard tug on the wire pulled it through an explosive compound and caused it to ignite. This, in turn, caused the gunpowder charge to burn. The tube directed the flame into the main demijohn.

When used to fire artillery, a gunner provided the hard tug with a lanyard. To duplicate this action in the torpedoes, McDaniel and Ewing connected the roughened wires in the friction primers to an external trigger line that linked pairs of demijohns. The idea was that when a boat hit the trigger line it would stretch it taut and then provide the tug to initiate the explosion. An ingenious system of floats, weighted pulleys, and adjustment lines allowed "torpedo" men on the shore to manipulate the demijohns so they remained hidden beneath the surface of the water.[36]

The torpedoes' practical trial came on the morning of December 12, when a five-boat Union flotilla cautiously steamed up the Yazoo River with the tinclad *Marmora* scouting the way. Aboard the *Cairo*, Commander Self-ridge heard the rattle of small arms fire apparently directed against the *Marmora* and ordered the *Cairo* ahead to provide support. Actually, sailors aboard the *Marmora* were firing at floating blocks of wood they suspected were torpedoes. In fact, they were buoys holding the submerged glass demijohns in place. Selfridge had orders not to run his vessel in among the torpedoes. Accordingly, he directed that boats be lowered so that the small craft could search for hidden explosives. Sailors mishandled the launching and this annoyed Selfridge. As he watched, an ensign aboard the *Marmora*'s cutter found a line, probably a trigger line, and cut it with his sword. A glass demijohn torpedo popped up. The ensign saw a wire, the adjustment line, connecting it to shore. Selfridge ordered it cut.

Everyone had been paying such attention to the torpedoes that no one noticed that the *Cairo*'s helmsman had allowed her bow to drift too close to shore. Irritated again, Selfridge rang for reverse engines and called out for the *Marmora* to get under way. The *Marmora*'s lieutenant hesitated; he had just seen hidden, possibly lethal danger close at hand. Impatiently Selfridge repeated his order and then, seeing the *Marmora* respond slowly, ordered the *Cairo* to push ahead. The *Cairo* had barely advanced when two explosions in quick succession rocked the boat. The ironclad had struck a trigger line which detonated one torpedo under her port bow and the linked torpedo just off her port quarter. The explosions hurled the port anchor in the air, dismounted a gun, and flooded the forward shellroom. A fourteen-year-old crewman recalled that water "rushed in like the roar of Niagara."[37] In twelve minutes the *Cairo* settled on the Yazoo bottom, the first armored vessel in the history of warfare to be sunk by a naval mine.

Young Selfridge did not appreciate his special place in naval history. Nine months earlier he had been in charge of the *Cumberland*'s forward battery when the ironclad *Virginia* sank her, another historical first. Years later he candidly acknowledged that perhaps on the Yazoo River he had pushed his ship "a little farther to the front than prudence dictated."[38] When Admiral Porter studied the case he, too, concluded that Selfridge had been imprudent, but that it was "nothing more than one of the accidents of war arising from a zealous disposition on the part of the commanding officer to perform his duty."[39] Believing that Brown had "got the river chock-full of torpedoes," Porter concluded that he dare not advance far up the Yazoo River.[40] In fact, at the time of the *Cairo*'s sinking, Brown had very few torpedoes to employ, but Porter could not know this. The initiative of two junior Confederate officers and the introduction of a technically advanced weapon had effectively sealed the best backdoor approach to Vicksburg.

Having dealt with Selfridge, Porter proceeded to Memphis. At this point in the war the admiral disliked West Pointers. To his mind, most had proven themselves pedantic and unpractical. Preparing to meet Sherman, he anticipated the worst. Because he expected a formal encounter, Porter dressed in full uniform coat. Sherman, on the other hand, appeared in a casual civilian blue flannel suit. Sherman immediately got down to business, interrupting his conversation with Porter to issue a stream of orders to get the expedition under way promptly. Impressed, Porter overcame the tradition of interservice rivalry to show himself willing to go more than halfway to cooperate with the army. But the presumed presence of torpedoes blocked a debarkation very far up the Yazoo River. In any event, Sherman wanted to land first on the Louisiana shore to cut the railroad leading west.[41] So it was that instead of steaming up the Yazoo River for a surprise landing, Christmas Eve found Porter's fleet and Sherman's men at Milliken's Bend, Louisiana, twenty miles above Vicksburg.

At Vicksburg, the city's elite gathered at Dr. William Balfour's Greek Revival mansion for a gala ball. Officers, dressed in their best uniforms, danced with Vicksburg's fairest while the garrison's commander, Major General Martin Luther Smith, watched approvingly. Some sixty-five-miles upstream a telegraph operator frantically tapped a message that a fleet packed with Yankees was steaming past him. The recipient, who manned a station across the river from Vicksburg, braved the storm-tossed river to arrive at the Balfour residence a little after midnight: "I was muddy and woe begone as I passed through the dancers and they gave me a wide berth, when I stopped in front on Gen. Smith, he scanned me critically and frowned with the exclamation, 'Well sir, what do you want?' " Apprised of the presence of a Union fleet, Smith turned pale and in a loud voice exclaimed, "This ball is at an end."[42] Smith ordered all available forces, about six thousand men, to man Vicksburg's defenses.

If Sherman had hurried, he enjoyed such a substantial numerical advantage that he might have overcome the city's defenses. Instead, his twenty-three thousand men did not even land until the day after Christmas and then probed cautiously on December 27 and 28. By that time substantial reinforcements had arrived at Vicksburg, including Lieutenant General Pemberton. Pemberton had responded quickly to news of Sherman's arrival. Knowing that Grant was in retreat, on Christmas Day Pemberton summoned troops from northern Mississippi. Two days later they arrived in Vicksburg and marched out to man the trenches confronting Sherman. Having skillfully reacted to Sherman's threat, Pemberton curiously preferred to remain in the city and allow his subordinates to determine Vicksburg's fate at a site three miles away.

Because of the navy's unwillingness to advance up the Yazoo and risk torpedoes, Sherman's troops had landed at a difficult site just a short distance up the river. To reach their objective they had to struggle through waterlogged ground known as Chickasaw Bayou. There were few routes inland, and all led to a line of hastily constructed Confederate defenses on the higher ground behind the bayou. Sherman was not keen about the prospects, but, commenting that "we will lose 5,000 men before we take Vicksburg, and may as well lose them here as anywhere else," on December 29 ordered an assault. Receiving the attack order, the commander of one of his assault units lamented, "My poor brigade!"[43] Likewise, the soldiers of the Twelfth Missouri could plainly see that a charge was going to be nearly suicidal. Lieutenant Kircher described the scene as they waited for the order to advance:

> I noticed various faces that almost visibly changed and got paler and paler. The eyes looked so hollow . . . And the hands gripped the rifle . . . and believed that they had found their own rescuer in that. Others looked terribly solemn and seemed impatient for the moment when they could sacrifice themselves. Still others, and so it was with me, were determined, pressed their lips together and stared at our flag.[44]

In spite of a gallant effort, the ensuing charge proved futile. It also displayed something extraordinary: 3,000 entrenched defenders easily repulsed an army eight times their number while inflicting 1,776 casualties and suffering only 187 losses themselves.[45] The terrain, with its restricted avenues of advance, had had much to do with this result. But there was a lesson here if anyone was keen enough to see it. For the first time in this war, defenders manning crude trenches and rifle pits had dominated the tactical battle.[46] The era of open field battles was rapidly drawing to a close. The path to Cold Harbor, Kennesaw Mountain, and Verdun could be seen in the footsteps of the doomed midwestern boys who charged at Chickasaw Bayou.

Many soldiers blamed Sherman for demanding the impossible. "It was complete madness of Sherman to think of such a thing," wrote one discouraged Illinois lieutenant.[47] An Iowa captain wrote to his wife about "a useless sacrifice of life" and how "our Generals do not understand their business and do not appear to care for the loss of life no more than were we so many brutes."[48] In contrast, the repulse of Sherman gave hope to Vicksburg's defenders. A Confederate artillery officer noted, "I do not think there is any chance for them ever to occupy Vicksburg. If they ever do, depend on it, it will be by the bad management of the general in command, which we fear here he is frequently guilty of."[49] An elated Tennessee officer observed the Union withdrawal and wrote in his diary: "Our enemy had gone . . . and Vicksburg still sat proud and free upon her impregnable hills."[50]

Sherman had now seen those "impregnable hills" up close and concluded that nature and Confederate engineering had made it "the strongest place I ever saw."[51] The need to extricate his forces from the Mississippi swamps after his failed assault depressed him. Admiral Porter encountered the dispirited Sherman and said, "You are out of sorts. What is the matter?"

Sherman answered, "I have lost seventeen hundred men, and those infernal reporters will publish all over the country their ridiculous stories about Sherman being whipped."

Porter responded, "Only seventeen hundred men! Pshaw! that is nothing; simply an episode in the war. You'll lose seventeen thousand before the war is over, and will think nothing of it. We'll have Vicksburg yet before we die. Steward, bring some punch."[52]

While Sherman could console himself with Admiral Porter's punch, the new regiments whose introduction to combat came at Chickasaw Bayou experienced profound despair. Formerly staunch fighters now muttered about compromise with the rebels on most any terms. The raw 120th Ohio had merely seen skirmish combat, yet one-third of its officers tried to resign after the debacle.

Not until January 8 did Grant learn of Sherman's repulse, and that via the amazingly indirect route of a Halleck dispatch reporting the news, which in turn had been picked up from a Richmond paper dated January 5.[53] Halleck ordered Grant to reinforce Sherman. This, coupled with the success of the Confederate cavalry and his concerns about McClernand, convinced Grant to abandon completely his overland march against Vicksburg. He would shift his base to the Mississippi River and stake everything upon a campaign based on that line.

THE DAY ON WHICH SHERMAN began to land his men at Chickasaw Bayou found Jefferson Davis forty-five miles to the east in the Mississippi capital. He had left Richmond to tour the West because it seemed that his strategic plan for his country to win the war was failing in the huge area west of the Allegheny Mountains. Twice the western Confederacy had denuded important garrisons in order to concentrate manpower for an offensive thrust. Defeat at Shiloh and General Braxton Bragg's failed Kentucky campaign had ensued. Undaunted, Davis continued to advise his Western generals about the manifest wisdom of concentrating strength from every command. Then Arkansas and Tennessee could be cleared of the invader, fortifications built to control the Mississippi, and a new offensive begun to recapture Helena, Memphis, and Nashville.[54] Davis appreciated that such an ambitious scheme hinged upon close cooperation among his generals. By now he should have also appreciated that such cooperation was unlikely to occur in the absence of firm direction from the commander in chief. Lieutenant General Theophilus Holmes commanded Confederate forces west of the Mississippi. To mount an intelligent defense of the Mississippi River Valley, Holmes's army needed to cooperate with Pemberton. Listing the recapture of Helena as one of Holmes's prime missions, which could not be done while cooperating with the armies east of the river, set the stage for a potentially unwise dispersion of effort.

When Davis journeyed west, he entered the newly created supercommand supervised by Lieutenant General Joseph Johnston. Davis intended for Johnston to provide the coordination that had been absent in recent campaigns. Following a battlefield wound in Virginia in the summer of 1862, Johnston had spent six months convalescing. During this time he observed the galling sight of his replacement, Robert E. Lee, leading his former command to glory. Disgruntled, he became a regular guest at Richmond social affairs hosted by a political group whose only glue was opposition to the commander in chief. The president's wife heard about Johnston's backbiting and reported the news to her husband. Davis understood that Johnston was no friend but, unwilling to go outside the limits imposed by seniority, found no alternative. So when Johnston regained his health, Davis selected him for the post widely regarded as the second most important in the entire Confederacy.

The Department of the West covered the entire area between the Appalachians and the Mississippi River.[55] Within this area Johnston enjoyed complete strategical, tactical, and logistical authority, yet the general still found the assignment overly limiting. He complained that the Mississippi was a departmental boundary that made no strategic sense. Defense of the river required close cooperation between Confederate armies on both riverbanks. Moreover, he asserted, coordinating the two major Confederate field armies within his department would be impossible since one was in Tennessee and the other at Vicksburg. Johnston maintained that they were too far apart for mutual support. He took his case to the secretary of war, who could only smile and explain that while he agreed with Johnston, the boundary came from the president and nothing could be done. So it was that Davis chose a general to take command in the decisive theater whom he distrusted and disliked, who returned these feelings in spades, and who forcefully doubted the job could be done. Davis expected Johnston to take field command whenever the general deemed it necessary. Johnston, on the other hand, saw his role as purely advisory to the two existing field commanders.

Traveling to his new assignment, Johnston quickly saw his fear confirmed regarding the coordination of forces across the Mississippi River boundary. Both he and the secretary of war urged Holmes to assist Pemberton at Vicksburg. Holmes, an officer whom Robert E. Lee had discarded as soon as possible and a man who had graduated third from the bottom of his West Point class, may have lacked strategic insight, but he well understood that the people west of the Mississippi had grown weary of serving as the eastern Confederacy's recruiting ground while their own homes fell to the Yankees. Holmes shared this parochial view. Accordingly, he told Richmond that a movement to Vicksburg would abandon Arkansas, expose Little Rock to the invader, and therefore he must decline. It was the typical limited vision of a detached general who did not want to exacerbate his own very real troubles by sending scarce resources to meet some distant threat. It was up to the higher authority in Richmond to assess all threats and allocate resources accordingly. This Davis failed to do. Instead, he deferred to Holmes, and by so doing undercut, in Johnston's mind, Johnston's ability to perform his job.[56]

Davis and Johnston arrived in Jackson, Mississippi, on December 19 and moved on to inspect Vicksburg's defenses. Throughout the war Joe Johnston seldom found a natural or man-made position that met his approval. So it was at Vicksburg, where he found that "the usual error of Confederate engineering had been committed."[57] An immense entrenched camp had been made instead of a compact fort. Thus, a defense required a large force instead of a small garrison. Likewise, the water batteries had been sited to prevent a naval bombardment of the town instead of being positioned to concentrate fire and prevent ships from steaming past. In Johnston's view these were critical mistakes. A meeting with Pemberton reinforced Johnston's notion that serious blunders were being made. Pemberton's concept of field operations "differed widely" from Johnston's strategy.[58]

The day after Christmas, President Davis addressed the Mississippi legislature in Jackson, the state capital. More than anything else, this address was why he had come home. He wanted to bolster Mississippi's martial spirit and encourage public support for the officers he had selected to defend Vicksburg. Characteristically, Davis began by attacking the enemy. Grant's army was "worse than vandal hordes," he proclaimed. He proceeded to praise the officers and soldiers assigned to Mississippi's defense and concluded with a ringing appeal: "Vicksburg must not fall."

He sat down to polite applause. To his secret chagrin the cry went up: "Johnston! Johnston!" The audience gave voice and the request became a demand. It was a delicious moment for Johnston. In contrast to Davis's lengthy address, Johnston spoke briefly: "Fellow citizens: My only regret is that I have done so little to merit such a greeting. I promise you however, that hereafter I shall be watchful, energetic, and indefatigable in your defense."[59]

Joe Johnston had about as complex a personality as any general officer in this war. He was careful to prepare a paper trail listing alibis for failure before actually meeting the enemy. In the coming months he continually returned to three themes: his command mandate was impossible, since Tennessee and Mississippi were too far apart for anyone to coordinate their respective military operations; substantial forces from across the Mississippi River—the vast region known as the Trans-Mississippi—should be transferred east; if the Union armies acted in concert, the Confederates would have to yield either Tennessee or Vicksburg.[60] Johnston's trail of alibis also reveals the mind of a top-notch strategist. Regarding the Trans-Mississippi, he believed that whatever was lost there because its defenders were absent in the East could be regained once Grant was defeated. More profoundly, his visit to Vicksburg had given him the insight to forecast the course of the coming campaign.

He informed his commander in chief that if Grant joined Sherman outside of Vicksburg the combined force could invest the citadel before Confederate reinforcements could gather to do anything about it. Pemberton's army would be unable to attack Grant because it was too dispersed guarding the batteries along the Mississippi and the backdoor entrance via the Yazoo. With Pemberton besieged inside of Vicksburg, the forces in Mississippi's interior would be inadequate and "could not break the investment."[61] Thus, Johnston judged it a question for the government to resolve, "Which is the most valuable, Tennessee or the Mississippi?"[62]

Ten days later his concept had further clarified. He distilled it in another message to Davis. Pemberton had 42,000 men, of which he considered 24,000 necessary to garrison Port Hudson and Vicksburg. This left 18,000 as a potentially mobile force. Confederate intelligence estimated that Grant had 38,000 troops, Sherman 30,000, and Nathaniel Banks (at Baton Rouge) 25,000.[63] These estimates were fairly accurate, their totals overwhelming. Furthermore, the Union's superior mobility granted by control of the river meant that a force could appear at Vicksburg before the Confederates in northern Mississippi could intervene. Johnston concluded, "Should a large portion of these forces act upon this river, they may invest our two positions, which would fall in the course of time, unless we have an active army to break the investment." Based on previous experience moving men from Tennessee to Mississippi, he again told the president that it would take too much time to perform such a transfer. The armies were not mutually supportive. He concluded with the observation that Van Dorn's raid had compelled Grant's retirement, but predicted he would soon return to the offensive.[64]

There was one other strategic notion that heavily influenced Confederate planning. Davis and Pemberton both regarded the interdiction of Federal shipping on the river more important than the maintenance of access to Confederate resources across the river. This idea had some basis in fact. Since the first settlers had crossed the Allegheny Mountains, their focus had been upon the Mississippi River as the outlet for their labor. Before the war, the midwestern states relied upon the river for most important commercial intercourse. By literally turning their back on the eastern seaboard, westerners had developed a set of shared interests based upon commerce on the Mississippi. From time to time this had prompted a call for a Northwestern Confederacy. Davis, like many Southerners, keenly followed all signs of Northern war weariness. If the South could continue to interdict the river, then perhaps the Northwest would split from abolitionist New England. This idea made the defense of Vicksburg even more important.

So Confederate strategy hinged upon holding Vicksburg and Port Hudson, another bastion some 110 air miles to the south. But merely holding these places was not enough. They were only useful insofar as their possession interdicted Federal shipping. This required artillery. Davis's visit to Vicksburg persuaded him that Pemberton was correct in requesting more heavy artillery. On December 23, Davis telegraphed Richmond: "There is immediate and urgent necessity for heavy guns and long range field pieces at Vicksburg."[65] On into 1863, Pemberton would repeatedly request additional heavy artillery, explaining to the president, "If enemy increases his fleets, you will have to increase my guns."[66] The authorities in Richmond complied as best as they could, but big guns were scarce and there were many threats to address.

With Sherman's repulse there was an opportunity to make last preparations to hold the Mississippi before the inevitable renewal of enemy pressure. Given that Joe Johnston believed he had found significant flaws in the

Confederate defensive scheme, now was the time to rectify them. But Johnston issued no orders to correct the deficiencies. Given that Johnston believed a Federal attack could come with startling suddenness and that communication and coordination between Vicksburg's defenders and the rest of the Confederacy would be difficult, now was the time to make contingency plans. This Johnston also did not do. From the time he toured the city's defenses until the crisis came, Joe Johnston did nothing useful to ensure Vicksburg's safety.

ON JANUARY 4, 1863, General McClernand assumed command of the U.S. Army forces above Vicksburg. Some of the soldiers who had participated in the botched assault through Chickasaw Bayou welcomed his arrival. One colonel observed that he did not know McClernand but he had to be an improvement over Sherman, for whom he felt "nothing but contempt and detestation," judging him "utterly unfit to lead an Army."[67] In McClernand's mind some tricky maneuvering had almost preempted him his due when Sherman brought the army to Vicksburg. However, now McClernand was in his rightful place as commander of what he styled "the Mississippi River Expedition." Raw ambition is not always the father of sound strategy. After all, in the words of the politically savvy Assistant Secretary of War Charles A. Dana, "McClernand's education was that which a man gets who is in Congress five or six years. In short, McClernand was merely a smart man, quick, very active-minded, but his judgment was not solid."[68] His lack of solid judgment became manifest when, having taken charge, he was unsure what he wanted to do with his expedition.

When Sherman proposed a thrust against a Confederate fort on the Arkansas River, McClernand concurred. It could not be done without the navy, so the two set out to secure Porter's cooperation. McClernand made a most unfavorable impression upon Porter and the admiral quickly lost all confidence in him. The admiral judged McClernand incompetent and considered it a crime that this man should lead the army when Sherman, a much more able officer, was present. Still, Porter overcame his antipathy and conducted the army to the Arkansas River.

Sixty miles above the mouth of the Arkansas River, 117 miles below Little Rock, was a small tongue of elevated ground. Here, just above flood level, in 1685 the French had built a trading outpost. Over time a small village known as the Post of Arkansas grew. In recent months it had served as a base for some Texas cavalry and had supported bushwhacking operations along the Mississippi River. Here also was Fort Hindman, a small, square, river defense fortification mounting eleven guns within casemates of heavy oak clad in railroad iron. Unlike the rebel fortifications along the Mississippi, Fort Hindman was low lying and thus presented a much more vulnerable target to naval gunfire. The Post of Arkansas really had little value to either side and certainly was not worth the division of Confederate infantry assigned to its defense. But somehow its commander, Brigadier General Thomas Churchill, a former Little Rock postmaster, received orders to defend it to the death. Churchill's stubborn determination kept the garrison in place on the night of January 9, 1863, when transports began to disgorge an overwhelming enemy force.

Late the next morning, Federal infantry marched to encircle Fort Hindman. One column blundered through the swamps and got lost while the other managed to drive in the rebel pickets. McClernand announced he was ready for the assault, so Porter's gunboats began their bombardment. They silenced Fort Hindman's artillery, but McClernand failed to attack. During the night, Churchill took advantage of the respite and drove his men furiously to complete a line of works to oppose a landward assault. The next morning, January 11, the Union forces began a combined land and naval attack. The infantry assault stalled before the stubborn defense. A Texas colonel reported that his brigade repelled three distinct charges. More than one thousand Federal soldiers were hit while making the attack.[69] Churchill was everywhere, waving his sword, urging his men to fight on. But the fleet again silenced the fort—the heavy naval artillery easily pierced the fort's six-foot-thick walls—allowing two ironclads to position themselves to deliver close-range fire against the rebel infantry. The defenders were in an untenable position: "The enemy's gunboats and batteries had now complete command of our position, taking it on the right flank, front and rear, literally raking the entire position."[70] There was no alternative but surrender.

Porter conned his flag steamer, the *Black Hawk*, upstream where sailors moored it against the fort's shattered casemates. As white flags appeared from within, Porter scrambled ashore to encounter Confederate Colonel John W. Dunnington. Dunnington was a former U.S. Navy lieutenant. He had served with the Confederate River Defense Flotilla until its destruction at Memphis. Since the Confederacy offered few naval commands, he had joined the army; even so, the memories of army-navy rivalry remained strong. He would be damned if he yielded to any grubbing footslogger and told Porter he wanted to surrender to the U.S. Navy.

Meanwhile, a lookout observing the action from a treetop near Mc-Clernand's headquarters informed the general of Fort Hindman's capture. McClernand galloped toward the fort, where he saw the gray defenders stacking their rifles and unhooking their ammunition boxes. Nearby, a thoroughly disgusted Churchill complained that he had not authorized any showing of the white flag. It did not matter. Dunnington had surrendered the fort, and so the men in the adjacent trenches would have to surrender as well. McClernand relished his victory. Unlike one of his soldiers who inspected Fort Hindman's shattered casemates and concluded, "Our gunboats have proven that they are extraordinary machines for destruction and death," McClernand overlooked the navy's contribution.[71] Likewise he ignored the fact that the idea to attack the Post of Arkansas had come from Sherman when he gleefully reported to Lincoln: "I believe my success here is gall and wormwood to the clique of West Pointers."[72]

The capture of Post of Arkansas had been a most agreeable sideshow. It removed 4,791 prisoners and perhaps 150 killed from the Confederate order of battle and eliminated a threat to the flank of any Federal force operating against Vicksburg. It also marked the end of McClernand's tenure as army commander. McClernand had greatly enjoyed the unfettered life of independent command and wanted to continue by taking his army into the Arkansas interior. Only a categorical recall order from Grant dissuaded him from engaging in such strategic stupidity. The Illinois lawyer had employed all his considerable political powers to persuade the Lincoln administration that he should command an independent expedition on the Mississippi River. Halleck, displaying more skill at bureaucratic infighting than he ever revealed in field command, overmatched him. By January 12, Halleck had confidently collected enough authority to authorize Grant to relieve McClernand of command of the Vicksburg expedition.[73]

Grant, in turn, considered McClernand's adventure a ridiculous diversion, an unnecessary "wild-goose chase."[74] Such was Grant's antipathy for McClernand that even after Sherman patiently explained the military merit of capturing the post, Grant remained obdurate. Sherman did appreciate that the excursion to the Post of Arkansas was a preliminary step for the difficult work ahead. Before the attack he wrote his brother that success in Arkansas would have a "good effect" on the main operation, but that "in the end Vicksburg must be reduced." He concluded, "It is going to be a hard nut to crack."[75]

3

Ebb Tide

This campaign is being badly managed. I am sure of it. I fear a calamity before Vicksburgh. All Grant's schemes have failed. He knows that he has got to do something or off goes his head.

> —General Cadwallader Washburn to his brother,
> Congressman Elihu Cadwallader, April 11, 1863
> (quoted in *Israel, Elihu and Cadwallader Washburn*)

GRANT ARRIVED to take personal command of the army on January 29, 1863. He found it located twenty miles above Vicksburg on the western shore where the Mississippi River carved a meandering crescent known as Milliken's Bend. Grant was well aware that his arrival coincided with the time when Federal fortunes were at a nadir. In Virginia, Fredericksburg's pointless slaughter and subsequent blundering compelled Lincoln once again to relieve the commanding general of the Army of the Potomac. In Tennessee, the rival armies had recently fought to a bloody stalemate on the banks of the Stones River at Murfreesboro. Here Major General William S. Rosecrans's army lay inert, gravely wounded. This left the Mississippi River Valley where, one way or another, Grant believed that his pending campaign against Vicksburg would be decisive. Another military failure on the heels of misfortune elsewhere would pave the way for Southern independence.

Yet nature seemed to have enlisted in the Confederate ranks. The winter of 1862–1863 was particularly rainy. The Mississippi and its tributaries rose to flood stage, forcing Grant's army to camp atop the levees within Milliken's Bend. Here they huddled; wet, miserable, and sick. Rampant camp diseases turned the levees into "almost one continual Graveyard."[1] A soldier counted 200 fresh graves in less than two miles. In five weeks the newly mustered 120th Ohio saw sickness reduce it from 850 men and 33 officers to about 350 men and 11 officers fit for duty. An Illinois soldier described how the sick were thrown on a boat "to be shiped north like hogs without protection, medicine, or enough to eat. A soldier is no more cared for in the army than a hog at home, if he lives all right, if he dies all the same."[2]

The high water and incessant rains also profoundly restricted maneuver. From a practical standpoint it made sense to return the army upriver to its Memphis base until the land dried out. This Grant did not do. He possessed a keen sense of the national scene and knew that there was growing dissatisfaction with operations in the Mississippi River Valley. Even the prowar *New York Times* complained that Grant "remains stuck in the mud of Northern Mississippi, his army for weeks of no use to him or to anybody else."[3] Grant realized that the people and the press would judge a return to Memphis as another retreat, as one more failure.

Also pressing upon Grant's mind was the knowledge that his own standing was shaky. In the recent past Halleck had shown himself to be no great admirer of his, and presumably he had the administration's ear. McClernand had nearly managed the feat of creating an independent army within Grant's geographic sphere of control. If Grant returned upriver he would be in direct telegraphic communication with Washington. It would open the door to any number of command changes or Washington-inspired strategic schemes. Grant wanted to avoid such meddling. For all its disadvantages, his base was mercifully isolated. Here the army was his alone to order as he wanted. Amid difficult subordinates, challenging geography, and hostile weather, what he wanted was clear: "to go forward to a decisive victory."[4]

How to go forward when most of the ground was under water was the problem. Even before he joined the army at Milliken's Bend, Grant's map study had led him to believe that "our troops must get below the city to be used effectively" because waterlogged ground shielded Vicksburg from an attack from the north.[5] Yet the manifest difficulties of "getting below" Vicksburg were such that Grant felt compelled first to investigate all other alternatives. Accordingly, during February and March Grant made two attempts to outflank the batteries at Haynes' Bluff, and thereby reach the dry ground behind the Yazoo River, and three attempts to outflank Vicksburg's big guns. One of the latter was a continuation of a project begun the previous summer when the Union fleets had visited Vicksburg. The three

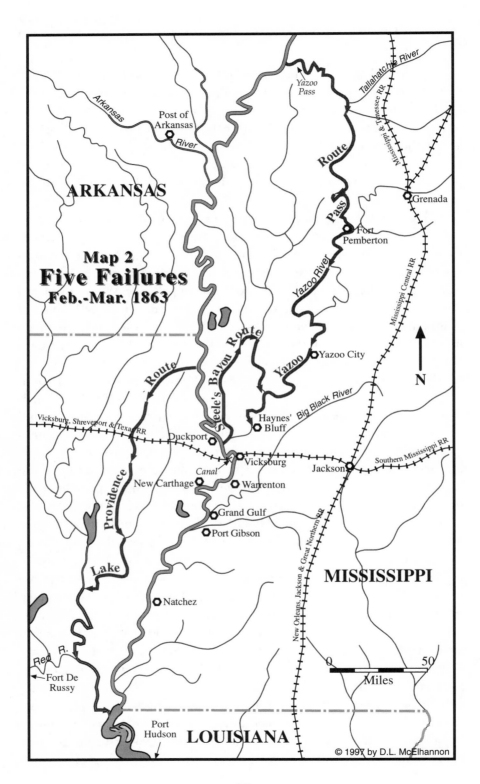

Map 2
Five Failures
Feb.-Mar. 1863

thousand or so soldiers who had accompanied the fleets had been insufficient to storm the city, so they had set to work digging a canal across the peninsula opposite Vicksburg. If successful, this canal would permit Union transports to bypass the city's batteries and allow an attack from below. Grant judged that the canal held little promise, but rather than have his men remain idle, he ordered them to keep digging. Thousands of Sherman's men proceeded to excavate the bayou ooze with spade, wheelbarrow, and dredging machine until abandoning the canal in March in favor of other, more promising approaches. Simultaneously, Union pioneers began an ambitious canal project at Duckport, Louisiana. The hope was that it would connect with a winding route through the Louisiana bayous to re-enter the Mississippi River twenty miles below Vicksburg. A sudden, unexpected drop in the water level in mid-April would cancel this labor.

At the same time, Major General James B. McPherson's corps worked on another scheme to outflank Vicksburg's defenses. They toiled to clear a 350-mile channel through Louisiana from Lake Providence into a complex maze of bayous that led to the Red River. If the troops completed the channel, they could steam down the Red, cross the Mississippi, and disembark south of Vicksburg. It would take a herculean effort, but in the absence of any better alternative it seemed worthwhile. While some of Grant's men labored to dig canals and clear overgrown channels west of the city, to the north naval units probed every possible route through the waterlogged land between Vicksburg and Memphis. The hope was to find a route passable by steamer eastward from the Mississippi River to the headwaters of the Yazoo River. Then transports could steam south to deliver the army behind Vicksburg. Some 325 miles upstream from the Confederate citadel, a mere 10 miles separated the Mississippi from the Coldwater River. Scouts reported that light draft ships could navigate the Coldwater and steam south to the Tallahatchie, the Yazoo, and reach the dry land above Vicksburg. To begin, Federal engineers blew a cut in the one-hundred-foot-high, eighteen-foot-thick levee to open an old channel called the Yazoo Pass to the Mississippi waters. The idea was that if Union pioneers could clear the channel, an army corps could follow.

Unfortunately for the Army of the Tennessee, the Confederates displayed alert anticipation and had begun obstructing the channel even before Grant's men commenced work on this approach. An Alabama soldier described the misery of operating in the Yazoo Delta: "We were four days and nights in the mud and water up to our knees . . . [we] went up the Yazoo River 100 miles without seeing land. The backwater of the Mississippi has covered the swamps for several miles. After we left the boat we had to go on flat boats two miles before we saw any land."[6] Toiling in the same conditions, by dint of prodigious labor Grant's soldiers managed to advance a few miles each day until they neared the Yazoo River. Here, on March 11, they encountered an obstacle that could not be conquered. This was Fort Pemberton, built on a narrow, five-hundred-yard-wide neck of land between the Tallahatchie and Yazoo Rivers. With the Yazoo Pass Expedition stalled before Fort Pemberton, Grant conceived one more effort to outflank Vicksburg's defenses from above the city.

Grant and Porter had reconnoitered yet another water route through Steele's Bayou. A tortuous journey along some two hundred twisting, turning miles eventually led to the Yazoo above the rebel fortifications at Haynes' Bluff. This approach seemed to be the most promising route yet. Admiral Porter threw his considerable energy along with major elements of his fleet into what became known as the Steele's Bayou Expedition. The expedition encountered nearly insurmountable obstacles, but Porter refused to give up. He drove his fleet through shallow, overgrown channels and stagnant bayous that were little better than ditches. At one point Porter entered a channel so narrow that there were only two feet of clearance on either side of his flagship. Low-hanging limbs toppled smokestacks and knocked apart the upper decks. By March 17, the log- and willow-choked channels had reduced his progress to about half a mile an hour. Even so, the fleet outstripped Sherman's infantry, who tried to follow in the gunboats' wakes. Two days later Porter's progress ceased altogether as swarms of Confederate sharpshooters forced naval working parties to seek shelter inside their vessels. It began to dawn on Porter that he could very easily lose his fleet here in the swamps. So perilous was his predicament—boats trapped in narrow channels, rebel axmen felling trees ahead and behind, enemy marksmen pinning the crews to the inside of their iron casemates, gunboats shuttered tight like frightened turtles—that Porter issued orders detailing how to scuttle his vessels to prevent their capture. He sent a bayou-wise former slave with a message to Sherman asking for help. Then the admiral put his fleet on half rations, covered the gunboats' iron platings with grease so boarders could find no purchase, loaded his cannon with grape and canister, and waited.

When Sherman learned of Porter's plight, he sent all available infantry on a forced march to the navy's rescue and set off by canoe himself to hurry along additional men. The Missouri colonel commanding the rescue party described the situation when he reached Porter: "I found the fleet obstructed in front by fallen trees, in rear by a sunken coal-barge, and surrounded by a large force of rebels."[7] When Sherman later arrived with additional troops, the sailors poured from their ironclads and cheered loudly. Sherman found Porter on the deck of one of his ironclads, standing behind a shield made from a section of smokestack, and altogether acting grimly determined to defend his vessel. Sherman realized that much of this was posturing. He recalled, "I doubt if he was ever more glad to meet a friend than he was to see me."[8] Protected by Sherman's infantry, sailors and soldiers cleared the narrow channel sufficiently to permit Porter's gunboats to retrace their route by unshipping their rudders and steaming backwards to the safety of the Mississippi River.

Sherman's men could not resist the opportunity to jibe the sailors with remarks like, "Jack, you'd better stick to the briny," and "How do you like playing turtle anyway," and "Better let the bushwhacking out to 'Old Tecump's' boys."[9] One of "Tecump's" boys was a major who commanded the army's sole regular battalion. He was a Mexican War veteran accustomed to the formal paperwork characteristic of the old army. After the expedition into the Yazoo he was somewhat bewildered by the seemingly aimless trekking through the bayous. He needed to write his report and asked one of Sherman's staffers to help: "I want you to tell me where I have been, how I went there, what I did, and if I came back the same way I went, or if not, how I did get back."[10]

Many shared the major's confusion, but there was no doubt that Porter's return marked Grant's fifth failure in two months to find a way to attack Vicksburg. Grant's soldiers were not particularly worried by all of this. The story circulated that a Confederate general interrogated a Union soldier captured in the Yazoo Delta and asked him:

"What in the thunder Grant expected to do in there?"

"Take Vicksburg," the prisoner coolly replied.

"Well, hasn't the old fool tried ditching and flanking five times already?"

"Yes, but he has thirty-seven more plans in his pocket, and one of them will get there now you bet."[11]

Whether the administration or the public would permit Grant to try very many more plans was doubtful. The string of failures came on the heels of Sherman's December debacle at Chickasaw Bayou and Grant's ignominious retreat after Van Dorn burned his base at Holly Springs. General McClernand tried to capitalize on Grant's predicament by writing to Illinois Governor Dick Yates to complain that "the republic is dying of inertia." He asked Yates to plead with Lincoln for a "competent commander" to lead the army.[12] The head of the navy was also discontented. Secretary of the Navy Welles summarized his department's attitude toward Porter with the observation that the admiral's accounts "are not satisfactory."[13]

The Northern papers were less prone to use understatement when expressing displeasure. Many clamored for Grant's removal, suggesting McClernand, John C. Frémont, David Hunter, and even George B. McClellan to replace him. Indeed, for three months Grant's army had floundered to no apparent purpose. So the drumbeat of criticism mounted. On March 12, a correspondent for the *New York Times* reported, "There is no symptom of any plan of attack upon Vicksburgh." Toward the month's end, the paper's field reporter, who by this time had concluded that Grant was unworthy of command, claimed, "Nothing visible . . . has been done lately toward the reduction of Vicksburgh."[14] The influential *Cincinnati Commercial* likewise declared that Grant had "botched the whole campaign."[15] The paper's editor, acid-penned Matt Halstead, took advantage of Grant's misfortunes to write to his friend Salmon P. Chase, Lincoln's secretary of the treasury, to warn that Grant was incompetent, a drunk, and a menace to the nation. Lincoln had stood by Grant in the past when he had confronted such charges, but how much longer he would continue to support him was an open question.

In mid-March 1863, Grant lacked the prestige that later became associated with his name. He had won a great victory at Fort Donelson, but that was more than a year before. His subsequent battle at Shiloh had been a bloodbath. Most people attributed the eventual Union success on that field to the providential arrival of a reinforcing army and the leadership of its commander, Major General Don Carlos Buell. In the minds of both the public and the Lincoln administration, Grant, like all the other commanders of the principal Northern armies, was on trial. With three months of dismal failure in the Mississippi swamps, his position as army commander hung by a narrow thread.

NINETEEN-YEAR-OLD Colonel Charles R. Ellet was something of a glory-seeker. At the beginning of February 1863, when Admiral Porter resolved to restore Union control of the river between Vicksburg and Port Hudson, Ellet cheerfully volunteered for the mission. This section of the Mississippi included the outlet for the Red River. The Red was a corridor by which Vicksburg, Port Hudson, and points east received provisions from Louisiana and Texas. To interdict this corridor, Ellet intended to take one of his high-speed rams on a nocturnal run past the Vicksburg batteries.

The need to make repairs delayed him until the sun had risen on February 2. Undaunted, Ellet conned his *Queen of the West* downriver through a wild barrage of rebel shot and shell. Apparently many of the Confederate artillery officers had spent the night drinking heavily at a Vicksburg dance hall and this affected their gunnery.[16] The *Queen of the West* rammed the Confederate steamer CSS *City of Vicksburg* while it was at anchor beneath Vicksburg's fortified bluffs. In characteristic Ellet style, the young colonel backed off to deliver a second blow but then received two hits that set fire to some of the cotton bales that provided extra protection for the ram's vulnerable topside. In addition, the discharge of the *Queen of the West*'s own bow gun ignited some more bales. The flames spread rapidly, forcing Ellet to flee for safety downriver. Eager to capitalize on his surprise passage of the batteries, Ellet quickly made repairs to the fire damage as well as twelve heavy shot holes and pressed on.

The next day the *Queen of the West* captured three Confederate steamers, two of which were loaded with supplies for the army. Ellet's appearance was unexpected and for a few days he enjoyed great success raiding the Confederate lifeline along the Red River. A shortage of coal curtailed his adventure, but upon learning that Porter was dispatching an ironclad to support him, and reluctant to share glory with anyone, Ellet set out on another raid. On February 14 an inexperienced pilot ran his vessel hopelessly aground while under fire from a minor Confederate battery. Worse, Ellet was unable to scuttle her. Although Ellet escaped, the rebels captured the ram and hauled her off for repair. The Confederates hardly had time to congratulate themselves when a new threat appeared. This was the new Federal ironclad *Indianola*, which had run the Vicksburg batteries on the night of February 12. Porter had selected this vessel because it was the only ship that could steam more than two knots against the Mississippi's current. But it could not steam anywhere without coal, and this proved the *Indianola*'s undoing.

To the rebels serving along the Red River, the *Indianola* presented a dire menace. Ironclads enjoyed a formidable reputation and this vessel, with iron casemates housing two eleven-inch guns firing forward and two nine-inch guns aft, overmatched anything the Confederates could bring against her. Her mere appearance spread alarm and confusion. "To attempt the destruction of such a vessel as the *Indianola* with our limited means seemed madness," recalled General Richard Taylor, "yet volunteers for the work promptly offered themselves."[17] Foremost among them was Taylor's chief of artillery, Major Joseph Brent. A lawyer by profession, Brent knew nothing about military affairs when the war began. He devoted himself to his new profession and by virtue of hard work mastered the technical side of the artillery service. While doing so he exhibited considerable administrative skill, initiative, and courage. In sum, he was very much like Ellet. So, at a moment of crisis when the *Indianola* controlled the South's navigation of the Mississippi River, Brent took command of the expedition to conquer the iron-shod behemoth or perish trying.

Under his driving leadership the Confederates quickly improvised a flotilla consisting of the *Queen of the West*, a steamboat named the *Webb* that was outfitted as a ram, and a tender. Thirteen men of the Third Maryland Artillery served the *Queen of the West*'s two bow Parrott rifles. A surplus of enthusiastic Texas and Louisiana infantry volunteered to crew the vessels, some literally smuggling themselves aboard in order to share in the adventure. They called themselves Brent's "Desperadoes." To help put them on their mettle, Brent harangued them on February 22, reminding them that like themselves, George Washington had fought for liberty.[18] With the fighting portion of the expedition ready, there remained one lack, stokers to shovel coal to feed the boats' boilers. This was work simply not to be done by Southern white men. The local planters had offered their slaves to dig earthworks, but steadfastly refused Brent's entreaties to work them as stokers. Exasperated, Brent sent a provost party ashore to impress a gang of slaves and shanghai them aboard. While 130 infantrymen waited, the slaves fired up the boilers and the boats steamed down the Red River to do battle.

On February 24, the unsuspecting *Indianola* was loitering just below the rebel batteries at Warrenton with two coal barges lashed to her sides. In the previous days Major Brent had exercised his vessels' guns and learned several things, including the fact that discharging the *Queen of the West*'s guns set fire to her protective cotton bales. Brent could and did order the cotton wetted thoroughly before battle, but could do nothing about another fact he had learned: rowdy Western infantry, who manned most of his artillery, did not overnight make skilled naval gunners. Accordingly, Brent appreciated that his flotilla could not engage in a gun battle against the foe. He resolved upon a nocturnal attack.

Around 10 P.M., the *Indianola*'s lookouts spotted the oncoming *Queen of the West*. The *Indianola* barely had time to clear for action before the *Queen of the West* approached at full speed. The ironclad managed to reverse direction and partially evade the blow, which sliced through the port coal barge. Briefly the *Queen of the West* held stuck into the coal barge, during which time her infantry swept the *Indianola*'s deck with rifle fire. When the *Queen of the West* was able to pull free, the *Webb* entered the battle. By now, of course, the Union sailors were fully alert, but a veil of clouds obscured the moon and made gunnery difficult. At seventy-five yards range, the *Indianola*'s two giant eleven-inch Dahlgren guns fired from her forward turret. The shots missed wildly and the *Webb* struck bow to bow. The impact knocked down most of the crew on both vessels but did little damage. The *Webb* tried again and this time managed to shear off the starboard coal barge. All the while the Confederate artillery fired. At one point when the *Queen of the West*'s bow rested on the *Indianola*, a Maryland sergeant fired his big Parrott rifle when it was so close to the ironclad's forward casemate that the Parrott's discharge enveloped her portholes in flames. Yet the shell failed to cause damage.

Aboard the *Indianola*, young Lieutenant Commander George Brown was in his first combat. He was a fighting fury as he struggled to defend his ship. The *Indianola*'s safety depended upon rapid, precise gunnery. She showed anything but. Her pilothouse offered very restricted vision through peepholes, so Brown climbed upon the hurricane deck to look for the rebel rams. Here he stood exposed to fierce musketry, which he ignored to call out orders to his pilots and to fire his pistol at the enemy pilots. He crouched down on his knees to speak through the gratings to his engineers, rose up to run repeatedly into the casemates to order his gunners to fire low and reserve their shots for a telling blow. At one point he aimed and fired one of the guns himself before returning to the hurricane deck. It was noble conduct, but Brown could have served his command better if he had remained a little cooler and done less himself. During Brown's frenzy, the *Queen of the West* circled and got up a head of steam sufficient to ram again. Two hasty shots from the Union vessel missed but distracted the *Queen of the West* sufficiently so that she merely delivered another glancing blow. As the ram slid past, the *Indianola*'s aft battery fired. One shot carried away a dozen cotton bales. Another shell entered the forward porthole and exploded, killing two men and wounding four while knocking out two fieldpieces.

Brown managed to fend off a fifth blow that hit the *Indianola* without consequence. Finally the *Queen of the West* rammed abaft the paddle box in a blow that crushed the *Indianola*'s frame, jarred loose some iron plate, and disabled her starboard engine. This left the *Indianola* helpless to evade the *Webb*, which delivered a death blow fair in her stern. With water pouring into her, voices cried out from the Union vessel announcing her surrender. So poor had been the Federal gunnery that only three shots had struck the two Confederate vessels. Still, because of the repeated rammings, the rebel rams were in sad shape. The *Queen of the West* was a near wreck, taking on water and listing to port so excessively that her starboard wheel almost rose out of the water. The *Webb* had her bow knocked off to within fourteen inches of the water line. As the *Indianola* filled, Brent ordered her towed to the opposite bank, where she settled on a bar with only her gun deck above water.[19]

The loss of the *Indianola* was a potential disaster for the Federal campaign against Vicksburg. If the rebels could salvage her they would possess an ironclad more powerful than the *Arkansas*. So confident had Porter been when he dispatched the *Queen of the West* and the *Indianola* that he had sent his other ironclads upstream on patrol. Upon learning of the twin disaster, the admiral could do nothing except assure his superiors in Washington that his plans had been perfect, the only blemish being the blunders of two hot-headed subordinates. Then luck and resourcefulness rescued Porter.

Two days after the loss of the *Indianola*, a false report of the arrival of another Federal ironclad came to the infantry lieutenant charged with guarding the *Indianola*. Since that vessel's capture, this officer and his handful of Tennessee infantry had been happily idling away their time foraging at a nearby plantation owned by Jefferson Davis's older brother. The lieutenant had orders to blow up the *Indianola* if the enemy appeared. Without taking the time to verify the report of a new enemy presence, the panic-stricken lieutenant destroyed the *Indianola*. In fact, what had occurred was that rebel lookouts had sighted a clever Union ruse, a wooden raft made up to resemble an ironclad monitor that had been launched in the current upstream of Vicksburg. It survived a slow drift past the city's batteries and seemed to be on its way to recapture the still-grounded *Indianola*.

The federal commanders could take small comfort from the success of this ruse. They had begun to appreciate that the Red River was a Confederate west-to-east supply highway guarded on its flanks by Vicksburg and Port Hudson. They knew that the U.S. Navy had again lost control of the Mississippi River between Port Hudson and Vicksburg, and that once more this highway was open.

AS THE 1863 CAMPAIGN SEASON got under way, Jefferson Davis could take considerable satisfaction with how well his handpicked defender of the Mississippi River valley was performing. Pemberton's repulse of Sherman and subsequent ability to disrupt Grant's multiple threats had even won praise for the Pennsylvania-born general from the local newspapers. So sanguine was Davis about Vicksburg's safety that he even pondered the merits of building a rail line between Port Hudson and Jackson, Mississippi.

Joe Johnston also judged that Pemberton had matters well in hand—so well, in fact, that he believed troops could be removed from Pemberton's command to help defend Tennessee. In the second week of January Johnston decided that Van Dorn's cavalry—the men who had spoiled Grant's strategy by burning his depot at Holly Springs—could best be employed by raiding into western Tennessee. Such raids would tie down numerous garrisons and prevent Federal troops from transferring east to the Union army that confronted Bragg in middle Tennessee. When Pemberton learned of this scheme he worried how, in Van Dorn's absence, he would defend northern Mississippi against Federal eruptions. Johnston assured Pemberton that Van Dorn's raids would also serve to interrupt any hostile movement into Mississippi. On February 7, 1863, the Confederate cavalry departed northern Mississippi.

At Vicksburg, the Confederates enjoyed unrestricted access to the Trans-Mississippi for less than three weeks following Colonel Brent's exploits against the *Indianola*. Then a new threat emerged from the south, with the return of Admiral Farragut. Union strategy called for a diversion to assist Grant's operations. It was intended to be a combined army-navy effort, but Major General Nathaniel Banks managed to bungle his assignment. This left Farragut to make the diversion alone. Accordingly, on the night of March 14, the admiral led his fleet upstream to pass Port Hudson's guns.

Almost a year before, Farragut had gone this way without trouble. Since that time, Confederate engineers had sited batteries with fourteen heavy guns on the bluffs. Annapolis graduate Marshal Smith, who had once served under Farragut, was in charge of the heavy artillery. He looked forward to giving Farragut a warm welcome. Farragut, in turn, anticipated trouble. He ordered his sailors to take down surplus spars, unscrew and stow all brass railings, and hang splinter nets. In order to operate their guns in the dark, sailors whitewashed decks and gun carriages so that ropes, equipment, and stands of ammunition stood out in sharp contrast. Since the only fighting would occur on the starboard side, Farragut had smaller gunboats lashed to the port side of his larger warships. Not only would this protect the more vulnerable gunboats, it would allow the gunboats to help pull the bigger vessels clear if they became disabled or should their deeper drafts cause them to run aground on the dangerous shoal known to exist on the western side of the sharp river bend. Aboard his own flagship, the admiral ordered that a speaking tube connect the pilot, who would be positioned in the mizzentop so he could see over the battle smoke and river mist, with the helmsmen at the wheel.

The rebels also displayed great ingenuity by erecting huge metal reflectors to project the light from shoreside bonfires into the river. The unexpected illumination from the bonfires confused Farragut's pilots as they tried to negotiate the river bend beneath Port Hudson. So bright was the light, so thick was the smoke, that Farragut and his pilot had to forsake visual references and conn the *Hartford* by compass alone. Meanwhile, Confederate batteries pounded his fleet. Marshal Smith could plainly see the Federal officers on the *Hartford*'s poop deck. He ordered the double-shotted eight- and ten-inch Columbiads discharged at point-blank range. When both friction primers failed, Smith ordered them replaced. They failed again and the *Hartford* passed. When a shell from another gun whistled overhead, it caused Farragut's son to duck. The admiral sternly rebuked him, "Don't duck, my son, there is no use in trying to dodge God Almighty."[20] Only the *Hartford*, along with the gunboat lashed to her side, managed to pass Port Hudson. The rest of his fleet received such punishment that they turned back. The rest, that is, except the old side-wheeler *Mississippi*.

Eleven years earlier the *Mississippi* had carried Admiral Matthew Perry to Japan. At Port Hudson she carried a twenty-five-year-old Annapolis graduate named George Dewey, who would earn immortality at Manila Bay in 1898. Dewey recalled: "The air was heavy and misty. Almost immediately after we were engaged, a pall of smoke settled over the river and hung there, thickening with the progress of the cannonading."[21] The *Mississippi* was last in the Federal line. In front of her the steam sloop *Richmond* had tried to follow the *Hartford* until it received a shot in her engine room that twisted a safety valve lever and filled the room with steam. The *Richmond* rapidly lost steam pressure. Four determined sailors tried to carry burning coal from the furnace to the engine room to reignite the starboard boiler. They could only work for a few minutes in the steam-filled room before collapsing. Although they earned the Congressional Medal of Honor by their gallant persistence, they could not restore boiler operation and the *Richmond* drifted back downstream. In the general confusion she fired a broadside by mistake into the *Mississippi*. The third vessel in the line, the *Monongahela*, and her consort, the gunboat *Kineo*, ran aground under heavy fire. For twenty-five minutes the *Kineo* labored to free the *Monongahela*. Meanwhile, rebel cannoneers shot apart her bridge, knocked out two broadside thirty-two-pounders and an eleven-inch pivot gun, and killed six men while wounding twenty-one. But for the presence of the *Kineo*, the *Monongahela* would have been destroyed.

So it was that by the time the *Mississippi* came up, the Confederate gunners had found the range. In the confusion, the *Mississippi*'s pilot misjudged the turn and ran her aground. Because of her protruding paddleboxes, she had no consort lashed to her side to assist her in getting off. The *Mississippi* did have an experienced crew of blue-water sailors who had spent hours drilling to prepare themselves for battle. "But," as Dewey remembered, "no amount of training could altogether prepare men for such a situation as we were in. With our own guns barking, and the engines pounding, and the paddle-wheels making more noise than usual, because we were aground, it was difficult to make commands heard." The experience of guiding a heavy-draught, oceangoing ship in the midst of battle smoke was new to Captain Melancton Smith. Smith was one of those old navy officers who were most comfortable following orders. Beneath Port Hudson's guns he exhibited great calm as he chain-smoked cigars, but little leadership.

The ship was quite literally a sitting duck target and all efforts to free her proved vain. Coolly lighting another cigar, Smith remarked to his executive officer, Dewey, "Well, it doesn't look as if we could get her off." Then came word that the forward storeroom, filled with all sorts of inflammable material, was on fire. Smith gave the order to abandon ship. Through it all the ship's crew continued to fire back at the flashes of light on the nearby bluffside. Indicative of the sailors' fighting spirit was Dewey's experience when he circulated to pass the order to abandon ship. Dewey encountered an ensign sighting a gun. "What are we leaving her for?" the ensign demanded. Dewey persuaded him to depart only after explaining that the ship was on fire. As the fire spread, the Confederates saw what they had accomplished. Dewey remembered that his ship's blaze served as "a signal to those on the bluffs . . . to break into that rebel yell which I then heard in full chorus of victory for the first and only time in my life. It was not pleasant to the ear."[22]

Farragut was now in a tight situation, his two ships isolated with Port Hudson astern and Vicksburg ahead. A weaker officer would have called the recent action a defeat and retired the way he came. Farragut continued upstream with the determination to interdict all rebel steamer traffic on the Mississippi. During the next weeks Farragut's two warships severed the flow of Confederate supplies from the Trans-Mississippi, intercepted large quantities of foodstuffs carried by rebel vessels, and prevented hostile land forces from utilizing the riverine highway to interfere with Grant's campaign. Through it all the admiral longed to return to familiar salt air. He worried about what was happening throughout his Gulf Coast command and particularly was anxious over rumors that enemy ironclads were preparing to take advantage of his absence and sortie from Mobile Bay. Had any disaster occurred anywhere along the Gulf Coast while he was operating on the Mississippi, the fault would have been his. Showing great moral courage, Farragut overcame such fears and maintained a lonely blockade of the Red River. He never received much credit for this, but his unflinching sense of duty did much to advance Grant's campaign.

The Confederates well understood the significance of Farragut's throttlehold. They worked feverishly to erect new batteries at Grand Gulf and at Warrenton to limit Farragut's reach. They built Fort De Russy on the Red River and armed it with cannon salvaged from the wreck of the *Indianola*. Whenever possible, commissary agents tried to cross the great river with herds of cattle and swine to feed the hungry eastern armies. But they had to guess where the Federal navy might appear and this guesswork made the regular maintenance of a supply line impossible.

Over time, the pressure of being isolated deep within enemy territory got to the admiral. He began to wonder if Grant would ever do something to relieve him. Furthermore, the Confederates seemed to be erecting batteries daily and Farragut wanted Grant or Porter to do something about them. Porter declined to cooperate with Farragut, explaining to the secretary of the navy that he could do nothing with his gunboats because the Vicksburg batteries could destroy most of the vessels Porter possessed without the gunboats being able to retaliate effectively.[23]

If Porter was unwilling, members of the always eager Ellet clan were not. General Alfred W. Ellet offered to run the rams *Lancaster* and *Switzerland* past Vicksburg to join Farragut. He asked the navy for help, only to receive an indignant refusal. To naval officers, the Ellets were former civilians, upstarts, crazy, and, what was worse, they were army. In the absence of assistance from the navy, Ellet took what steps he could to reduce risks. He ordered the rams to carry a skeleton crew, to keep the lifeboats on the starboard rail away from the enemy guns, and to hang knotted ropes on both sides. This last measure was a grim reminder of the machinery's vulnerability: in the event the boilers burst, the crew could leap overboard to avoid the scalding steam and cling to the ropes.

General Ellet had intended the run to occur at night. By the time the rams were fully provisioned it was near daylight. As the rams cautiously began their run, an unfortunate puff from the steam vents reverberated downstream and alerted the rebel gunners. Throwing caution to the wind, Colonel Charles R. Ellet, who, having returned after his loss of the *Queen of the West,* now commanded the *Switzerland,* ordered full steam ahead in an effort to outrace the guns. Initially, it seemed to work, as the first twenty or so shots missed wildly. But as the rams neared Vicksburg the rebel gunners found the range: "Shot after shot struck my boat, tearing everything to pieces . . . A few hundred yards behind us the *Lancaster,* under command of Lieutenant Colonel John A. Ellet, still steamed steadily down, but I could see the splinters fly from her at every discharge."[24] The *Switzerland* was in trouble. A ten-inch shell plunged through her deck into her center boiler. As suffocating steam filled her pilothouse, Colonel Ellet heard cries of exultation from the gunners on the bluff. The *Switzerland*'s pilots, one of whom had run the batteries once before, stood to their posts while the ram drifted downstream. Meanwhile, as planned, the crew, including three badly scalded former slaves, either climbed into the boats or took to the water and hung onto the ropes until the ram cleared the fire zone.

The *Lancaster* was less fortunate. A heavy shot struck the pilothouse, carrying away one of the pilot's feet. Additional shot repeatedly struck at the waterline. The *Lancaster*'s commander, John Ellet, describes what happened next: "At this time I entertained the most sanguine expectations of getting my vessel past in safety; this though, however, was speedily dispelled by a heavy shot which exploded the steam drum and enveloped the entire vessel in a terrible cloud of steam."[25] The crew fled to the bow, where a breeze shielded them from the hot steam. Another shell punctured a large hole in her hull. The pilot remained at the wheel trying to steer until a shot shattered the wheel itself. The pilot went below to try to control the tiller ropes by hand while Ellet inspected the hull. It was hopeless. The *Lancaster* was caught in an eddy and filling fast. John Ellet ordered her abandoned as the water washed over her decks. The Confederates continued to shell their lifeboats as they headed for the Louisiana shore.

The entire affair had been extremely brave and extremely foolhardy. Porter had been absent up the Yazoo River when General Ellet sent the rams on their run. Upon his return, the admiral was white hot, demanding by what authority General Ellet had launched this mission. A minor breach of paperwork protocol soon gave Porter the chance to charge Colonel John Ellet with "disrespect" and order his arrest. Farragut likewise denounced Ellet's rashness, commenting that by running the batteries in the daylight he had merely afforded the enemy target practice. The destruction of the *Lancaster* raised the number of major vessels sunk or captured to five in the new campaign to control the waters between Vicksburg and Port Hudson.

BY THE THIRD WEEK OF MARCH there was no doubt that the Army of the Tennessee's camps in the sodden bayou country were unhealthy and getting worse. Exposure to relentless rains increased sickness, reducing many regiments to half strength or worse. Some units fared better than others. A German soldier in the Twelfth Missouri boasted, "Overall, one finds that the regiments consisting mostly of Germans have better health than those consisting of Americans or Irish. First of all, the German stomach is better attuned to sauerkraut and root plants and therefore can stand pretty much everything."[26] Diligent officers and attention to camp sanitation made a difference, but even so veterans later recalled these times as the worst ever experienced during the war. The soldiers would have been even more discouraged if they had known that apparently Grant himself was running out of ideas. On March 22 he wrote General Banks that the failure of his various flanking expeditions meant "there is nothing left for me but to collect all my strength and attack Haynes' Bluff. This will necessarily be attended with much loss, but I think it can be done."[27]

That very day from his desk aboard the *Hartford*, Admiral Farragut was pondering Grant's dilemma and had reached a very different conclusion. It was a "delicate" matter for a naval officer to suggest anything to a general, but Farragut believed that Grant should go downstream and capture Grand Gulf. He could then leave a garrison there and continue on to attack Port Hudson in conjunction with Banks.[28] Porter deeply doubted the wisdom of such an approach. He had befriended Sherman and Sherman had persuaded him that there was nothing to do but return the army to Memphis and renew the overland campaign by again advancing along the railroad.

In this climate of increasing anxiety, on March 25 Grant received the latest batch of Southern newspapers. With considerable interest he read that Vicksburg depended upon supplies from west of the Mississippi. He shared this news with Porter. It confirmed Porter's suspicions that when the navy held the outlet to the Red River it had possessed a choke hold. Porter now confidently told Farragut that if the navy controlled the Red River outlet, "It is death to these [Confederate] people; they get all their grub from there."[29] Farragut's concerns about the strengthening rebel batteries below Vicksburg had helped focus Grant's attention downstream. The confirmation that Vicksburg's survival depended upon supplies from west of the river was another link in the chain of reasoning that was leading Grant to a radical, new strategy.

The succession of failures had not unbalanced the commander of the Army of the Tennessee. He had long suspected that he needed to somehow get his army below Vicksburg as a first step to coming to grips with his foe. Thus, four days after perusing the newspapers, Grant ordered McClernand to march his corps south through Louisiana along the western shore of the Mississippi River. The objective was the town of New Carthage, Louisiana, twenty miles below Vicksburg. In Grant's mind, a force at New Carthage could be moved across the river to strike at either the Warrenton batteries or Grand Gulf. It could then move downstream to unite with Banks against Port Hudson. Meanwhile, Grant himself, with the remaining two-thirds of his army, would tie most of Pemberton's infantry to Vicksburg's defenses. In sum, an advance to New Carthage would both address Farragut's concerns about the growing menace posed by Confederate fortifications and oblige the Lincoln administration's desire for cooperation with Banks. But Union infantry at New Carthage were valueless unless there were transports to ferry them across the river and one or two gunboats to provide fire support. Accordingly, Grant explained his intention to Porter and asked the admiral to consider whether some of his vessels could run Vicksburg's batteries.

Porter replied that he was ready to cooperate. Whether he was willing was another matter. Porter explained that instead of sending only one or two vessels he would want to send a flotilla of his best ironclads. Once below the city, they would lack the motive power—they could only make about two knots against the current—to return upstream fast enough to avoid destruction from the Confederate heavy artillery at Vicksburg. Furthermore, after sending the flotilla past Vicksburg there would be insufficient vessels remaining to support an attack against Haynes' Bluff. In conclusion, Porter told Grant that a run past the batteries represented an irrevocable commitment to a campaign against Vicksburg from below the city.[30]

No competent commander wanted to stake everything upon one toss of the die if there was any other option. So, on April 1, Grant joined Porter aboard a gunboat to examine up close the possibility of storming Haynes' Bluff by a direct assault. His inspection convinced him it could not be done without an immense loss of life. He told Porter, "This, then, closes out the last hope of turning the enemy" from above.[31] Satisfied that he had evaluated all alternative strategies, Grant next exhibited surpassing moral courage by choosing a path from which there could be no return. Henceforth, he devoted all his energy to a downriver campaign. He intended to attack Vicksburg from below after bypassing the city by marching his entire army south along the river's western bank and then crossing to the Vicksburg side of the river.

FOR THREE MONTHS Lieutenant General Pemberton had defended Vicksburg against multiple threats. As April came he continued to believe all was going well. He wanted more heavy artillery but little else. On April 4 he telegraphed Davis and said, "I see nothing unfavorable in present aspect of affairs."[32] There were annoyances, but they hardly seemed important when weighed against the Confederate successes. Whenever it rained hard, a common occurrence during this unusually wet spring, portions of the railroad running east from Vicksburg washed out. The need to make frequent repairs along this "wretched" railroad, as Pemberton called it, inhibited the accumulation of food stocks in Vicksburg.[33] Railroad inefficiency meant that greater reliance had to be placed upon moving supplies by water. Back in January, when the U.S. Navy departed from the mouth of the Yazoo due to a coal shortage, Confederate quartermasters had availed themselves of the opportunity to send steamers up the Yazoo to collect supplies from the region that served as Vicksburg's commissary. Porter's subsequent unexpected return isolated the steamers from the city, leaving only two government-owned steamers assigned to the duty of collecting foodstuffs to stockpile at Vicksburg. The general who commanded in northern Mississippi had refused to release idle steamers to collect locally raised, abundant, and cheap corn for Vicksburg. Even had steamers been available, Pemberton's commissary department seemed unable to resolve a quarrel with local planters regarding the collection of corn because the army bureaucrats insisted that it be shelled and sacked and the planters refused.[34] Pemberton had experienced similar problems in the past and could attribute them to turf wars among competing army officers or the normal tensions among civilians and soldiers when living in a garrison state.

There were some other commercial transactions occurring in Vicksburg about which Pemberton was unaware. War had interrupted normal commercial intercourse and brought scarcity to many parts of the South. For those so inclined it also brought opportunity. A Vicksburg newspaper correspondent saw "boat after boat" arrive at the city's wharves carrying nothing "but sugar and molasses." Businessmen shipped these commodities east, where they were in great demand. The clarity of hindsight allowed the correspondent to conclude, "The importance of provisioning Vicksburg was forgotten in the thirst for speculation."[35] Nature had blessed Vicksburg by surrounding the city with regions of farm bounty. More than three months before, Pemberton had ordered Vicksburg provisioned so that an army could defend it for at least a five-month siege. As spring came to Mississippi, this job had yet to be done.

4

The Hazardous Enterprise

The news is here, of the capture, by our forces of Grand Gulf—a large & very important thing.

—Abraham Lincoln, May 8, 1863
(in *The Collected Works of Abraham Lincoln*, vol. 6)

At THE BEGINNING OF APRIL, Admiral Porter told Grant he would need several weeks to prepare for his run past Vicksburg. In the meantime, the army would march south through Louisiana. As Grant counted noses, he knew that he had about only thirty-six thousand men for his next move against Vicksburg. Because of Joe Johnston's skillful placement of some thirteen thousand hard-riding cavalry troopers, the threat to Federal communications in western Tennessee tied down sixty-two thousand more soldiers under Grant's command.[1] Grant also knew he could call upon some of them as reinforcements if the move through Louisiana succeeded, but he correctly estimated that Pemberton had a force about numerically equal to his own disposable strength. So he would begin his climactic make-or-break campaign without the advantage of numbers. Unlike all other Union army commanders, mere numerical equality did not deter him. He judged his force "abundant" for the work ahead.[2]

Moreover, while Pemberton could utilize the rail lines and superior roads on the dry, eastern side of the Mississippi, Grant's soldiers would have to traverse waterlogged ground. The Louisiana side of the great river was full of flood channels, bayous, and swamps and crisscrossed by natural levees atop of which ran the few primitive roads. It was a land better suited to the alligator and the catfish than to an army corps. Spring rains were frequent. At night temperatures plummeted and men awoke to find their campsites covered in frost. In addition, the army corps assigned to lead the way was commanded by McClernand, the general in whom Grant had the least confidence.

When Grant assumed personal command of the army back in January, McClernand was happily referring to himself as "Headquarters, Army of the Mississippi." A quarrel ensued—all very proper, with both Grant and McClernand disputing the issue formally on paper—but Grant knew how to play the army bureaucrat. He bested his lawyer opponent and managed to assert command authority. Although removed from independent command, the politician-general remained the army's senior corps commander, and about McClernand's seniority Grant could do nothing. The beginning of April found McClernand's Thirteenth Corps at Milliken's Bend. It would be a logistical nightmare to move McPherson's Seventeenth Corps through the already overcrowded staging area. Politics, adherence to the dictates of seniority, and logistics compelled Grant to depend upon his least dependable senior officer to execute what was certain to be a difficult march.

To his great credit, McClernand energetically threw himself into the task. In the face of rebel sharpshooters, McClernand personally reconnoitered routes of advance. At one point McClernand, two other officers, and three enlisted men rowed a skiff through a bayou to examine up close a possible roadway through the flooded land. When Confederate pickets opened fire, the six men took shelter behind a levee. Worried that the major general was about to slide inadvertently into the water—or so they claimed—some of the men hustled behind McClernand to prop him up. McClernand, mistaking their action for cowardice, exclaimed: "Damn you, stand fire, don't you run, stand fire, damn you!"[3]

Under normal circumstances, the march to New Carthage would have taken two days, but the terrain was anything but normal. To begin with, most of it was under water, and that which wasn't quickly became a boggy morass beneath the frequent rains and the soldiers' boots. Horse teams, eighteen strong, struggled to pull a single gun. One of General John Logan's men recalls that the route was "strewn with wrecks of wagons and their loads and half-buried guns." Another soldier counted twenty-eight vehicles badly mired along one three-mile section of road.[4] Men floundered in knee-deep mud, sometimes not even marching two miles during an entire day. The stagnant backwaters bred ferocious clouds of insects. "I can tell you," wrote an Illinois private to his family, "the mosqetoes was very bad . . . so that it kept me busy to keep them from taking me prisoner."[5]

The bayou's numerous branches required bridging and there were no bridging materials available. Applying the frontier spirit of makeshift, the midwestern boys tore down houses and barns to build floating bridges, trestle bridges, corduroy roads, or whatever was necessary in order to continue the advance. Dirty as hogs, wet and often cold, lousy and poorly fed, they persisted and took pride in their accomplishment. After a winter of frustration, they were happy to be on the move again. When the sun shone they gazed about at a delightful country in full spring glory. They marveled at the climbing roses, blooming magnolias, and most of all at corn already three feet high. Then the rain returned, making life miserable once again.

If McClernand was Grant's least trusted subordinate, there was no doubt that the man he trusted most was Sherman. On April 8, Sherman told Grant that the march through Louisiana was a mistake. He recommended that the entire army—except for perhaps ten thousand men—be returned to Memphis, and the overland campaign down the Mississippi Central resumed. Sherman reassured his friend that he would support him zealously regardless, but his letter was anything but confidence inspiring. Compounding Grant's troubles was knowledge that henceforth he would be operating under the close scrutiny of Lincoln administration spies.

Unlike the situation in the East, only occasionally did Lincoln intervene in the Mississippi River Valley campaign. The fact that Grant's army was not connected to a telegraph line undoubtedly prevented some meddling. Letters and telegrams from Grant to Washington took anywhere from eight to sixteen days. Still, indicative of Lincoln's concern was a telegram he sent to General Stephen A. Hurlbut in Memphis: "What news have you? What from Vicksburg? What from Yazoo Pass? What from Lake Providence? What generally?"[6]

Unbeknownst to Grant, Lincoln was "rather disgusted" with Grant's efforts to outflank Vicksburg.[7] Still, during April Grant received no communications from the president. In contrast, the commander of the Army of the Potomac, Joseph Hooker, who was also in the midst of preparing an offensive, received a five-day visit from Lincoln, a presidential memorandum on his planned campaign, and five telegrams or letters during a two and one-half week span preceding his advance. What Grant received instead was Charles Dana and Lorenzo Thomas.

Officially, Dana was a special commissioner detailed from the War Department to investigate the pay service in the western armies. Everyone knew that he had really come to report to the president and secretary of war about Grant. Dana arrived at Milliken's Bend on April 6. Some of Grant's junior officers immediately wanted to toss him in the Mississippi, but the army's adjutant general, thirty-two-year-old Lieutenant Colonel John A. Rawlins, prevailed. Rawlins was a man of good sense, simple manners, and fierce independence. He had no technical knowledge of war, but was an observant, intelligent man. In an army of champion cursers he exceeded most and was not reticent in expressing an opinion. If he thought Grant was misstepping, he would chide the general in no uncertain terms even to the point of cursing Grant to his face. Bemused staffers believed Rawlins to be guilty of insubordination many times a day, but his behavior did not seem to faze Grant, who said Rawlins was "more nearly indispensable to him than anyone else."[8]

Rawlins's sternest purpose stemmed from having seen his father's fall to alcohol. Rawlins had developed a lifelong, violent antipathy to demon drink. A sincere patriot, he believed he could best serve his country by keeping Grant away from alcohol. Rawlins told another staff officer, young Lieutenant Colonel James Wilson, "There are lots of men in this army, some on Grant's staff, who not only drink themselves but like to see others drink, and whenever they get a chance they tempt their chief, and I want you to help me clean them out."[9] While "cleaning them out," Rawlins also guided his chief through many social and political entanglements.

Rawlins insisted that Dana be accorded proper hospitality and so Grant accepted Dana into his military family. Dana was a Harvard-educated, polished New Englander. Grant was anything but. In spite of their differences, Dana found that Grant conveyed, in some difficult-to-explain manner, the impression of a solid, capable leader. Long after the war Dana was still trying to describe this plain, unremarkable man. He was "the most modest, the most disinterested, and the most honest man I ever knew, with a temper that nothing could disturb . . . Not a great man, except morally; not an original or brilliant man, but sincere, thoughtful, deep and gifted with courage that never faltered." Dana also noted that "when the time came to risk all, he went in like a simple-hearted, unaffected, unpretending hero."[10] As April advanced, and Grant's time to risk all approached, Charles Dana had concluded that the Army of the Tennessee was in capable hands.

Fifty-eight-year-old Adjutant General Lorenzo Thomas typified the old army officer. An undistinguished West Point graduate, he had fought in the Seminole War and served in staff positions thereafter. This experience reinforced his notion that strict adherence to orders was a peerless virtue. The

War Department sent him to Grant with several duties in mind. Overtly Thomas was to institute the new policy of forming freed black men into fighting regiments and to dismiss or commission officers based upon their support for this policy. This he did with enthusiasm—he was an ardent abolitionist—and with characteristic old army directness. He circulated among Grant's rear area camps and delivered long, thundering abolitionist speeches in which he explained what the government expected. When he finished, Thomas asked those who opposed the order to move one step from the ranks. Amid some considerable shuffling, impelled by the strength of their prejudice, a few men came forward. Thomas promptly ordered them arrested and given time in the guardhouse to revise their opinions.

Soldiers tended to hear in Thomas's words that which they wanted to hear. Lieutenant Henry Kircher, who in no way wanted to serve with black soldiers, concluded from one of Thomas's speeches that "the soldiers are not to think that these [black] regiments are to be equal to the white regiments . . . for they are a subordinate race and would be used chiefly for such labors as previously fell as a burden to the white soldiers."[11] Lieutenant George Dodd Carrington wrote, "Bully for the Darkey Regiments. It's fun to see the Black Boys get their cartridge boxes on upside down, They don't know a belt from a hole in the ground. But seem very willing to learn."[12]

Some soldiers, including men of the 120th Ohio, stood around their camps muttering that they would not "fire a gun for this d——d abolition war" and earned stern rebukes from their officers.[13] Crusty Brigadier General A. J. Smith told anyone who would listen that he hated abolitionists worse than the devil and "if Jesus Christ offered to take him to heaven if he would become an abolitionist he would reply, NO! Mr. Christ, I beg to be excused. I would rather go to hell than be an abolitionist."[14]

Thomas's offer that diligent white volunteers, including enlisted men, could serve as officers in the new black regiments was a shrewd stroke that did much to defuse a potentially explosive situation. A soldier observed that those who had most bitterly denounced the policy of arming the blacks often showed the most energy trying to gain a commission in a Negro regiment.[15] But mostly it was the soldiers' sense of duty, a soldier culture that subordinated specific issues to the cause of victory, that made them tolerate the new situation.

In between delivering rousing abolitionist speeches, Thomas evaluated Grant. During the unhappy recent winter, rumors had flown about Washington that the incompetent Grant was frequently drunk and that his inattention to duty was slowly killing his army in the Mississippi swamps.

Thomas, to his credit, undertook an open-minded assessment. A jolly evening sharing punch with Admiral Porter, who fervently supported Grant, helped persuade him that all was well. After less than a week on the ground, Thomas reported that the army was "in very fine condition, unusually healthy."[16] Rawlins's good sense and Porter's punch helped, but in the end Grant's shining capacity converted two potentially intrusive and hostile men into allies, thus allowing the general to focus on the enemy across the river.

CONFEDERATE POLITICAL LEADERS west of the Mississippi had long felt that Jefferson Davis paid too little attention to their plight. Since so many of the guns and munitions their forces required came from the East, they believed that their very survival depended upon maintaining a connection across the Mississippi River. Finally, as spring came it seemed that Davis had awakened to their needs. The Confederate commander in chief informed Arkansas politicians that "the preservation of communication between the States on the East and West banks of that river is of primary importance" both militarily and politically.[17] To the Arkansas governor, he wrote his strongest statement yet on the importance of holding Vicksburg: "I assure you that you can not estimate more highly than I do the necessity of maintaining an unobstructed communication between the States that are separated by that river." The only issue, Davis continued, was how best to dispose the available troops. Here, too, Davis had reached a conclusion: "I have deemed the defense of Vicksburg and Port Hudson as indispensable."[18]

Although Davis might now deem the Confederate strongholds on the Mississippi "indispensable," such was the poverty of resources available that in reply to Pemberton's appeal for more heavy guns all he could do was to order four Columbiads to be transferred from the Alabama River and two heavy rifled guns to be sent from Richmond.[19] If he could not offer more material support, he could at least give moral encouragement. Some Mississippians still protested about having their fate in the hands of a Yankee. To one of them Davis wrote, "I selected General Pemberton for the very important command which he now holds from a conviction that he was the best qualified officer for that post then available, and I have since found no reason to change the opinion I then entertained of him."[20]

Davis's opinion of Pemberton rose even higher when, on April 11, Pemberton jubilantly announced, "I think most of Grant's forces are being withdrawn."[21] Pemberton had reached this conclusion after analyzing intelligence from a variety of sources. From a general in northwest Mississippi came scouts' reports that empty steamboats were being sent from Memphis to extricate Grant's army and carry his soldiers to reinforce Rosecrans in Tennessee. Pemberton also learned that the enemy had given up the effort against Fort Pemberton on the headwaters of the Yazoo River and was retreating rapidly. Simultaneously, Major General Frank Gardner reported that the threat against Port Hudson had receded. Then scouts informed Pemberton that on April 7 two separate convoys loaded with troops had departed upriver from Vicksburg.

The Pennsylvania-born general also had received reports about the Yankee movement through Louisiana. Initially, the only Confederates to resist McClernand's advance belonged to the Fifteenth Louisiana Cavalry Battalion. They were partisan cavalry, accustomed to hit-and-run, guerrilla-style operations.

On April 4, Brigadier General John Bowen sent Missouri soldiers from Grand Gulf, the site of newly built batteries below Vicksburg, to reinforce them. Since the Missouri men had left their home state to help block the Union drive on Corinth, Mississippi, back in 1862, two-thirds of them had fallen in battle or to disease. Yet the surviving nucleus remained a highly effective fighting force. The first days of April featured a type of riverine warfare between partisan cavalry, Missouri veterans, and McClernand's Union forces that would be familiar to American soldiers who fought in Vietnam's Mekong Delta 105 years in the future.

From these initial clashes, Pemberton received a report that McClernand, with perhaps fifteen thousand men, was present in Louisiana and that he might be en route to Natchez. In any event, Pemberton was reluctant to commit too much strength across the river for fear that Federal warships would cut them off. He told Bowen to continue his delaying operations if possible but that there was nothing in Louisiana important enough for Bowen to risk losing his command. On April 9, Pemberton telegraphed the War Department that he had received unconfirmed reports of "a movement under McClernand, in large force, by land west of river and southward. Much doubt it."[22]

At this time Pemberton had in hand fairly accurate intelligence. He had made the timeless error of focusing on enemy intentions instead of capabilities. The collection of steamers at Memphis was to support Grant's campaign through Louisiana. The movement of ships upstream from Vicksburg was to relieve traffic congestion on the river. The reported sightings of loaded transports involved a brigade-sized Union force charged with securing Grant's lines of communications. Grant was abandoning the approach to Fort Pemberton to concentrate on his latest outflanking effort. Banks was stripping forces from below Port Hudson to embark on a campaign into the Louisiana interior, after which he intended to return to Port Hudson. In assessing all of this, Pemberton fumbled badly.

With the reported end to the threat against the Mississippi River, General Johnston and President Davis were naturally eager for Pemberton to return to Tennessee the reinforcements he had previously received. Before obliging them, Pemberton had to consider one more piece of intelligence. Colonel Francis Cockrell, who commanded the Missouri soldiers confronting McClernand, had thirdhand news—the original source was a Louisiana woman who was actively collecting information about the invaders—that Grant was in Richmond, Louisiana, and that some of his officers had boasted that they intended to "get below Warrenton and cut off all supplies, and then starve us out." Cockrell added that such a maneuver was well within Yankee capabilities because of the combination of a decent road and the network of waterways that would support small boat traffic.[23] Cockrell had done a superb job of forecasting what was to come.

Pemberton ignored Cockrell's report. He telegraphed Johnston: "Will forward troops to you as fast as transportation can be furnished—about 8,000 men. Am satisfied Rosecrans will be re-enforced from Grant's army."[24]

WITH THE TIME APPROACHING when the army would attempt to leapfrog over the Mississippi River, Grant's responsibilities grew larger. Supporting him was a too small and too unprofessional staff. Much that he should have been able to delegate he had to do for himself. Overwork was taking a visible toll. A visiting friend commented on how his face was becoming ever more deeply lined. His tension-induced sick headaches were more common. Admiral Porter, who had grown to like and respect Grant, confidentially wrote that while working "like a horse" Grant was wearing himself out and was not well.[25] Yet one night when McPherson expressed concern and invited the general to take a break, Grant replied that McPherson could best help by giving him a handful of cigars and leaving him alone so he could continue his map study.

By now, criticism of Grant had become a regular feature in the eastern newspapers. Then, as now, congressmen and people in the administration carefully scrutinized a handful of news outlets to monitor the nation's mood.

On April 16, the *New York Times* correspondent wrote, " . . . [T]oday we are as far from taking possession of Vicksburgh as when we landed here in the middle of last January."[26]

Against this backdrop, Grant convened a council of war aboard Porter's flagship. He explained what he proposed to do and solicited comment. Mc-Clernand was not present but had provided written support for Grant's plan. The army professionals, led by Sherman, disagreed. Citing the Swiss strategist Henri Jomini, a Napoleonic Wars veteran whom every West Point graduate held in deep respect, Sherman argued that Grant's plan violated numerous strategic dictates. Grant listened patiently. When they had finished he told them that he had not changed his mind. He concluded the meeting by saying, "You will be ready to move at ten o'clock tomorrow morning."[27]

There was no ignoring that as much as the unfolding campaign was a gamble for Grant, so it was a high stakes roll for the navy and Admiral Porter. Once already in this campaign a Confederate ironclad had emerged from one of the many rivers feeding into the Mississippi to wreak havoc. Porter regularly received reports that other enemy ironclads and rams were under construction, near completion, or about to sortie against him. Yet Grant's plan required him to divide his fleet and send the best vessels downstream to a position between two powerful enemy fortresses. Once there, Porter had to rely upon the army to extricate him. It could easily become a trap, and if Porter lost his fleet because of army bungling the blame would be his. The logistical problems alone were staggering. Every shot his fleet fired, every bushel of coal burned, could be replaced only by hauling shot and powder overland through the bayous or running a coal barge past Vicksburg's batteries. Furthermore, if any of Porter's ships received significant battle damage there would be no machine shop to make repairs. Quite simply, this was not an operation Porter believed wise or necessary.[28] Some might have dragged their feet or worked to foil the plan in a myriad of undetectable ways. But that was not Porter's style. He understood that for a combined navy-army operation to succeed, it needed unity of command. Even though Grant had no authority over him, he willingly deferred to the general's wishes and ordered his subordinates to obey orders from Grant or Sherman as if they came from himself. Then he focused on the all-important run past the Vicksburg batteries scheduled for the night of April 16.

PEMBERTON'S CONFIDENCE that Grant seemed to have given up his futile efforts and withdrawn toward Memphis buttressed the spirit of Vicksburg's people. They were blithely unaware of the momentous events taking place upstream. Elegantly dressed women flounced through the streets to shop for last-minute apparel in anticipation of Major Watt's forthcoming ball. On their arms strutted gray-clad men, notable among them the gay officers of the river batteries who were particularly proud for having helped repulse the detested Yankees. On the evening of April 16, carriages brought Vicksburg's society to the ball. Here music played and drink flowed while upriver Ulysses Grant stood smoking a cigar as he gazed at the fleet as it departed to run the gauntlet of Vicksburg's heavy guns. Julia Grant sat in a chair next to him while one of the couple's young children sat on the lap of Colonel Wilson. The scene reminded an observer of a theater party waiting for the curtain to rise.

Darkness would provide concealment. One of Porter's officers recalled how at Island Number Ten his ironclad had diverted the exhaust steam into the paddle wheel housing to muffle the steam engines. To enhance stealth, Porter ordered all his ironclads rigged so. All livestock—essential hens and goats, ubiquitous canines—were sent ashore so there would be no untimely cluck, bleat, or bark. For extra protection, Porter also ordered each ironclad to lash coal-filled barges to their port sides, the side facing enemy fire, to protect hulls. Sailors stacked hay or cotton bales or sandbags around vital machinery and magazines. Since they had been purposely built to fight bows on along narrow rivers, the ironclads featured thin, stern armor. Accordingly, sailors stacked the stern decks with wet hay bales and slung heavy logs around the stern waterline. The frail transports received double bulwarks of cotton and hay.

In order to maintain silence, Porter ordered the ships to drift with the current. From his vantage point in the lead vessel, the *Benton*, Porter could see that neither light nor sound leaked from his fleet as it approached Vicksburg's frowning bluffs. The admiral hoped that the city's gala would occupy the guard's attentions. He had just remarked to the *Benton*'s captain that it seemed they would slip past unnoticed when a dazzling light illuminated the scene. It was 11:16 P.M.

So sudden and surprising was the illumination that at first the *Benton*'s captain thought that Vicksburg itself was on fire. In fact, vigilant rebel pickets had detected the fleet in motion, crossed to the shore opposite the city, and set fire to several previously prepared buildings and stacks of tar barrels. The blaze backlit Porter's fleet. In case that was not enough, they also fired a signal rocket. Then the first of Vicksburg's thirty-four heavy artillery pieces opened fire.[29]

So ferocious was the firing that men sixty miles away heard the cannon's detonations. Aboard the warships, the Confederate shot and shell rattled against the iron siding like hail. Fortunately, the *Benton* had an experienced pilot who had previously taken the *Essex* past the batteries. It was a frightening din, but not particularly deadly. It seemed worse when the ironclads drifted to within twenty yards of the shore. At point-blank range Confederate riflemen leaned over the levee, aimed at the ships' portholes, and fired. However, although rifle fire could wound and kill, it could not sink. And the cannon fire from the heavy guns was surprisingly ineffective. In part this was because the ironclad's own broadsides provided concealing smoke, causing most of the rebel shots to miss high. Also, Confederate artillery munitions were seldom of satisfactory quality, so that their strikes lacked penetrating power. Nonetheless, one thirty-two-pounder round passed through the *Benton*'s corner where her side and stern joined, grazed a machinery housing, penetrated four inches into her cylinder timber, and rebounded back into her stateroom. A large rifle bolt struck her port casemate just above her number eight port, passed through two and one-half inches of iron, and gouged out a six-foot by six-foot section of interior planking. These two shots hinted at what could take place.

The vessels behind the *Benton* did not enjoy the advantage of surprise. The *Lafayette*, second in line, had the former Confederate steamer *General Price* attached to her starboard side. This made maneuver difficult. At one point her helmsman lost control in the eddies and ran directly under the Vicksburg bluffs. Later her pilot became disoriented in the gunsmoke and glare from the burning buildings and pointed her upstream. Once she straightened out and the crew ran out her guns, an officer aboard had a good view through the portholes at "the rebel batteries, which now flashed like a thunder-storm along the river as far as the eye could see."[30] Nine of those flashes sent heavy rounds that struck home effectively. Several rifled artillery shots actually penetrated through the *Lafayette*'s armor. The unarmored *General Price* was hit thirteen times. Twice heavy rifle shells exploded within, destroying her officers' quarters and setting her afire. In spite of being badly cut up in her upper works, the *Price* suffered only three sailors slightly wounded.

From the river bluffs, Major J. T. Hogane saw the "yankee gun boats slowly steaming down the river; nearer they came with almost a death-like motion, slow, and in harmony with the black, lithe, sinuous gliding of the river."[31] The bonfires behind the Confederate artillery and from across the river illuminated the ironclads as they passed. One after another the big guns thundered. The shells for the ten-inch Columbiads weighed 128 pounds, yet even they seemed to have little effect. Overall, the rate of fire was slow. To the extent the Confederates concentrated their fire, they directed it against the van vessels. Consequently, the four Pook Turtles in the middle did not fare too badly. Only four shots hit the *Louisville*, while five struck the *Mound City*, including one round that passed cleanly through both iron casemates. Five shots passed through the *Pittsburgh*'s upperworks and two hit at her waterline. But for the extra log protection there, these shots would have entered her magazine. A particularly tense moment occurred when the *Louisville* and *Carondelet* tangled, but by cutting away the attached coal barges the ships came free. The last ironclad in the main column, the *Carondelet*, performed an inadvertent pirouette directly across from the Confederate batteries. One heavy shot struck her, bending two iron plates and slightly wounding four men.

Three unarmored army transports fared much worse. Porter had hoped that gunsmoke and battle confusion would shroud them. Just in case, he told Lieutenant Commander James Shirk in the ironclad *Tuscumbia* to trail the column and force the transports on should they balk. Sure enough, when the fire illuminated the river and the barrage commenced, two transports reversed course. Under heavy fire, Shirk shepherded them back into position. Shell fire set ablaze the transport *Henry Clay*. Once on fire she seemed to attract all attention. Hospital steward James Worthington was aboard a barge being towed by the *Henry Clay*. The steamer's erratic movements convinced him that the captain and pilot were drunk. As the pilot tried to press through the gauntlet, cannon fire knocked out her engines. Worthington described the scene: " . . . the boat was allowed to drift down amongth the cannon balls . . . It seemed, when the bluffs of the town were lighted by the blaze of artillery, like going down into the Lower Regions."[32] When the burning steamer became unmanageable, her crew jumped into the Mississippi to save themselves while Worthington's barge floated to safety.

In the smoke and confusion the *Tuscumbia* ran aground. She backed off and collided with the transport *Forest Queen*. From the heights above sailors heard the rebel gunners' jubilant cheers. The Confederate artillerymen heaved their weapons furiously to try to hit the two vessels. But few guns could train on these vulnerable targets. If the gunners depressed the barrels sufficiently, the shot literally spilled out the muzzle before the gun could be fired. One round did penetrate below the *Tuscumbia*'s waterline, but vigorous pumping controlled the leak. A shot cut in two a pilot aboard the *Forest Queen*. The surviving pilot pushed the carcass aside and continued.

Another shot sliced through a steam pipe and disabled the *Forest Queen*, but she managed to drift clear of the Confederate fire. She took on fourteen inches of water before Shirk was able to tow her to safety on the Louisiana shore.

Aboard the *Benton*, which had now passed through the danger zone, someone in a small boat called "Benton ahoy!" It was Sherman. The general asked, "Are you all right, old fellow?" Porter replied, "Come on board and see." A quick survey showed one sailor's leg cut off by a roundshot and a half-dozen shell and musket wounds. The *Benton* itself was undamaged. Pleased and satisfied, Sherman said that there were soldiers on the Louisiana shore ready to help if any assistance was needed. With a cheery good-night, he set off to visit the rest of the fleet "to find out how the other fellows fared."[33] In fact, the other fellows had fared very well. During the two and one-half hours the fleet had been under fire, a total of about forty-seven shots had struck the ironclads without doing significant damage. The entire fleet suffered only one fatality and had fifteen crewmen wounded.[34]

The entire Vicksburg campaign hinged upon the effectiveness of Vicksburg's big guns. The purpose of defending this place was to interdict movement along the river. John Pemberton's supposed experience using artillery against ships had been the prime reason he had been appointed to this command. Yet in spite of the best efforts of Vicksburg's gunners and of Pemberton himself, Porter's fleet had passed the Confederate fortifications with little loss. Although Pemberton had typically been absent from the scene of decision, from the vantage point of his Jackson headquarters he partially comprehended the significance of Porter's success: "I regard navigation of Mississippi River as shut out from us now."[35] The lieutenant general well knew that he could no longer supply his command from the Trans-Mississippi. He also realized that Grant apparently was not sending reinforcements to Tennessee and that, therefore, neither should he. Nineteen-year-old gunner Hugh Moss, who manned a battery on the Vicksburg waterfront, reached a deeper conclusion. He wrote in his diary, "Their object, I think, in going below is to cross troops and try and get in the rear of Vicksburg."[36]

Pemberton quickly apprised the Confederate high command in Richmond of the alarming news that the Federal fleet had passed Vicksburg's batteries. By nature the Confederate president was not one to solicit advice. But in matters of strategic importance, no one stood higher in his esteem than the commander of the Army of Northern Virginia. By necessity, Robert E. Lee had to concentrate on the military situation in the East. Still, Davis relied upon Lee's opinion regarding the defense of the entire Confederacy.

Thus the president found it reassuring to learn Lee's assessment of the significance of Porter's run past Vicksburg. Lee had read about it in a report that claimed that the Federal ships had suffered badly. Thus, Lee told Davis that the enemy "can derive no material benefit from it."[37] Furthermore, Lee expected that the additional heavy guns he knew were on the way to Vicksburg would prevent any repeat performances.

ON APRIL 20, Grant issued Special Order Number 110 in which he formally committed his army to the task of achieving a foothold on the Mississippi's east bank. The march through Louisiana would continue accordion-style; McClernand in the lead, then McPherson, then Sherman. As soon as one corps cleared the road the next one would move up as rapidly as possible. Special Order Number 110 required a great deal of work to be performed, and once again it seemed that a perverse Mother Nature marched under a rebel banner.

The entire winter, the Mississippi and its tributaries had run high and greatly limited Grant's freedom of maneuver. Grant planned to take advantage of the situation to float necessary supplies through the interlinked bayous and channels extending from Milliken's Bend south. Even more important, the skiffs, flatboats, and small steamers required to ferry soldiers across the Mississippi were to use this route. Then water levels fell. Consequently, either the army could stockpile supplies for the assault crossing by relying upon slow-moving wagon train convoys—McClernand estimated this would take thirteen days—or the supplies themselves could be loaded aboard steamers and risked against Vicksburg's guns. It was one thing to send ironclads to escort steamers past the batteries and quite another to send unarmored, unescorted vessels. Nonetheless, this is what McClernand suggested. He told Grant that "the loss of a few transports in running the blockade" paled in comparison to the advantages.[38] Grant agreed.

On April 22, six more transports and twelve barges ran the batteries. Their regular civilian crews balked at the danger, so infantry volunteers manned the vessels. One hundred sixteen men from a single regiment presented themselves as experienced pilots, engineers, firemen, or deckhands. The competition for places was so keen—volunteers were offered a thirty-day furlough if they survived—that men offered hard cash to the chosen few for the opportunity to brave the enemy fire.[39] Each transport had a crew of twenty-five volunteers. Under the supervision of Colonel Clark Lagow of Grant's staff, they placed double tiers of cotton bales around the machinery and piled sacks of grain on the deck to prevent plunging shot from piercing the boilers. The crews rigged fire hoses to the pumps and placed water buckets in the hold and on deck. The pilots agreed to hug the eastern shore as closely as possible in the hope that the enemy guns would be unable to depress sufficiently to hit them. One transport had a civilian pilot whose background was unknown. The transport's commander nominated a Missouri sergeant to serve as second pilot and gave him orders to stay alert. If the civilian wavered, the sergeant was to kill him. Major General John Logan took this one step further. Many of the volunteers came from his division. He told them before embarking, "I want no faltering, if any man attempts to leave his post, I want him shot on the spot."[40]

Having taken all possible precautions, Colonel Lagow boarded a steamer—officers worth their salt in this war, whether staff or line, shared their men's danger—and ordered the transports to cast off once the moon went down. The vessels kept their steam up but hid their boiler's fires beneath tarpaulins. They drifted downstream slowly about four miles before being detected by the rebel picket boats shortly before midnight. The pickets gave the alarm and again ignited large bonfires to illuminate the vessels. A Union officer recalled that it was so bright he would have had no trouble reading a newspaper from the hurricane deck of his steamer. By the time the transports were opposite the Vicksburg courthouse it seemed as though a veritable storm of shot and shell was erupting from the city. The steamer *Tigress* was particularly unfortunate. Solid shot pounded through her deck and exited through her hull. A shell exploded in the captain's stateroom, sending splinters flying in all directions. One splinter knocked down the colonel commanding the vessel. Soon the *Tigress* was taking on water and responding sluggishly to her rudder. Still, it seemed she would make it until a shot from the upper battery raked her from stern to bow, ripping a huge gash in her side. Water filled her engine room waist deep, but her engineer clung to his post in an effort to coax her safely to shore.

As before, Sherman was in the river below Vicksburg: "The first boat to arrive was the *Tigress*, a fast side-wheel boat which was riddled with shot and repeatedly struck in the hull. She rounded to, tied to the bank and sunk a wreck . . . The next was the *Empire City*, also crippled but afloat, then the *Cheeseman* that was partially disabled, then the *Anglo-Saxon* and *Moderator*, both of which were so disabled that they drifted down stream catching the Warrenton batteries as they passed." Overall, the damage to the transports was such that Sherman concluded that running the guns "was a desperate and terrible thing."[41] The *Tigress* had carried Grant to Pittsburgh Landing when the sounds of Confederate thunder alerted him that his Army of the Tennessee was under attack and in grave danger at Shiloh. At Vicksburg she carried the army's medical supplies. Holed thirty-five times, she sank beyond salvage. The Army of the Tennessee could endure without her, but the sick and wounded would suffer and some would die because the *Tigress* had sunk. In addition, six of the ten barges were lost. Admiral Porter provided carpentry stores to the army mechanics, who immediately began to repair the riddled steamers and surviving barges.

There was a recent law in the United States by which Congress authorized the president to reward personal valor with a medal. The medal's design featured a star, each of whose five points held a cluster of laurel leaves representing victory and oak leaves symbolizing strength. In the star's center was Minerva, the Roman goddess of wisdom and war, holding the shield of the Union to dispel Discord. Two infantry volunteers who crewed the transports—Ohio Private Henry Casey and Illinois Lieutenant James Vernay—earned the Congressional Medal of Honor for their valor on this night. Again the position of the pilot had proven exceptionally dangerous. One pilot died from an abdomen wound suffered while conning his steamer.

The transports had made their run during a windless night. Thus the smoke from the heavy Confederate guns failed to disperse and this made accurate gunnery difficult. In addition, the gunners again exhibited poor fire discipline. As had been the case on the night of the sixteenth, whenever their fire damaged a target and it slowed, everyone seemed to pile on. It was easier to hit a helpless target and most satisfactory to see tangible evidence—timbers flying, smokestacks toppling—of the cannons' destructiveness. But by concentrating on the cripples, they allowed the other steamers to slip by. The Confederate river batteries fired 391 shots that night, but managed to sink only the *Tigress*. Nonetheless, they had sufficiently battered the transports to henceforth cause Grant to forbid additional attempts by unarmed steamers to run the guns. In coming days some tugs and barges carrying supplies would try the blockade, but after April 22 Grant possessed enough shipping—seven transports and fifteen or sixteen barges—below the Vicksburg and Warrenton guns to ferry his army across the Mississippi.

A junior Confederate officer well summed up the altered strategic situation caused by the concentration of shipping below Vicksburg when he wrote in his diary, " . . . [T]he crisis of this war is fast approaching."[42]

General Grant would have agreed with this assessment. The day after the transports made their run, he shifted his headquarters downriver to direct personally the army's assault crossing of the Mississippi River.

Grant's strategy continued to alarm Sherman. Both he and Grant knew that the supply line through Louisiana was a single, poor road, "a narrow levee, hemmed in with water on each side, and with space barely sufficient to set up tents between the roadway and the water."[43] Much of the route was liable to become a quagmire whenever it rained and it seemed preposterous for an entire army to rely upon it. Once across the Mississippi no one knew how the army would be supplied. The difference between the two men was that Grant was willing to accept the risk whereas Sherman was not. Sherman confided to his brother that he felt "less confidence" in Grant's plan "than in any similar undertaking of the war."[44] Porter continued to share Sherman's doubts. It seemed to him that his gunboats' run past Vicksburg had merely exchanged one set of troubles for another.

So it was that with the campaign's crisis approaching, Grant was sanguine about success while Sherman and Porter, two very competent military men, were dubious. Grant had acquired a key insight back in 1861 that now served him well. The then Colonel Grant had marched his men across twenty-five miles of deserted countryside where, for all he knew, the enemy might be lying in ambush to destroy his regiment. As Grant approached the enemy's position, "my heart kept getting higher and higher until it felt to me as though it was in my throat. I would have given anything then to have been back in Illinois, but I had not the moral courage to halt and consider what to do; I kept right on." In the event, he found that the Confederates had abandoned their camp in haste. As Grant reflected, a novel thought occurred that forever altered his approach to war. Henceforth, "I never experienced trepidation upon confronting an enemy . . . I never forgot that he had as much reason to fear my forces as I had his."[45] In April 1863, as in 1861, Grant "kept right on."

For the Army of the Tennessee, the first fruits of Porter's successful run past Vicksburg came on April 17. Until that date and despite overwhelming odds, units belonging to Bowen's Missouri Brigade had been conducting a tenacious delaying action along the Louisiana shore. Concerned that Porter's gunboats would cut off his detachments on the far shore, Bowen ordered them to return to Mississippi while they still could. By the evening of April 17, the Missouri men were back at Grand Gulf. Because of the navy, for the crucial last two weeks in April, the Army of the Tennessee faced no significant Confederate opposition as it slipped south through the

Louisiana bayous. However, the winter spent in sodden encampments continued to take a toll. When the unhappy news of one midwestern boy's fate reached the folks back home, a father passed the word throughout the family: "You may have herd that my son Newton had Died down near there he was sick a bout 10 days with the Tifoid fever & chronic Diareah he was taken sick on a march while going from Millecans Bend to Grand Gulf."[46]

Across the river, following Porter's run, General Pemberton appreciated that Grant had the capacity to try to cross the Mississippi somewhere between Vicksburg and Grand Gulf. But this was just one of several possibilities. Then, on April 27, General Bowen informed him that "all the movements of the enemy during the last twenty-four hours seem to indicate an intention on their part to march their army still lower down in Louisiana . . . then to run their steamers by me and cross."[47] By correctly divining Grant's strategy, Bowen had presented Pemberton with a priceless gift if he had the wit to use it. The problem was that at the time when Bowen came to his revelation, what wits Pemberton possessed were concentrated elsewhere. Specifically, the Pennsylvanian judged that a Union cavalry column marauding through the Mississippi interior was a more serious threat and he wanted it eliminated.

READERS OF THE *New York Times* awoke on May 18 to headlines proclaiming Colonel Benjamin Grierson's safe arrival at Baton Rouge and the end of "The Great Cavalry Raid Through Mississippi."[48] *Harper's Weekly* followed suit, providing its readers with a full front-page portrait of the colonel in its June 6 edition. For too long Northerners had read about the exploits of enemy cavaliers, men like Jeb Stuart, Bedford Forrest, and John Morgan. The account of Grierson's sixteen-day raid was something new and refreshing.

There could hardly have been a less likely cavalryman than the thirty-seven-year-old Grierson. Music was his first love. During the decade preceding the war, he first floundered to support his family as a music teacher and then as a small store owner. There was little demand for musicians on the Illinois frontier of the 1850s. As a store owner he sold too much on credit, and quit after five years virtually penniless. When the call for volunteers came in 1861, Grierson joined the infantry. He feared and detested horses, having been kicked in the face at age eight and suffered two months of blindness from his injury. Naturally the military bureaucracy transferred him to the mounted arm. He sought service elsewhere only to rebuffed by Halleck himself, who "jocularly remarked that I looked active and wiry enough to make a good cavalryman."[49]

Dawn of April 17, 1863, found the reluctant cavalier departing the southwestern Tennessee town of LaGrange in command of 1,700 troopers belonging to the Sixth and Seventh Illinois and Second Iowa cavalry. Grierson's troopers were one of five raiding columns Grant had arranged to divert attention from his pending crossing of the Mississippi. The carefully synchronized expeditions set out across a front extending from Memphis to middle Tennessee. Of them all, Grierson's force had the most important objective: the east-west railroad linking Pemberton at Jackson with Confederate forces to the east.

From the raid's onset Grierson commanded with considerable intelligence. For the first three days he dodged scattered rebel patrols and rode south. At this point, five miles from Pontotoc, Mississippi, he mustered his command at 3 A.M. to cull horses and men who might encumber further movement. The 175 or so troopers selected, along with their saddle sore or lame mounts, styled themselves the "Quinine Brigade." Sick or weakened they might be, but Grierson believed the Quinine Brigade could still serve. Escorting the prisoners captured to date, it countermarched north, taking careful measures to obliterate the main column's tracks. Meanwhile, Grierson proceeded along side roads to avoid detection.

In Jackson, on April 20—three days after Grierson set out—Pemberton issued his first series of orders to intercept and destroy Grierson. Already Confederate cavalry was chasing the Federal calvary. One detachment managed to engage the raiders. At a crossroads skirmish, the commanding Confederate officer sent his men in with the order to "make 'em holler." The rebels attacked, were defeated, and forced to retire at the double quick. A private dashed by the officer and exclaimed, "Well, Captain, we made one of 'em holler."

"What did he say, Tom?"

"He said, 'Forward, skirmishers.'"[50]

Now operating deep in enemy country, at midnight on April 20 Grierson took the bold decision to divide his command. He detached the Second Iowa with orders to strike east against the Mobile & Ohio Railroad and then return home. He hoped they would attract the pursuit and permit him to make an unmolested strike against the Southern Railroad. As the Quinine Brigade had done the previous day, the Iowa troopers took pains to simulate the passage of a much larger force. Gunners turned the one piece of artillery in four different places to make it seem that an entire battery was with them. On rain-soaked ground, the deceit worked handsomely. The pursuing Tennessee cavalry had not been taken in by the Quinine Brigade's ruse. This time, when they reached the telltale marks left by the artillery, they had no doubt that the tracks represented Grierson's entire column. Had they proceeded another few hundred yards they would have again found tracks left by the main Union body. Instead, the Tennessee troopers turned to follow the Second Iowa.

The next day, having advanced another forty miles toward his objective, Grierson studied his map to anticipate likely enemy responses. He guessed that yesterday's ruse would have been detected by now. He needed another day to reach his objective. Deciding that the Mobile & Ohio Railroad would still be a prime Confederate concern, he detached a single company to ride thirty miles southeast to feint toward that railroad. Captain Henry Forbes, the officer assigned this mission, had no illusions about the risks involved. He explained matters to his company and said that any trooper who believed himself unfit for a hard march-gallop could withdraw without prejudice to his record. A handful of troopers reluctantly acknowledged that their horses were failing. At the head of thirty-four stalwart Company B troopers, Forbes then set off. No one anticipated that he would be absent for five days and four nights, during which time he and his men slept for only eighteen hours. Company B would travel some three-hundred miles through enemy country, thoroughly alarm and confuse the region's defenders, and miraculously reunite with Grierson well after the colonel had given up all hope of seeing them again.

The same day, April 22, that Forbes set off on his independent mission, Pemberton concluded that the raiders had evaded the pursuing cavalry. He became increasingly alarmed about the threat to the rear. A network of small bases and depots lay scattered in front of the raiders. It represented the carefully husbanded logistical sinew Pemberton needed to fight a summer campaign against Grant. Unwilling to weaken his own army, Pemberton ordered an infantry brigade commanded by Brigadier General Abraham Buford to intercept the raiders. The next day, Pemberton received a report that a heavy enemy column was approaching the Mobile & Ohio near the town of Macon. He concluded that this force represented the raider's main blow. In fact, it was Forbes and his thirty-four troopers. Pemberton ordered available troops to concentrate on the railroad and defeat the raiders.

On Friday, April 24, Grierson's raiders were six miles from their objective. Key to their ability to penetrate so deep into rebel territory had been the service of Grierson's "Butternut Guerrillas." At the raid's outset, Grierson had formed a scouting detachment of young, intelligent, and reckless troopers. They dressed in Confederate-style wear and rode ahead of the column to scour the countryside for intelligence. It proved to be the simplest of matters for the Butternut Guerrillas to encounter a rebel soldier and chat him up about which bridges were burned or the whereabouts of formed Confederate forces. Then came a request to admire the soldier's fine weapon, his willingness to hand it over for inspection, and a pistol point denouement: "You, sir, are my prisoner."

On April 24, three Butternut Guerrillas entered Newton Station, a small depot on the Southern Railroad east of Jackson. They ascertained that it was largely undefended and that two trains were due in shortly. One scout drew pistol and shouted "Remain inside! Don't come out on peril of your lives."[51] On came the Illinois cavalry to seal off the town and hide in the tall grass near the railroad. As the scouts nonchalantly watched, a twenty-five-car train eased onto a siding. Suddenly, on signal, a line of mounted riders swept in and captured the train. It carried material for repairing rail lines and building Vicksburg's fortifications. Hustling the prisoners out of view, the cavalry hid again while the scouts resumed their loitering posture. In a few minutes the Jackson-Meridian passenger train carrying refugees from Vicksburg approached Newton Station. As the engine slowed, a scout sprang up the locomotive's steps and pointed a pistol at the engineer. This train included four freight cars loaded with ammunition and weapons and six with commissary and quartermaster stores. The raiders burned the loaded cars, after which Grierson set them to cutting telegraph lines and burning bridges and trestleworks. Throughout the war, cavalry showed little aptitude for such physical labor. Usually their destructive efforts could be readily repaired. But at this juncture every day was important. Anything that inhibited the arrival of Confederate reserves was useful.

With the destruction of the rail line at Newton Station, Grierson's mission was done. What remained was to escape intact. This Grierson did in style by employing a variety of ruses. He allowed a prominent citizen to overhear a discussion of planned routes of march, relaxed the guard so he could escape, and then headed off in a different direction. He feinted at multiple objectives while actually taking the route least expected by retracing the road the command had just taken. He sent a telegraphic report to Pemberton falsely describing his command's location. In spite of such measures, the Illinois cavalry would be out for another eight harrowing days before arriving within friendly lines at Baton Rouge. The final twenty-eight hours saw them march seventy-six miles, fight four skirmishes, and narrowly avoid capture when trapped against a swollen river.

Grierson's sixteen-day raid was an outstanding example of what intelligent, resourceful leadership could accomplish. His troopers had inflicted some one-hundred casualties, captured over five hundred prisoners, and destroyed much valuable Confederate property, while losing only three killed, seven wounded, and fourteen missing or captured. More importantly, the raid diverted units belonging to Pemberton's strategic reserve. Consequently, they would be unavailable to oppose Grant's crossing of the Mississippi River. Likewise, Wirt Adams's cavalry marched in pursuit of Grierson and away from the Mississippi at Grand Gulf just as Grant was beginning his crossing operations. Their absence blinded General Bowen, the officer charged with defending Grand Gulf. However, the raid's surpassing impact was on Pemberton himself. At a time when he needed to devote all his energy and talents to divining Grant's true line of approach, he spent time trying both to defend his own rear and to trap the meddlesome raiders. Indicative of his preoccupation were his actions on April 27, when he sent seventeen messages to a variety of commands concerning Grierson and not one addressing the Union buildup in Louisiana.

Grierson's ability to raid deep in the Confederate rear surprised Pemberton.[52] Confederate soldier Edward Fontaine concluded, "Nothing proves more fully the incompetency of our Generals than the miserable disposition of the forces appointed to defend the State. This raid is the most successful the Yankees have yet made, and is a disgrace to our State."[53] Grant would write in his memoirs that the raid "was of great importance, for Grierson had attracted the attention of the enemy from the main movement against Vicksburg."[54] Sherman, who was always sparing with his compliments, called it "the most brilliant expedition of the war."[55] Victors are often too fulsome in their praise for subordinates. Still, all in all the newspapers were correct in describing it as a "wonderful cavalry exploit." Perhaps the leader of Company B's independent foray, Captain Forbes, summed it up best. Using words that could have applied to the entire Army of the Tennessee, he wrote: "The men who did this work were a year and a half from the plow-tail, and their chief claim to consideration is that they were representative men—fair types of our American citizen-soldiery."[56]

FOR MORE THAN THREE WEEKS the Army of the Tennessee's objective had been New Carthage. However, when Grant arrived near that town on

April 23—the day before Grierson attacked Newton Station—it was obvious that he could not use this area as a staging ground for an invasion across the river. It, like much of his tenuous supply link back to Milliken's Bend, was under water. Already McClernand—again displaying commendable energy—had found an alternative, a road leading to a place called Perkins's plantation, about eight miles below New Carthage. This route would require another two thousand feet or so of bridge construction, but Grant's westerners were becoming quite skilled at this. Accordingly, Grant ordered the route put in order to permit the passage of an army and its trains. That evening an anxious Admiral Porter arrived to confer about how best to cross the river.

In Porter's mind things were not going well at all. It seemed to him that the army was no closer to its goal. The admiral did not appreciate the difficulty of the army's trek through Louisiana. To his way of thinking, all the army did was march a mile or two and then encamp. Its slow pace was allowing the rebels too much time to erect fortifications at Grand Gulf and elsewhere. Twice the navy had reconnoitered Grand Gulf. Viewed up close, the Confederate works there looked formidable. Given time, Porter warned that they could erect an impregnable citadel. Meanwhile, Porter's fleet had no secure source of supplies. It was a thoroughly wretched state of affairs and it depressed the admiral. Further darkening Porter's thinking was an encounter the previous evening with a civilian informant. Playacting the role of a Union sympathizer, the civilian had claimed that the Confederates had anticipated Grant's maneuver and had been preparing for six weeks. He said that Confederate troops and artillery were marching from Vicksburg to Grand Gulf as fast as they could. Twelve thousand were already there, with more coming on. Porter informed Grant of this distressing news, adding that he recommended against a direct assault on Grand Gulf. As he explained the next day in a candid letter to Secretary of the Navy Welles, "I see no certainty of a successful landing of our army on the Mississippi side."[57]

Porter had fallen for a ruse that Confederate generals everywhere—in this case probably General Bowen—employed with great success. They sent "primed" deserters or "Union loyal" civilians across the lines with exaggerated reports of their own strength. Their tales imposed caution and delay. So was the case when Porter's anxiety persuaded Grant that he had best take a look at the situation himself. The next morning, Porter and Grant examined Grand Gulf from the deck of the onetime Confederate ram *General Price*. Grant judged the position less formidable than did Porter. Still, he took an extra day to send Colonel Wilson and a regiment of infantry to the river's east bank to reconnoiter the land above Grand Gulf. If Wilson found suitable roads leading inland, then Grand Gulf would not have to be tackled directly. Wilson went, returned, and reported that if there were roads they were under water. There was nothing for it but to attack Grand Gulf.

Grant also concluded that Perkins's plantation was too far away from Grand Gulf to serve as a staging area for the invasion. The time it would take his transports to complete a round trip and bring reinforcements was excessive. His first wave would be in peril for too long to a potentially over-whelming Confederate counterattack. Grant thus ordered the army on an-other downriver march across waterlogged terrain and around one more bayou to a place called Hard Times, located just above the bend where Grand Gulf was perched. Once he reached Hard Times, his line of com-munications would extend sixty-three miles back to Milliken's Bend. U. S. Grant was not a man given to introspection. Yet perhaps even he smiled at the irony of the name "Hard Times." Nine years before, he had left the army in near disgrace, his resignation induced by his growing alcoholism. He had tried to support his family on a farm aptly named "Hardscrabble" and had failed. Now his army's base for its great cross-river gamble echoed the farm name from that difficult time.

Porter and Grant agreed that the navy would silence the batteries at Grand Gulf and provide cover while the army made an assault crossing. Confidentially, Porter doubted the wisdom of this scheme. Grant, he wrote, "seems to think these soldiers will assault a hill two hundred feet high, at an angle of 60 degrees—they cannot and won't do it."[58] Porter preferred to run past Grand Gulf and cross the army below. But he did not argue and in-stead made plans to assure that the navy did its part.

No Federal officer appreciated the real strength of Grand Gulf. Con-federate engineering had proved uneven during this war, but here it ex-celled. The key was Fort Cobun, dug into the side of a steep knoll known as Point of Rock. The Mississippi River flowed toward Point of Rock and then turned sharply south to continue past the fire-gutted village of Grand Gulf. Situated forty feet above the river, Fort Cobun's four guns—one of which was a heavy eight-inch Dahlgren—dominated this turn. A communi-cations trench protected by a double line of rifle pits connected these works with another fortification three-quarters of a mile downstream. This was Fort Wade, named after the colonel who commanded the artillery in Bowen's division. Fort Wade was twenty feet above the river line and fea-tured two heavy guns, including a one-hundred-pounder Blakely rifle and an eight-inch Dahlgren along with two rifled thirty-two-pounders. Below

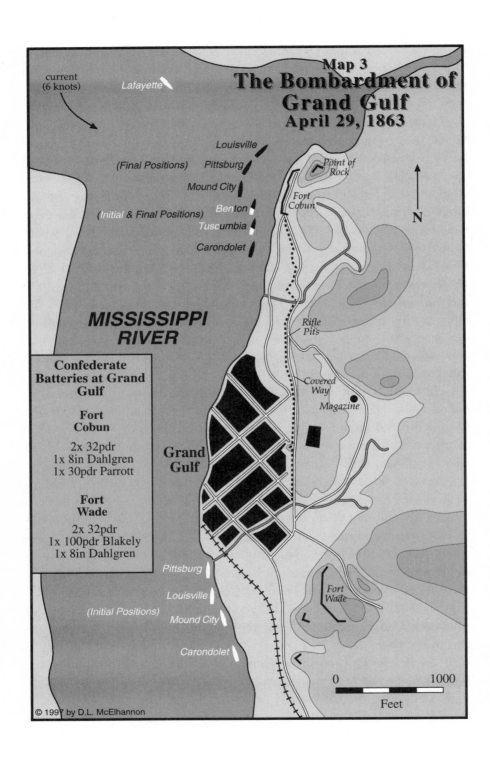

Map 3
The Bombardment of
Grand Gulf
April 29, 1863

current (6 knots)

Lafayette

Louisville

(Final Positions)   *Pittsburg*

Mound City

(Initial & Final Positions)   *Benton*

Tuscumbia

Carondolet

Point of Rock

Fort Cobun

N

Rifle Pits

MISSISSIPPI RIVER

Covered Way

Magazine

Confederate Batteries at Grand Gulf

Fort Cobun

2x 32pdr
1x 8in Dahlgren
1x 30pdr Parrott

Fort Wade

2x 32pdr
1x 100pdr Blakely
1x 8in Dahlgren

Grand Gulf

Pittsburg

Louisville

(Initial Positions)   *Mound City*

Carondolet

Fort Wade

0   1000

Feet

© 1997 by D.L. McElhannon

Fort Wade was a redan surmounting a detached hill. From here the Confederates could deliver enfilade fire against any infantry trying to land on the Mississippi shore. Tough Missouri infantrymen backed by five field-pieces manned both the rifle pits and a trench line along the blufftops. Although the defenders numbered only about four thousand men—one-third the strength claimed by Porter's civilian informant—they were well positioned to command the river in all directions. Most significantly, the rebel artillery sat behind earthen banks up to forty feet thick that were proof against any artillery. Adding to the difficulty of attacking this position was the presence of six-knot currents and three-knot return eddies that made boat steering extremely difficult.

Porter's plan called for his four Pook Turtles to pass within one-hundred yards of Fort Cobun, spray the works with antipersonnel rounds, and proceed downstream to silence Fort Wade. Meanwhile, Porter in his flagship *Benton*—the "old war horse," as sailors fondly called her—and the new iron-clads *Tuscumbia* and *Lafayette* would tackle the upper battery at Fort Cobun. Should any vessel receive a shot in her machinery, the commander was to drop anchor and continue the fight. Federal infantrymen would remain ready aboard steamers and barges to conduct an amphibious assault when Porter gave the signal.

At 7 A.M. on April 29, the Mississippi Squadron slipped anchors and steamed down to bombard Grand Gulf. A volunteer officer, Lieutenant William Hoel, who was an ex–Mississippi River pilot, led the way aboard the ironclad *Pittsburgh*. The Pook Turtles showered Fort Cobun with shrapnel, then carried on toward Fort Wade while Porter's division took station in front of the upper work. Once in position to fire, the unpredictable currents caused the ironclads to swing wildly, forcing the big *Benton* to present first bow, then starboard, then stern to the rebel guns. It was very difficult to lay the guns accurately while the boats swerved about.

However inaccurate, the sheer volume of fire from the gunboats' eighty-one cannons awed the defenders. To a veteran Arkansas soldier the bombardment beat anything he had experienced, including pitched battles at Elkhorn Tavern and Corinth. Worse, the Confederates sensed that their return fire was ineffective, with most of their rounds apparently glancing off the ironclads' armor. After two hours of firing the gunboats began literally to smother the defenders' cannons. So many rounds struck the embrasures that the rebel gunners had to dig repeatedly to clear them. One naval shell struck their commander, Colonel William Wade, in the head and killed him at the post named in his honor. Slowly the Federal fire drove the Confederate artillerymen from their guns and dismounted two of Fort Wade's thirty-two-pounder rifles.

Once Fort Wade had been silenced, Porter signaled for the four Pook Turtles to join him in the battle against the upper fort. Once again the Union pilots displayed high courage as they battled both the currents and the Confederate artillery. When a bolt entered the *Tuscumbia*'s pilothouse the pilot refused to relinquish the wheel until he fainted from blood loss. Aggressively, Porter directed his ironclads to close within fifty yards of Fort Cobun. Under the ensuing barrage and the fire from volunteer infantry sharpshooters, the rebel gun crews feared to expose themselves and declined to push the remaining gun forward into its firing bay. With a severely restricted field of fire, this gun shot wildly. Yet the defenders were inflicting more damage than they realized. One shot from Fort Cobun penetrated the *Benton*'s pilothouse, wounding the pilot and shattering the wheel. An eddy swept the temporarily unmanageable *Benton* close in under the cliff and held her in place with her stern facing the enemy guns. Lieutenant Hoel, the commander of the *Pittsburgh*, interposed his ironclad between the *Benton* and the shore guns. The *Pittsburgh* lay within ten paces of the battery and during the next ten minutes suffered a severe pounding, losing six killed and eight wounded.

Nonetheless, Federal persistence paid off. By about 1 P.M. the Confederate fire had all but ceased. Grant slipped downstream aboard a small tug to meet the *Benton* and confer with Porter. Porter's fighting blood was up. He had just fought a difficult action for more than five hours, but at last he seemed to have accomplished his mission. He told Grant that it was perfectly safe to land his troops. Grant disagreed. In his mind, the rebel gunners had just stood toe to toe with ironclad gunboats. Frail, unarmored transports stood no chance against such a foe. Furthermore, what lay behind the fortifications and along the wooded bluff was impossible to discern. Grant told Porter that even with the heavy guns silenced the Confederates might still have hidden field batteries that could inflict great loss upon infantry in steamers, open boats, and barges. Rather than assault, he preferred to march his men farther downstream where they could reembark, cross the river, and take the batteries from the rear.

Grant's new plan angered Porter even though it was the same scheme that Porter had originally preferred. It meant that his fleet had sacrificed for nothing. The admiral gave the withdrawal order, but vented his spleen in the general order he later issued. In it he praised his sailors' conduct and concluded, "It is not our fault that the enemy's guns and munitions of war are not in our hands. Ours is the duty to silence batteries; it can not be expected that we shall land and take possession."[59] Fortunately for army-navy relations, Grant was long gone when Porter wrote these words.

Following the battle, five of Porter's seven ironclads recorded how many rounds they had shot. At mostly point-blank range they expended 1,729 "fires," most of which were heavy artillery projectiles including one-hundred-pounder rifles and eleven-inch guns. For comparison, consider that the famous October 14, 1942, Japanese shelling of Guadalcanal—"the Bombardment," as it became known—featured two battleships with sixteen heavy guns delivering about nine hundred fourteen-inch shells. By any standard, the U.S. Navy's bombardment of Grand Gulf was stupendous. Unlike the Japanese battleships, Porter's ironclads endured an intense return fire. The *Benton* was hit forty-seven times. In its gallant effort to draw fire from the flagship, the *Pittsburgh* received most of its thirty-five hits. But nothing equaled the battering taken by the poor *Tuscumbia*. Confederate cannon struck her eighty-one times. These three vessels had eighteen killed and fifty-six wounded.[60] The rest of the fleet reported only one sailor wounded.

By battle's end the *Tuscumbia* was a drooping hulk—"torn to smash"— with her stern hanging seven and one-half inches too low and her bow one and one-half inches out of plumb. Her trial by combat had revealed design and construction flaws. When an enemy shell exploded in her forward turret it threw sparks into the shell room and magazine passages. Rounds that hit the forward turret started the bolts that secured the armor plating. Investigation revealed the "outrageously bad manner" by which contractors had fastened the armor to the backing using very short drift bolts.[61]

After Porter retired upstream, the Federal infantry climbed off the transports to resume the march down the Mississippi's western shore. Meanwhile, the navy's remaining task was to get the transports past Grand Gulf so they could ferry the army across the river. Porter decided that at dusk his warships would again engage Grand Gulf at close range while the transports hugged the opposite shore and tried to slip downstream.

On the bluffs overlooking the river, the Confederate gunners had counted noses—losses had been surprisingly light, with only three killed and some eighteen wounded—returned to their pieces, and cleared the dirt and debris from their guns. When the Union fleet reappeared they returned fire as best they could. It was not very effective. More importantly, screened by the fleet, the transports passed unhurt. For all their success in thwarting a direct assault, the gunners at Grand Gulf, like those at Vicksburg, had failed in their larger purpose of interdicting Federal passage of the river. One of Bowen's Arkansas soldiers who had watched the fight at Grand Gulf appreciated the significance of this:

> Yankees have a force of some 30,000 men on the other side of the river, opposed to about 6,000 or 7,000 of our men, on this side. It is their object to effect a landing on this side [of] the river, and move round in rear of Vicksburg. I fear they will make it.[62]

WHETHER THE YANKEES would "make it" or not depended to a large extent upon Confederate countermoves. On April 28, the day before Porter's ironclads dueled with Grand Gulf, General Pemberton was at his Jackson headquarters trying to comprehend Grant's strategy. For three months he had performed without significant misstep. Recently, he had expended much attention dealing with Grierson, but he had not ignored Bowen's April 27 prediction that Grant would try to force a crossing of the Mississippi below Grand Gulf. Pemberton dutifully forwarded the warning to Joe Johnston and asked Bowen if he had enough men to "hold your position" and if not, what was "the smallest additional force" Bowen required.[63]

Pemberton's responses to Bowen's warning do not reveal the mind of a confident general. Essentially, he was abdicating responsibility both up and down the chain of command. It was Pemberton's duty to assess risks and make decisions. Instead, while passively informing his superior of the situation without recommending any action, he threw that duty upon his subordinate. Moreover, by emphasizing Bowen's need to hold Grand Gulf, he failed to address the consequences of a Federal crossing further downstream. To Bowen's great credit, he responded to Pemberton's lack of decisiveness by advising that "every man and gun that can be spared" be sent to Grand Gulf.[64]

Pemberton commanded an effective force of about 54,000 men divided into four major commands. Twenty-six thousand of them manned the defenses from the fortified bluffs on the Yazoo River to the Warrenton batteries below Vicksburg. General Bowen's Grand Gulf garrison numbered 6,000. Major General Frank Gardner commanded 12,000 effectives at Port Hudson. At the opposite end of the line, Major General William Loring was on the upper Yazoo around Fort Pemberton with 5,000 effectives.[65] Another 5,000 men were scattered in northern Mississippi. By straight-line measurement, two hundred miles separated Fort Pemberton from Port Hudson. Pemberton appreciated that in an emergency it was difficult to move Port Hudson's garrison rapidly because that post lay fifty-eight miles from the

Mississippi Central rail depot.[66] All in all the Confederate position was too extensive for 54,000 men to defend. Everything reduced to how Pemberton distributed his force.

Pemberton decided that 5,000 men were all he could spare to support Bowen and alerted the commander of the Vicksburg garrison to hold them in readiness.[67] That subordinate, Major General Carter Stevenson, had responsibility for a twenty-two-mile front from the Warrenton battery below the city to Haynes' Bluff above. Stevenson was far from a military genius. He had graduated fourth from the bottom of his West Point class. He had no combat experience in this war beyond supervising Vicksburg's batteries. But Stevenson understood that his artillery line along the Mississippi was the essential point around which all else pivoted. He was most reluctant to do anything to weaken it. For the previous five days he and Pemberton had conducted a debate by telegraph regarding the relative importance of the Union threats above and below Vicksburg. On this Tuesday, April 28, Stevenson reluctantly complied with Pemberton's order, but warned his chief that an unknown Union force remained across the river from Vicksburg. It might constitute the main Federal attack while the activities at Grand Gulf provided a diversion.

On April 29, Pemberton remained uncertain about which was the greater threat, the Union force opposite Vicksburg or opposite Grand Gulf. Perhaps he would have been well advised to focus exclusively on this salient issue. Instead of defending himself from Grant, he spent time defending himself from Johnston. Pemberton believed that a recent telegram from Johnston implied some degree of censure concerning his conduct during Grierson's raid. Consequently, he occupied a portion of the day providing a detailed justification of his decisions. Then battlefield reality intruded; he learned that the telegraph wire to Grand Gulf was down. In the absence of current news from Grand Gulf, Pemberton made his finest command decision during the Vicksburg campaign by ordering Stevenson to send the five-thousand-man mobile reserve to support Bowen, along with extra ammunition for the big guns at Grand Gulf. Yet Pemberton still remained fixated on the direct threat against his river defenses. He was more concerned about Grand Gulf's ability to withstand a naval attack than any threat from further downriver. As the day progressed, news that a Federal amphibious force had entered the Yazoo River and chugged upstream to near Snyder's Bluff further complicated Pemberton's strategic chessboard. Confederate fortifications atop the bluff controlled access to the Yazoo River and the back door approach to Vicksburg. The appearance of Federal forces here might represent the main attack that Stevenson feared.

Pemberton did not know that this activity on the Yazoo constituted another of Grant's diversions. Grant's tortuous supply route through Louisiana could only handle limited traffic. Most of McClernand's Thirteenth Corps was near its southern terminus poised for the river crossing. McPherson's Seventeenth Corps was hustling along in McClernand's wake. This left Sherman's Fifteenth Corps waiting for the route to clear, and Grant did not want anyone sitting idle. He proposed that Sherman make a feint along the Yazoo, but left it to Sherman's discretion whether or not to carry it out. Grant added that such a feint could easily be misconstrued by the folks back home and implied that reporters would write that it was another failure.

Hardly anything could have put Sherman more on his fighting mettle than the hypothetical howls of detested reporters. As Grant anticipated, the challenge of ignoring them was not something Sherman could resist. "Does General Grant think I care what the newspapers say?" Sherman exclaimed. Thoroughly riled, Sherman continued by saying that the "sneaking, croaking, scoundrels" in the press were a worse enemy than the "secesh."[68] Having vented his spleen, the red-haired general set about arranging the required diversion. As he told Grant, "You are engaged in a hazardous enterprise" and he would do what he could to help.[69]

So it was that Pemberton received reports during April 30 that Union warships and transports remained active near Snyder's Bluff. Reports claimed at least five enemy infantry regiments had already landed although, so far, the defenders appeared to have matters in hand. Indeed, as affairs above Vicksburg turned out, the Confederate defenders required no extra help. Sherman landed some men who maneuvered noisily, the U.S. Navy received another battering from fortified blufftop batteries with one boat being struck forty-six times, and then the Federals were gone.

Contrary to Sherman's postwar claim, the feint failed to pin any of Pemberton's reserves in place. However, it occupied the attention of both Carter Stevenson in Vicksburg and Pemberton in Jackson during a critical time when both should have been focusing on Grand Gulf. When Pemberton telegraphed Stevenson the order to dispatch the reserve to Grand Gulf, Stevenson was at Snyder's Bluff. Because of his absence, the reserve did not leave Vicksburg until 7 P.M., eleven hours after Porter attacked Grand Gulf. At another time such a delay would not have mattered, but just now, every hour was precious to the Confederate war effort. How precious became clearer late on the next day, April 30, when Pemberton received one more message from Bowen. It told him that Union forces had crossed the Mississippi below Grand Gulf. With the scales removed from his eyes, Pemberton called in his outlying detachments and took the train for Vicksburg. The crisis was at hand.

THE NIGHT OF APRIL 29 found the Federal transports moored along the Louisiana shore four miles below Grand Gulf. McClernand's infantry bivouacked nearby on whatever dry ground they could find. Grant supposed that he would have to continue their march south until arriving opposite the town of Rodney. His map showed that a road connected Rodney with Port Gibson. However, he had sent cavalry patrols to scour the Louisiana countryside and collect information about conditions on the opposite shore. One patrol brought him a slave who provided valuable intelligence: there was a good landing at Bruinsburg, several miles upstream from Rodney, from where a firm road ran some twelve miles to Port Gibson. Grant immediately recast his plans and decided to cross the Mississippi opposite Bruinsburg. Even though this river crossing represented a literal leap onto an unknown shore, Grant decided to place all his hope in its success. That night he ordered his friend Sherman to march with two divisions to join him. This decision meant that there was not enough strength left upriver to accomplish anything important. Whatever was to happen would happen below Vicksburg.

For the crossing the Navy mobilized everything that had safely passed Vicksburg's guns. Troops crammed aboard gunboats, battered transports, coal barges, and scows. Even Porter's flagship, the *Benton*, served as a ferry. Still, only one division could cross at a time and no one knew if the Confederates held the opposite shore in strength. At 8 A.M. the invasion armada cast off. A band aboard the *Benton* played "The Red, White, and Blue," prompting soldiers and sailors alike to cheer enthusiastically. With some apprehension the armada approached Bruinsburg. The *Benton* signaled "Prepare to land" and steamed bows on into the eastern bank. Holding their rifles at the ready, Hoosiers belonging to the Twenty-fourth and Forty-sixth Indiana ran ashore. There was no one there except one civilian, who they detained lest he broadcast news of the invasion.

By noon most of McClernand's 17,000-strong corps had completed the unopposed landing. It was not flawless. Someone blundered and failed to issue rations to McClernand's men before they embarked, thus causing a four-hour delay within the bridgehead before soldiers advanced inland. Nonetheless, the greatest amphibious operation in American history to date was under way. Ferrying operations continued through the night taking men, horses, equipment, and supplies to the eastern shore. By the end of April 30 a 22,000-man army composed of McClernard's and McPherson's corps had crossed the river.

The successful coordination of the march down the Louisiana shore, followed by a crossing of the Mississippi River, was a remarkable achievement reflecting high credit on Grant and his staff. Although Grant had a West Pointer's skepticism about the ability of civilian officers, he showed greater flexibility than any other army leader in letting competent civilians rise to their level. The smooth unfolding of the Mississippi crossing contrasts sharply with what would take place within the presumably more professional Army of the Potomac in 1864, when it experienced endless confusions and delays during its bungled crossing of the James River. After four frustrating, floundering months the Army of the Tennessee had accomplished something great and its commander knew it. Grant explained in his memoirs that once his army landed at Bruinsburg, "I felt a degree of relief scarcely ever equalled since. Vicksburg was not yet taken it is true, nor were its defenders demoralized . . . But I was on dry ground on the same side of the river with the enemy. All the campaigns, labors, hardships and exposures . . . that had been made and endured, were for the accomplishment of this one object."[70]

Whether "this one object" was enough was unclear. General Sherman, having completed his feint and returned to Milliken's Bend, remained dubious. Grant's successful river crossing meant he had progressed farther than Sherman had believed possible. Even so, Sherman continued to doubt Grant's strategy. He wondered how Grant could possibly maintain his army in a position between two enemy-held fortresses. As he explained to his wife:

> If the capture of Holly Springs made him leave the Tallahatchie, how much more precarious is his position now below Vicksburg with every pound of provision, forage and ammunition to float past the seven miles of batteries at Vicksburg or be hauled thirty-seven [actually 63] miles along a narrow boggy road.[71]

No professional soldier would have disputed Sherman's analysis. It was a matter of perspective. Grant was at the end of an exceedingly precarious supply line, isolated in hostile territory, positioned between Port Hudson and Vicksburg—two well-fortified, enemy-held citadels—outnumbered by his enemy, and with an unfordable river to his rear. Few generals would have considered this anything but a trap. Grant judged it an opportunity.

Part 2

The Shot-Torn Ground

5

The Battle of Port Gibson

Just before a man goes into battle he feels a sort of dread or secret anxiety but just as soon as he gets under fire this feeling is all gone and he goes to shooting at the enemy as though he were shooting ducks . . . If a man falls dead beside him he don't mind about it but keeps on firing as though nothing had happened.

—William H. Parks, Twenty-ninth Wisconsin, June 18, 1863
(Parks-Towle-Ferguson Family letters, Civil War
Miscellaneous Collection, *MHI*)

GENERAL JOHN BOWEN appreciated that while his men had done very well indeed against the Federal navy, once the fleet passed Grand Gulf he had to redeploy promptly. If the Yankees crossed the river and then headed toward Vicksburg, they would march along roads leading to the small town of Port Gibson, about seven miles inland from Grand Gulf and thirteen from Bruinsburg. If they captured Port Gibson, the defense of Grand Gulf would be untenable and Bowen would have to relinquish it. Bowen was a stubborn man. Pemberton had ordered him to hold Grand Gulf and he intended to obey. Three days earlier he had carefully scouted the land around Port Gibson and selected the best defensive position available. It was to this position that he sent his available manpower at 1 A.M. on April 30.

As the morning progressed, first came rumors and then confirmation: Grant was ashore at Bruinsburg! Once he knew that the Yankees were headed inland, Bowen rode to Port Gibson to confer with Brigadier General Martin Green, who commanded the forces there. As Bowen and Green considered the proposition they realized that the enemy could advance along two roads. The main thoroughfare was the Rodney Road. A position along the ridge top just east of Magnolia Church seemed the best ground to hold in order to block this road. Two and one-half miles northwest of the church was a suitable position to defend the other likely route Grant might use. This was the Bruinsburg Road. The Confederate commanders resolved to defend both roads, and then Bowen returned to Grand Gulf. During the day, Green perfected his dispositions by placing his own brigade on the Rodney Road and assigning Brigadier General Edward Tracy's 1,500-man Alabama brigade to hold the Bruinsburg Road. Tracy's men were part of the reinforcements Pemberton had sent from Vicksburg. They had marched forty miles in twenty-seven hours to reach Port Gibson.

Green was a veteran of four field battles but had never held independent command. That evening, as rumors came that the foe was drawing near, he grew restless. At 12:30 A.M. on May 1 he visited his outpost line at the Shaifer house. He found the women of the house frantically packing their best possessions onto a wagon. Green reassured them that no enemy would be here until daylight at the earliest. He had barely spoken before a crash of musketry sounded with bullets hitting the wagon and one striking the house. It was the Yankees, coming fast.

The Union soldiers whose volley sent the Shaifer women flying in panic to Port Gibson were Iowa men belonging to Colonel William Stone's brigade. Stone had last been in Mississippi one year before as a prisoner of war. Following his exchange, he wanted revenge and so was well forward with his advance patrol. Concluding that he confronted an isolated outpost, Stone sent for additional men and pressed on. He encountered Green's main battle line on the high ground east of Magnolia Church. A lively skirmish ensued. Stone had little idea what he faced. However, the boom from Confederate artillery and flashes from a formed rebel battle line persuaded him to retire rather than commence a nocturnal engagement.

Since 4 P.M. on April 30, General McClernand had been driving his corps through the night toward Port Gibson as fast as possible. To facilitate rapid movement, the cavalry, the horses belonging to all officers beneath general, and all baggage and excess equipment had been left on the west bank. Officers walked with their men. At least one divisional general rode a requisitioned mule. Speed was important because Grant hoped that McClernand could seize the bridges over Bayou Pierre north of Port Gibson before the Confederates reacted. Consequently, regiments marched for five hours until 9 P.M., when they enjoyed a thirty-minute supper break. Then they slung knapsacks and marched all night before stopping for breakfast at 7 A.M. about four miles from Port Gibson.

At 2 A.M., McClernand himself rode toward the sounds of firing around Magnolia Church. Like Colonel Stone, McClernand waited for daylight to clarify the situation. Dawn lit a country comprising "a series of irregular ridges, divided by deep and impassable ravines, grown up with heavy timber, undergrowth, and cane."[1] The complex terrain imposed a heavy tactical burden on the Union and Confederate leaders. From battle's beginning to end, officers on both sides had trouble understanding their own position relative to supporting, friendly units and had even less comprehension of how lay the opponent. At the Shaifer house, McClernand stood at a road junction: a plantation road headed off to the west and joined the Bruinsburg Road; the Rodney Road ran southeast to Magnolia Church. Exceptionally rugged terrain separated the Bruinsburg and Rodney roads. McClernand ordered Brigadier General Peter J. Osterhaus to take his division and attack along the Bruinsburg Road. McClernand would supervise the main effort toward the church. It was an awkward position requiring the Union soldiers to fight in diverging directions. Those facing Magnolia Church had their backs to the Confederates on the Bruinsburg Road. Osterhaus's men had their backs to the rebels at Magnolia Church. Both Federal forces would have open flanks.

General Green confronted a more vexing challenge. Since McClernand's men were between his two wings, he had to operate along exterior lines. Four road miles separated the wings, making it very difficult to coordinate their efforts. In the event, even a mounted courier would take two hours to complete a round trip from one wing to the other. Far worse, although reinforcements were marching hard to support him, at battle's start Green had about one thousand men at Magnolia Church while Tracy had fifteen hundred on the Bruinsburg Road. Shortly after 6:30 A.M. an artillery duel announced the beginning of the Battle of Port Gibson.

With the exception of the Third Maryland Artillery, no Confederate unit had traveled farther from home to participate in the defense of Vicksburg than Virginia's Botetourt Artillery. Thirteen months earlier, General Kirby Smith, then commanding in east Tennessee, had requested that the best prepared and available battery be sent from Richmond to Knoxville, Tennessee. At that time, the newly formed Botetourt Artillery had been still fitting up. Nonetheless, it was more advanced in its drill than any other, so it took the cars west. Later, as part of Stevenson's Division, it transferred to Vicksburg at the tail end of Sherman's operations in December 1862.

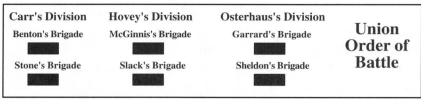

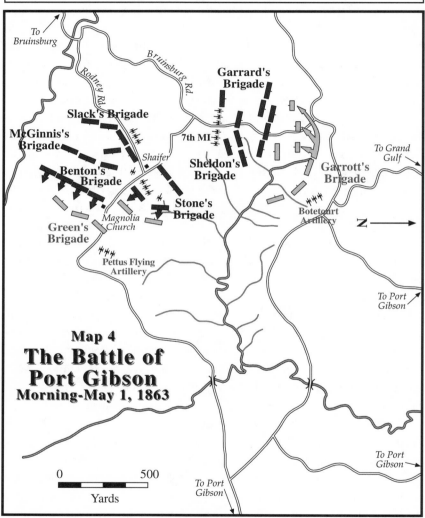

To Bruinsburg

Rodney Rd.

Bruinsburg Rd.

Garrard's Brigade

Slack's Brigade

McGinnis's Brigade

7th MI

Shaifer

Sheldon's Brigade

To Grand Gulf

Garrott's Brigade

Benton's Brigade

Stone's Brigade

Magnolia Church

Green's Brigade

Botetourt Artillery

N

Pettus Flying Artillery

To Port Gibson

Map 4

The Battle of Port Gibson
Morning–May 1, 1863

0   500

Yards

To Port Gibson

To Port Gibson

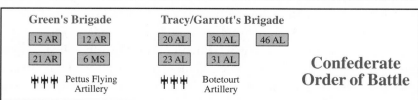

Assigned to Tracy's brigade, the battery participated in the grueling twenty-seven-hour march to the battlefield. When one section deployed on a ridge overlooking the Bruinsburg Road on May 1, 1863, the Virginians entered their first battle in defense of the southern confederacy. They were about 650 miles from home.

One thousand yards away, the Seventh Michigan Battery deployed six ten-pounder Rodman rifles on a hilltop and opened fire on the Botetourt Artillery. At this range an artillery duel favored rifled guns over smooth-bores. But weeks of drill paid off for the Virginia gunners. They managed to fire their twelve-pounder Napoleons accurately and kill two and wound two more Michigan artillerymen. Nonetheless, after a forty-five minute preparatory barrage, Osterhaus's leading infantry brigade advanced.

General Osterhaus was an immensely popular figure among the German soldiers who served in his division. Much as the German soldiers in the East liked their Franz Sigel, so those who served in the West were fond of their Peter Joseph. He had attended a Berlin military school and served in the Prussian infantry before emigrating to Missouri in 1848. He enlisted in a Missouri regiment as a private and soon received promotion to major. As a colonel he had fought at Wilson's Creek and commanded a brigade at Pea Ridge. Although a combat veteran, his prior service had been in a distinctly subordinate capacity. Port Gibson marked the first time he led a division in combat. Moreover, his was a semi-independent command, since McClernand had chosen to supervise personally the combat on the Rodney Road. Whether Osterhaus was fully competent for the task was an untested proposition.

His men entered a maze of overgrown ravines where it proved impossible to maintain unit alignment. A Union soldier recalled, "We moved up over ridges, through canebrakes, ravines, over ditches which were nearly impassable"[2] Two hundred yard gaps opened up between some of the Union regiments as officers lost all sense of direction. The initial attack merely managed to drive in the Confederate skirmish line. Osterhaus reinforced his battle line with another brigade. Again the Federal soldiers scrambled forward, only to go to the ground when they encountered Tracy's main infantry line. A noisy, long-range firefight ensued. However, some bluecoated marksmen wormed their way forward and began to shoot down the exposed gunners of the Botetourt Artillery. With men and horses dropping fast, the battery's commanding officer, Lieutenant Philip Peters, three times requested infantry support and permission to withdraw his caissons to a less exposed position. After declining twice, Tracy finally came to battery to see the situation for himself. A cheerful Botetourt gunner offered the general a chaw of tobacco; just then a bullet hit Tracy in the back of the neck. Tracy fell hard onto his face crying out "O Lord!" His wound was mortal. Tracy was the first Confederate general to die in defense of Vicksburg.

Thrust into command by the bullet that felled Tracy, Colonel Isham W. Garrott of the Twentieth Alabama had no idea what the Confederate battle plan was. He sent a courier to Green for instructions. In the meantime, Garrott resolved to hold his ground because "the enemy was in our front, and I knew of no order to retire." Two hours later came orders endorsing Garrott's decision. The colonel was to defend his ground "at all hazards."[3] During this time the artillery pounding continued. Amidst exploding shells Lieutenant Peters remarked, "This is hot." The battery sergeant recalled what took place: "William Couch #2 at right hand Napoleon, was first to fall, cut almost in two at the waist. David Lipes was second, shot just above the left eye while ramming down a charge. Frederick C. Noell shot in the top of the head."[4]

The battery's six-pounder section arrived to reinforce the battered Napoleon section. The battery officers revealed their inexperience by cramming all four guns into a restricted area with poor fields of fire. Jammed together, the battery made a splendid target. Federal artillery fire knocked out one six-pounder before it could fire a shot. Several more shells blew the wheel off one of the Napoleons. The crew attached a new one only to have a shell split the gun's axle. Another shell exploded, killing Peters and the just-arrived lieutenant who commanded the six-pounders. By 10 A.M. Garrott ordered the surviving two guns to retire.

For five and one-half hours Osterhaus had accomplished little. During much of that time he shuffled his regiments left and right in an effort to form an organized battle line in the overgrown ravines. It was admittedly a time-consuming matter as regiments easily became disoriented—the Sixty-ninth Indiana and Forty-second Ohio exchanged volleys in one wooded ravine—but finally as noon approached Osterhaus's deployment was complete. He had twelve artillery pieces in position to support his attack. The defenders had none. His infantry outnumbered the Confederates at least three to one. Then, instead of ordering a charge, Osterhaus called for reinforcements.

THE RODNEY ROAD ran atop a narrow ridge from the Shaifer house to Magnolia Church. The ground fell sharply away from both sides of the road. A tangle of undergrowth—vines, briars, and nearly impenetrable canebrakes—filled the adjacent ravine bottoms. A ridge bisected the road at roughly right angles where the church stood. Green's skirmish line occupied this ridge. Further east a second ridge also bisected the road. Here was Green's main battle line. From his position Green could readily see that he was grossly outnumbered. He immediately sent a courier spurring to Tracy's command to request a regiment and a section of artillery. Meanwhile, during the first hours of daylight, Union patrols belonging to Brigadier General Eugene Carr's division probed the thickets and ravines adjacent to the Rodney Road while the experienced eye of Carr himself tried to make sense of the terrain. When Osterhaus's artillery announced that the battle on the Bruinsburg Road had commenced, McClernand ordered Carr to begin what he planned would become his major effort.

Carr's men easily carried the Magnolia Church ridge. The main rebel line lay two hundred yards further on, separated from the Federal position by a deep ravine. Carr's men swarmed through the thickets and stabbed at Green's left flank. Green was in trouble. He had concentrated his strength directly on the road since he assumed that the Federals would utilize the open ground here to make at attack. Only a handful of skirmishers held his left. Moreover, his artillery support—the Pettus Flying Artillery—had unwisely consumed their ammunition in a profitless duel with the Union artillery. As Carr's line surged forward the Pettus Flying Artillery withdrew. At this point General Bowen reached the field. A Mississippi lieutenant saw him ride "up in our immediate front. He was covered with blood, but had not been wounded. His horse had been hit in the thigh, and its switching tail was showering him with blood." It was the first of four horses that would be shot out from under Bowen. To buy time until reinforcements arrived, Bowen resolved to attack the Federal batteries that were deploying on the Magnolia Church ridge. He requested permission from the colonel of the Sixth Mississippi to lead the unit personally. In a loud voice Bowen said, "Attention! Battalion!" The Mississippi soldiers rose to their feet. Pointing his sword at an enemy battery, Bowen said, "Follow me! Let's take that battery!"[5] At the canter, Bowen headed for the Union artillery.

It was a desperate thing to ask, but the Confederate infantry—including the regiment sent by Tracy, the Twenty-third Alabama—gave it their best try. The attack collapsed under the weight of canister-firing artillery. Bowen told Green to hold on for another hour—it was now about 9 A.M.—and galloped off to locate reinforcements.

McClernand had intended to attack Green's left flank. Bowen's counterattack caused him to alter his plan. He was steadily receiving reinforcements a division at a time, which allowed him to always retain one division in reserve. McClernand decided to mass his strength for a power punch against Green's center. While maneuver away from the road was tedious and slow, massing along the Rodney Road did not prove a panacea. There was so little open ground that the Union regiments were stacked three and four deep. There were insufficient places for the Federal artillery to deploy; as a result, many guns stood idle. Sometime after 10 A.M. McClernand's line lurched forward.

Brigadier General Alvin Hovey's division spearheaded McClernand's advance. They were tired men, having been on the march since 3 P.M. the previous afternoon, with only a one-hour break for breakfast. They threw their knapsacks in a pile by a fence, detailed the usual handful of men—the otherwise useless ones who would shirk if sent into battle—to guard them, and marched toward the rebel position. Hovey directed the Thirty-fourth Indiana and Fifty-sixth Ohio against the two-gun section of the Botetourt Artillery that had arrived from the other wing to reinforce Green. Hovey's infantry charged forward through fierce shell fire, lost their alignment as they crossed a split-rail fence, and then were staggered by musket volleys fired by an unseen foe. When they came within 150 yards of the Botetourt's twelve-pounder howitzers, the Virginia gunners switched to canister. Their withering fire stopped the attackers 80 yards from their objective.

From the woods to the left, the Ninety-seventh Illinois, along with Stone's brigade, appeared. Their long line overlapped the rebel position. Hovey shouted out "Forward!" and this time the Federal surge proved irresistible. On the left, Stone's people rushed a wood line defended by the Twenty-third Alabama, sent that unit reeling, and captured its battle flag and numerous men. On the right, Brigadier General William Benton's and Brigadier General George McGinnis's brigades drove the Fifteenth and Twenty-first Arkansas regiments into the ravines. Two Indiana soldiers shot and wounded the color-bearer of the Fifteenth Arkansas and seized his flag. In the center, the attackers shot down all but two of the Botetourt horses, so the section could not retire. The crew tried to hand haul the guns to the rear, but the section commander, Lieutenant William Norgrove, realized that they were not going to make it. He ordered the guns double shotted with canister for a last defense. Federal fire cut down the gunners before they could fire. Elements of three Indiana regiments then stormed the battery, each forever after claiming that they had captured it unaided! One of the attacking regiments, the thoroughly drilled Zouaves of the Eleventh Indiana, had received some artillery instruction early in the war and now put it to good use by manhandling the howitzers about and discharging them into the backs of the routing Confederates. Norgrove himself had often said he would never be taken prisoner. The Federals surrounded him. Someone called out to surrender. Norgrove replied with a sword stroke and fell mortally wounded when a ball pierced his body.

As Green's scattered command ran to the rear, jubilant Federal soldiers swarmed the ridge. They admired their trophies—two battle flags and two twelve-pounder howitzers—and looked up to see a command group riding toward them along the road. Soldiers began to cheer as they recognized Generals Grant and McClernand and Illinois governor Richard Yates. McClernand exulted to an aide, "A great day for the northwest!"[6] Yates and McClernand could not resist the opportunity and delivered impromptu stump speeches to their soldier-constituents. Grant, who since his arrival on the field had been leaving tactical control in McClernand's hands, waited until the politicians were done and then suggested that perhaps McClernand ought to see about driving the rebels from the field. Indeed, had the facts been known the celebration might have been less fevered. Two Federal divisions had conquered a position held by about 1,200 Confederates and had taken the better part of an entire morning to do it. The hardest fighting lay ahead.

Across the line and away from the celebration Lieutenant William Thompson of the Sixth Mississippi lay among the Confederate wounded. A shell had exploded nearby, sending a piece of shrapnel against Thompson's head and knocking him unconscious. "When I came to, my hair was all bloody, my face was covered with blood and mud, I was . . . dizzy with pain." He dragged himself rearward toward the hospital and stumbled headfirst into a water-filled hole. Fortunately, someone pulled him out and handed him over to a bandsman charged with hauling the wounded off the field. Amidst a fierce shelling they worked back along the Rodney Road to encounter a black servant holding two horses belonging to field officers. The bandsman shoved the lieutenant atop a horse and they set off. Before they traveled more than a few paces a cannonball killed the horse. In the fall, Thompson again landed on his head. He finally reached the hospital, where the regimental surgeon was busy removing a soldier's leg. "The blood-curdling screams" caused Thompson to thank "god that I had been hit in the head!"[7] The doctor examined the lieutenant and told him he had a skull fracture. He went to a large demijohn, poured a full glass of whiskey, and told Thompson to drink it. Treatment completed, the doctor told his assistants to take the lieutenant to a hospital in Port Gibson and moved on to minister to the other wounded. Such was Confederate field surgery at the Battle of Port Gibson.

While Lieutenant Thompson was heading for the rear, Green's surviving soldiers encountered General Bowen near the junction of the Bruinsburg and Rodney roads. They had retired about a mile and were already rallying. Bowen judged that they could continue to reorganize while performing a speed march to reinforce the hard-pressed defenders on the Bruinsburg Road. Bowen intended to hold the Rodney Road with the just-arrived brigade commanded by Brigadier General William Baldwin. This brigade was another part of the five-thousand-man force that Pemberton had judged he could spare to help Bowen hold Grand Gulf. Like Union Colonel Stone, General Baldwin had tasted defeat and capture once already in this war when he had been part of the garrison of Fort Donelson. Port Gibson was his first combat since his exchange. His task on this field was to defend a position carefully chosen by General Bowen.

Bowen realized that Green's men had suffered because they manned a ridge top that included too much open, exposed space. They had been vulnerable to Federal marksmen firing from concealed locations in the overgrown ravines. He applied his recently gained knowledge by stationing the Seventeenth Louisiana south of the Rodney Road along the edge of a triangular wood that jutted forward toward the direction the Yankees would approach. Two powerful twenty-four-pounder howitzers occupied this salient in a position from where they could enfilade any attack against the adjacent unit to the left of the triangular wood. That unit was the Fourth Mississippi, which occupied a wood line overlooking an open field. Four twelve-pounder howitzers belonging to Guibor's Missouri battery occupied a ridge behind the Fourth Mississippi, from where they could bombard the open field.

Forty-year-old Captain Henry Guibor was a Mexican War veteran. Before the war, his battery had been part of the Missouri State Guards. So the battery enjoyed the double benefit of being trained by a combat veteran and placed within a prewar organization that took military service seriously. In many places nationwide, the state militia served more as a social than a military organization, but not so in Missouri. Missouri militia drilled against the backdrop of bitter conflict along the Missouri-Kansas border. More than a few officers and men had participated in the prewar fight in "bleeding Kansas." Their practical know-how had helped instill spirit and discipline. Guibor's battery, along with three Missouri infantry regiments who also traced their lineage to the State Guards, had been part of the Grand Gulf

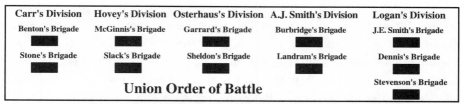

Map 5
The Battle of Port Gibson
Afternoon–May 1, 1863

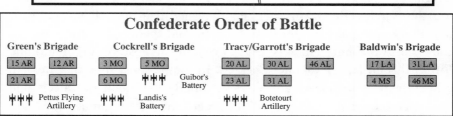

garrison. Recalled at 10 A.M., they had sped the eight miles to join Bowen. Bowen sent the Sixth Missouri to help on the Bruinsburg Road. The remaining two regiments he placed in an overgrown creek bottom behind the left flank of the Fourth Mississippi. On the opposite flank, to the right of the Rodney Road, another of Baldwin's regiments manned an overgrown ridge top while the remaining regiment stood in reserve eight hundred yards to the rear. Two guns belonging to the Pettus Flying Artillery that had managed to find ammunition deployed with the reserve regiment. In sum, Bowen had weighted his defense on the left because he anticipated that it would be here that the main Union blow would land. So stood no more than four thousand rebel soldiers on the afternoon of May 1. A mile away, having completed his speechifying, McClernand was preparing to attack with a force swollen to three and one-half divisions, numbering more than sixteen thousand men.

The Union approach march to the new Confederate position proved time consuming. Again there was the thick underbrush, dense canebrakes, and ravines where men had to hand-pull themselves up the steep sides by clinging to root and ledge. Upon encountering the Confederate skirmish line, the senior officers tried to make sense of the rebel position. It seemed to them that they confronted the most formidable position yet and so they hesitated. When the Union line finally advanced over the crest line, the heretofore concealed Confederate twenty-four-pounder howitzers opened up. They literally blasted the attackers apart. All order dissolved as men sought shelter in nearby gullies. For ninety minutes a firefight raged. At last McClernand decided to switch tactics, or rather revert to those that had previously proven successful. He again massed his units until he had twenty-one regiments concentrated on an eight-hundred-yard-long front. Then the Illinois politician ordered a frontal attack against the Confederate center.

From the salient where the big howitzers stood, Bowen saw McClernand's preparations. He also saw the Yankee line continue to extend to the south, where it overlapped his own left flank. This was a potentially fatal development for Bowen's army because about a half mile in that direction was the Natchez Road. If the Federals reached that road, they could pour into Port Gibson and cut off Bowen's men, and there was nothing Bowen could do to prevent it. It was time to commit his reserve, the Third and Fifth Missouri led by Colonel Cockrell. In the personal style that western soldiers expected, Bowen and Cockrell briefly explained to officers and men what they required. Cockrell's two regiments set off through the canebrakes in full expectation of winning the battle. Bowen omitted to mention that he hoped Cockrell's maneuver would go undetected, which was fortunate since it did not.

General Hovey saw Cockrell's Missouri men, formed in column by battalion, moving through a hollow leading to the Union right flank. Hovey hurried to the threatened flank and ordered all four batteries assigned to his division to shift to counter the Confederate threat. He was unable to reach his rightmost infantry brigade, commanded by Colonel James Slack, before the rebels struck. The rebels, reported Slack, "came down at a charge, with terrific yells, and could not be seen, because of the very thick growth of cane, until they reached a point within 30 yards of my line."[8] Amazingly, Cockrell's warriors almost succeeded in collapsing the Union flank. But even as they drove back one line of Federal troops a new line emerged. A Missouri officer remembered that "the continuous roll of small guns was appalling, almost drowning the fierce discharge of the artillery. The noise was so incessant that no orders could be heard; and the bullets flew so thick that hardly a leaf or twig was left on the bare poles of what had been a diminutive forest when we entered it."[9]

For close to an hour the two Missouri regiments fought it out with ten different Union regiments. In the end, the combination of Hovey's twenty-four-gun artillery line, stalwart fighting by several Union regiments including the green Twenty-ninth Wisconsin, which refused to be stampeded by a surprise flank attack, and vastly superior Union strength prevailed. When Cockrell's men sullenly withdrew, they encountered Bowen astride his horse next to where the regimental colors had been planted as a rallying point. The Missouri men did not particularly like Bowen since he was something of a martinet. Bowen did not particularly like their loose discipline. But Cockrell's charge moved Bowen to commend the survivors. He said, "I did not suspect that *any* of you would get away, but the charge *had* to be made, or my little army was lost."[10]

The effort to defeat Cockrell sapped McClernand's resolve. Having had his first thrust repelled by superbly sited and well-hidden enemy cannon and then having had to commit most of his reserves to repel a howling counterattack, McClernand gazed at the rebel line and wondered what additional horrors lay hidden. Not knowing what to do, he did very little. His inaction worried Bowen. He wondered why the obviously superior Union force had not pursued Cockrell. Concerned that McClernand was merely pinning him in place while working around his flank toward the Natchez Road, Bowen ordered Baldwin to probe the Union line. Following a short preparatory bombardment, at 4 P.M. Baldwin's men moved forward. A storm of shot and shell sent them reeling back to their start line. Bowen realized that the enemy was still present in overwhelming force.

An inconclusive firefight continued all along the line that gradually forced the Confederates to retire a short distance. Desultory fighting might have continued until dusk but for the actions of renowned Federal artillerist Captain Samuel De Golyer of the Eighth Michigan Battery. De Golyer was well known for his aggressive fire and move tactics. Attached to Brigadier General John Stevenson's brigade of Logan's division, his battery had reached the field several hours earlier. At that time McClernand had been clamoring for reinforcements. Although Grant doubted McClernand could usefully employ more men on his already crowded front, Grant had sent him Stevenson's brigade. Stevenson's infantry entered the line opposite the triangular woods where the rebel twenty-four-pounders had stood.

Stevenson ordered De Golyer to deploy to provide covering fire for a charge. Instead of moving to the nearest high ground and blazing away, De Golyer had his battery horses haul his six guns to just below the crest. Here, hidden from Confederate view, his gunners loaded with canister and prepared to manhandle the guns over the crest line when De Golyer gave the word. The surprise appearance of a canister-firing battery at close range overwhelmed the weary defenders and permitted Union infantry to overrun the triangular woods. Bowen finally realized that this was a fight he could not win and at 6 P.M. ordered Baldwin and Cockrell to retreat.

A long, nocturnal march lay before Baldwin's brigade. When they arrived at Bowen's rallying point on the north bank of Bayou Pierre at 9 A.M. on May 2, they had completed a remarkable twenty-seven hours in which they had marched eight miles to the battle, fought for seven hours, and then retreated twenty-one more miles.

BACK ON THE BRUINSBURG ROAD, not until 3 P.M. did Osterhaus receive the reinforcements he judged necessary to launch an attack. This was John Smith's brigade of Logan's division.

Thirty minutes earlier, Colonel Garrott had received reinforcements as well in the shape of Green's rallied brigade and the four-hundred-man Sixth Missouri, commanded by feisty Colonel Eugene Erwin. The newly arrived general outranked Garrott. Exercising the prerogative of rank, Green did not consult with the colonel when he deployed the reinforcements to extend Garrott's left. This made sense in that Green knew that McClernand's large force was active in that direction. But just now Garrott needed help on his opposite flank because it was here that Osterhaus had massed his force.

When Osterhaus charged Garrott's right his men confronted the same terrible terrain that had plagued the Federal effort all day. In the maze of ravines an inconclusive firefight took place. After throwing a blanket over his shoulders to hide his rank insignias from Confederate sharpshooters, corps commander McPherson worked his way forward to reconnoiter the Confederate position. He found a covered approach and sent Smith's brigade to exploit it. After a hard scramble—the men had to let themselves down into the ravines by holding onto boughs and grapevines—Smith was in position for a charge. Slowly, superior numbers told and the bluecoats drove the Confederate right flank backward.[11] Meanwhile, along the Confederate left, both sides were content to engage in some long-range shooting until the impetuous Colonel Erwin resolved to win the battle by himself. On his own initiative, the colonel raised his saber and roared "Forward!" Erwin led the Sixth Missouri on a wild bayonet charge that scattered the surprised Federal skirmish line and recaptured the two disabled guns belonging to the Botetourt Artillery. But Erwin was entirely unsupported. From the shelter of a fence line, the Forty-ninth Indiana fired a deadly volley at thirty yards range into Erwin's people. The Sixth Missouri took shelter behind a ridge and for the next ninety minutes engaged in a musketry duel with the Indiana regiment. Much like his colonel, twenty-two-year-old Missourian Matt Moore was not content to sharpshoot at long range. Moore advanced to an exposed place fifteen paces from the Union line, from where he shot down Federal officers and standard-bearers while his mates passed forward loaded muskets.

At 5 P.M. General Green received an order to hold his ground until sunset and then use his judgment and retreat if necessary. Sensing that Osterhaus's buildup was reaching the critical stage, Green ordered a retreat. Overlooked was Erwin's Sixth Missouri. By 5:30 P.M. the isolated Sixth Missouri was the last rebel outfit still holding its position. Recognizing that he was about to be swamped by overwhelming numbers, Erwin arranged a tactic to extricate his men. After having his surviving captains explain to the men what was expected, Erwin bellowed loudly the orders: "Attention battalion! Fix bayonets! Forward double quick, march!"[12] While the nearby Federals braced for the charge, the Missouri men filed to their left flank out of harm's way and then withdrew from the field. Fortunately for them, Bowen, who had no idea of their whereabouts, kept faith by holding a bridge along his line of retreat until nightfall. When Erwin's men marched out of the forest murk to rejoin the brigade, Bowen completed his withdrawal and burned the bridge behind him.

Port Gibson had been an altogether amazing battle. For twelve hours fewer than 7,000 Confederates had held their ground against a force that by mid-afternoon numbered 24,000 men. Back during Grant's hardscrabble days living in Missouri, he and Bowen had been neighbors and friends. In his report, Grant complimented his former neighbor, describing Bowen's defense as "very bold" and "well carried out." Although not given to boastfulness, Grant could not help but add, "My force, however, was too heavy for his, and composed of well-disciplined and hardy men, who know no defeat, and are not willing to learn."[13] The battle's significance lay not in the losses endured, although individual units had suffered severely. In its first field battle the Botetourt Artillery lost four of its six guns and one-third of its manpower, including all three section lieutenants killed. Incomplete Confederate reports—neither Cockrell's two Missouri regiments nor the hard-fighting Sixth Mississippi submitted returns—listed 787 casualties, including 387 missing.[14] The Army of the Tennessee lost 875 men, of whom only 25 were missing, while claiming the capture of 580 men.

The battle of Port Gibson was important because the Union victory secured Grant's bridgehead over the Mississippi River. Furthermore, a campaign's first battle has an exaggerated impact on the morale of the rival armies and on the minds of the opposing commanders. A Union officer wrote that "our army is in fine spirits, flushed with victory achieved at Port Gibson. Entire confidence is felt in the Generals commanding."[15] This had been the first battle for the 124th Illinois. Although the regiment mostly remained in reserve, at battle's end they advanced to fire two volleys into the rear of the retreating Confederates. The soldiers knew that they had not done much, but nonetheless felt good about themselves when Grant rode up to say "You have behaved yourselves well."[16] These words helped brace them for the far more difficult combat to come. In contrast, before the battle a Confederate lieutenant had circulated among his men and assured them "that we would run Grant and his boys back over ole Mississippi before they knew what had hit them."[17] This was a typical prebattle fight talk. Instead of running Grant over the river, the rebels faced defeat and demoralizing retreat. Baldwin's brigade marched all the way back to Vicksburg, where it arrived at 5 P.M. on May 4, weary and discouraged. Overall, Bowen's defense had been skillfully and gallantly performed, but it was not a battle that needed to be fought. Bowen's "little army" alone could not hope to save Grand Gulf and the general himself would have better served his men if he had retired behind Bayou Pierre from the outset.

For most of the battle Bowen had been outnumbered on the order of 3 to 1. He had fought such a masterful offensive-defensive delaying action that one wonders what might have transpired if the three infantry brigades Pemberton sent in fruitless chase of Grierson had been present with Bowen. It is even conceivable that a sizable portion of the entire army could have been present instead of remaining behind their fortifications at Vicksburg and elsewhere to fend off imaginary threats. The fact that they were not was Grant's reward for a carefully planned and well-executed series of feints and diversions. As bad as was the terrain and as courageously as Bowen's men fought, the Army of the Tennessee was bound to win the Battle of Port Gibson because of its commander's superior prebattle strategy.

In contrast, Pemberton had little impact on the battle beyond forwarding reinforcements and ammunition and urging Bowen to "whip" the enemy. Even after Bowen reported by telegraph at 5:30 P.M. on May 1 that he would have to retire after confronting a force he judged "overwhelming," Pemberton petulantly replied that Bowen had said he would fight and asked, "Why have you changed your mind? You have now about 9,000 men, and you ought to attack before he can greatly increase his strength."[18] How nine thousand men were supposed to defeat a far superior force Pemberton did not say. On the day of the Battle of Port Gibson, the Confederate lieutenant general did come to an important strategic realization. At last he comprehended the true significance of the Union ability to run Vicksburg's batteries. While requesting heavy reinforcements he explained to Jefferson Davis that the "enemy's success in passing our batteries has completely changed character of defense."[19] Whether Pemberton had the mental flexibility to adjust to the new situation was the pressing question. He needed to ask himself what was Vicksburg's value if it could not interdict the river? After Grant crossed the river, he needed to change his focus from holding the city to defeating Grant's army.

Behind each impersonal statistic listing battle losses was a human story. On May 9, an Alabama captain found time to write Cassia Roberts with news about Port Gibson that for her was much more important than any issue of higher strategy:

> I suppose that you have heard the painful intelligence which I am now about to impart to you. [At Port Gibson, about ten o'clock] your husband, Luke R. Roberts was struck by a minnie ball in the neck, near the shoulder. This

wound we found to be mortal. He was carried back a few hundred yards where he could get medical attention. The doctors say that they could do nothing for him but wished to carry him to the hospital; he told them no, that he knew he could not live long and wished to die on the battlefield. They granted his request.[20]

UNAWARE THAT BOWEN had retired behind Bayou Pierre, Grant ordered McClernand to renew his attack at daylight. Remembering how the day before they had not detected a Confederate presence until receiving a volley in their faces, the Union soldiers probed cautiously. Nearing the junction of the Rodney and Bruinsburg roads they saw the unmistakable signs of an enemy on the run: dead men and horses, abandoned equipment, and discarded muskets littered the ground. The soldiers switched from skirmish line to march column and headed for Port Gibson, only to find that McPherson's people had beaten them there.

Grant had accompanied McPherson into Port Gibson. He realized that the pursuit could go no further until the Little Bayou Pierre bridge, which had been burned by the retreating Confederates, was rebuilt. After giving Colonel Wilson this task, Grant read a Southern newspaper and for the first time learned about Grierson's successful raid. While Grant digested this agreeable news, Wilson's work crews feverishly constructed a rickety bridge. Although their first effort failed, they completed a 12-foot-wide and 166-foot-long bridge using timbers taken from a nearby cotton gin and mill. They corduroyed the bridge approaches, which traversed a dangerous patch of quicksand, and announced that the bridge was ready. From start to finish the entire operation required a mere four hours, which was good because their commanding general was in a big hurry. As the infantry approached the bridge Grant was there to urge them on: "Men, push right along; close up fast, and hurry on."[21]

Grant hoped his men could capture the suspension bridge at Grindstone Ford. At 7:30 P.M. on May 2 his hard-marching men reached the ford, only to find the bridge on fire. The energetic Wilson set the men to extinguishing the blaze. Making a quick reconnaissance in the fading light, Wilson saw that enough of the original structure remained to serve as a foundation for a new bridge. During a dark, stormy night Union pioneers salvaged timbers and beams, lashed them to the suspension rods with telegraph wire, and rebuilt the bridge. By dawn of May 3 it was ready for the infantry.

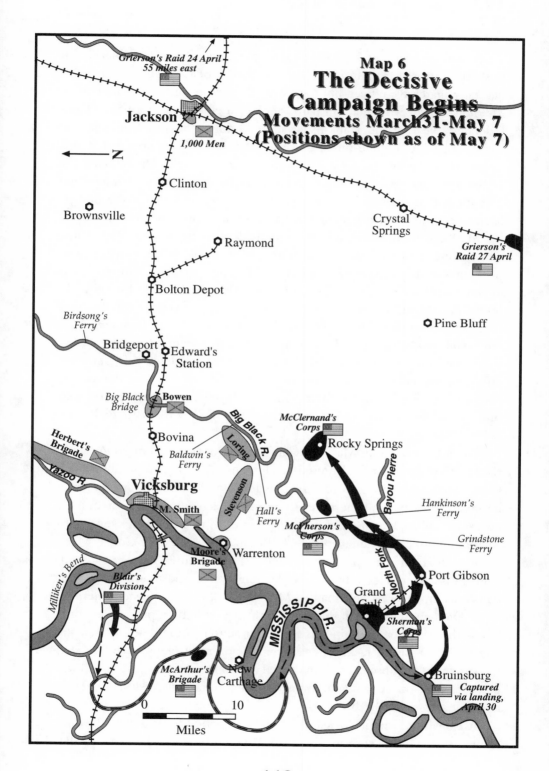

Map 6
The Decisive Campaign Begins
Movements March 31-May 7
(Positions shown as of May 7)

Grierson's Raid 24 April
55 miles east

Jackson

1,000 Men

← N

Clinton

Brownsville

Crystal Springs

Grierson's Raid 27 April

Raymond

Bolton Depot

Birdsong's Ferry

Pine Bluff

Bridgeport

Edward's Station

Big Black Bridge

Bowen

McClernand's Corps

Rocky Springs

Bovina

Baldwin's Ferry

Loring

Big Black R.

Bayou Pierre

Hankinson's Ferry

Herbert's Brigade

Yazoo R.

Vicksburg

J.M. Smith

Stevenson

Hall's Ferry

McPherson's Corps

North Fork

Grindstone Ferry

Port Gibson

Moore's Brigade

Warrenton

Milliken's Bend

Blair's Division

Grand Gulf

Sherman's Corps

MISSISSIPPI R.

McArthur's Brigade

New Carthage

Bruinsburg

Captured via landing, April 30

0   10

Miles

119

Logan's division crossed the bridge, overcame a rebel roadblock, and pushed on toward Hankinson's Ferry on the Big Black River. Logan was a naturally aggressive officer, but lest he falter, McPherson accompanied him. McPherson drove the column hard, hoping to cut off the retreating Confederates. Nearing the Hankinson's Ferry bridge, the van regiment, the Twentieth Ohio, double-timed ahead. They reached the bridge just as a Confederate demolition team was preparing to destroy it. Up galloped De Golyer's Eighth Michigan Battery. Covered by the battery's barrage, the Twentieth Ohio stormed the bridge. With its capture Grant had a bridgehead across the last major natural obstacle between his army and Vicksburg.

McPherson's blitzkrieg-like advance had encountered little opposition. There were, however, substantial numbers of hostile soldiers in the area. Back on May 1, the day of battle at Port Gibson, Pemberton had sent word of Grant's entry into Mississippi to Jefferson Davis and Joseph Johnston. To Johnston the issue seemed clear: with Grant safely across the river, the campaign hinged upon beating his army. To do that he advised Pemberton "to unite your whole force."[22] Initially it seemed that Pemberton agreed. He summoned units from throughout his command and ordered substantial reinforcements rushed south to support Bowen. On May 2, once Pemberton realized that Bowen had retired from the Bayou Pierre line, he ordered Bowen to abandon Grand Gulf and retire across the Big Black River. Bowen obliged.

By mid-morning on May 3, a Confederate force numbering more than sixteen thousand men had united at Hankinson's Ferry. As senior officer, General William Loring assumed command. Pemberton had given Loring no instructions beyond the order to be on the lookout for Bowen and "if necessary, fall back across Big Black."[23] At this time, Loring enjoyed a substantial numerical advantage over McPherson's Seventeenth Corps, which numbered about eleven thousand men. Furthermore, the Seventeenth Corps was spread out along the road leading from Grindstone Ford. A sudden attack might well have mauled McPherson or even achieved something more. On the other hand, if the recent fight at Port Gibson proved anything, it was that the area's terrain was far better suited to the defense than the attack. Still, a Lee, a Jackson, or a Grant would most likely have hazarded the stroke. In the absence of firm central direction, Loring, who after all was merely a divisional commander, was unwilling to take the risk. He ordered a retreat across the Big Black.

Meanwhile, back in Vicksburg, Pemberton tried to deal with the consequences of Grant's surprise appearance south of the city. He realized that his orders permitting Loring to retreat across the Big Black left the state capital vulnerable. On May 2, he told Mississippi governor John J. Pettus to remove the state archives from Jackson and ordered the head of the Jackson Arsenal to ship the machinery to safety in Alabama. Whether Pemberton was being prudent or defeatist is unclear, but there is no doubt that he lacked confidence in his ability to conduct field operations. Lacking confidence, he earnestly sought to follow orders by taking to heart Johnston's recommendations that he concentrate his forces to defeat Grant.[24] He informed President Davis that to gather sufficient force he wanted to evacuate Port Hudson.

Concentrating manpower was one thing, employing it was quite another. Pemberton's only idea was to prepare defensive positions behind the Big Black River while trying to figure out what Grant was up to. As in the past, Pemberton remained in the rear. He told Loring, who continued in command of the field force behind the Big Black, that if battle seemed imminent he would come down, but that in the meantime he would direct events from Vicksburg. War's inherent uncertainty continued to vex Pemberton. He complained to General Stevenson that he needed constant and frequent reports because otherwise he would be "unable to act with any satisfaction or certainty."[25] To reduce uncertainty, Pemberton sent out scouting parties but learned little of Grant's intentions. Here was the ageless problem when a general decided to defend a river line: the river provided a shield for his army, but it also formed a curtain obscuring what his enemy was doing on the far side. In the absence of certain intelligence and for fear of making a misstep, Pemberton remained passive. Because Pemberton exhibited absolutely no initiative, he left Grant free to perfect his dispositions.

THROUGHOUT THE CAMPAIGN various Confederate outfits, ranging from bushwhackers to regular units, had been trying to interfere with Grant's campaign by intercepting supply steamers on the Mississippi River. Generally, Admiral Porter's vigilant gunboats, particularly his shallow-draft tinclads, prevented the rebels from accomplishing much. On May 3, Lieutenant William Ritter and his section of the Third Maryland Artillery sprung a neat ambush. Confederate scouts reported that a heavily laden transport was coming downriver. Ritter masked his guns at a place where the current ran close to the bank and waited. The steamer's captain and crew had been up late the previous night drinking hard. They did not keep a wary lookout. When their vessel, the *Minnesota*, came close to shore the Maryland gunners fired two shots which cut the *Minnesota*'s tiller rope and broke a piston rod. The hungover crew raised the white flag and met the rebels "at the head of the saloon steps, and politely requested their captors, in true Western style, to 'take a drink.'"[26] While such successes were pleasing, particularly to the Marylanders who happily removed from the *Minnesota* flour, bacon, canned oysters, and whiskey, they were too infrequent to disrupt the Union flow of supplies. Downriver, one day prior to Ritter's ambush, a more formidable obstruction to Grant's progress had disappeared in smoke and flame.

At dawn on May 3, the noise from three tremendous explosions washed over the ears of Union sailors at Bruinsburg. Porter suspected that the detonations meant that the Confederates had blown up their magazines at Grand Gulf. He took the fleet upstream to investigate. Seeing that the enemy had departed, the fleet tied up against the shore and Porter gave his people liberty time to explore the fortifications that had defied their ironclads four days earlier. Porter was well pleased: clearly Grant was making progress, and there was now one less Confederate stronghold blockading the river. Leaving four ironclads at Grand Gulf, Porter steamed downstream to join Farragut's ships, which were maintaining their lonely patrols above Port Hudson.

Like his army, General Grant had been traveling light and fast. He rode a borrowed horse. He had no servant. His entire baggage kit consisted of a toothbrush. He had worn the same clothes for a week. Riding to Grand Gulf, Grant found that the opportunity to bathe, shave, and change clothes aboard one of Porter's ironclads was most welcome. Refreshed, Grant turned to paperwork. The most important news came from Banks. Both Halleck and Lincoln had wanted Grant to cooperate closely with Banks, and Grant had dutifully tried to comply. With two enemy-held fortresses standing between them, it proved very difficult to communicate. It took twenty-eight days for couriers to complete a round-trip between headquarters, by which time the strategic situation could change enormously. Earlier in the campaign, Grant had intended to capture and hold Grand Gulf and then detach McClernand's corps to help Banks capture Port Hudson. Reading Banks's letter, Grant learned that the Massachusetts politician-general expected to return from his expedition into Louisiana and to be ready to operate against Port Hudson by May 10. But Banks's letter was twenty-three days old and Grant was skeptical.

Grant now confronted a momentous decision. He had achieved a somewhat secure bridgehead in Mississippi—secure from enemy attack but reliant upon a precarious line of communications stretching through the Louisiana bayous back to Milliken's Bend. The Army of the Tennessee was between two fortified Confederate citadels with its back to the continent's greatest river—in other words, situated in the dangerous position that Sherman had warned him about. Also entering Grant's calculus was the knowledge that both the nation's general in chief and commander in chief wanted him to work with Banks against Port Hudson before tackling Vicksburg. By all measures the prudent, conventional solution was to hold a fortified bridgehead at Grand Gulf and send McClernand to Port Hudson. But whereas Grant could endure uncertainties imposed by Confederate generals, having worked so hard to get to Grand Gulf he was loath to accept the uncertainties of cooperating with Banks. Grant had campaign experience directing converging columns against a common target and he knew it was an exceedingly chancy proposition. When, as would be the case against Port Hudson, the columns began one hundred miles apart and were commanded by unprofessional, political generals, the risks rose. Even if Banks kept to his optimistic forecast, it still meant an idle week for the army. Delay did not suit Grant. It would undo what he had done and give the rebels time to regain their balance, to reinforce and to fortify. He discarded the Port Hudson notion and resolved to act alone against Vicksburg. It was the greatest decision of his military career.

Having secured Grand Gulf, Grant had to pause to stockpile supplies. Already McClernand's corps had nearly run out of rations. Although Grant was running this campaign on a logistical shoestring, it still would take time to amass the essentials. Before he could strike inland he needed more men and had to accumulate ammunition and hardtack. To complete these logistical preparations as soon as possible, Grant labored until near midnight sending out a stream of orders. He had already told the quartermaster at Milliken's Bend to dispatch rations and forage "with all expedition" because "time is of immense importance." Now he wanted working parties to improve the roadway down to New Carthage because "everything depends upon the promptitude with which our supplies are forwarded." To Sherman, who was hustling his men south to join Grant, he wrote, "It is unnecessary for me to remind you of the overwhelming importance of celerity in your movements."[27] Unconsciously Grant was emulating the great Napoléon with his attention to logistical detail and rapid movement. Like

Napoléon, he sensed that once he had his opponent off balance, he could complete the job if he hurried.

At this time Grant made one other key decision. It represented the final maturation of a thought that had been percolating in his mind since the previous December when, after the destruction of his base at Holly Springs, he had learned that he could subsist his army on the countryside. In the forthcoming campaign he planned to take from the land as much food and forage as possible. Nevertheless, he would still need some sort of supply train. Army wagons, after driving down the sixty-three miles from Milliken's Bend to Hard Times, could form a nucleus for a supply train. Grant resolved to take the balance from the enemy. Grant sent detachments swarming through the countryside to collect vehicles and draft animals. Over the coming days his gleeful westerners returned with everything from huge, long-coupled wagons with racks designed to carry cotton bales to small, finely made carriages intended to convey the plantation gentry. When hitched to horses, mules, and oxen and loaded with cartridge boxes and hardtack, it made a rather unmilitary looking train. Certainly the spit and polish Army of the Potomac would have been appalled to be seen with such a thing. But it was serviceable, and that was all that mattered.

WHILE GRANT ADDRESSED formidable logistical problems and Pemberton worked to defend the Big Black crossing sites, President Jefferson Davis battled poor health. Stress and overwork drove the Confederate commander in chief to his sickbed during much of May. Already ill with bronchitis, stress brought a recurrence of neuralgia. Doctors feared he would lose the sight in his one good eye. Davis was not one to bow to physical problems. Bedridden or not, he continued to manage the war. On May 4 he briefly ventured outside for the first time in weeks, only to suffer a recurrence three days later that left him prostrate.

Davis had more than occasional flashes of strategic insight. On the day he retired to his sickbed he sent Pemberton his strategic analysis. Davis judged that Grant's lack of vehicular transportation would compel him to seek a junction with the fleet once he ventured inland. The president correctly appreciated Grant's ultimate need to rely upon the fleet in order to restock vital supplies. However, Davis misestimated the duration of any inland operation, wrongly predicting it could not last more than a few days. Then, in what proved to be a fateful conclusion, Davis responded to Pemberton's request to abandon Port Hudson in order to concentrate strength.

He wrote: "To hold both Vicksburg and Port Hudson is necessary to a connection with Trans-Mississippi."[28] Pemberton immediately ordered Gardner to return to Port Hudson and "hold it to the last" while resolving to do the same at Vicksburg.[29]

Davis also addressed Pemberton's request for reinforcements, noting that Beauregard could spare five thousand men. The only other manpower source was three thousand or so exchanged prisoners from the Post of Arkansas. Nothing better illustrates the poverty of Confederate resources than this: At a time when Vicksburg—one of the places the Confederacy had to hold if it were to win this war—was gravely threatened, exchanged prisoners represented three-eighths of the available reinforcements. Furthermore, so thoroughly had the Federal war machine cut connections with the Trans-Mississippi that Pemberton would have to rely upon the U.S. Navy to ferry the exchanged prisoners to him.

In Pemberton's view, the dual dictates of defending Vicksburg and feeding his command required that his army stay close to the Hill City. He suspected that Grant would drive directly on Vicksburg via Warrenton while feinting against the Big Black Bridge. To defend against the Warrenton threat, to defend the various crossing sites over the Big Black, and to keep a reserve near a supply depot, Pemberton lost the concentration he had earlier achieved. As of May 7, nine brigades occupied a twenty-mile-long front behind the Big Black facing south and southeast. Bowen's two brigades guarded the Big Black Bridge. Pemberton's remaining four brigades manned the river defenses against the unlikely possibility of a Union direct storm of the city. Two brigades, numbering about five thousand men, were trekking north from Port Hudson while another five thousand reinforcements from Beauregard were due in Jackson. Excluding Beauregard's men, Pemberton had about thirty-seven thousand soldiers to confront Grant's similarly sized army.

But Pemberton had a secure base and Grant did not. Once Grant resumed his advance, as long as the Army of the Tennessee kept moving it could live off the land. If Pemberton managed to slow its momentum or pin it in position, Grant's army faced annihilation.

6

Blitzkrieg through Mississippi

The crisis to decide the fate of Vicksburg has nearly arrived.

—Gabriel M. Killgore, Seventeenth Louisiana, May 5, 1863
("Vicksburg Diary: The Journal of Gabriel M. Killgore,"
Civil War History 10, no.1)

ON MAY 7 THE ADVANCE BEGAN. Grant's goal was to isolate Vicksburg from outside assistance by severing its rail connection. The army's initial objective was the small town of Rocky Springs. From there McClernand and Sherman would hug the Big Black River as closely as possible and head northeast to get on the Vicksburg and Jackson Railroad somewhere between Edwards Station and Bolton Depot. McPherson's corps would march on a parallel route further east to Raymond, at which point it would head toward Jackson to destroy the railroad. Flexibility remained a hallmark of Grant's strategy. He did not know how Pemberton would react. He believed that after the army had completed a few day's march, Pemberton would have to tip his hand. At that point he intended to adjust his own strategy.[1]

Baggage and equipment had been stripped to a minimum to promote rapid marching. Still, soldiers slung over their shoulder and back "the blanket roll, the knapsack, haversack and canteen. The cartridge box, cap box and bayonet scabbard all strung at the waist belt, 40 ounces of leaden bullets with the powder and bullets wrapped in paper to form cartridges." A handful of caps and three days rations completed the load.[2] The Army of the Tennessee had an established tradition of victory and the men were cheerful. A Union-loyal Missouri private wrote that the ongoing maneuver is "one of the best moves that has been made . . . we have entered the very heart of their country . . . you may tell your copper heads that I say they are gone up and if they don't believe it just add a little more simpathy for their southern brothers for god knows they need it . . . I expect we will have a big battle in a few days in which I expect to be on the winning side."[3]

The Union men marched through a virgin country that had not been stripped by the passage of hungry armies. It was a naturally fertile region. Loyal planters had responded to Richmond's pleas to replace cotton with food crops and these crops provided ample animal fodder since Grant's army entered it at a bountiful time of year. It was a land of abundant corn, hogs, cattle, sheep, and poultry and the soldiers took all they could find. A farmer appeared at Grant's headquarters to complain that an Iowa regiment had taken all of his livestock excepting a goose and an old mule. Grant inquired of General A. J. Smith, who commanded the Iowa men, if the charges were true. Smith hotly denied them, calling them a "damned lie." He continued, "I know my boys too well. If it had been the 13th Iowa they'd have taken everything."[4]

Grant's army moved rapidly. An Ohio colonel wrote that his regiment marched hard for eleven consecutive days, sometimes until one or two in the morning. For thirteen days he slept out of doors with no opportunity to change clothes. For everyone, there was little time to eat and less to sleep. Even generals catnapped when and where they could. On one moonlit night an Illinois soldier saw something rolled up in a blanket in a fence corner. Wishing to have some fun, he left the ranks to give the bundle a kick and exclaimed, "Hello, old fellow! Where did you get your whiskey?" To his horror General Sherman emerged from the bundle, prompting the man to disappear back into the ranks.[5] The pace of operations left little time for foraging. Later the legend would grow that this was a time of plenty for all. In fact, the men marching in a column's middle and rear found that the preceding soldiers had gleaned all the easy-to-find food. An Ohio soldier relates that his only ration was flour and salt, to which he added water and cooked "slapjacks . . . which lie on a man's stomach like cakes of lead."[6] The flour and salt that nourished the army were available because Grant retained a supply line back to Grand Gulf. This fact, too, would become clouded by hazy postwar recollections. Grant himself wrote in his memoirs that he abandoned his supply line after May 3. In fact, on a regular, almost daily, basis through mid-May, wagon trains numbering up to two hundred vehicles hauled ammunition and rations from Grand Gulf to the front.[7]

The Big Black River continued to act as a shroud concealing Grant's movements from Pemberton. By May 7 the Confederate commander had begun to appreciate that the Army of the Tennessee was sidling up the river and suspected that its target was the Big Black Bridge. But he took no decisive steps to intercept Grant's march and instead continued to prefer waiting behind the river barrier. General Loring believed this unwise. He proposed an offensive to catch Grant's army while it was regrouping for its final lunge against the railroad. Loring argued that it was important to take action before Grant perfected his dispositions and that, furthermore, an attack would have the virtue of surprise. "They don't expect anything of the kind," Loring explained, "they think we are on the defensive."[8]

Just now Pemberton did not welcome advice from his subordinates. May 10 found him working hard to coordinate his command's movements. But as the pressure built, he was becoming muddleheaded, and to his mind Loring's conduct did not help. Pemberton did not address Loring's notion for an offensive. Instead, when Loring made an honest error and moved part of his command contrary to Pemberton's wishes, Pemberton sent a complaining message that he was having "great difficulty in having his views comprehended."[9] From first impressions Loring had not thought highly of his "Yankee" superior. Pemberton's strategy during the first two weeks of May, with its march and countermarch, massing of forces and dispersal, was not elevating Loring's opinion of his commanding officer.

The next day Bowen gave Pemberton a report from an officer who had ridden around and through Grant's lines counting noses and chatting up soldiers the whole time. That officer judged Grant's force to number about forty thousand infantry and two thousand cavalry, which was pretty close to the truth. Pemberton had spent some time hectoring his subordinates for reliable information. Now he possessed it. The following day, May 11, the lieutenant general resolved that if the enemy moved on Jackson he would "advance to meet them."[10] But when Pemberton actually considered doing this, the difficulties overwhelmed him. He believed himself largely outnumbered. If he crossed the Big Black to engage Grant, several things might happen and all of them were bad. Grant might use one of the adjacent river crossings to strike in behind him or he might circle around Pemberton's flanks. While Pemberton was busy marching east, Union forces might storm Vicksburg from the west. In all these cases the Yankees would capture Vicksburg. To prevent this, Pemberton judged that he needed to leave substantial forces guarding the city and the adjacent river defenses, the Big Black crossings, and both his flanks. Thus, his strike force would be necessarily small, which, in turn, made him reluctant to do anything more than remain behind the Big Black.[11]

Pemberton was perfectly prepared to have his subordinates take the offensive. He ordered Texas Brigadier General John Gregg, who commanded one of the brigades sent from Port Hudson, to attack Grant's rear. If Grant turned on Gregg, he told Bowen to cross the Big Black and attack to support Gregg. This was a risky scheme, and one that if worth doing would seem sensible only if Pemberton committed his whole force. But this he could not bring himself to do. He took half steps when the situation called for decisive action and thereby allowed his opponent the chance to defeat his detachments piecemeal. Even as he pondered his tepid offensive actions, he began to realize that his orders to Gregg might involve peril. On May 12, Pemberton dispatched a courier to Gregg with additional advice: "Do not attack the enemy until he is engaged at Edwards or Big Black Bridge." How Gregg was supposed to determine this moment, with Grant's entire army between his isolated brigade and the Big Black, Pemberton did not say. Pemberton continued his instructions with words that revealed much about his own perception of the perils of field command. Reflecting his own insecurity, Pemberton wrote, "Be ready to fall on his rear or flank at any moment. Do not allow yourself to be flanked or taken in rear. Be careful that you do not lose your command."[12] By day's end Pemberton decided that it was time to depart Vicksburg and assume field command of his army. Meanwhile, by the time Gregg received this fatuous communication, he had already fought the Battle of Raymond.

BY MAY 10, Grant remained unsure as to how Pemberton intended to resist his drive on Vicksburg's lifeline, the railroad east through Jackson. But he sensed that "many days cannot elapse before the battle will begin which is to decide the fate of Vicksburg."[13] From Grant's perspective, the sooner that battle came the better, because he was uneasy about the difficulty of feeding his army. The next day, May 11, he told McPherson, "We must fight the enemy before our rations fail."[14] Toward that end he had his three corps continue their advance, with McClernand paralleling the Big Black River, Sherman in the middle, and McPherson on the eastern flank heading toward the crossroads at Raymond.

On the day Grant issued these instructions, Gregg's veterans entered Raymond to the acclaim of the townspeople, who greeted them as saviors because it seemed that the Yankees were coming on hard. Gregg's orders demanded that he exercise his judgment. Pemberton had explained that he believed it likely that any Union advance through Raymond toward Jackson represented a feint in favor of an advance toward the Big Black. Accordingly, he told Gregg that if that officer confronted overwhelming force he was to retire to Jackson. On the other hand, if Grant turned toward the Big Black, Gregg was to attack him in flank and rear.[15] A more experienced field general than Pemberton would have recognized that this war had already proven that an isolated infantry brigade could not attack divisional- or larger-sized hostile forces and win. A less aggressive subordinate than Gregg would have proceeded with greater caution.

Early the next morning Gregg awakened to the report that a force of unknown size was rapidly advancing toward him. Because cavalry screened the enemy column, it was impossible to say how large it was. Besides being an instinctively aggressive officer, the fact that he had once been forced to surrender to the detested Yankees at Fort Donelson still gnawed at Gregg. Thirsting for revenge, he was inclined to think that he faced the feint that Pemberton had told him to expect. When one of his scouts brought the additional intelligence that the approaching column numbered 2,500 men or so, he was certain. He would smash this detached column and then, with reinforcements he knew were marching to join him, continue to attack Grant's rear. Like their general, most of the infantry in Gregg's 3,000-man brigade had surrendered to Grant at Fort Donelson fifteen months before. As they deployed overlooking a bridge on Fourteenmile Creek, many believed that revenge was at hand.

The densely covered terrain that had helped Bowen resist a much larger force at Port Gibson worked against the Confederates at Raymond. When a Federal force appeared near the bridge about 10 A.M., Gregg could not accurately estimate its strength because of the thick woods. From a commanding knoll, his three artillery pieces, belonging to Bledsoe's Missouri Battery, opened the battle by firing on the Union advance guard. These soldiers belonged to the Twentieth and Seventy-eighth Ohio. As the Ohio men had marched toward the battlefield they had passed an old woman leaning on a fence, smoking a corncob pipe. She had said, "Y'all be back this way before long. They're waiting for you uns up yonder."[16] The column laughed and marched on to put the woman's prophecy to the test.

The Missouri battery's opening shots brought corps commander James McPherson spurring to the fore. Thirty-four-year-old McPherson was a Grant favorite. McPherson had graduated first in his West Point class. Although his war service involved staff and engineering duty, his shining

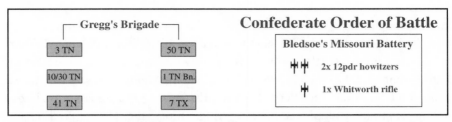

Confederate Order of Battle

Gregg's Brigade

3 TN	50 TN
10/30 TN	1 TN Bn.
41 TN	7 TX

Bledsoe's Missouri Battery

2x 12pdr howitzers

1x Whitworth rifle

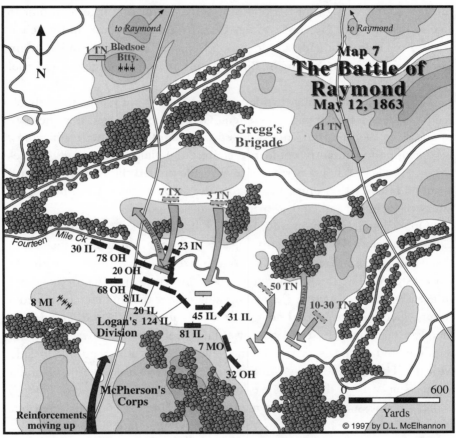

to Raymond

to Raymond

1 TN Bledsoe Btty.

N

Map 7
The Battle of Raymond
May 12, 1863

41 TN

Gregg's Brigade

7 TX

3 TN

Fourteen Mile Ck

30 IL

78 OH

23 IN

20 OH

68 OH 8 IL

8 MI

50 TN

10-30 TN

20 IL 124 IL

45 IL 31 IL

Logan's Division

81 IL

7 MO

32 OH

McPherson's Corps

Reinforcements moving up

0 — 600

Yards

© 1997 by D.L. McElhannon

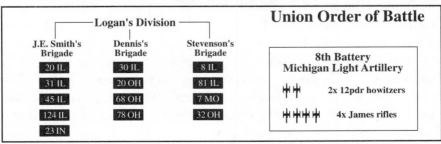

Union Order of Battle

Logan's Division

J.E. Smith's Brigade	Dennis's Brigade	Stevenson's Brigade
20 IL	30 IL	8 IL
31 IL	20 OH	81 IL
45 IL	68 OH	7 MO
124 IL	78 OH	32 OH
23 IN		

**8th Battery
Michigan Light Artillery**

2x 12pdr howitzers

4x James rifles

competence caused Grant to nominate him for higher command. Grant's wife had personally sewn his general's stars to his uniform. When McPherson arrived on the battlefield it marked the first time he held independent battle command. Looking across the creek valley, McPherson saw the smoke from the Confederate artillery. Through the gaps in the trees he made out a line of infantry deployed along a ridge top. Like Gregg, McPherson misjudged the strength of the opposing force, estimating it to total four to five thousand men. He sent couriers to hurry up his column and watched while his leading brigade deployed and crossed the creek and Captain De Golyer's Eighth Michigan Battery unlimbered to engage the rebel artillery.

The ensuing long-range artillery duel was noisy but not particularly effective except for its impact on General Gregg. Gregg judged that the two-to-one odds Bledsoe confronted spelled ultimate doom. If he lost his guns, his unsupported infantry could not contest the field. Accordingly, he resolved to attack. While a portion of his brigade pinned the Union force with a frontal attack, other units would cross the creek to take the opposing infantry of its right flank and overrun De Golyer's guns.

Opposing Gregg's men were sixty-five hundred men belonging to John Logan's division. Two of Logan's brigades had deployed and advanced into the woods before Gregg attacked. A third remained in reserve with De Golyer's guns. The thick undergrowth contributed to an initial deployment so ineptly managed by the Federal brigadiers that the first contact pitted a surging Confederate battle line against hastily formed, isolated Union regiments. Encouraged by the sword-wielding Gregg, who had recruited the regiment and served as its colonel, the Seventh Texas advanced side by side with the Third Tennessee. "Our line rushed forward at double-quick and a short distance from the woods we received a volley from a line of battle," wrote a Tennessee officer. "Our men though falling fast never faltered but still advanced and rushed into the timber yelling like demons."[17] The Twenty-third Indiana had crossed the creek and was blundering forward through a thicket when the rebels struck. Because the regiment's skirmishers were not far enough forward to give a proper warning, the attack came as a surprise. "All at once, the woods rang with the shrill rebel yell and a deafening din of musketry," recalled a nearby Federal officer.[18] The Twenty-third broke in the face of this charge. When the fleeing men ran past the Twentieth Ohio, that regiment began to waver as well. At this critical moment Logan arrived. "For God's sake men, don't disgrace your country," Logan thundered.[19] His charismatic presence helped steady the men. A point-blank firefight ensued at such close range that men were burned by the powder discharged through the muzzles of opposing riflemen.

For nearly two hours the close-range firefight continued. A Union soldier wrote:

> We dropped on the ground right there and gave those Texans all the bullets we could cram into our Enfields, until our guns were hot enough to sizzle. The gray line paused, staggered back like a ship in collision which trembles in every timber from the shock. Then they too gave us volley after volley, always working up toward us, breasting our fire until they had come within twenty, or even fifteen paces. In one part of the line some of them came nearer than that, and had to be poked back with the bayonet.

At times during the two-hour combat the fight became personal:

> One officer, not more than thirty feet from where I stood, quietly loaded up an old meerschaum, lit a match, his pistol hanging from his wrist, and when he had got his pipe well agoing, he got hold of his pistol again and went on popping away at us as leisurely as if he had been shooting rats. Why that fellow didn't get shot I don't know. The fact is when you start to draw a bead on any chap in such a fight you have got to make up your mind mighty quick whom you'll shoot.[20]

So far, Gregg's frontal pinning attack had succeeded famously. Because of the blundering Federal deployment, his men had encountered only isolated regiments and never more than two abreast, although there were thirteen Union regiments present. Consequently, Gregg still believed that he faced only one brigade. Thus, all that remained was to execute his flank attack and sweep the field. Lieutenant Colonel Thomas Beaumont, commanding the Fiftieth Tennessee, one of the regiments charged with carrying out the flanking thrust, was just now reaching a quite different conclusion. Beaumont had crossed the creek only to encounter two regiments charged with protecting Logan's flank. Looking to his right, the colonel saw additional Union regiments and correctly concluded that the Confederates were battling a force much larger than Gregg supposed. He halted and dispatched a courier to apprise Gregg of the situation. The Confederate commander of the adjacent Tenth and Thirtieth Tennessee Consolidated Infantry, Colonel Randall MacGavock, whose attack was to occur after Beaumont's regiment advanced, likewise halted.

Beaumont's message never reached Gregg. Gregg did sense that his attack was stalled and so called up his reserve regiment, the Forty-first Tennessee, from Raymond. It was not enough. Finally numbers began to tell. A Union counterattack drove the Seventh Texas back to Fourteenmile Creek. From this natural defensive position Texas riflemen killed the commander of the attacking Twentieth Illinois. A soldier in the regiment recalled suddenly being struck by a Confederate bullet: "Was knocked from a left in front to a right in rear all of a flutter regained my feeling, found blood flowing very freely. Prayed for mercy, life & victory."[21] As the soldier dragged himself to the rear he saw the Sixty-eighth Ohio join the attack. Hand-to-hand combat was uncommon in this war, but here in the streambed of Fourteenmile Creek a wild melee occurred "with loaded guns, bayonets, & fists & clubs, butt end of muskets oh! dear but the men fought desperately on both sides."[22] Historian Ed Bearss describes the bizarre tactical situation in the creek bed: "The Federals held the bed for about 125 yards east of the bridge, firing north, and the Rebels held it for another 100 yards beyond, firing south."[23] Because a curve in the creek separated the two forces, neither realized that the enemy was nearby. The Third Tennessee, which had surged across the creek, began to receive a galling fire upon its flank and rear. It held its ground for nearly an hour, but as the pressure built its colonel realized that if his regiment remained in place it risked annihilation. He ordered a withdrawal, which turned into a difficult run along a gauntlet of fire from both flanks. The intense flank fire compelled the Tennessee men to ignore their wounded comrades' piteous entreaties and abandon them. Shattered and bleeding—the regiment lost fully a third of its strength during its charge and withdrawal—the Third Tennessee reformed on its ridge-top start line.

Similar pressure forced Beaumont's Fiftieth Tennessee backward, which left MacGavock's regiment isolated on a bare hilltop in the Confederate center, the target of most of the Federal artillery on the field. As a thickening cloud of shells exploded overhead, Federal infantry began to work their way around MacGavock's flanks. His position was untenable. To retreat might jeopardize the entire brigade. MacGavock resolved to attack. MacGavock was a tall man who wore a long, gray, scarlet-lined cloak. Habitually, when danger most pressed, he threw his cloak back as if preparing to get down to work. So he did here. No sooner had he shouted out the order to charge than a bullet struck and killed him. The cloak that had long inspired his men had provided an unmistakable target and now his life's blood spilled on its scarlet lining. His vengeful regiment overthrew the nearest Union regiment, but unsupported it could not hold its position long. Slowly the Union line drove it back.

A unified and vigorous Federal advance would have swept the field. Gregg's remaining battleworthy unit, the First Tennessee Battalion, managed by bluff alone to outface the Union left. The tangled terrain and the jumble of misaligned units kept the Union right from pressing hard. Even the normally well-directed Federal artillery contributed little. None of McPherson's twenty-two cannon advanced across the creek during the battle.

Gregg's battered brigade—incomplete returns showed 515 casualties; the Seventh Texas alone lost 158 out of the 306 men who began the battle—retired through Raymond toward Jackson. McPherson's men, who had lost 442 casualties, were content to occupy the town and call it a day. The western soldiers had fought with characteristic savagery. A Federal colonel reported that in front of his regiment he found seven dead rebels behind a log that had been pierced by seventy-two bullets. Illinois sergeant Ira Blanchard related that "behind every tree, in every hollow, or behind every log some poor fellow had crawled away and died."[24] It fell to the surviving comrades and relatives to report the news to home:

My Dear Cousin Em,

It is with sad feelings that I inform you of Victor's death. He was shot through the head, killing him instantly. He died without a groan or struggle. [We lacked time] to make a box to bury him in, so we wrapped him in his blanket and laid him in his grave.[25]

The commanding officers had been unequal to the challenge of controlling a fight in the wooded terrain. For most of the battle neither Gregg nor McPherson knew where their regiments were positioned. McPherson had performed poorly in his first independent command, having committed his regiments piecemeal. He never managed to launch a coordinated attack to take advantage of the three-to-one superiority he enjoyed for the second half of the battle. In contrast, Gregg had displayed an aggressive tactical touch that would propel him the following winter to the command of the Army of Northern Virginia's elite shock unit, the Texas brigade.

The significance of the Battle of Raymond lay in its impact upon Grant's strategy. He had been trying to anticipate Pemberton's movements by a combination of active patrolling and reading the most current local newspapers. Gregg's obstinate defense alerted him to the rebel buildup at Jackson. Once more he revised his plan. He would sever regular communications with Grand Gulf after one last supply convoy departed from that place. Instead of moving against Edwards Station, he determined to make a ninety-degree wheel and deal with Jackson so as to secure his flank and rear from enemy interference. Because he did not know the strength of the Confederate force he would confront, Grant decided he required his whole army to attack Jackson. This scheme meant he would be turning his back on Pemberton. Grant calculated carefully: Nothing Pemberton had done so far indicated that he was an aggressive leader; consequently, Grant believed he could deal with Jackson and return to fight Pemberton before that general realized what was afoot. It was an audacious plan of Napoleonic vision. By virtue of careful logistical preparation followed by rapid marching, Grant had achieved the central position Napoléon cherished. Having interposed his army between the two Confederate wings, Grant intended to use the central position in Napoleonic style by defeating one wing and then countermarching to defeat the other before the two wings could cooperate. To accomplish this he would have to contend with a general widely recognized as one of the most skillful strategists on the North American continent. Lieutenant General Joseph Johnston was coming to Jackson.

BECAUSE HE CONSIDERED Tennessee the key front, Johnston had remained at Bragg's headquarters in the south-central Tennessee rail hub of Tullahoma as the crisis on the Mississippi mounted. As of May 9, Johnston still had neither learned about the results of the Battle of Port Gibson nor had he any idea of Grant's whereabouts. Then he received an order to proceed immediately to Mississippi to attend to the developing crisis. Although weakened by a monthlong illness, Johnston dutifully boarded the train the next morning and headed for Jackson. It was not a fast journey. May 13 found him at a rail station fifty miles east of Jackson, where he received a telegram from Pemberton dated the previous day. The first news Johnston had received since May 1, it outlined a rapidly deteriorating situation. Pemberton explained that the Yankees were apparently moving in heavy force against the railroad at Edwards Station. Pemberton announced that he intended to fight but judged himself largely outnumbered. These were unnerving tidings. Arriving in Jackson, Johnston conferred with General Gregg about the strategic situation. Gregg told him that four enemy divisions commanded by Sherman occupied Clinton, ten miles to the west. To oppose them, Gregg elaborated, there was a mixed force numbering six thousand men composed of his own battered brigade, some Mississippi militia, and the advance elements from Beauregard.

The presence of these latter stemmed from a decision made on May 2, when Secretary of War James A. Seddon had ordered Beauregard to send eight to ten thousand men to Pemberton. Old Bory responded that he could send only five thousand men because "to reduce this command further might become disastrous."[26] At least Beauregard sent two brigades composed of his best men, including an artillery lieutenant named Rene Beauregard, the general's son. The reinforcements had taken seven days to reach Jackson by riding the cars along the South's rapidly deteriorating railroads. When everyone en route arrived, Johnston could expect to have twelve thousand men by May 14.

After digesting all of this, at 8:40 P.M. Johnston sent a message to Pemberton: "Major-General Sherman is between us, with four divisions, at Clinton . . . If practicable, come up on his rear at once. To beat such a detachment, would be of immense value."[27] It seemed that Johnston, the celebrated strategist, had determined that when Grant interposed his army between two Confederate forces he had stepped into the jaws of a trap. Then Johnston fired off an entirely different message to Richmond and this one revealed his true assessment: "I arrived this evening, finding the enemy's force between this place and General Pemberton, cutting off the communication. I am too late."[28] Johnston ordered the city evacuated and dispatched Gregg to cover the retreat. He specified that the direction of retreat would be toward Canton, which was northeast of Jackson. Thus he would not be in position to cooperate with Pemberton should that general follow his suggestion to attack toward Clinton.

ON THE NIGHT OF MAY 12, Pemberton edged closer to the front by departing Vicksburg to travel to Bovina, a rail depot about six miles east of the city. During the day of May 13, the dreaded uncertainty characteristic of field command haunted Pemberton. Pemberton had little idea where Grant was and in what direction he was moving. He ordered Loring to conduct a reconnaissance in force to learn these things. If Grant was moving on Jackson, Pemberton was considering attacking his rear and cutting his communications. Since any advance jeopardized Vicksburg, he required "accurate information" from Loring that he could "rely on before making this move."[29] Until the situation clarified, Pemberton was not going to budge.

While Pemberton spent May 13 trying to determine Grant's whereabouts, the Army of the Tennessee commenced its wheel toward Jackson.

This maneuver placed a particular strain on McClernand's corps. The previous day it had been within four miles of Edwards Station and patrols had been in skirmish contact with the Confederates. General Loring, acting as field commander in Pemberton's absence, commanded some twenty-two thousand men around Edwards. McClernand had only three divisions present, numbering thirteen thousand men. Neither general realized the true state of affairs. Upon receiving orders to march toward Jackson, McClernand resolved to make a diversion to cover his disengagement. On May 13 he aggressively sent a division to within two and one-half miles of Edwards Station. This maneuver overawed Loring. McClernand was thereby able to disguise his withdrawal and retire to Raymond unmolested. Not until 5 P.M. did Loring realize that McClernand had departed from the area. By 8 P.M. he informed Pemberton that he had no doubt that the enemy was marching on Jackson.

As McClernand's men filed east they crossed a small stream known as Bakers Creek. They did not know that they would return to this position in three days to fight the campaign's decisive encounter.

FOR MANY UNION SOLDIERS the march toward Jackson was hard and fast. On May 13, the Thirteenth Illinois covered forty miles in twenty-four hours, stopping for only two hours of rest. Soldiers from the Twentieth Ohio stole mules from nearby farms to carry footsore men who could not keep up. Grant himself set an example by being constantly on the move, accompanying first one corps commander and then another to ensure the movement proceeded as planned. Because he genuinely liked Sherman and McPherson, he continued to spend the most time with them, preferring to deal with McClernand through written dispatches. He paid little attention to his own nourishment. His son recalls that his father's table during this period was the worst he ever saw. On the evening of May 13 Grant wrote orders for the capture of Jackson. He set McClernand the task of wrecking the railroad west of the capital. McPherson would use the Clinton Road and move on Jackson from the northwest while Sherman marched along the Raymond Road to approach Jackson from the southwest. All movements were to begin at dawn.

May 14 brought heavy rains. As two Union corps converged on Jackson, General Gregg followed Johnston's orders and deployed his rearguard to cover the efforts to evacuate public property from the city. Initially Gregg had no idea that Sherman was heading his way and consequently stationed all of his force to oppose McPherson on the Clinton-Jackson road. His command comprised his own brigade that had fought at Raymond and the forces Beauregard had sent from the Atlantic Coast. Prominent among the new arrivals was thirty-one-year-old Brigadier General States Rights Gist, whose birth name bespoke his South Carolina family's devotion to the cause. The defense of Jackson would require more than devotion, however, because the approaching Union forces vastly outnumbered the defenders.

McPherson's corps contacted Gregg on the Clinton-Jackson road about 9 A.M. The Federals drove in the Confederate pickets and deployed into battle formation. But the torrential rains made the cautious McPherson reluctant to order an assault because he feared that if his men opened their cartridge boxes their ammunition would receive a ruinous soaking. Because of McPherson's hesitancy, when Gregg learned that another Federal column was also approaching Jackson, he was able to detach a scratch force to contest its advance.

Around 11 A.M. Sherman's leading division contacted this detachment on the Raymond-Jackson road. Two Union batteries rapidly deployed and delivered an accurate, twenty-minute-long bombardment that overwhelmed the rebel roadblock. The Confederates retired to a woods where they rallied. Again Sherman's vanguard deployed and swept forward. The Confederates did not care about the position; they were fighting for time. Accordingly, they withdrew before contact to a line of fieldworks that surrounded the city. Within these works were ten field guns served by Mississippi State Troops. Their fire brought the Federals up short. It was 1:30 P.M. The Confederate rear guard had done well to delay an entire corps for two and one-half hours.

While subjected to an intermittent Confederate shelling, Sherman conferred with Grant. Exhibiting a growing fear of assaulting an entrenched enemy, Sherman proposed that he halt the advance and send a regiment to probe the rebel flank. Grant customarily allowed his corps commanders to fight their own battles and accordingly endorsed Sherman's tactics. As the rain of enemy shells continued, Grant and Sherman rode among the soldiers to keep them steady. Meanwhile, the flanking regiment literally walked through an unmanned sector of the rebel defenses and approached from the rear the works facing Sherman's main body. A quick charge carried the day against a skeleton force that had been left to man the artillery and cover the Confederate retreat.

Over on McPherson's front, when the rain let up at 11 A.M., McPherson ordered Brigadier General Marcellus Crocker's division to advance. Crocker was a frail, tubercular man who was often on the sick list—except when battle was imminent. Grant considered him to be one of his finest divisional commanders and now he showed why. His division moved forward through shot, shell, and sharpshooter fire until reaching a wooded ravine some five hundred yards from the Confederate line. From this volume of fire Crocker judged that he confronted a relatively small force. After his men paused to gather breath, he ordered Colonel John Sanborn's brigade to "fix bayonets and charge through the ravine and all the way to the batteries."[30] With banners unfurled, Sanborn's line went forward at the double. There was the brief run through the beaten zone where men fell to canister and musketry, and then a bitter, close quarters fight between State Rights Gist's Twenty-fourth South Carolina and the Union Tenth Missouri in which the latter showed that Missouri valor was not limited to the men who fought for the South. A Wisconsin artillerist recalled that here as well, "Generals McPherson and Crocker were in the thickest of the fight, taking things as coolly as though there was no danger."[31] Numbers prevailed and the defenders retired to the entrenchments surrounding Jackson. By the time McPherson reorganized his command and sent out scouts to probe the works, the enemy was gone. A little before 2 P.M., Gregg had learned that the army's wagon trains were safely under way and had ordered a general retreat.

At the Battle of Jackson, Gregg had again displayed fine tactical skill while both McPherson and Sherman had exhibited excessive caution. And for the third time the significance of the battle lay not in the butcher's bill that listed 300 Union casualties and an estimated 845 Confederate losses along with seventeen cannon. As had occurred at Port Gibson and Raymond, Grant had concentrated overwhelming force against unsupported Confederate detachments. At Jackson, only one division in each of the two Federal corps did much fighting. But Grant had not known how strong a force he would confront and so had two-thirds of his entire army available and McClernand within supporting distance just in case. Since crossing the Mississippi, Grant had combined mass with flexibility and speed to achieve a central position. He then took advantage of his position by driving Johnston from the rail lines that converged on the state capital before Johnston had time to gain his bearings.

In response to the crisis on the Mississippi, Confederate reinforcements from three different commands had boarded the cars and rushed toward Jackson. Grant's bold descent on Jackson caused Johnston to stop the pending convergence. While personally accompanying Gregg's defeated forces on their march up the railroad northeast of Jackson, Johnston ordered the remainder of Beauregard's reinforcements to halt east of Jackson, well out of harm's way. Likewise, Johnston ordered two brigades sent from Bragg's Army of Tennessee to wait in Meridan, Mississippi, eighty-five miles east of Jackson. A brigade from the Port Hudson garrison that was thirty-five miles south of Jackson countermarched away from the capital. In time these forces could reconcentrate, but for the next several days Grant could afford to ignore them and focus on Pemberton and Vicksburg.

So sudden had been Grant's blitzkrieg that some of Jackson's inhabitants did not realize what had taken place. That afternoon, accompanied by Sherman, Grant entered a factory where the mostly female employees were busy weaving tent cloth for the army. The presence of the generals attracted no attention until Grant finally commented that he reckoned they had done work enough. He permitted the women to take with them what cloth they could carry and then ordered the factory burned.

Out in the city streets, the Army of the Tennessee thoroughly enjoyed its brief stay in Jackson. Flying from atop the capitol dome was the flag of the Fifty-ninth Indiana. Beneath it, soldiers found it was agreeable to be in the capital of a Deep South state and most satisfactory to be told by captured Confederates that they were hard soldiers, far tougher than the eastern Yankees whom the prisoners had confronted on previous fields. Soldiers found an abandoned silk flag from a rebel cavalry outfit. On one side it had the inscription "Claiborne Rangers," on the other "Our rights." Just now those rights did not include property, because many victors took to looting and delighted in watching how the city's poorer inhabitants reacted: " . . . these women would go into stores after our soldiers had smashed in the doors and load themselves with as much as they could carry away, of calico, shoes, hoop skirts, large bolts of factory cloth, thread . . . They were not content with one load but came again and again."[32] Jackson's poor particularly relished the sacks of wheat flour the soldiers scattered in the streets, commenting that it was a high-priced delicacy they had not eaten for more than a year.

That night Grant established his quarters in the capital's best hotel. From the lobby he had a clear view of the State House, where Jefferson Davis had pledged that the Confederate military would defend Mississippi from the enemy's "worse than vandal hordes." Grant slept in the room where Joe Johnston had reputedly slept the previous night. But there was not time for loitering. At dawn the next day the men slung knapsacks and marched west toward Vicksburg—all the men, that is, except for Sherman's corps, who remained to wreck the railroad and destroy other public property, and so began to hone the incendiary skills that they would carry with them when Sherman led them through Georgia and the Carolinas.

ABOUT THE TIME McPherson and Sherman were preparing to attack Gregg's outnumbered defenders at Jackson, John Pemberton was thirty-five miles to the west, preparing to depart Bovina to join his army at Edwards Depot. He had no particular plan in mind, since all he had learned from Loring's reconnaissance in force the previous day was that the Yankees had been present near Edwards and then they were gone. A courier delivered Johnston's message recommending an attack against Sherman at Clinton.

Although Grant was maneuvering deep within the Confederate rear on ground familiar to many rebels and where every farmer and soldier's wife was a willing source to report Yankee movements, Pemberton had few clues as to Grant's true whereabouts. He accepted Johnston's claim at face value and promptly responded that he would move toward Clinton at once. But, as he explained to Johnston, he doubted the plan's wisdom: "In directing this move, I do not think you fully comprehend the position that Vicksburg will be left in."[33] In making this response it was clear that Jefferson Davis's directive to hold Vicksburg ranked foremost in his mind.

Moreover, Pemberton did not move at once. As the morning of May 14 progressed, he entertained serious doubts. Having arrived at Edwards Station, and before he placed his army in motion, Pemberton availed himself of the traditional habit of the weak general by convening a council of war. Pemberton read Johnston's note to his assembled generals. He then stated that he believed the army's great duty was to defend Vicksburg. Furthermore, he thought that he had insufficient strength to attack Grant's main force. Pemberton warned that if the army advanced, it could be defeated— and this would be disastrous. In sum, Pemberton told his generals, to adhere to Johnston's scheme would be "suicidal."[34]

Here was a pitiful display which did not inspire confidence in his subordinates. Johnston, on the other hand, was a famous and respected general. Duty and personal preference converged. The majority of Pemberton's generals favored Johnston's proposition. Then Loring outlined a different scheme. He proposed to attack Grant's line of communications, which reportedly was guarded by an isolated division. A minority of the generals endorsed Loring's plan. Pemberton did not care for Loring's scheme because it, too, would place Vicksburg at risk. He argued once more in favor of defending the line of the Big Black River. He failed to persuade anyone. Because his subordinates were eager for action, Pemberton yielded. The army would march according to Loring's scheme. Writing after the war, Joe Johnston described Pemberton's state of mind perfectly: "Although adverse to both opinions, General Pemberton adopted that of the minority of his council, and determined to execute a measure which he disapproved, which his council of war opposed, and which was in violation of the orders of his commander."[35]

Having spent most of two days deciding what to do, Pemberton capped his dismal performance by deciding that the next day would be soon enough to begin. He sent word to Johnston about his plan, attended to some administrative business, and went to bed. So it was that one day after the lieutenant general had told Johnston that he was already under way toward Clinton, Pemberton's army prepared to lurch forward in an entirely different direction, and in an effort to find and sever Grant's nonexistent line of communications.

At the time when Pemberton convened his council of war, the entire Federal force across the Mississippi River numbered about forty-four thousand men. The Confederates had an approximately equal number. The crucial difference was that the Union field army was well concentrated within a few hours march of one another, while the Confederates lay scattered into three major groups—the Vicksburg garrison, Pemberton's field army, and Johnston's force—with no two of them within mutually supporting distance.

Sometime after Pemberton recited Joe Johnston's message to his council of war, another very interested party was also reading it. To ensure safe arrival, Johnston had sent the message in triplicate. One of the three couriers was a Federal agent. His presence at Johnston's headquarters was the result of a clever scheme hatched by Grant's old comrade from Shiloh, General Stephen Hurlbut. Several months earlier, Hurlbut had evicted a man from Memphis on charges that he entertained rebel sentiments. Hurlbut publicly proclaimed that he was taking this action as a warning to all inhabitants of Federal-occupied territory not to trifle with Federal force. Having thus established his pro-rebel credentials, this man had little difficulty worming his way into Confederate service as a special courier. Given Johnston's dispatch, he rode straight to the Union army. Blessed by this intelligence coup, Grant had a very good idea of what his opponents were about and was able to take appropriate countermeasures. His intention was simple: He would smash Pemberton's force before Johnston recovered to reinforce it.

Grant's plan called for Sherman to remain in Jackson to complete the destruction of the railroad and other military installations while his other two corps marched toward Edwards Station. During May 15, McPherson's Seventeenth Corps would march west along the railroad to Bolton's Depot while McClernand's Thirteenth would concentrate on a line from Bolton's Depot to Raymond. From this staging area, Grant would have thirty-two thousand soldiers ready to advance the following day along three roads converging on Edwards Depot. Somewhere along these roads Grant expected to encounter Pemberton in the act of carrying out Johnston's orders.

In contrast to Confederate performance, the Army of the Tennessee was under way between 4 and 5 A.M. on May 15. The approach march went off without a hitch. By day's end Grant was well satisfied. He had concentrated seven divisions and done so without subjecting too many men and draft animals to long, punishing marches. Although on any given day over the past ten, men had marched hard and eaten very little, most marches had ended early enough for the soldiers to have time to forage and rest. There had been hard bursts, like the march to Jackson, but they had produced battlefield victories or material successes. Even when physically weary, men who knew they were winning remained eager. Because of his deft handling, on the evening of May 15 the Army of the Tennessee was a physically and morally powerful fighting force.

While Grant's two corps advanced toward Pemberton, the morning of May 15 found Joe Johnston ten miles outside of Jackson accompanying his infantry as they retreated to the northeast. A tired courier spurred up to him bringing the latest from Pemberton. The message had been sent more than fourteen hours earlier and its content angered Johnston. He learned that instead of marching to unite with him, Pemberton was heading off to cut Grant's supply line and was marching in a direction that increased the distance between the two Confederate forces. The fact that Old Joe was not blameless of this latter sin bothered him not at all as he wrote out a new order to his wayward, erstwhile subordinate: "Our being compelled to leave Jackson makes your plan impracticable. The only mode by which we can unite is by your moving directly to Clinton."[36] Johnston added that he would join Pemberton at Clinton with about six thousand men.

Having directed Pemberton upon a perilous path across the front of Grant's army in order to join his own force, Johnston now issued orders regarding his own route of march. To reach Clinton and unite with Pemberton, Johnston's column had to march northwest. Incredibly, and to his great discredit, Johnston ordered his column to continue northeast. Each step took them further away from Pemberton.

Some thirty miles to the east, Pemberton's army remained inert throughout the morning of May 15. Sloppy staff work had failed to stockpile adequate food and ammunition at Edwards Station. Finally, at 1 P.M., a day and a half after having received orders to march, all was ready and Pemberton's army got under way. The commanding general's lack of experience at conducting field operations and his subordinates' lack of faith in his ability now caused additional delay. In spite of being in the near presence of the enemy, and knowing that they were going to march, no one had taken the routine precaution of scouting possible lines of advance. The assigned route was found to be impassable due to muddy roads and to a swollen ford at Bakers Creek. By the time the generals agreed upon an alternative, daylight was fast dwindling.

The ensuing movement proved to be a tiring, start-stop-start sort of march, "much confused" by rain, bad roads, and darkness."[37] So slowly did the column proceed—the van division commanded by Loring had to contend with an inaccurate map atop everything else—that Stevenson's rearmost division did not even depart until 5 P.M. When Wirt Adams's cavalry, operating in front of the column, encountered Union forces east of Bakers Creek, it was near dark. Not wanting to bring on a nocturnal engagement, Pemberton halted the army. Although the soldiers had been up since early dawn, the march had covered a mere six miles. The march was so disjointed that Bowen's men did not reach their campsites until 10 P.M., while Stevenson's soldiers did not halt until 3 A.M.

Only Loring's van division was able to settle down at a decent hour. Softened by garrison life, many Confederate soldiers were badly worn by two weeks of active campaigning. During the day the men of Winfield S. Featherston's brigade had learned of the loss of Jackson. The news caused the evening conversation around the campfires to turn sour. The brigade that hailed from Mississippi took Jackson's fall hard. In addition, some of Loring's contempt for Pemberton had worn off on their commander. At Featherston's headquarters officers blamed Pemberton for the loss of their capital, calling the Pennsylvania-born officer incompetent and, even worse, a traitor.[38] These were not sentiments to put men in a fine, fighting frame of mind.

Yet most soldiers seemed in good spirits, eager to come to grips with the invaders. During the afternoon's march there had been few stragglers, a sure sign of high morale. At no time since the campaign's start had so many Confederates been concentrated in one place. The soldiers took heart from the visible evidence of their own strength. A Tennessee lieutenant wrote on the eve of battle about his comrades:

> These are effective men, Men that are fightening for their property of their families for their rights . . . such men can't be subjugated, unconquarable with too much hatred to even wish for peace, all joyful and full of glee marching perhaps right into the jaws of death. Ah, will the GOD of battles give this splendid army to Lincolns hords who have robbed the defenseless women and children of the staff of life . . . No the God of Battles has given us Victory.[39]

Whether or not there would be a victory, there seemed little doubt there would be a battle. From the campsites of Bowen's division, the glare of enemy campfires could clearly be seen to the east. Loring's pickets likewise reported the Yankees' near presence, information Loring personally relayed to Pemberton.

But the lieutenant general seemed oblivious. Overnight he kept his army in march column, not battle formation. This meant that the supply wagons and cattle herds were intermixed with the fighting formations. A disgusted Confederate brigadier later described the army as jammed along the road, in a "huddle."[40] Furthermore, Pemberton issued no orders to alter the next day's march. He intended to proceed to search for Grant's line of communication.

On May 16, before his army had moved far, the Army of the Tennessee forced it to deploy for battle, thus beginning the campaign's decisive encounter.

7

To the Crossroads

Every human instinct is carried away by a torrent of passion, while kill, kill, KILL, seems to fill your heart and be written over the face of all nature—at this instant you hear a command . . . "Fix bayonets, forward charge!" and away you go with a wild yell.

—Charles Longley, Twenty-fourth Iowa ("Champion's Hill," MOLLUS Papers—Iowa, vol. 1)

SUNRISE ON MAY 16 illuminated three Union columns marching west toward Edwards Station. On the southernmost route, the Raymond Road, came A. J. Smith's division followed by Major General Frank Blair's division. One and one-quarter miles of wooded terrain separated them from an adjacent column to the north. Here on the Middle Road marched Osterhaus's division followed by Carr. General McClernand, who commanded both of these columns, rode with the troops on the Middle Road. Another mile and three-quarters further north was the Jackson Road, which ran from the state capital through Clinton and continued until it merged with the Middle Road. The leading division on the Jackson Road was Hovey's division, which also was part of McClernand's corps. Trailing Hovey were Logan and Crocker of McPherson's Seventeenth Corps. Given that the three Union columns were moving along roads separated by rugged terrain, they would have difficulty coordinating their actions if, as Grant expected, they encountered the enemy. All seven divisions, numbering about thirty thousand men, had gotten an early start, which was good because with the rain over, the day promised to bring the return of heat and humidity.

The roads on which the two northernmost columns marched eventually merged at a point usefully referred to as "the Crossroads." From the Crossroads, the road headed west to a bridge at Bakers Creek and then continued to Edwards Station. A plantation road, the Ratliff Road, ran southwest from the Crossroads along the spine of a wooded ridge for two and one-quarter miles to intersect the Raymond Road. One and one-quarter miles west of this intersection the Raymond Road also crossed Bakers Creek. It was at this site that high water had blocked the Confederate march the previous day, and the ford remained impassable during the morning. This then was the road net that was to have a dominant impact on the battle: three roads—from south to north the Raymond, Middle, and Jackson—along which Grant's army marched to contact the Confederates; an important intersection—the Crossroads—where the Jackson and Middle roads joined; the Ratliff Road, which provided lateral communication for Pemberton's army; and two routes heading east over swollen Bakers Creek toward Edwards Station.

Eight hundred yards northeast of the Crossroads, in the direction from which approached Hovey, Logan, and Crocker, the Jackson Road crossed the crest of Champion Hill. This hill, which was to give the Union name for the battle, was the highest ground on the battlefield. It was the property of the Champion clan, whose family farmhouse was about one-half mile away. The hill was clad in a forest cover, brightened by blooming magnolia trees. A clearing on its top, where cotton had once grown, provided a useful artillery position. The ridge along which ran the plantation road featured denser undergrowth and a thicker stand of trees. Ravines and gullies bisected both this ridge and the slopes of Champion Hill. In the bottomland east of the plantation road was Jackson Creek. At the point where the Raymond Road crossed it, Jackson Creek was not a significant obstacle. Along both creek banks between the Raymond and Middle Roads was thick underbrush. Overall, while the terrain was neither as overgrown nor as cut up as that encountered at Port Gibson and Raymond, it was still difficult, confusing ground on which to maneuver.

General Pemberton had spent the night at the Ellison plantation, east of where the Raymond Road crossed Jackson Creek. Here an anxious Colonel Wirt Adams found him shortly after 7 A.M. Adams reported that his cavalry screen was again skirmishing with the enemy on the Raymond Road. While he contemplated the colonel's news, a weary courier arrived bringing the latest from Johnston. It had taken him twenty-two and one-half hours to find Pemberton. Pemberton again read the recommendation

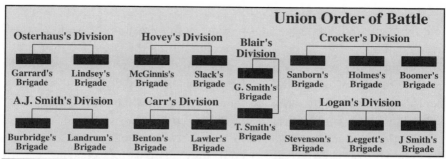

Union Order of Battle

Osterhaus's Division
- Garrard's Brigade
- Lindsey's Brigade

A.J. Smith's Division
- Burbridge's Brigade
- Landrum's Brigade

Hovey's Division
- McGinnis's Brigade
- Slack's Brigade

Carr's Division
- Benton's Brigade
- Lawler's Brigade

Blair's Division
- G. Smith's Brigade
- T. Smith's Brigade

Crocker's Division
- Sanborn's Brigade
- Holmes's Brigade
- Boomer's Brigade

Logan's Division
- Stevenson's Brigade
- Leggett's Brigade
- J Smith's Brigade

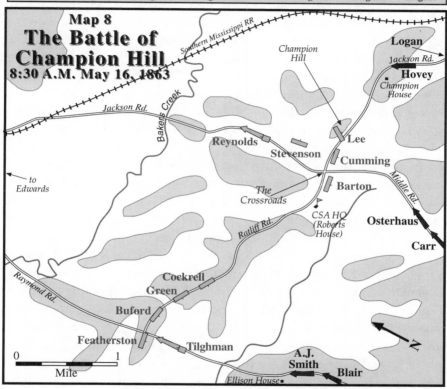

Map 8
The Battle of Champion Hill
8:30 A.M. May 16, 1863

Southern Mississippi RR

Champion Hill

Logan

Jackson Rd.

Hovey

Champion House

Jackson Rd.

Baker's Creek

Reynolds

Stevenson

Lee

Cumming

to Edwards

The Crossroads

Barton

Middle Rd.

Ratliff Rd.

CSA HQ (Roberts House)

Osterhaus

Carr

Cockrell

Green

Buford

Raymond Rd.

Featherston

Tilghman

N

0   1
Mile

A.J. Smith

Blair

Ellison House

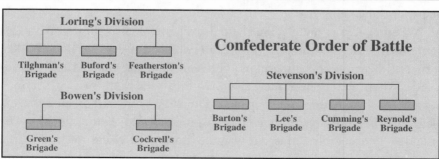

Confederate Order of Battle

Loring's Division
- Tilghman's Brigade
- Buford's Brigade
- Featherston's Brigade

Bowen's Division
- Green's Brigade
- Cockrell's Brigade

Stevenson's Division
- Barton's Brigade
- Lee's Brigade
- Cumming's Brigade
- Reynold's Brigade

149

that he march to Clinton in order to unite with Johnston, the same proposal which had been the subject of deliberation during the council of war nearly forty-eight hours ago. This time Pemberton decided to obey. Ignoring the growing sounds of skirmish fire, already thickened by the boom of cannon, Pemberton ordered his army to countermarch back to Edwards Station. From there they could continue toward Clinton.

On first inspection his decision seems remarkable. He was adopting a plan that he previously had rejected after labeling it "suicidal." Clearly Pemberton had no real intention of rejoining Johnston. For him, the overriding consideration was that by reversing his line of march he was drawing closer to Vicksburg. He had never wanted to march his army east over the Big Black in the first place. He felt renewed confidence now that he had orders to return to Edwards Station. Like a horse gone barn sour, Pemberton could not endure heading any direction except back to his base. So began what one Confederate brigadier later called "a hustle to extricate ourselves from the predicament."[1]

Pemberton might have managed to break contact with Grant's army, had not General Loring intervened just at this moment. Loring took grim pleasure in the advice he was about to impart. The escalating sounds of combat had convinced him, or so he said, of the need to form a line of battle astride the Raymond Road to oppose the oncoming Yankees. Pemberton agreed and chose Brigadier General Lloyd Tilghman's brigade, since it was closest to the enemy. After examining the ground, Pemberton ordered Tilghman to take position blocking the road. He ordered Loring to support Tilghman with his other two brigades. Riding back west, Pemberton encountered General Featherston, with whom he had a brief conversation. One of Featherston's aides, Lieutenant William Drennan, sensed that Pemberton was off balance. He "looked as if he was confused, and he gave orders in that uncertain manner that implied to me that he had no matured plans for the coming battle."[2]

Whether it was merely the natural excitement of orchestrating a first battle or whether Pemberton was indeed confused is unclear. What is clear is that at this time the disharmony between Pemberton and Loring resurfaced. When Pemberton met again with Loring and two of Loring's brigadiers, an ugly encounter ensued. Drennan overheard Pemberton explain that the army was to move to join Johnston and then outline how he intended to accomplish this. He wanted Loring's division to provide the rearguard. Pemberton said something that Drennan did not hear and Loring "rather testily" replied, "Gen'l Pemberton you did not tell me this last night." Pemberton responded, "Yes, Loring, you know I did." According to Drennan, "Their manner was warm."

Here was a shameful scene. In the face of the enemy and in front of their staffs, the army's two senior generals disputed strategy in a venomous fashion. It was the continuation of a long-simmering feud. As a result, Drennan wrote, "there was no harmony—no unity of action, no clear understanding of the aims and designs of our army." When the two generals were done, Drennan and another officer who witnessed the exchange agreed that Loring would "be willing for Pemberton to lose a battle" if that caused Pemberton "to be displaced."[3]

While the generals argued, Tilghman's brigade occupied a ridge-top position overlooking Jackson Creek. Here its attached battery enjoyed a fine field of fire across open, gently rolling ground all the way to the Ellison plantation. Meanwhile, Bowen's division, the next division to the north, deployed along the ridge parallel to the Ratliff Road to secure Loring's left flank. Pemberton had summoned the commander of his third division, Major General Carter Stevenson, to explain the vital task he required Stevenson to perform. Stevenson's division had been the army's rear. Since Pemberton had resolved to countermarch, it now became the van. The lieutenant general told Stevenson to cover the extrication of the army's trains, which at this moment were jammed along the Jackson Road, and to ensure their safe return to Edwards Station. Accordingly, Stevenson deployed some of his division between Bowen and the Crossroads and set the army's teamsters to the laborious task of turning the wagons around.

This then was the Confederate position at 8:30 A.M. Pemberton wanted to withdraw to Edwards Station, but the proximity of the Union forces had caused him to order the partial deployment of his army. He commanded a force of three divisions positioned along a two and one-half mile front atop a wooded ridge in the order, south to north, of Loring, Bowen, and Stevenson. This army numbered about twenty-three thousand men divided into nine infantry brigades, two cavalry regiments, and fifteen batteries. The batteries contained sixty-six artillery tubes, the majority of which were short-range, six-pounder smoothbore cannon and twelve-pounder howitzers. If given time, Pemberton possessed the strength to defend his position, which local topography rendered naturally formidable.

GENERAL MCCLERNAND ROSE EARLY on May 16 and rode toward Bolton to confer with McPherson. He looked forward to the stimulating prospect of independent battle command. His orders from Grant were to "feel" the enemy but to avoid bringing on a general engagement until McPherson could support the battle.[4] Since his Thirteenth Corps units were advancing on all three roads toward Edwards Station, McClernand knew that first contact would involve forces he commanded. Thereafter, how to "feel" the enemy was up to him. McClernand entertained big plans. He told McPherson that if his corps was able to defeat whatever enemy forces it encountered, and if his fellow corps commander pushed his men hard along the Jackson Road to support Hovey, McPherson would then be perfectly positioned to pitch into Pemberton's left rear. In making this proposal, McClernand was stretching the command latitude he enjoyed as senior corps commander. It was really up to the army commander to make such plans. If it was a typically bombastic proclamation, it was also sound strategy. Had McClernand adhered to it and done his part, the results would have been devastating for the Confederate army. Having briefed McPherson on his Napoleonic vision, McClernand returned to the Middle Road to oversee his impending triumph.

Meanwhile, the day's first combat occurred on the Raymond Road. A little before 7 A.M. a detachment of the Fourth Indiana Cavalry, acting as the advance guard for A. J. Smith's division, encountered Adams's Mississippi Cavalry. The Mississippi troopers' job was to detect the enemy and then slow him down. This they did well. Their belligerent presence imposed caution on Smith. A prewar cavalry officer, Smith enjoyed the reputation of being a bold, sometimes reckless commander. However, rather than pushing ahead to overwhelm the Mississippi cavalry, he worried about the presence of hidden enemy infantry somewhere nearby. Accordingly, Smith ordered his leading brigade, commanded by Brigadier General Stephen Burbridge, to deploy and advance. It was this advance that had caused Adams to gallop west along the road to inform Pemberton that the enemy was in contact. Burbridge drove in the rebel cavalry, who retired behind an infantry roadblock manned by soldiers of the Thirty-fifth Alabama and Twenty-second Mississippi.

Unwilling to bring on a general engagement until more men were up, Smith then halted. Burbridge deployed the six ten-pounder Parrotts belonging to the Seventeenth Battery, Ohio Light Artillery. For the next ninety minutes the battery shelled the rebel roadblock while Federal infantry patrols probed the position. In his official report, Burbridge would claim that if properly supported he could have easily driven through all opposition and reached Edwards Station by evening, but that Smith's orders prevented him. In any event, it is apparent that neither his brigade, which suffered just sixteen wounded during the entire day, nor Smith's other brigade, which lost six wounded, were aggressively handled.

On the Middle Road, Union soldiers heard the sounds of Smith's combat. They continued west with troopers of the Third Illinois Cavalry scouting to their front. About one and one-half miles east of the Crossroads, dismounted pickets belonging to the Twentieth Mississippi Mounted Infantry fired at them. The clash occurred on hilly, thickly wooded terrain. Not knowing what he confronted, General Osterhaus, like A. J. Smith, proceeded cautiously. He detached an infantry regiment from Garrard's leading brigade to support the cavalry and put the remaining three regiments on alert. Meanwhile, the Confederate mounted infantry retired to a position six hundred yards east of the Crossroads, where stood a roadblock initially manned by some Tennessee infantry.

Finding his advance checked at this roadblock, Osterhaus rode forward to scout. He saw that his cavalry could do no more and ordered them off the road to the left, where they could provide a link with the Federal troops moving on the Raymond Road. He reinforced his leading regiment, the Seventh Kentucky, with the Forty-ninth Indiana. There was not much open ground, so only one artillery section belonging to the Seventh Michigan Battery found a firing position. Covered by the bombardment of these two ten-pounder Parrotts, the Seventh Kentucky and Forty-ninth Indiana went forward.

By this time, one of Pemberton's staff officers had taken nine Georgia infantry companies belonging to Brigadier General Alfred Cumming's brigade to relieve the Tennessee infantry at the roadblock. The Georgia infantry easily repulsed the first Federal advance. Osterhaus committed the remaining two regiments of Garrard's brigade. Although possessing a four-to-one superiority, Garrard's men failed. The terrain contributed to the success enjoyed by the Georgia infantry. But it is apparent from the brigade's casualty list, which numbered sixty-eight men for the entire day, that the attack was not forcibly pressed. As had occurred at Port Gibson, Osterhaus seemed unable to bring superior force to bear effectively. Nor did he utilize his second brigade, which remained idle in reserve for the next ninety minutes.

With Osterhaus's division stalled at the roadblock, the entire Union advance on the Middle Road ground to a halt. McClernand feared to bring on a general engagement and doubted there was favorable ground to deploy his second division, Carr's, which was trailing Osterhaus. Consequently he held it in reserve. He sent two aides spurring to order Hovey to advance "cautiously but promptly" and then awaited developments.[5] Seemingly, McClernand's Napoleonic intentions had not survived the first contact with the foe.

AFTER DEPLOYING LORING'S DIVISION astride the Raymond Road, Pemberton rode to his left, where he made his battle headquarters at the Isaac Roberts house, just south of the Crossroads. It was 9 A.M. and all seemed well. His trains, composed of nearly four hundred heavy wagons, had moved over Bakers Creek. He had a formed battle line along a strong ridge-top position. Confederate infantry had successfully checked the Federal advances on both the Raymond and Jackson roads. In neither place were the adversaries in close contact. There seemed to be every opportunity to retire his army from the field and march it to Edwards Station. From his ridge-top headquarters, Pemberton could hear the continuing sounds of skirmishing on his right flank and at the Georgia infantry's roadblock.[6] He had trouble evaluating what all this firing signified. It seemed to engage his entire attention and convinced him that the main Union effort would come against his own right.

Thirty minutes later Pemberton received further good news when Stevenson reported that the trains had moved off and the Jackson Road was open "and free for the passage of troops."[7] Pemberton's scheme called for a steady sidle to the army's left toward the Crossroads. In succession, each of his army's brigades would march to the Crossroads, deploy, await the arrival of the next brigade, and then withdraw toward Edwards Station. This process was already under way. One of Stevenson's brigades—Tennessee soldiers commanded by Colonel Alexander Reynolds—had departed the Crossroads to escort the wagons and been replaced by Brigadier General Stephen Lee's brigade. Whereas Pemberton focused on the known threats and entirely overlooked the possibility that additional Federal forces might be advancing on the Jackson Road, the very capable Lee did not.

Lee was a thoroughgoing professional who had won his spurs under the gaze of Robert E. Lee. As soon as his brigade reached the Crossroads, he sent a six-company patrol out the Jackson Road. Its leader was Lieutenant Colonel Edmund Pettus, the younger brother of the Mississippi governor. Pettus descended from the crest of Champion Hill and marched about eight hundred yards to a grove of trees near the Champion house, where he concealed his men. Meanwhile, Lee deployed his Alabama infantry and its supporting artillery to guard the Crossroads. Shortly after 9 A.M., Pettus spotted a strong enemy column approaching rapidly. He sent a courier spurring up Champion Hill to inform Lee. Lee reacted quickly by shifting his brigade eight hundred yards from the Crossroads to the crest of Champion Hill. He relayed the information to Stevenson and to General Cumming, whose Georgia brigade was on his right, and then waited for the Federal advance.

The arrival of a Union force on the Jackson Road—it was Hovey's division—entirely changed the engagement's tactical calculus. Until this point, Pemberton's army had been comfortably facing east. Now Hovey was appearing at nearly a right angle to this front. Hovey was operating under McClernand's order to move "cautiously." Accordingly, he had some of his cavalry escort scouting the way. These Indiana troopers reported that an infantry and artillery force blocked the road atop Champion Hill. Hovey sent a message to McClernand asking whether he should attack. In the meantime, he deployed his leading infantry brigade, which flushed Pettus's patrol from the woods and sent it scuttling back up the slope, and awaited developments.

On the Middle Road, McClernand pondered Hovey's news. Like his divisional commander, he felt unable to bring on an engagement until he received permission from Grant. Therefore, he told Hovey to hold his position while sending a message to Grant describing the situation and asking whether he should advance. So it was that the battle hung fire—from the Union perspective because Grant had issued orders not to engage until his forces were concentrated on the field, from a Confederate perspective because Hovey's arrival had surprised Pemberton and caught his army trying to withdraw to Edwards Station.

AROUND 5 A.M. two railroad workers had been ushered into Grant's headquarters in Clinton. They had just passed through Edwards Station and brought fabulous intelligence. They told Grant that Pemberton had massed a force totaling twenty-five thousand men and that he intended to attack. This remarkably accurate estimate agreed with the information Grant had previously received from his double agent. Certain that he would soon have a battle, Grant sent a courier galloping to Jackson to recall Sherman. Escorted by only a few orderlies, he then rode west at a fast clip. He passed through the rear elements of McPherson's Seventeenth Corps. While trotting past one brigade he called out to its commander, John Sanborn, "Colonel, we shall fight the battle for Vicksburg to-day" and urged him to march quickly.[8] Continuing west, Grant saw that the wagons belonging to

Hovey's division blocked the road. He ordered the wagon masters to move off so the combat troops could pass. It was to prove to be one of those small decisions that paid handsome dividends.

Accompanied by McPherson, Grant arrived at the Champion house around 10 A.M. Here he listened to General McGinnis report on the Confederate position. McGinnis commanded the brigade that led Hovey's divisional column. An Indiana cavalry sergeant had taken McGinnis to within two hundred yards of the bald top of Champion Hill. Based upon his reconnaissance, McGinnis told Grant that the enemy occupied a naturally strong position. Undaunted, General Hovey requested permission to attack. Hovey was one of the army's aggressive generals. He had devoted himself to soldiering, and unlike many volunteer officers, made "it his business to learn the military profession."[9] But Grant held him in check pending the arrival of McPherson's people.

Federal caution gave the Confederates a breathing space, an opportunity to make tactical adjustments before close action began. As we have seen, Lee took advantage of this lull to occupy Champion Hill. Likewise, Carter Stevenson appreciated the seriousness of the threat from the Jackson Road. As he watched Hovey deploy, he sensed the vulnerability of Lee's left flank. Accordingly, he began redirecting his command while sending repeated warnings to Pemberton that Union forces were massing against him.[10] However, even though Pemberton's battle headquarters was only three-quarters of a mile from the crest of Champion Hill, Pemberton took no personal action to address the threat.

From his vantage point atop Champion Hill, Lee watched the Federal buildup with increasing anxiety. He could contend with Hovey's division, which was in plain view in the meadows below. When Logan's division deployed on Hovey's right, Lee had to adjust again by shifting his infantry a half mile to the northwest along a wooded spur of Champion Hill. There was not time to recall Pettus, which meant that the brigade occupied its new position minus 12 percent of its strength. Along a wood line overlooking Logan's division, Lee deployed his five Alabama regiments; from Lee's left to right the 23rd, 30th, 46th, 31st, and 20th. His soldiers propped their guns on a rail fence and prepared for combat. The brigade extended over nearly three-quarters of a mile and was without any reserves.

Earlier, one of Pemberton's staff officers had found the remnants of the Botetourt Artillery feeding their battery horses on the plantation road. He said they were urgently needed on the army's left. Hastily bridling the horses, the Botetourt Artillery reversed direction. The staff officer directed them to the old cotton field atop the hill. Here the gunners unlimbered their six-pounder smoothbore and twelve-pounder Napoleon, the only two pieces that had escaped the Port Gibson debacle. They could see no friendly troops—Lee having moved off to the northwest—and did not know that at this time General McGinnis was closely reconnoitering their position.

Lee's leftward sidle also posed a dilemma for the neighboring brigade commanded by General Cumming. Cumming was a combat veteran and had been wounded back east at Malvern Hill and again at Sharpsburg. But he was unknown to his brigade, having assumed command less than a week before, and scarcely knew his field officers. Moreover, his Georgia infantry had never been under close-range fire, and some had never been under fire at all. Cumming realized that he simply did not have enough men to stretch from the Crossroads all the way to Lee's right flank. Accordingly he divided his brigade and left the Fifty-sixth and Fifty-seventh Georgia along with Waddell's six-gun battery at the Crossroads, where they faced east toward Osterhaus. He moved with the remainder to Champion Hill, where he discovered that his own leftmost regiment, the Thirty-ninth Georgia, as well as four companies of the adjacent Thirty-fourth Georgia, had moved off with Lee's brigade. Apparently inexperience and unfamiliarity with its commander was causing the brigade to lose tactical cohesion even before the serious shooting started.

Furthermore, the brigade was much reduced by detachments. Nine of Cumming's companies continued to occupy the roadblock on the Middle Road. Two companies had been detailed to build a bridge where the Raymond Road crossed Bakers Creek. This left Cumming with two companies from the Thirty-fourth Georgia and six from the Thirty-sixth Georgia to defend Champion Hill. He hurriedly summoned a twelve-pounder Napoleon section from Waddell to buttress his defense and recalled the men who had wandered off after Lee. Because there were Federal troops both to the east and the north, Cumming had to station his infantry on Champion Hill in an L-shaped formation. When he had reassembled his command, he had seven companies of the Thirty-ninth and four of the Thirty-fourth facing north and two companies of the Thirty-fourth and six of the Thirty-sixth facing east. About fifty yards in front of the L, the ground dropped away sharply. In the absence of a rebel skirmish line, this meant that an attacker would be sheltered from most musket fire until arriving at nearly point-blank range. Furthermore, the slopes of Champion Hill were heavily wooded and Cumming had no time to detach skirmishers onto these slopes. Thus,

Cumming's infantry would have little warning before the attackers were on top of them.

Carter Stevenson was alive to the growing menace to his left flank. Earlier he had dispatched a regiment from Brigadier General Seth Barton's brigade and two guns from his divisional artillery to guard the upper Bakers Creek bridge. Just before the Union assault, he rushed the brigade's remaining four regiments at the double to secure Lee's left flank. The ground between Champion Hill and Bakers Creek was too broken to permit the brigade's artillery to accompany the infantry. Consequently, the Cherokee Georgia Artillery unlimbered its four ten-pounder Parrotts near the Jackson Road to Barton's left rear. Four guns from Company A, First Mississippi Light Artillery joined them. These guns, particularly the rifled Parrotts, could enfilade Logan's infantry when they advanced against Lee.

To recapitulate the Confederate tactical deployment when Hovey and Logan attacked: Carter Stevenson's division had Reynolds's brigade already off the field, having led what was supposed to be a withdrawal to Edwards Station; Barton's brigade was moving to occupy the bottomland between Bakers Creek and the ridge spur occupied by Lee's five regiments; Lee's brigade faced north; Cumming's brigade—charged with defending the battlefield's two key features, the Crossroads and Champion Hill—was fragmented into four separate elements, with two companies building the bridge at Bakers Creek, nineteen companies atop Champion Hill, twenty companies guarding the Crossroads, and nine companies manning the roadblock on the Middle Road. There was a three-hundred-yard-wide gap between the rebels on Champion Hill and at the Crossroads. Cumming's deployment, if it can be so dignified, had occurred within eyesight of Lieutenant General Pemberton's headquarters. Although he was present at his headquarters at this time, Pemberton neither examined the ground from the vantage point of Champion Hill nor conferred with Stevenson or his subordinates during this time.

AROUND 10 A.M. General John Logan had met with Grant and McPherson at the Champion house to receive instructions. He had an eye for display. Wearing his full dress uniform, he departed the house to straddle a superb white horse and course the fields west of the Champion house and rejoin his division. He passed behind Brigadier General Mortimer Leggett's brigade, which was in battle formation to Hovey's right. To Leggett's right rear was General John Smith's brigade, while General John Stevenson's brigade stood in reserve. Standard tactical practice called for combat brigades to maintain a double line of skirmishers to their front. One of Smith's units assigned this duty was Company A, Twentieth Ohio. Typically, fighting soldiers piled their knapsacks somewhere to the rear before advancing. Company A had yet to receive this order. Spotting Logan, one of the Ohio men called out, "Shall we not unsling our knapsacks?" Besides knowing how to make a dramatic spectacle, Logan understood how to inspire with a dramatic utterance. "No," he snarled, "damn them, you can whip them with your knapsacks on!"[11]

At 10:30 A.M. Grant judged that he had a sufficient force on the field to begin the battle. He gave McPherson tactical control of the attack and ordered the advance to begin. From behind Hovey's line, Grant watched McGinnis's men walk forward five hundred yards through an artillery barrage fired by the four guns atop Champion Hill. Operating under orders to "feel" the enemy, the battle line then lay down to give time for their skirmishers to accomplish their task. Hovey's skirmishers climbed the sloping meadow and entered the woods, where they exchanged fire with Pettus's Confederate skirmishers.

Hovey's pause to allow the skirmishers to advance gave Captain John Cook of the Fifty-sixth Ohio time to catch up with his men. Cook had been too ill to march and had fallen behind. With battle looming, and although still obviously weak, he rejoined his comrades, telling them, "I am going in with the boys if it is the last thing I ever do."[12] Meanwhile, the divisional skirmishers slowly drove Pettus's skirmish line up Champion Hill. The lush Mississippi vegetation, with its tangle of vines and underbrush, and the numerous gullies and ravines slowed all movement. Logan's men had even greater difficulty struggling through the more broken terrain between the hill and Bakers Creek. In addition, the rebels fought well. Nearly every Federal soldier who wrote about the battle commented on the severity of the hour-long skirmish combat.[13]

In Civil War parlance, "feeling" the enemy meant locating the enemy's main line of resistance. When Confederate regular volleys began to thicken the single shots fired by their skirmishers, the Union skirmishers had done their job. By 11:30 A.M. Hovey and Logan informed McPherson that they had driven in the opposing skirmish line. McPherson ordered them to storm the hill.

At this time Pemberton had no idea what was about to beset him. As the firing built up along Carter Stevenson's front, he believed his men were getting the best of it. He sent Stevenson a discretionary order that if the en-

emy faltered, "to push him vigorously." To complete his unrealistic ap-
praisal of the situation, Pemberton sent word for Bowen and Loring to advance on their front and "drive" the enemy.[14] In the event, Bowen waited
for Loring to initiate the drive while Loring absolutely refused to obey the
attack order. Had they followed Pemberton's instructions, the Vicksburg
campaign would have ended on this day with the destruction of the Confederate field army. As it was, Carter Stevenson, instead of pushing the enemy, was about to be pushed himself very hard.

Covered by friendly artillery fire, twenty-one Union infantry regiments
numbering ten thousand men swept forward along a mile and one-half
front.[15] Opposing them were perhaps sixty-five hundred men, who a Confederate staff officer described as "composed of the last regts from Georgia
and Alabama, very ignorant men, far away from their homes, [who] had
been marched heavily for the past few days."[16]

Initially, Hovey's two brigades oriented on the Jackson Road and advanced abreast of one another until a jog in the road caused them to di-
verge. Continuing upslope, they assumed a crescent-shaped formation.
Climbing to within three hundred yards of the crest, they began receiving
artillery fire. The shelling came from the two Virginia guns and two twelve-
pounder Napoleons from Waddell's battery. The guns occupied a poor position, able to see Hovey's approach only by "peering through little open
spaces" in the trees.[17] When they did see a target, the Botetourt gunners
cut their fuses as short as possible so the shells would burst as soon as they
left the muzzle. Before the Union troops disappeared from view, the guns
also managed to fire a double round of canister.

Making skillful use of the ground, McGinnis's men climbed through
the fire to within seventy-five yards of the cannon. Here they found shelter in the dead ground just under the crest. McGinnis considered the situation. His brigade lapped around the Confederate L-shaped defense. From
where he stood, his men would charge southwest against one side of the L.
He knew that the defenders would be able to fire only one volley before
his men were on them. Accordingly, he told the nearby soldiers of the
Twenty-ninth Wisconsin that after they had advanced a few paces he would
chop his sword downward as a signal to fall flat on the ground. McGinnis
hoped that the defender's volley would pass harmlessly overhead. Then the
men would rise up and charge. He ordered his soldiers to fix bayonets and
led them to the assault.

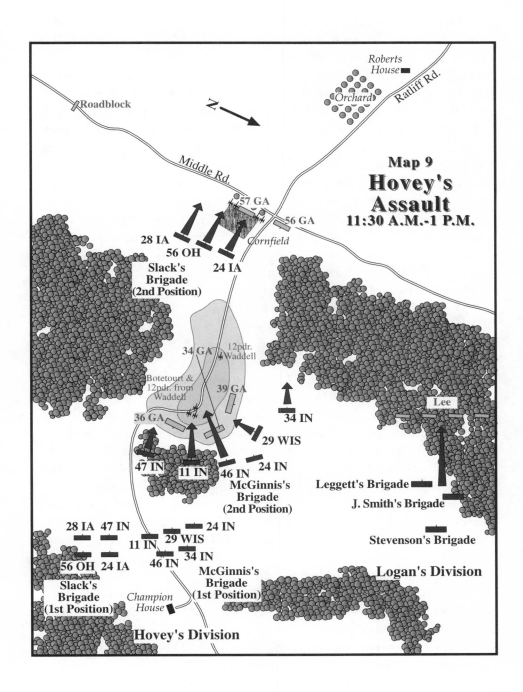

Roberts
House

Orchard

Ratliff Rd.

Roadblock

N

Middle Rd.

Map 9
Hovey's
Assault
11:30 A.M.-1 P.M.

57 GA

56 GA

28 IA

56 OH

Cornfield

24 IA

**Slack's
Brigade
(2nd Position)**

34 GA

12pdr.
Waddell

Botetourt &
12pdr. from
Waddell

39 GA

34 IN

36 GA

29 WIS

Lee

47 IN

11 IN

46 IN   24 IN

**McGinnis's
Brigade
(2nd Position)**

Leggett's Brigade

J. Smith's Brigade

28 IA   47 IN

24 IN

29 WIS

11 IN

34 IN

Stevenson's Brigade

56 OH   24 IA

46 IN

**Slack's
Brigade
(1st Position)**

*Champion
House*

**McGinnis's
Brigade
(1st Position)**

Logan's Division

Hovey's Division

161

His scheme worked perfectly. Cumming reported that "the attack broke upon us with great impetuosity and vehemence, in overwhelming force, and in a manner wholly unexpected and unlooked for, no driven in pickets, or scattering shots to give warning."[18] The defenders, the Georgia soldiers of the Thirty-ninth and Thirty-fourth regiments, fired when they saw their enemy appear, but most of their shots passed over the heads of McGinnis's infantry. The return fire from the Twenty-ninth Wisconsin crippled them. Here fell Colonel J. T. McConnell of the Thirty-ninth Georgia with a serious wound which disheartened his combat-inexperienced men. Moreover, the Union fire enfiladed the position of those defenders who faced east, so that many shots that missed the men immediately to the front found other targets. Then the Twenty-ninth Wisconsin charged the northern face of the L. The Thirty-fourth Georgia broke on contact. Cumming desperately tried to stop the rout, but since he was virtually unknown to them, the Thirty-fourth ignored him and carried the Thirty-ninth Georgia with them as they fell back.

While McGinnis conducted his charge from the north, the Eleventh Indiana employed a different assault tactic. Using their Zouave training, they tried to advance stealthily, taking care not to rattle their equipment. Officers delivered orders in an undertone and ordered the final rush to be conducted with the bayonet alone. Moving forward, the Zouaves saw one of the rebel guns turning to face them. Ignoring orders, they spontaneously fired and then charged to contact the salient from the east. Caught with discharged weapons and badly outnumbered, the Georgians fought a brave but brief hand-to-hand struggle around the rebel guns. Exhibiting a fine command of tactics, McGinnis committed the Forty-sixth Indiana into the breach. Meanwhile, the Eleventh Indiana nimbly turned to the left, where they enfiladed the Thirty-sixth Georgia. The combination of the Zouaves' destructive fire and the fact that some charging bluecoats had penetrated as far as his colors behind his center caused the Thirty-sixth Georgia's colonel to order a retreat.

Because of the difficult terrain, Colonel James Slack's brigade, on McGinnis's left, had been unable to keep pace. Pettus's skirmishers continued a stubborn, fighting retreat. One of their bullets mortally wounded Captain Cook, the sick officer who had insisted upon "going in with the boys." Advancing to within two hundred yards of the Crossroads, the Union soldiers looked across a cornfield to see an artillery-studded Confederate battle line. This was the Fifty-sixth and Fifty-seventh Georgia and two sections of Waddell's battery. They had been facing east to block the Middle Road, but

Osterhaus's inactivity allowed them to reface to confront Slack. Slack's brigade had to pass through the bombardment of Waddell's guns in order to close. Sergeant Charles Longley of the Twenty-fourth Iowa described the scene: "Onward and upward you go; thicker and faster the hissing hail . . . Suddenly the added elevation brings into view a battery, and the same instant the horrid howling of grape and canister is about us." While the Georgia infantry manned a rail fence bordering the cornfield, Waddell tried to withdraw his guns before Slack charged. Federal marksmen fired at the battery horses. The Iowa sergeant recalled how "a full artillery team catches the eye just long enough to see a leader fall and the six horses almost stand on end as they go over and down in struggling confusion." The battery lost too many horses and was unable to limber and withdraw.

Spearheaded by the Twenty-fourth Iowa, Slack's brigade used fire-and-move tactics to surge across the cornfield toward the guns. Reliving his experience, Sergeant Longley recalls seeing

> a gray-clad enemy marking their line at but a few rods distant. You note one, perhaps, striving to find shelter behind a slender tree—he is reloading, and hastily withdrawing his rammer, uncovers the upper part of his body—instantly you aim and fire, and when he falls backward, throwing the useless gun over his head, you . . . scream aloud in the very frenzy of self congratulation.[19]

The Georgia infantry retired to the Middle Road and then turned to face Slack's charging Federals. Resting their muskets on the fence rails, they fired a heavy volley. An Ohio soldier recounted:

> Henry Richards, fell, shot through the brain. A little further along, as we halted to give them a volley, my brother, John Henry Williams, was shot through the heart . . . The comrade on my left had his arm shot off. Other comrades in the company were being hit, but there was no halt.[20]

Instead of firing off a last canister round as Slack's men approached, Waddell unwisely ordered his gunners to manhandle their guns to the rear. The two supporting Georgia regiments, along with some of the men who had defended Champion Hill, tried to contest the advance. Here, Confederate colonel Elihu Watkins—who, like Ohio Captain Cook, had risen from his sickbed to be with his men—fell severely wounded. The spirited charge of the Twenty-fourth Iowa overran the guns. An Iowa soldier recalled: "The Rebs ran like sheep. Our boys did nobly but paid dearly for ground gained."[21] Near his headquarters at the Roberts house, Pemberton emerged to rally the Fifty-sixth and Fifty-seventh Georgia, who took cover behind some nearby corn cribs. But Slack now possessed the Crossroads.

Over on the Confederate left, Lee's Alabamians had been doing very well in their fight against Logan's division. Using a rail fence to steady their muskets, they had managed to hold off Leggett's brigade during a thirty-minute firefight. An Ohio officer remembered that the bullets flew so thick that when a staff officer came to speak with a regimental colonel, the staffer "involuntarily and unconsciously screened his eyes with one hand, as one would shield his eyes from a driving rain."[22] However, when the gunners of Company D, First Illinois Artillery manhandled their four twenty-four-pounder howitzers to within four hundred yards of Lee's line, the rebel infantry risked being slowly shot apart. Consequently, Lee ordered his Twenty-third Alabama to charge the guns. It was a mistake. Major Charles Stolbrand, Logan's divisional chief of artillery, observed the movement and rode to General John Smith. In his thick German accent, Stolbrand alerted Smith to the threat, adding, "By damn it they vant mine guns." Smith had the Forty-fifth Illinois and Twenty-third Indiana in near support of the howitzers. He grimly replied, "Let 'em come, we're ready to receive them."[23]

Just before the Alabama soldiers charged, Logan and McPherson dashed up. Like his subordinate, McPherson appreciated the impact of a good display. Today he wore his full dress uniform and rode a beautiful black horse. The young corps commander was not prone to using profanity. Riding behind the infantry, he steadied the men, saying "Give them Jesse boys, give them Jesse." Logan was less restrained. Rising in his stirrups he said, "We are about to fight the battle for Vicksburg . . . We must whip them here or all go under the sod together. Give 'em hell."[24] Fire from the big-throated howitzers and the supporting infantry sent the Twenty-third Alabama reeling. Then Lee's right flank began to unravel as well.

When McGinnis's brigade captured Champion Hill they had retained their order. The Twenty-fourth Indiana and Twenty-ninth Wisconsin wheeled to the right to exploit their success by attacking toward Lee's right flank. Lee learned about their approach and seized a battle flag to rally Cumming's Georgia infantry. It was futile. A Confederate ordnance officer saw "bodies of men, some without hats, their guns thrown away," claiming that they were the only survivors from their company. They ignored all the officers and kept running.[25] McGinnis's flank attack caused Lee's rightmost regiment to retreat. Then the adjacent unit broke as well. Both regiments fell back some seven hundred yards to the Jackson Road, where they re-formed. Lee recognized that it would be fatal to continue to hold the fence line against Logan. He ordered his remaining three regiments to retreat to the new line parallel to the Jackson Road.

General Logan, riding well forward with his leading troops, had carefully observed the hour-long skirmish preceding the fight between Leggett and Lee. He recognized that the Confederate left—at this time Lee's left flank, because Barton's men were not yet up—was dangling in the air. General John Smith's brigade already partially overlapped the Confederate left. To exploit the situation thoroughly, Logan summoned his reserve brigade as well. John Stevenson's brigade was formed in handy battalion columns, a formation that permitted rapid movement and easy deployment. Stevenson hustled his men through the fields to the Union right, but just before they arrived where Logan wanted them, they found that the enemy had beaten them to it. The Confederates looming before them were Barton's Georgia brigade, men who had just completed more than a mile-long jog at the double.

Barton's men came up just before Lee retreated. Barton saw John Stevenson's westerners occupying a woods and preparing to charge against Lee's left flank. Barton kept the Fifty-second Georgia in reserve and immediately committed his other three regiments to a charge against Stevenson. It enjoyed initial success and drove Stevenson's skirmishers back for several hundred yards. But Stevenson's battle line held firm and checked the rebel advance. Then Barton saw Stevenson's brigade begin to outflank his own left. He summoned his reserve, but the Fifty-second Georgia could not effectively contest the progress of an entire Union brigade. As the bluecoats continued to wrap around his flank, Barton sent a courier galloping to the Bakers Creek bridge to recall the Forty-second Georgia, which had been detailed as bridge guards. In spite of these reinforcements, Barton could not hold because another enemy brigade began to enfilade his right flank.

These soldiers belonged to Leggett's brigade. When Lee withdrew, it left a void to their front. When the order came to advance, Color Sergeant Morely of the Twentieth Ohio led the way, running so fast that his comrades had trouble keeping up with him. Leggett's brigade entered the void and turned to the right to pour a heavy, destructive fire into Barton's flank. The musketry killed the colonel of the Forty-third Georgia. Leggett pressed the attack. An Illinois soldier described how his regiment "rushed right up to them [they] had now become terror-stricken at our boldness, crouched down in the channel of the creek, held up their hands and begged for mercy."[26]

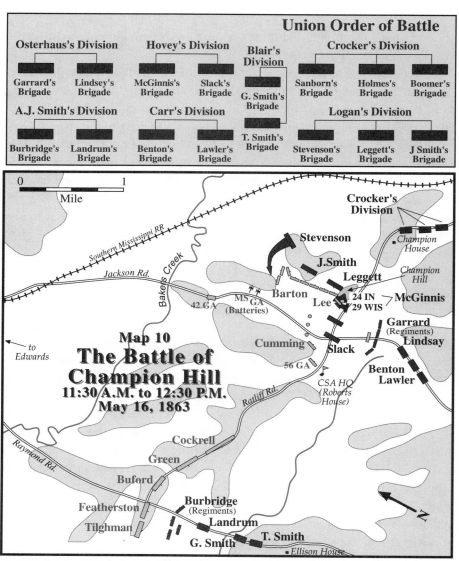

Union Order of Battle

Osterhaus's Division
- Garrard's Brigade
- Lindsey's Brigade

Hovey's Division
- McGinnis's Brigade
- Slack's Brigade

Blair's Division
- G. Smith's Brigade
- T. Smith's Brigade

Crocker's Division
- Sanborn's Brigade
- Holmes's Brigade
- Boomer's Brigade

A.J. Smith's Division
- Burbridge's Brigade
- Landrum's Brigade

Carr's Division
- Benton's Brigade
- Lawler's Brigade

Logan's Division
- Stevenson's Brigade
- Leggett's Brigade
- J Smith's Brigade

Map 10
The Battle of Champion Hill
11:30 A.M. to 12:30 P.M.
May 16, 1863

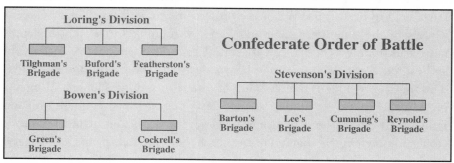

Loring's Division
- Tilghman's Brigade
- Buford's Brigade
- Featherston's Brigade

Bowen's Division
- Green's Brigade
- Cockrell's Brigade

Confederate Order of Battle

Stevenson's Division
- Barton's Brigade
- Lee's Brigade
- Cumming's Brigade
- Reynold's Brigade

166

Barton's routed men fled west along the Jackson Road and surged across the creek. Logan's soldiers thoroughly enjoyed chasing the fleeing rebels and scooped up prisoners by the handful. It seemed as though each man "corralled" two or three foemen. One German soldier of the Twentieth Illinois proudly strutted up to his comrades with eight prisoners. After the battle Barton, in turn, would proudly cite his brigade's 42 percent loss rate as proof of how hard it had fought. Indeed, the brigade lost 58 killed and 106 wounded. However, 80 percent of the brigade's losses were missing men, most of whom were captured.

Meanwhile, John Stevenson's men spied a Confederate artillery position on the crest of the ridge to their left front. Officers redirected the brigade's three regiments toward those guns: "Forward, guide left, march." The regiments wheeled to the left in line abreast with the Eighty-first Illinois on the right, the Thirty-second Ohio in the center, and the Eighth Illinois on the right. After a few steps the men of the Thirty-second Ohio—a unit whose veterans had served in Virginia, where they had been compelled to surrender ignominiously to "Stonewall" Jackson at Harper's Ferry, and had lived with the shame ever since—raised the shout "Go in, Harper's Ferry cowards."[27] They ignored their officers' commands to remain "Steady, steady" and charged impetuously up the hill. Simultaneously, Logan, who always seemed to have his finger on the battle's tactical pulse, ordered John Smith's brigade to join the attack.

On the hilltop stood eight guns belonging to Company A, First Mississippi Light Artillery, and the Cherokee Georgia Artillery. The Mississippi gunners stood somewhat apart and to the left of the Georgia battery. As the Union line surged toward them, Carter Stevenson's chief of artillery, Major Joseph Anderson, ordered the gunners to switch from shell to canister, and then to double canister. The Mississippians were clearly shaken by the rout of the Georgia infantry and their aim was poor. In addition, the rolling terrain offered considerable shelter to the charging infantry. One attacker remembers that John Stevenson's brigade crossed two deep, narrow ravines "and this going down or up hill almost all the time of our advance prevented the artillerymen from getting our range."[28] The Mississippi Light Artillery managed to fire only four canister rounds before Stevenson's men entered point-blank range. The Union infantry fired a volley at thirty yards range that ripped through the battery, killing most of the horses, numerous crew, and Major Anderson. Still, the Mississippi gunners exhibited amazing tenacity. Battery Captain Samuel Ridley suffered multiple wounds while serving a gun single-handedly. Section commander Lieutenant Frank

Johnston had his horse shot out from under him in the first volley. He rose to serve another gun whose crew had already fallen. Recognizing that he could not extract his guns because of the loss of his horses, Ridley ordered Johnston to get the men out if possible. As he turned his horse to the rear, Illinois Sergeant Freeman Campbell called out, "See me shoot that fellow." The sergeant fired and Ridley fell dead. The Mississippi battery lost seventy-four of eighty-two men in its desperate defense, but the westerners could not be denied. Spearheaded by the Eighth Illinois and Thirty-second Ohio, the Federal soldiers overran the guns. The "Harper's Ferry cowards" had achieved vindication. Shortly thereafter, McPherson rode up to compliment Lieutenant Johnston for his gallant effort.[29]

About the time Lee's brigade retired to their second position, the Cherokee Artillery had been dueling with a Federal battery six hundred yards to its front. A Georgia gunner recalls, "we fired fifteen or twenty rounds from each gun, but it was hot work. Shot shell and shrapnel flew thick and fast around us. Here fell Hutchens, killed, and Lumpkin and Anthony mortally wounded."[30] The battery shifted position. While awaiting orders they saw John Stevenson's brigade emerge from the woods about two hundred yards away and overrun the Mississippi battery. From the rolling ground directly in front came John Smith's brigade. Smith's soldiers could see their objective: the battery on the hill; the infantry supports below, their brownish-yellow uniforms "almost the color of the ground they were hugging."[31]

Smith's brigade advanced quickly and found the dispirited Georgia infantry were fought out. An Illinois soldier recalled that they "threw down their arms and begged for mercy." So feeble was the infantry resistance that the Cherokee Artillery only had time to unlimber two Parrott rifles and fire one charge of canister before Smith's men arrived. The Illinois soldier remembered, "When we had nearly reached the top of the hill the rebels commenced to limber up. They had to go through the gate. Our colonel gave the order to shoot the horses. I shot one horse in the gateway and we shot from one to three horses from each gun."[32] Captain Van Den Corput had positioned his battery in a terrible tactical position. Fallen horses obstructed the only passage through which the battery could withdraw. A Georgia gunner recalled that with "the infantry flying in disorder from the field, many of the cannoneers had failed to stick to their guns, and the Yankees were close upon us, Capt. Van Den Corput told his men to take care of themselves" and they fled.[33]

Everywhere they looked, Logan's men saw dazed or fleeing Confederates, "single and in squads, officers and men hiding in the ravines and among the underbrush and when called upon to surrender they promptly obeyed."[34] After detailing men to guard the prisoners, the Union regiments began to reform. In the aftermath of excitement and battle, soldiers realized that they were very hungry. One Illinois soldier "picked out a clean looking" Confederate corpse, emptied his haversack, and sat down beside the body to eat a fine lunch of corn bread and beef.[35] Some of the other jubilant victors mounted the battery horses and galloped about waving their hats. In the proud words of one Illinois soldier, "Our regiment killed the captain of the battery, got his sword and belt, and took the guns."[36] They had reason to rejoice. Smith and Stevenson's brigades had captured two enemy batteries and the latter claimed about 1,300 prisoners as well. More importantly, John Stevenson's brigade now sat athwart the Jackson Road, Pemberton's line of retreat.

It was 1:30 P.M. Back at the Champion house, medical personnel had converted Grant's headquarters to a field hospital. A surgeon saw Grant and his staff arrive and the general dismount. The roar of battle clearly indicated that Stevenson's brigade was outflanking the defenders. The surgeon saw Grant take a cigar from his mouth and heard him tell an aide, "Go down to Logan and tell him he is making history today."[37] So far that history included the thorough thrashing of Carter Stevenson's division, the capture of sixteen cannon and numerous prisoners, and the occupation of the battlefield's key features.

8

The Hill of Death

Our men will have to fight these western men there and they are the best
fighters they have.

> —Warren Magee, Thirty-ninth Mississippi, April 19, 1863
> ("The Confederate Letters of Warren G. Magee,"
> *Journal of Mississippi History* 5, no. 4)

AROUND 2 P.M. General Pemberton awoke to the developing crisis. He
responded to Carter Stevenson's request for reinforcements by sending
aides to "tell General Bowen to move up at once to assist Stevenson" and
tell Loring to move his division—minus the Twelfth Louisiana Infantry and
Adams's cavalry, who would remain at the ford—"to the assistance of
Stevenson, and crush the enemy."[1] Once already, when told to attack the
forces to their front, Bowen and Loring had declined. Again neither general
complied. Loring replied that "he was threatened by a cavalry force in front
and that if he moved, the enemy would flank him on the right."[2] So Loring stayed put and sent a major to tell Pemberton why. Bowen personally
informed Pemberton that he, too, confronted a heavy force to his front and
dared not move.

In the time it took for this exchange, Stevenson's situation deteriorated
badly. Thereupon, Pemberton categorically ordered Bowen to send one
brigade to Stevenson's left and follow it with his other brigade. Marching
along the Ratliff Road came Colonel Francis Cockrell's brigade—about
twenty-five hundred men in five infantry regiments, Missourians all—including those veterans who had fought so splendidly at Port Gibson. At Port

Gibson only three regiments had been present, yet with two of them Cockrell had delivered a ferocious flank attack that required the attention of ten Federal regiments and twenty-four guns to contain. What Cockrell could achieve when fighting with his entire brigade was about to be demonstrated.

At the double, the Missourians pushed through throngs of flying Georgians and entered the fields west of Pemberton's headquarters. By this time Slack's men had captured the Crossroads, causing Pemberton to redirect the brigade toward that vital intersection. As the Missourians passed the lieutenant general they found breath enough to give him a cheer. Moving toward the Crossroads, Cockrell saw the Fifty-sixth Georgia standing firm. He ordered his leading regiment, the Fifth Missouri, to deploy on the Georgians's left, with the balance of his brigade to form on the left of the Fifth Regiment as they came up. The twenty-four-year-old brigade bugler, Samuel B. Lyons, sounded the signal to begin the deployment from road column to battle line. His notes had hardly ceased when the Georgians dissolved before the onslaught of Slack's Federals. These were the same Union men who had borne the brunt of Cockrell's flank attack at Port Gibson. To their mutual surprise, they encountered one another again.

Because the Fifth Missouri was caught in the act of deploying, at first the advantage lay with Slack's people. At a range of fifty yards they fired a punishing volley into the right flank of the Fifth Missouri. The Fifth Missouri recoiled, but the men remained steady. They fired back into the smoke, loaded while moving away from the foe, formed up behind a fence line, and for the next fifteen minutes exchanged regular volleys with Slack. When the Fifth Missouri retired, it exposed the right flank of the adjacent regiment, the Third Missouri. Union muskets enfiladed the Third Missouri. It was too much for some, including a twenty-three-year-old lieutenant with the warlike name of John Paul Jones. Panic-stricken, Jones bolted from the ranks while his regiment retreated to escape the awful flank fire. The Third joined its sister regiment at the fence line and turned to face the enemy. It was an altogether inauspicious introduction to the battle for Cockrell's brigade, and it made more than one Missouri rebel mad.

Private John Dale of the Fifth Missouri bounded over the rail fence toward the foe and screamed, "Come on Company I, we can whip the God damn Yankee sons-of-bitches!"[3] Company I cheered and followed the belligerent private. The regimental color party joined them. Then the entire regiment surged forward and this caused the Third Missouri to advance as well. The spontaneous counterattack regained the position where the Fifty-sixth Georgia had stood. Cockrell realized that the Union strength was on his right, so he countermarched his own two left flank regiments, the Second and Sixth Missouri, to the opposite flank, where they formed up under heavy fire. Again the Union troops charged and seemed about to overwhelm the Fifth Missouri when Cockrell's last regiment came panting up the Ratliff Road. A sergeant in the Fifth Missouri recalled, "Just as luck would have it the 1st Missouri Regiment came up and poured a volley of musketry into them and prevented them from flanking us, which they were doing rapidly and had got within ten paces of us on the right and nearly that close all along the line."[4] At that moment no one realized that the tremendous charge of Hovey's division had reached its high-water mark.

The First Missouri's colonel, Amos Riley, noticed that Slack's men still overlapped his right flank and were only forty yards distant. "I immediately moved my two right companies to the right and rear forming a line at right angles with the Regiment. After firing two rounds into the enemy, Brigadier General Bowen who was in the rear of the left of my Regiment ordered me to charge." The First Missouri advanced at the double but did not make much headway until Bowen's second brigade entered the fray.[5]

General Green's brigade deployed on the right of the Missouri brigade. Spotting an old acquaintance, Colonel Cockrell rode through the bullets to shake hands with Colonel Elijah Gates, whose First Missouri Cavalry (dismounted) held Green's left. Cockrell exclaimed that he was very glad to see him "for he had been under a desperate fire."[6] While this brief reunion took place, five Missouri companies that had been detached as skirmishers trotted along the Ratliff Road toward the sounds of the firing. They passed Pemberton's headquarters and heard the sound of female voices singing "Dixie." Glancing over, they saw a group of ladies assembled in the yard of the Isaac Roberts house. The women were singing and cheering to encourage their heroes. Next, five Missouri batteries numbering twenty guns trundled into position behind Bowen's infantry, unlimbered, and opened fire. With that, Bowen's five-thousand-man division completed its deployment.

The division possessed substantial tactical advantages. Had Hovey's division been intact, Bowen would have outnumbered it five to four. But Hovey had already suffered significant combat losses and was weakened by the need to escort prisoners and wounded comrades to the rear. Moreover, it had just completed a long charge over rugged terrain which had caused a considerable jumbling of the ranks. Lastly, the division's two brigades were not in mutual support. McGinnis remained on Champion Hill while Slack was at the Crossroads. Neither had artillery support. In sum, five thousand

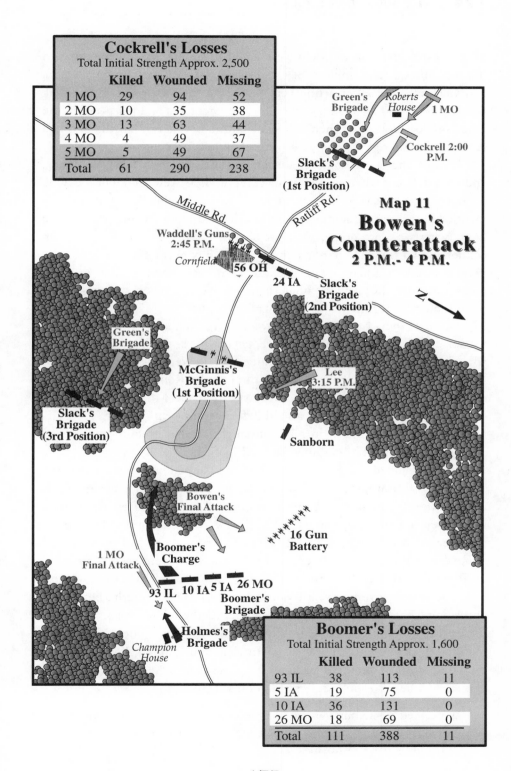

Cockrell's Losses
Total Initial Strength Approx. 2,500

	Killed	Wounded	Missing
1 MO	29	94	52
2 MO	10	35	38
3 MO	13	63	44
4 MO	4	49	37
5 MO	5	49	67
Total	61	290	238

Green's Brigade

Roberts House

1 MO

Cockrell 2:00 P.M.

Slack's Brigade (1st Position)

Middle Rd.

Ratliff Rd.

Waddell's Guns 2:45 P.M.

Cornfield

56 OH

24 IA

Map 11
Bowen's Counterattack
2 P.M.- 4 P.M.

Slack's Brigade (2nd Position)

N

Green's Brigade

McGinnis's Brigade (1st Position)

Lee 3:15 P.M.

Slack's Brigade (3rd Position)

Sanborn

Bowen's Final Attack

16 Gun Battery

1 MO Final Attack

Boomer's Charge

93 IL   10 IA   5 IA   26 MO
Boomer's Brigade

Holmes's Brigade

Champion House

Boomer's Losses
Total Initial Strength Approx. 1,600

	Killed	Wounded	Missing
93 IL	38	113	11
5 IA	19	75	0
10 IA	36	131	0
26 MO	18	69	0
Total	111	388	11

173

of the best soldiers on the field were about to counterattack about sixteen hundred disorganized men of Slack's brigade. At 2:30 P.M., Bowen, Green, and Cockrell—the latter acting very much the gallant cavalier by holding both his reins and a large magnolia flower in one hand and his sword in the other—rode before their men and signaled the advance. The Missouri and Arkansas infantry gave voice to a wild rebel yell and charged.

Initially there was some confusion in the Fifty-sixth Ohio as officers and men debated whether the approaching soldiers were friend or foe. One company correctly identified the target and began shooting. Officers demanded they cease. A lieutenant in the Fifty-sixth Ohio related that "as we knew what we were doing, we kept on firing." Yet the company captain cautioned that they had better stop because "they may be our men." A corporal insisted, "Captain, take a look at them." By now the rebel line had come near and the captain shouted, "Up boys and given them h——."[7] Soon the entire regiment was firing as fast as possible.

Ahead of the advancing rebels lay a high rail fence. "With one impulse we seized the lower rails of the fence, gave a lift and a heave, and sent it sprawling," a Missouri soldier remembered.[8] Bowen's skirmishers stayed well forward, darting from tree to tree through the Roberts's family orchard until they reached a point across the road from the Fifty-sixth Ohio. Because the Fifty-sixth Ohio had a solid defensive position behind a fence, its musketry deflected the main rebel onslaught against its front and caused the Confederate battle line to lap around its flanks.

To the right of the Fifty-sixth Ohio, the Confederates confronted the Twenty-fourth Iowa, the unit that had spearheaded the charge against Waddell's battery. The Iowa regiment occupied a more exposed position in some open timber. As was so typical of Civil War combat in wooded terrain, each regiment perceived it fought alone. "Our regiment had no support," wrote Israel Ritter of the Twenty-fourth Iowa. "We were soon outflanked on Right & Left Fell back though in no great haste."[9] The Twenty-fourth Iowa's retreat uncovered the Fifty-sixth Ohio, causing it to retire before the onrushing Confederates. "In a moment," recalled a Ohio soldier, "we were under the most scorching fire from two or three sides. Under this fire our men fell thick and fast." The Fifty-sixth yielded its ground slowly, with the men frequently stopping to load and fire. The Ohio soldier described what happened when Bowen's artillery found his regiment:

> As I turned to fire, my musket being at prime, a bullet from the enemy struck the barrel of my gun, the ball exploding. Four small pieces were buried in the back of my hand . . . My Enfield was in the right place to

save me from the fate of my comrades. About the same time one of our boys had the top of his cap shot off his head; another had his canteen and haversack shot off, and another had the side of his pants below the knee cut off, all by pieces of shells bursting among us.[10]

Some of these shells may have been fired by Waddell's battery. When Cockrell's brigade overran the Crossroads they recaptured the battery's four guns in a desperate hand-to-hand grapple.

Pemberton sent a detachment from Company A, First Mississippi Light Artillery to collect the pieces. The detachment found that Captain Waddell and a handful of his own men had recrewed the guns and were enthusiastically blasting away into the backs of Slack's retreating men.

While Cockrell drove through the Crossroads, Green's brigade moved forward in tandem on their right. Many of the Federal soldiers Green initially encountered had unloaded muskets and this permitted Green to push forward rapidly. After passing the Crossroads, the fighting raged along the eastern slopes of Champion Hill, where Slack's brigade contested each tree, stump, and log. Slack's stubborn resistance stalled Green's advance but at great cost. Here fell with a mortal wound Corporal David Evans, the soldier who had captured the colors of the Twenty-third Alabama at Port Gibson. The Twenty-fourth Iowa, having suffered most of its 189 casualties by now, dissolved as an organized regiment, leaving gallant individuals and decimated squads to continue the combat. The fight surged back and forth across the wooded ravines. Private Pudic, of the Nineteenth Arkansas, ignored officers' calls to return to the ranks, and spearheaded the rebel advance by staying twenty to thirty yards in front of his regiment. At one point the Nineteenth Arkansas surmounted a rise to see a long blue line climbing toward them. An Arkansas soldier described what took place when his regiment fired at a range of eighty feet: "Never before nor since have I ever witnessed such a sight. The whole line seemed to fall and tumble headlong to the bottom of the hill. In a moment they came again, and we were ready and again repulsed them. And again and again for several hours in this way we held them at bay."[11]

Cockrell's brigade made better progress. Sergeant William Ruyle of the Fifth Missouri wrote:

We gave them the Missouri yell . . . and gave them a charge in Missouri REBEL style. We routed them and took after them, in about three hundred yards we came on to another line who were lying down over the hill, they raised on their knees and gave us a fire, we kept crawling on them until we got, in many places, within ten paces of them.

They soon gave way in wild disorder. We again gave the Missouri Yell and took after them. In a short distance we came to another line where I was wounded in my left arm with a ball and had to go off the field.[12]

The second line whose fire sent Sergeant Ruyle to the rear was McGinnis's brigade. Atop Champion Hill General McGinnis had briefly enjoyed the full flush of victory. His brigade had stormed the high ground, captured the enemy guns, and seen the backs of their enemies. To encourage the Confederate retreat, McGinnis called for artillery. Since there was not much open ground for artillery to operate, the general requested only a two-gun section. Until this point Union artillery had been supporting the attack as best they could from the fields below the hill. Eager to participate further in the action, battery Captain James Mitchell brought a section of his Sixteenth Ohio Battery up the hill. It was a decision that cost him his life. His two guns had barely deployed when he saw a heavy Confederate battle line advancing "at a quick step, their bayonets glistening in the sun."[13]

McGinnis's infantry saw them, too, and opened fire just as some of Cockrell's men were crossing a fence line. One of McGinnis's men described how "men tumbled, fence rails flew wildly through the air. The gunners . . . now cut loose double shotted with grape and canister completely mowing down the enemy. They stood in manfully for at least twenty minutes then turned and fled."[14] Having failed in their first rush, the Confederates began softening up the defender's line before trying again. From a nearby ravine, some Missouri marksmen picked off the battery horses. Sensing his section's vulnerability, Captain Mitchell shouted out "limber to the rear" and then toppled dead from his horse.[15] Cockrell's men charged again. The surviving Ohio gunners managed to fire sixteen rounds, including six double shotted with canister. The canister ripped through the Missouri infantry. A horrified Missouri private wrote that the blood in the ruts of the road "ran in a stream, as water would have done, after a hard rain." An Ohio gunner related that "though the slaughter was appalling, still on they came, they were determined to break our line at this point at any cost." Twenty-six-year-old Missouri Captain Norval Spangler, who had recently recovered from a serious wound received at Iuka, fell while leading his men against Champion Hill. Referring to the recent news of the death of a Confederate hero, Spangler said just before he died, "I guess I'll take supper with Stonewall Jackson tonight."[16]

Six color-bearers of the First Missouri were hit while urging their comrades forward. Thus inspired, Cockrell's warriors overran the two Ohio guns and recaptured two of their own (the other two having been previously re-moved by some Union troops). Still the fighting continued as McGinnis and Bowen fought back and forth around a log cabin atop Champion Hill for at least sixty minutes. When the color-bearer of the Twenty-fourth Indiana fell, Lieutenant Colonel Richard Barter rushed up to lift the colors from the ground and literally wave it in the face of the charging rebels. Confederate fire shattered the flagstaff and severely wounded Barter. Running low on ammunition, McGinnis's men rifled the cartridge boxes of the fallen. Three times during this bloody hour McGinnis asked for reinforcements but none came.

Finally, superior Confederate numbers told. It was the first pitched bat-tle one of the Union soldiers had ever experienced: "I tried to keep cool, and determined to fire no shot without taking aim; but a slight wound in the hand ended my coolness, and the smoke of the battle soon made aim-taking mere guessing." Suddenly someone shouted out to look behind the regiment. It was the rebels. The Confederates called out "Surrender!" but McGinnis's men "ran, and ran manfully."[17] The Twenty-fourth Indiana, oc-cupying McGinnis's right, lost 40 percent of its strength during the fighting on Champion Hill. It stubbornly contested three distinct positions until the rest of the line yielded. As it withdrew downslope, a survivor remembered, "We began to imagine that the day was nearly won for our enemies."[18]

The recapture of the Crossroads and the crest of Champion Hill gave John Pemberton something he had not had since the campaign began: his army now possessed the initiative. It is doubtful that the lieutenant general appreciated this. At any rate, to exploit the success required reserves, and in spite of Pemberton's prolonged efforts, they simply seemed unavailable.

Back at 2 P.M., when Pemberton had categorically ordered Bowen to the Crossroads, he had also ordered Loring to close up on Bowen's right. Lor-ing did sidestep his division to the left, with Brigadier General Abraham Bu-ford's brigade moving to occupy Bowen's former position, General Feather-ston replacing Buford, and Tilghman withdrawing to a ridge astride the Raymond Road.

As Bowen's attack gathered momentum, Pemberton seemed to expect that Loring would appear momentarily. Pemberton sent staff officers to hurry him along. At Loring's headquarters, Lieutenant Drennan had wit-nessed what transpired when Pemberton's couriers arrived. He had over-heard Loring, Tilghman, and Featherston "engaged in quite an animated conversation" about the Pennsylvania-born general in which "they all said harsh, ill natured things, made ill-turned jests in regard to Pemberton and when an order came from him, the courier who brought it was not out of hearing, before they would make light of it and ridicule the plans he proposed."[19] Confronted with such hostility, Pemberton's couriers failed to move Loring and his brigadiers. As time passed, Pemberton and his staff became increasingly anxious over his wayward subordinate's nonappearance. Accordingly, Pemberton dispatched one of his most prestigious staff officers, the army's inspector general, Major Jacob Thompson, to summon Loring.

Thompson told Loring, "General Pemberton desires you to come immediately and with all dispatch to the left, to the support of General Stevenson, whatever may be in your front."[20] Loring asked if Pemberton was aware that a heavy enemy force was in his front. Thompson knew not, but added that if Loring failed to comply with the order it was his responsibility. It was an extraordinary situation, the penultimate fruits of the feud between the lieutenant general and his ranking subordinate. While Carter Stevenson struggled manfully to stabilize his front and support Bowen, and Bowen heroically attacked Grant's center, Loring remained perfectly content to do little. Major Thompson returned to find Pemberton rallying some Georgians behind Bowen's line. Over the din of battle the inspector general related his unsatisfactory exchange. Pemberton sent yet another aide to explain to Loring why he was badly needed and to tell him to put Buford and Featherston "into the fight as soon as possible."[21]

Around this time, about 3:15 P.M., two of Lee's Alabama regiments came up to support Cockrell's left. The rallied Georgians also returned to plug a void that had developed between Cockrell and Green. But in Loring's absence, it was clear that if the battle were to be won, Bowen's division would have to proceed largely unaided. From the vantage point on Champion Hill, Cockrell's men could see Grant's headquarters at the Champion house. Nearby stood a wagon train, seemingly available for the taking. All that was required was an advance of another six hundred yards and Grant's center would be ruptured. Cockrell's line charged downslope, driving off the regiments manning McGinnis's center and left. These Union soldiers tried to halt and reform in the meadow from where they had begun their assault. To one running Union soldier the pursuing Missouri rebels sounded like "ten thousand starving and howling wolves."[22]

ABOUT THE TIME the Union skirmishers first advanced into the woods at the base of Champion Hill, Colonel George Boomer's brigade led Marcellus Crocker's division onto the field. Because of Grant's order to clear the road, the division had made rapid progress to arrive just before the battle began. Crocker's men were in high spirits. They felt good about themselves and about their general. The previous day they had cheered lustily when Crocker rode by and it seemed to make the frail general "feel gay."[23] While probing the woods south of the Jackson Road, Colonel Clark B. Lagow of Grant's staff arrived with the order "to move instantly" to support Hovey.[24]

Grant's order requiring Boomer's countermarch came about because of the situation on Champion Hill. When McGinnis's brigade began to shatter, General Hovey desperately sought help. Hovey was unfamiliar to the officers of the Seventeenth Corps, so no one listened to his appeals until Grant became aware of the situation and recalled Boomer's fifteen hundred men. Crocker found Boomer's men approaching at the double and shouted to Boomer, "For God's sake put this brigade into this fight."[25] In a performance that matched that of Cockrell's brigade, Boomer's soldiers deployed at the run even while many of McGinnis's men retired through them. Under Grant's gaze, they charged uphill with the Ninety-third Illinois resting its left on the Jackson Road and to its right the Tenth Iowa, Fifth Iowa, and Twenty-sixth Missouri. Just below the hillcrest the brigade encountered a solid gray wall of troops. A musket duel between Cockrell and Boomer ensued, and now, related an Iowa soldier, we "killed each other as fast as we could."[26]

Inspired by Boomer's arrival, Colonel Dan McCauley of the Eleventh Indiana seized his regimental colors, ordered his men to follow, and ran forward until he fell with a serious wound. "The infantry fire of the rebels was appalling," remembered a Union soldier.[27] For forty minutes Boomer's brigade checked Cockrell's advance and while so doing suffered the heaviest brigade casualties endured by Grant's army during the battle. More than one in three were hit by enemy fire, including the major commanding the Twenty-sixth Missouri, who fell mortally wounded. Moments later the senior captain dropped dead as well. A survivor recalls, "Here we fought, loading and firing rapidly, every officer and soldier at his post, shouting and cheering each other."[28] The brigade sensed it was fighting alone, with no support on its left. In spite of heavy losses and its feeling of isolation, only eleven men in the entire brigade were reported missing during the battle.

When he realized that Boomer's fresh troops had stalled Cockrell, General Bowen turned to his other brigade to see if it could reignite his advance. Green's brigade still was fighting Slack's dauntless soldiers across the wooded ravines south of Champion Hill. On Green's left, Colonel Gates's First Missouri Cavalry (dismounted) occupied one ridge while across a deep ravine Slack's people occupied another. "Three times," Gates reported, "I tried to drive them from their position, but my men were not able to ascend the hill on which the enemy's line was formed."[29] Nonetheless, Bowen ordered Green to try to turn Boomer's left.

The combination of Green's advance and a turning move by some of Cockrell's Missourians around Boomer's left flank exposed the Ninety-third Illinois to a dangerous enfilade fire. Half of the regiment's left flank company fell to Confederate fire. From the heights at two-hundred-yard range, rebel gunners who were crewing the two guns captured from the Sixteenth Ohio Battery also targeted Boomer's men. Overwhelmed, the brigade withdrew downslope along the Jackson Road. An Iowa private saw the regimental colors on the ground, its bearer wounded or dead. He yelled to a comrade that "it is a shame—the Fifth Iowa is running!" With an oath his comrade seized the flag and dared him to help defend it. The two soldiers tried to rally the regiment, "We might as well have yelled to a Kansas cyclone."[30] The battle's crisis was at hand. After the sternest fighting, Bowen's division had overcome all resistance except for a remnant of Slack's brigade which continued to hold the woods southeast of Champion Hill. Now Cockrell's and Green's warriors entered the open fields beneath Champion Hill to thrust against Grant's center.

Ulysses S. Grant had faced rout and near ruin at Belmont, Fort Donelson, and Shiloh. Now, as then, he retained his balance. The artillery offered the closest reserve at hand. Grant ordered his chief of artillery to assemble three batteries on a rise northwest of the Champion house.[31] He sent a courier to recall Stevenson's brigade, which at this moment still possessed a chokehold on the Jackson Road near the Bakers Creek crossing. Then he saw two regiments of fresh soldiers belonging to Crocker's remaining brigade commanded by Colonel Samuel Holmes, marching at the quick pace up the Jackson Road. Evaluating the situation, Grant characteristically focused on his enemy's, rather than his own army's, peril. "Hovey's division and Boomer's brigade are good troops," he told an officer, "and if the enemy has driven them, he is not in good plight himself. If we can go in again here and make a little showing, I think he will give way."[32] Grant intended Holmes to make his "little showing" and ordered him to advance up Champion Hill until stopped by the enemy.

As Grant completed these dispositions, Bowen's soldiers emerged onto the fields at the base of the hill. The combination of Slack's continued resistance on Bowen's right and the presence of two regiments commanded by Colonel John Sanborn, who occupied a gully on his left, limited Bowen's thrust to a narrow frontage that probably did not exceed four hundred yards. Once they entered the open they presented a clear target to the Union cannon. A Wisconsin gunner wrote:

> Batteries opened upon the rebels with telling effect. For a few minutes there was but one continuous roar of cannon, while the woods were full of bursting shells. The infantry meanwhile were not idle, but were also pouring in a destructive fire upon them. They could not long withstand this, no troops could, but soon gave way and commenced a precipitate retreat, leaving their dead and wounded on the field.[33]

The First Missouri, led by Colonel Amos Riley, achieved the deepest Confederate penetration of the day. Because he had heard that the prized Union wagon train was parked just over a rise near the Champion house, Riley charged his men three times up this slope, only to fail each time. Soldiers of the Sixth Missouri got as far as Hovey's ambulance wagons where, recalled a Missouri soldier, "one bloody wretch in a white shirt drew down his gun on me, but the blanket I had . . . arrested his Minie ball, and before I could pull on him another Yank got me in the side."[34] Colonel Tom Dockery of Green's brigade often volunteered his "legion," as he called his Nineteenth Arkansas, for hazardous duty. He particularly relished charging a battery and led his men to within thirty paces of the Federal gun line while having two horses shot out from under him. But the Union cannon provided the tactical trump to finally stop Bowen's amazing men.

The Confederates of Carter Stevenson's division who still remained on the heights could catch glimpses of Bowen's fight. An officer inquired who those troops were? The reply came, "They are Missourians going to their death."[35] Still moved by what he had seen, Stephen Lee wrote thirty-seven years later, "The firing of two lines of battle could be distinctly seen, and this terrible artillery fire, showered incessantly shot and shell on the entire line of the Confederates. But even this did not drive the division back."[36]

Under cover of the Union cannon, Boomer's brigade and many of Hovey's people rallied. Not only were Bowen's men receiving fire from three sides, but as they reached into their cartridge boxes they found few remaining bullets. Many of the Confederates had fired seventy-five to ninety rounds. Officers scurried to the rear to replenish their supply, but someone, probably Stevenson, had blundered. Earlier in the day, when the army's wagon train had withdrawn from the field, Bowen's ordnance train, with its ready reserve of ammunition, apparently accompanied it. This compelled Bowen's people to scrounge ammunition from the dead and wounded.

Grudgingly the division retired to the wooded slopes. Had they been granted a breathing space, they might have held the base of the hill. But before Cockrell and his regimental officers could tie in their units with the divisional artillery, Holmes's brigade charged.

The emperor Napoléon, who probably conducted more battles than any general in history, once observed that when a battle hung in the balance, the intervention of even a small but fresh unit often had a decisive impact. His observation became contained in the aphorism "the last battalion will decide the issue."[37] At Champion Hill, the Seventeenth Iowa and Tenth Missouri had a combined total of about five hundred men. Their charge tipped the balance.

As they surged uphill they encountered some of Slack's men who had never yielded their position. Not realizing that the thin line he saw represented the Fifty-sixth Ohio's survivors, Colonel Holmes called out to an officer to rally "those stragglers." The officer replied, "These are the men who have fought this battle; there are no stragglers here." Holmes doffed his hat to the powder-blackened survivors and acknowledged the correction: "True enough, there are no stragglers on this line."[38] Slack's weary Twenty-eighth Iowa joined with the Seventeenth Iowa and "the boys raised the Iowa shout" and pressed the charge.[39]

Bowen's soldiers were nearly fought out and Holmes's attack broke their spirit. Even as they retreated their fire remained lethal. A skirmish line comprised of the best marksmen covered Green's withdrawal. A private in the Nineteenth Arkansas describes seeing a Federal regiment eighty yards away—it was Holmes's Tenth Missouri—led by a mounted officer. The regiment advanced toward him and five other sharpshooters: "When they had covered about half of the distance between us, Billy Watts knelt beside a little oak tree and fired . . . the officer fell as if dead."[40] The other marksmen also fired. Three bullets knocked Lieutenant Colonel Leonidas Horney, the commander of the Tenth Missouri, from his horse, killing him instantly. One of the Arkansas sharpshooters then began to reload and tripped and fell, his head facing downslope. "The next instant they were at us with bayonets. I raised on my right elbow just as a big fellow was in the act of thrusting his bayonet through me and fired. The muzzle of my gun was within four feet of his breast and loaded with a Springfield rifle ball and a steel ramrod."[41] The rebel sharpshooter thus killed his adversary.

Holmes's charge inspired nearby Union soldiers. Soon Boomer's brigade, Sanborn's two regiments, and many of Hovey's men joined in a general advance that regained the crest of Champion Hill. About the time

Bowen's division had charged Hovey's gun line, General Cumming had managed to rally the majority of his 34th, 36th, and 39th Georgia regiments in a position west of the Crossroads. Cumming led them toward Champion Hill, where they encountered Bowen's men retreating before the resurgent blue tide. Already weakened physically and morally by their initial defeat atop the hill, the shaken Georgia regiments found the sight intimidating. They broke badly and fled all the way back to the recently rebuilt lower bridge across Bakers Creek.

For the second time this day, the rout of the Georgians left Lee's brigade in peril. By an exhibition of near reckless disregard for his own safety, Lee had managed to gather most of his brigade in a position covering the Jackson Road midway between the Crossroads and Bakers Creek. On several occasions he rallied regiments by grabbing their standards and imploring soldiers to stand firm. Bullets tore into his clothing, he received a slight shoulder wound, and he had three horses shot out from under him. Lee managed to rally two regiments, the Twentieth and Thirty-first Alabama, which participated in Bowen's assault while his remaining three regiments held their ground against Leggett.

The prolonged firefight between Lee and Leggett caused the Thirtieth Illinois to run out of ammunition. With two fresh regiments belonging to Sanborn's brigade available, Leggett brought up the Fifty-ninth Indiana to relieve the Thirtieth Illinois. Either Lee or the colonel of the opposing Confederate regiment, the Forty-sixth Alabama, mistook this exchange for a Union retreat and tried to capitalize by making a violent charge. The adjacent Thirtieth Alabama joined in. The two Confederate regiments surged out of the woods and began to climb a fence bordering an open field. Their solid line provided an unmistakable target to Captain De Golyer's battery. De Golyer had been leading his Michigan gunners with characteristic verve, twice displacing forward without infantry support while yelling "Come on boys! Forward Boys!" His six-gun battery opened on the Alabamians with canister "and completely annihilated men and fence . . . Such terrible execution by a battery I never saw. It seemed as if every shell burst just as it reached the fence, and rails and rebs flew into the air together."[42]

The Fifty-ninth Indiana added musketry to help repel the charge. When the Forty-sixth Alabama's color-bearer fell in front of its line, Sergeant Ford dashed forward to capture the colors. Then Leggett's brigade and Sanborn's two regiments counterattacked into the woods. The blue tide swamped the Alabama regiments with an advance so vigorous that it trapped the Forty-sixth Alabama in a ravine. Regimental Colonel Michael

Woods surrendered to the Fifty-ninth Indiana and Fourth Minnesota, with the latter regiment alone scooping up 118 prisoners. To compound the brigade's trial, about this time Lee learned that the Georgia troops on his right had again broken. There was nothing to do but retreat with the remnants of his brigade as best he could.

It was 4 P.M. Lee's collapse would have posed a serious threat to General Bowen had not a more critical emergency suddenly materialized. As Bowen's division was being driven off Champion Hill, several of Green's officers reported to Bowen that a powerful Federal column was advancing on the Middle Road and nearing the Crossroads. If it reached that intersection before Bowen could safely extricate his men from the combat on Champion Hill, the division was lost.

WHILE THE BATTLE'S DECISIVE ACTION was taking place on Champion Hill, McClernand's divisions remained inert. If Loring's shocking behavior bewildered Pemberton, McClernand's lethargy puzzled Loring. Since dawn, Loring and his generals had seen the Federal buildup on the Raymond Road. At times it seemed that battle would be joined. The artillery duel pitting twelve Union cannon against Loring's twenty-two guns occasionally became intense. An Ohio infantryman lying down in support of the Union batteries related, "The Rebels had an excellent battery and good gunners, they put the shells in fast and thick." When the shelling drove some gunners from their pieces, it prompted a call for volunteers from the Eighty-third Ohio. Although "it was a hot place to go into," remembered an Ohio man, six soldiers responded.[43] They helped maintain the cannonade but there was no follow-up advance by the infantry. Union passivity allowed Loring to sidestep to his left and leave just Tilghman's four infantry regiments to check twenty bluecoated regiments on the Raymond Road.

Whereas Loring's willful conduct kept his division from entering the battle, McClernand's conduct stemmed from Federal inability to coordinate action on the three roads leading to the Confederate position. About noon, Grant had received McClernand's 9:45 A.M. query asking if he should attack. Grant replied with both a written answer and later with several verbal messages, all of which told McClernand to attack if the opportunity presented. McClernand did not receive any replies until after 2 P.M., more than four and one-quarter hours after sending his query. In the absence of orders, his forces on the Middle Road, like those on the Raymond Road, continued to skirmish but did not press the combat. A more able officer might have marched to the sound of guns—the din of pitched battle on Champion Hill was audible for several hours before Grant's reply arrived. Instead, McClernand adopted the lawyerly course of strictly adhering to orders.

Unleashed by Grant's reply, at 2:30 P.M.—about when Bowen's men released their spirited rebel yells and charged—McClernand ordered an advance along the Raymond and Middle roads. The politician-general later reported that soon his units "became hotly engaged" and that "the battle was raging all along my center and right."[44] He exaggerated greatly. On the Middle Road, Osterhaus's division had confronted the roadblock manned by nine Georgia companies for seven hours. Osterhaus had found the ground adjacent to this roadblock a "chaos of ravines and narrow hills" so thickly wooded that infantry companies lost sight of one another once they moved off the road.[45] He fearfully expected an attack at any moment and even took the precaution of having his artillery load with canister and occupy a rearward position where they could provide a rallying point if a sudden attack drove his infantry backward.

When McClernand did order him to advance, the extent of the Confederate bluff became apparent. Osterhaus's men rolled over the roadblock with ease. The surge carried the leading Federal infantry to the edge of a woods from where they could plainly see the Crossroads and the Confederates fleeing back from Champion Hill. Osterhaus, who to his credit was well forward with his men, also saw a rebel brigade. It was Buford, moving north along the Ratliff Road. Convinced that this represented a dire threat to his left flank, Osterhaus halted his division in a defensive posture and asked for reinforcements. His excessive caution caused him to miss an opportunity to crush a weak opponent.

A LITTLE AFTER 3:00 P.M., while his staff officers were off looking for Loring, Pemberton saw Carter Stevenson's line begin to dissolve again. Pemberton rode to Stevenson to tell him to expect Loring's arrival momentarily and to ask if Stevenson could hold on. The experience of seeing his division break for the second time had unnerved Stevenson. He replied that he was fighting "from 60,000 to 80,000 men" and he could not hold.[46] The lieutenant general pledged to go find Loring and bring him to Stevenson's assistance. He headed south on the plantation road, where he encountered Buford. It was the army's largest brigade, numbering 3,005 men divided among eight infantry regiments. Pemberton detached the Twelfth Louisiana to support Green and sent the balance to bolster Carter Stevenson.

Colonel Thomas Scott, the commander of the Twelfth Louisiana, found Green's right wing "retiring from the field in great confusion." Scott positioned his regiment at right angles to their line of retreat and ordered an advance. The Twelfth Louisiana encountered heavy fire from Garrard's brigade of Osterhaus's division, which was moving up the Middle Road toward the Crossroads. Scott employed marching fire until he came within forty yards of the foe. His opponents included the Forty-second Ohio. The Forty-second Ohio did not know that the enemy was present until they received a volley from only a few paces ahead. Alarmed by the fact that his regiment had lost contact with adjacent units, the acting regimental commander ordered a hasty retreat. When the Confederates seemed to be chasing them, the withdrawal almost became a rout.

Colonel Scott, in turn, correctly appreciated that he actually did confront a much superior hostile force. "Finding that the contest was too unequal," he reported, "I determined to try cold steel. I caused the firing to cease, bayonets to be fixed, and ordered my men to make a steady advance in line without yelling, that they might hear my commands."[47] Scott's bold front overawed Garrard, prompting him to retire his brigade to a better defensive position. Osterhaus, in turn, perceived that the situation was so serious that he reported to McClernand that Garrard's brigade was "hard pressed" and asked for reinforcements.[48]

Meanwhile, Osterhaus's other brigade, commanded by Colonel Lindsey, advanced on Garrard's left. Lindsey had only two regiments in hand because Osterhaus had summoned the Forty-second Ohio to support Garrard and his remaining regiment to guard the artillery. Lindsey's direction of march had been personally scouted by General Osterhaus. Osterhaus had seen some of Loring's men, as well as a rebel battery, on a commanding elevation off to the southwest. He perceived that these forces were positioned to confront A. J. Smith's division. Nonetheless, instead of thinking offensively, he judged Lindsey's regiments inadequate "to repel or resist the numerous force of the enemy" and asked McClernand for reinforcements.[49] In the event, McClernand sent forward one of Carr's regiments, but before it arrived Lindsey had already moved forward.

Although Lindsey faced few opponents beyond a thin skirmish line, his two regiments failed to coordinate their advance. Entering an open field, they encountered hostile fire, lost their alignment while crossing a drainage ditch, and diverged in two directions. Halted and reformed, they then charged into the woods. Here they encountered some enfilade fire from one of Loring's batteries. After some hesitation, Lindsey continued his advance.

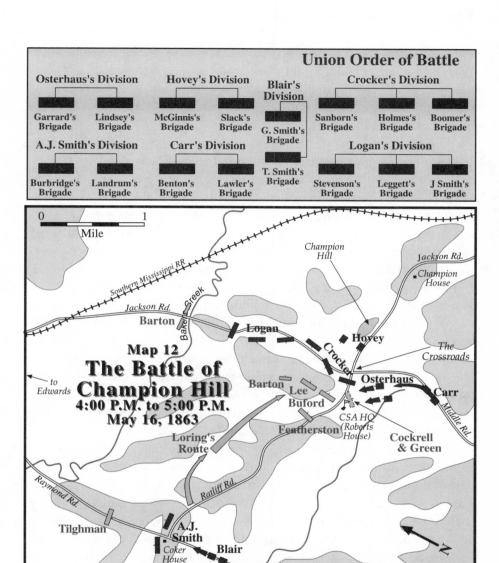

Union Order of Battle

Osterhaus's Division

Garrard's Brigade   Lindsey's Brigade

A.J. Smith's Division

Burbridge's Brigade   Landrum's Brigade

Hovey's Division

McGinnis's Brigade   Slack's Brigade

Carr's Division

Benton's Brigade   Lawler's Brigade

Blair's Division

G. Smith's Brigade

T. Smith's Brigade

Crocker's Division

Sanborn's Brigade   Holmes's Brigade   Boomer's Brigade

Logan's Division

Stevenson's Brigade   Leggett's Brigade   J Smith's Brigade

---

0   1
Mile

Southern Mississippi RR

Jackson Rd.

Champion Hill

Jackson Rd.

Champion House

Barton

Logan

Crocker

Hovey

The Crossroads

Map 12
The Battle of Champion Hill
4:00 P.M. to 5:00 P.M.
May 16, 1863

to Edwards

Barton

Lee

Buford

Osterhaus

Carr

Middle Rd.

Featherston

CSA HQ (Roberts House)

Cockrell & Green

Loring's Route

Ratliff Rd.

Raymond Rd.

Tilghman

A.J. Smith

Coker House

Blair

N

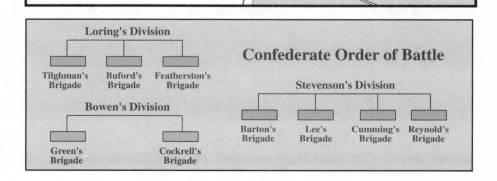

Loring's Division

Tilghman's Brigade   Buford's Brigade   Featherston's Brigade

Confederate Order of Battle

Bowen's Division

Green's Brigade   Cockrell's Brigade

Stevenson's Division

Barton's Brigade   Lee's Brigade   Cumming's Brigade   Reynold's Brigade

---

187

What transpired provides a hint of what would have happened had Osterhaus mounted a coordinated attack. Lindsey encountered no formed opposition during a two-mile forward surge and captured more prisoners than his two regiments had men.

During May 16, two full divisions operated on the Middle Road under the gaze of the corps commander. Both before and after receiving Grant's order to attack, McClernand failed to utilize them properly. Throughout the day, Osterhaus perceived imaginary threats that kept him from advancing. After he did move forward, he broke up his command's integrity by making numerous detachments. McClernand never launched a coordinated charge to come to grips with his foes. Of the two divisions under his personal supervision, Osterhaus lost seventeen killed, eighty-seven wounded, and twenty-six missing, a casualty rate of under 5 percent, and Carr's division had one man killed and two wounded.

While Union forces on the Middle Road groped cautiously ahead against the bold bluff of Colonel Scott's Twelfth Louisiana, Scott's brigade commander, General Buford, continued his march along the Ratliff Road. Having lost one of his strongest regiments to Pemberton's intercession, Buford now lost another when General Bowen intercepted the Thirty-fifth Alabama, took it under his personal command, and told its colonel to follow one of Bowen's aides. The colonel dutifully obeyed until General Green took control and directed the regiment toward the right of his brigade to support his artillery. The Missouri artillery had retired from Champion Hill to the cornfield northeast of the Crossroads. Reassured by the Thirty-fifth's solid presence, the artillerists worked their guns with renewed vigor, firing shell, shot, and canister at the advancing bluecoats. Sergeant R. H. Gaines of the Twenty-third Alabama contributed by single-handedly manning an abandoned twelve-pounder howitzer that had belonged to Waddell's battery. He fired off some twelve rounds before General Green noticed his labor. Green obtained four volunteers, Georgians of Cumming's brigade who refused to join their brigade's stampede, and sent them to assist Gaines. The combination of the artillery and the Thirty-fifth Alabama slowed the Federal pursuit until the gunners ran out of ammunition and withdrew. Immediately thereafter, Union infantry worked around the flanks of the Thirty-fifth Alabama and compelled it to change fronts to face the fire. The Thirty-fifth's colonel described the scene:

> At this time our friends gave way and came rushing to the rear panic-stricken. I rushed to the front, and ordered them to halt, but they heeded neither my orders nor those of their commanders. I brought my regiment

to the charge bayonets, but even this could not check them in their flight. The colors of three regiments passed through the Thirty-fifth. Both my officers and my men, undismayed, united with me in trying to cause them to rally. We collared them, begged them, and abused them in vain.[50]

Finally the regiment received orders to withdraw. It had tried to stanch the flow, too little, too late.

During the time his Thirty-fifth Alabama conducted its rearguard action, Buford marched the balance of his brigade at the double toward the Crossroads. They arrived around 4 P.M. to see Bowen's division falling back in disorder. While still in road column, Buford's brigade began receiving fire from Federal skirmishers hidden in the woods ahead. From Champion Hill came artillery fire. Simultaneously, broken Confederate troops rushed pell-mell through his column. Despite these trying circumstances, Buford was able to deploy his brigade. Its mere presence checked the Federal advance. Up came Union artillery, while bluecoated infantry began to work around both of Buford's flanks. He retired a half mile to the southwest where, to his surprise, he encountered Featherston's brigade and Major General Loring.

THE BACK AND FORTH EXCHANGE of orders and excuses between Pemberton and Loring had lasted until nearly 4 P.M., by which time the Confederate position was quite desperate. John Stevenson's brigade had returned to the scene of its earlier success and again cut the road leading to the Bakers Creek bridge. Worse, even as Bowen's men sullenly conducted a fighting withdrawal, Osterhaus advanced toward the Crossroads. Still having no clue as to Loring's whereabouts, Pemberton considered the situation. He saw that "the enemy's vastly superior numbers were pressing" his center and left back into a series of old fields behind Champion Hill. He believed that if his men could not defend a wooded ridge top they could not hold the open flatland. "I felt it to be too late to save the day," Pemberton later reported, "even should Brigadier-General Featherston's brigade . . . come up immediately." Accordingly, Pemberton ordered his army to retreat via the Raymond Road over Bakers Creek. Pemberton knew that Tilghman's brigade was blocking a Union force on the Raymond Road. He sent Tilghman an order "to hold the Raymond road at all hazards" until the army completed its withdrawal.[51] Then Pemberton continued his ride to search for Loring.

When one of Pemberton's staff officers finally located Loring, the major general was leading Featherston's brigade in road column along an obscure farm track. "I told him he was on the wrong road and going in the wrong direction; instead of going north, he was going west." Loring asked the officer to lead the way; the staffer replied he was unacquainted with any of the roads except the Ratliff Road on which he had already ridden. Exasperated, Loring gave the order "Forward."[52] Loring was on a seldom-used farm track that roughly paralleled the Ratliff Road. The reason he chose this route was never explained, although apparently he was acting on the advice of a local guide.[53] What is certain is that at the time Loring finally resolved to march to the army's left, the Ratliff Road provided the most direct way. Furthermore, this route was familiar to Loring's command—the division had marched over it the previous evening—and had already been used on this day by Bowen's division and Buford's brigade of Loring's division. Neither Pemberton nor his staff knew of the existence of the farm path that Loring chose to follow. Loring did not bother to inform his commanding officer that he was under way along this obscure route. Thus, through no fault of his own, Pemberton literally lost track of Loring at a critical time.

Loring blissfully followed the farm track as it meandered first northwest and then turned northeast until arriving on a ridge overlooking what had been Carter Stevenson's extreme left. It was a little before 4 P.M. Probably with some satisfaction, Loring recalled how his gaze took in "the whole country on both sides of the road covered with the fleeing of our army."[54] Having willfully helped to create the chaotic scene about him, Loring resolved to retrieve the situation by attacking! In fact, his notion had merit. At a minimum, an attack would cover the nearby retreating forces. Loring also hoped to recapture the upper Bakers Creek crossing, and even dreamed of possibly winning the battle outright.

Then John Taylor, Pemberton's aide-de-camp, arrived to provide information that disabused Loring of his grand scheme. Taylor reported that Pemberton had ordered a retreat. Another officer confirmed the news and said that Pemberton wanted Loring to act as rear guard. With John Stevenson's brigade controlling the upper bridge over Bakers Creek, Pemberton's army had to retreat over the rebuilt Raymond Road bridge and an adjacent ford. McClernand's and Osterhaus's bumblings had caused them to miss one chance to prevent this retreat. There was one other Union chance on the Raymond Road itself, where two Union divisions enjoyed a fivefold numerical advantage over a single Confederate brigade commanded by Brigadier General Lloyd Tilghman.

Tilghman was not one of Pemberton's admirers, probably, according to army rumor, because Pemberton had wanted to relieve him of command until Loring interceded on his behalf. What is certain is that earlier in the day Tilghman had enthusiastically participated in a mocking conversation about the lieutenant general's talents. The forty-seven-year-old Tilghman also was not one of the army's cerebral luminaries, as witnessed by his graduating third from the bottom of his class at West Point. He was a pugnacious, fighting officer, however, and this was exactly what the Confederate army needed just now.

When McClernand ordered Osterhaus to advance he had simultaneously sent word to A. J. Smith to "attack the enemy vigorously."[55] It took almost two hours for this order to reach Smith and during this time he did not budge. Instead, an artillery duel between Tilghman's eight cannon and the guns of the Chicago Mercantile Battery and the Seventeenth Ohio Battery continued until after 5 P.M. It was a noisy, fierce-seeming exchange that inflicted little damage. Shortly thereafter, Union General Burbridge, who had deployed his brigade on the reverse slope of the Coker house ridge, from where they could support the artillery but remain sheltered from hostile fire, sent a skirmisher party forward. They occupied some slave huts two hundred yards in front of the Confederate battery and began trying to pick off the rebel gunners. Their fire attracted Tilghman's attention.

Dressed in a new fatigue uniform, he rode over to the guns. Captain John Cowan's Mississippi battery was inexperienced and its officers had remained mounted in the positions prescribed by the drill manuals during the artillery exchange. Tilghman commented with good humor to Cowan, "I think you and your lieutenants had better dismount. They are shooting pretty close to us, and I do not know whether they are shooting at your fine grey horse or my new uniform."[56] Tilghman ordered his seventeen-year-old son to take a squad and drive the enemy sharpshooters from the nearby slave huts. To set an example, Tilghman then dismounted and said to Cowan, "I will take a shot at those fellows myself."[57]

He had done this once before at Fort Henry, where he and a handful of artillerymen had fought heroically against an overwhelming ironclad flotilla. So he contributed here, helping to site a howitzer while providing instructions for cutting the fuse. A Federal shell exploded nearby. Tilghman remarked, "They are trying to spoil my new uniform."[58] Shortly thereafter another shell exploded, sending a fragment through the general's breast and on through his adjutant's horse, killing both. Tilghman was the second Confederate general to die in defense of Vicksburg.

A soldier in the Twenty-sixth Mississippi who was thirty feet from where Tilghman fell remembered that

> the wildest confusion then prevailed for a short time, and but for the appearance of the daring, one-armed General Loring on his fast-racing, nick tailed roan horse there is no telling what might have happened. General Loring moved quietly a little to the right, where there were a few trees and a rail fence, and said: "Boys, don't let those d——n Yankees have that battery." . . . We stayed there under the fire of sharpshooters and bombshells until nearly sundown.[59]

While Tilghman's Mississippi artillerymen secured the Raymond Road, Pemberton's army retreated over Bakers Creek. Panic had overtaken some units. But Bowen's stalwarts, portions of Lee's brigade, and Buford and Featherston—who had yet to be engaged—retired in good order. After crossing the creek, Pemberton told Bowen to deploy on the west bank and hold his position until Loring retired. Then the dejected lieutenant general rode west with his staff toward the Big Black River Bridge.

Most of the Federal pursuit pressure developed after Union forces captured the Crossroads. Spearheading the advance to this intersection were Holmes's two regiments. Continuing its dazzling performance, the Seventeenth Iowa drove off the gunners manning Waddell's four guns and recaptured them along with the colors of the Thirty-first Alabama and 175 men. General Grant rode to the Crossroads hard on the heels of Crocker's and Hovey's victorious warriors. A Confederate prisoner, Arkansas sharpshooter Private A. H. Reynolds, remembered that he was "dressed in a fatigue suit with a blouse coat, similar to those worn by the private soldiers. He wore no insignia of rank." Although not prone to the prominent display typical of many Civil War generals, periodically throughout the day Grant had been well forward to direct his soldiers. On a shot-torn field, his conduct put him at risk. "From the direction we fired and the time that elapsed after out last volley," sharpshooter Reynolds related, "I am satisfied that General Grant and his escort were in range of our rifles and in line with that volley."[60]

DURING THE CIVIL WAR there were very few successful pursuits following a pitched battle. After the repulse of Bowen, Grant recognized that he possessed a fine opportunity if he could orchestrate an effective pursuit. Because of Crocker's and Hovey's battered conditions, he assigned pursuit duties to McClernand's much fresher men. Most of Carr's division had spent the entire day cooling their heels behind Osterhaus. McClernand selected them to lead the pursuit. Carr divided his force by sending Brigadier General Michael Lawler southwest and Brigadier General William Benton west. Lawler encountered Loring's rear guard, whose presence forced him to deploy. Then the Confederates nimbly evaded contact and withdrew toward the lower bridge and ford. Realizing he could not overtake them, Lawler ended his pursuit after capturing about five hundred stragglers and a dismounted cannon.

Meanwhile, Benton crossed Bakers Creek accompanied by Generals Carr and McClernand. McClernand now conceived a stroke that he believed would complete Pemberton's destruction. Informed by scouts that a Confederate force was heading toward him from Edwards Station, he ordered John Stevenson—who on his own initiative had also crossed the creek—to stop it. He sent Benton downstream to sever Pemberton's lifeline. Stevenson easily dealt with the force moving from Edwards Station. It belonged to Colonel Reynolds's brigade, the unit assigned to escort the Confederate trains off the field. After discharging this duty, Reynolds had turned his men around and marched cross-country toward the sound of the guns. Upon contacting Stevenson's bluecoats, Reynolds reversed course once more. Although harried by the Union's Sixth Missouri Cavalry, who opportunely snapped up some 150 stragglers and two wagons, Reynolds managed both to extricate his own brigade and then to cover the withdrawal of the army's trains.

The key element in McClernand's scheme, Benton's brigade, arrived on Bowen's flank. Bowen's exhausted division was still without ammunition. Even though only one of Loring's regiments had safely passed over the creek, Bowen withdrew when Benton approached. He sent a courier to Loring apprising him of this unwelcome turn of events. Exhibiting soldierly resolve, Loring initially seemed determined to cut his way across the creek. Then he changed his mind. The presence of hostile forces to his right and rear and the growing darkness worried him. But foremost in his mind was the knowledge that Pemberton would retire to Vicksburg and he wanted no part of that. This represented the maturation of an idea that had been growing in his mind. After conducting his two infantry brigades to a spot near the Jackson Road, he had returned to Tilghman's brigade in time to rally it after that officer's death. At that time he said to battery Captain Cowan, "I intend to save my division as I have been cut off by defeat of General

Stevenson, I want your battery to hold this position until sun down or captured."[61]

When he learned that the army's line of retreat was in peril, Loring saw his way clear to "save" his division and separate himself from the detested Pemberton. A soldier in the Thirty-first Mississippi related: "Gen. Loring came riding down our lines close up to us, and was encouraging the boys and told us that we had been sold, but he would be ———— if we should be delivered, and called on all to follow him and he would take us out."[62] Loring was unfamiliar with the road net and so relied upon a local physician to guide him. Initially the route paralleled Bakers Creek. The rebels found the going very difficult through the muddy bottomland. Compelled to switch to a seldom-used plantation path, Loring's column passed within a few hundred yards of the Coker house, where A. J. Smith's division was encamped. It was now full dark. Although some three hundred stragglers wandered into Smith's camps and were captured, Smith's division capped a dismal day by failing to detect the passage of Loring's division. Although the rebels had to abandon twelve cannon, their caissons and limbers, and seven ammunition wagons, Loring escaped with his men and horses unmolested.

Later in the evening, Loring had another opportunity to try to rejoin Pemberton when he reached the next downstream ford on Bakers Creek. However, a fire glow in the sky to the northwest convinced Loring that the enemy had captured Edwards and thus he was too late for an unopposed march. The next day he made a halfhearted last attempt, only to be deterred when local guides claimed that he would have to fight his way through the Yankee army to reach Pemberton. Instead, Loring marched to unite with Johnston. He managed his march poorly, losing three-eighths of his division, some three thousand men, as stragglers before arriving in Jackson on May. 20.

THE TWO DIVISIONS of Pemberton's army which did retreat to the west side of Bakers Creek were in a fearful state. A Confederate officer wrote:

> I saw scores and hundreds of men coming wildly along with no regard to order, with Artillery men who had lost their guns, riding frantically along, Officers without command vainly inquiring where such and such a regiment was, men without hats or guns rushing at full speed, poor wounded, men hobbling along, and asking for a surgeon, teamsters shouting and swearing at their mules, with the distant roar of an occasional shot.[63]

Adams's Mississippi Cavalry covered the withdrawal. Amid building pressure, one well-mounted trooper lost his nerve and galloped to the rear shouting to his comrades, "I can't hold my horse." Trooper Munford Bacon retorted, "Boys, I will give $1,000 for one of them horses you can't hold."[64] The ensuing laughter helped steady the unit.

On the east bank of Bakers Creek, additional Union infantry formed up to join the pursuit. Grant appeared and rode along one column. A Federal veteran remembered the scene:

> Every hat was in the air, and the men cheered till they were hoarse; but, speechless, and almost without a bow, he pushed on past, like an embarrassed man hurrying to get away from some defeat. Once he stopped, near the colors, and, without addressing himself to any one in particular, said: "Well done!"[65]

The Federal pursuit carried to Edwards Station. Entering the village, soldiers saw a railroad train loaded with ammunition and provisions burst into flames. This was the work of Confederate demolition teams. There were few other prizes to glean, so the army settled in for the night. Many went to sleep hungry. Living off the land was well and good as long as the army could spread out over the countryside. The need to concentrate for battle had prevented the dispatch of far-ranging foraging parties. Soldiers in McGinnis's brigade found their campsite "preoccupied . . . covered with dead and wounded men."[66] All night long, men of the ambulance corps disturbed their rest as they searched by torchlight for soldiers requiring medical attention. For the surgeons, battle's end meant the start of an arduous night of work. An Ohio surgeon reported that he "operated until 3 A.M. never worked harder." The next morning he rose at 5 A.M. and operated until 9 P.M.[67]

The battle had nearly wrecked Hovey's division. An Eleventh Indiana soldier caught the mood of many when he wrote in his diary: "May 17. Yesterday was a terribly bloody day for our division . . . My dear fried Wm. Pitman died this afternoon, he suffered much from his wound but said that he felt prepared to die; he was a noble boy and a brave soldier."[68] On Sunday, May 17, Union soldiers buried their fallen comrades. The battlefield resembled "a charnel house," recalled one survivor.[69] An Indiana soldier described how the next day he and his comrades buried the Confederates "in lots of twenties, thirties and upward, as was most convenient."[70] Among the slain was James Fogle of the Eleventh Indiana. At the end of April Fogle had written home about the likelihood of a big battle with its attendant heavy losses. The next letter his family received came from a comrade: "I told the boys to have him buried by himself so you can get him if you come soon. If you do not come soon it will be a bad job as he was buried without a box or coffin, it was impossible to do otherwise."[71]

The victorious Army of the Tennessee meticulously recorded its battle casualties. It lost 410 killed, 1,844 wounded, and 187 missing.[72] The figures clearly showed which units had done the fighting: of the four divisions operating under McClernand's command, Blair's division had no losses; Carr's division had 1 killed and 2 wounded; A. J. Smith's had none killed and 25 wounded; and Osterhaus's suffered 130 total casualties. In contrast were the losses endured by each of the three fighting divisions, four of whose regiments individually had higher losses than the aggregate of the four divisions controlled by McClernand. Logan's three brigades, continuing their superb fighting record from Port Gibson to Raymond to Champion Hill, lost 406 men. In the fighting on Champion Hill, Crocker's three brigades lost 665 men while Hovey's two brigades suffered 1,189 casualties. Their losses made Champion Hill the "Hill of Death." General McGinnis's brigade reported the following regimental percentage losses: 11th Indiana, 36 percent; 24th Indiana, 40 percent; 34th Indiana, 11 percent; 46th Indiana, 24 percent; 29th Wisconsin, 23 percent.[73] Colonel Slack's brigade lost 31 percent of its men. The division's three green regiments—the 29th Wisconsin and the 24th and 28th Iowa—had performed like veterans.

After Bakers Creek, as the Confederates named the battle, Confederate officers submitted incomplete returns and some filed no returns at all. Among the latter, for example, was Company A, First Mississippi Light Artillery, the battery overrun by General John Smith's brigade. Writing after the war, a battery lieutenant reported his outfit lost 74 of 82 men. The incomplete figures list 3,801 losses—381 killed, 1,018 wounded, and 2,411 missing—or approximately 16 percent of the entire army.[74] Including Loring's abandoned artillery, Grant's westerners captured twenty-seven field guns.

Like those of their adversaries, Confederate losses were unevenly distributed. General Featherston managed to carry out his vendetta against Pemberton and lose only 3 men from his brigade. Loring's entire division seems to have lost only 120 men on the field. Colonel Reynolds's brigade, which escorted the trains off the field before the battle really began, reported no killed or wounded and 143 men missing, most of whom the Federal cavalry snapped up during the pursuit. In Carter Stevenson's three fighting brigades, Barton lost 901 men, Lee 814, and Cumming 995. A staggering 72 percent of these loses were men reported missing, most of whom surrendered. In Bowen's division, the officers of Green's brigade provided no unit breakdown of casualties. Green's aggregate losses were 66 killed, 137 wounded, and only 65 missing. Colonel Cockrell's brigade suffered 65 killed, 293 wounded, and 242 missing. No rebel unit on the field had more men hit by enemy fire than Cockrell's First Missouri, which lost 29 men killed and 94 wounded. Overall, these figures underscore what Bowen's well-led, highly-disciplined, veteran force could accomplish. Although the division had to extricate itself from the meadows beneath Champion Hill while surrounded on three sides by the enemy and when out of ammunition, its aggregate missing were half the number reported individually by each of Carter Stevenson's three inexperienced brigades. Indicative of the rawness of Stevenson's men was the fact that Federal burial parties entered one ravine to find numerous dead Georgia soldiers, most of whom had been shot in the head, wearing fancy white slouch hats. Although sometimes forced to wear undyed uniforms that appeared white, veteran soldiers tried to avoid wearing anything that made them prominent targets.

General Pemberton lost the battle for several reasons, the most important of which was his failure to concentrate a sufficient field army. He left more than 40 percent of his available manpower west of the Big Black River, most in defensive positions at Vicksburg. Had General Martin Smith's and General John Forney's two divisions with their eleven thousand men been on the field, Grant would have been caught in a serious bind. Bakers Creek was Pemberton's first field battle and he performed poorly. His concept for his intended morning pullback was faulty. The notion of having each brigade move in succession to a designated point, deploy from road column into battle line, and then repeat the procedure in reverse when the next brigade arrived was unnecessarily time consuming. A far better scheme would have been to designate a rear guard and order it to hold the Crossroads until the entire army passed safely. The unhappy consequence of Pemberton's order was the stretching of Stevenson's division from near Edwards Station to the Crossroads and down the Middle Road where stood the nine-company infantry roadblock. It was impossible for Stevenson and his brigadiers to conduct operations wisely along such an elongated front. Consequently, things were overlooked that should not have been. In spite of this, once his supply train safely retired, Pemberton could have broken contact and retreated. He lacked the judgment and flexibility to appreciate his opportunity. His fixation on the Union threats against his right and center while ignoring the buildup against his left, his unrealistic tactical solution in which he ordered Bowen and Loring to attack the foe to their front, and his inability to nourish Cockrell's stunningly successful charge were all signs of his incapacity.

A Confederate soldier spoke for many when he wrote in his diary:

> May 16   Today proved to the army and the country the value of a general. Pemberton is either a traitor, or the most incompetent officer in the Confederacy. Indecision Indecision Indecision We have been badly defeated where we might have given the enemy a severe repulse. We have been defeated in detail, and have lost, O'God! how many brave and gallant soldiers.[75]

Compounding Pemberton's difficulties was execrable Confederate staff work. Pemberton allowed his staff officers to deploy many of the skirmish patrols. They did this by collecting companies from a variety of regiments and this upset regimental integrity. General Cumming in particular suffered from the numerous detachments that subtracted a fifth of his men from his battle line. When Cockrell recaptured Waddell's guns at the Crossroads, they sat for ninety minutes behind Confederate lines within eyesight of Pemberton's headquarters. Pemberton ordered them to be withdrawn, but again Confederate staff work proved defective and nothing was done. Thus the guns were there to be taken again at the end of the day. Somehow Bowen's ammunition wagons followed the ordnance train's early exodus from the field, leaving Bowen's warriors to scrounge ammunition from the dead and wounded. Although the battle occurred in a region that provided many recruits for Pemberton's army, not to mention the presence of loyal citizens including the women who gaily sang "Dixie" from the front yard of Pemberton's battle headquarters, no one adequately tapped local knowledge to learn about the field's road net. The army stumbled blindly the day before the battle. During the combat, Pemberton entirely lost track of Loring when that general marched along a farm track that was unknown to Pemberton and his staff.

Turning to the Federal side, Grant's corps commanders did not greatly distinguish themselves. At the top, McPherson performed competently while McClernand strictly adhered to his orders and failed to display initiative. At the more junior level, Hovey, Crocker, and Logan and their brigade commanders performed as very able subordinates. To the army commander must go the greatest credit. General Grant's prebattle strategy concentrated a force on the field that enjoyed a nearly three-to-two advantage. During the battle itself, Grant was very active. At key moments while the combat raged along the slopes of Champion Hill, numerous soldiers recalled seeing Grant. They described him as being just behind the front lines, from where he calmly watched the fighting and issued necessary orders. Grant's presence when Holmes's two regiments delivered their pivotal assault prompted someone to call out that Grant was watching them. "At once we set up a yell, every man shouting at the top of his voice, and this we kept up."[76] Grant's prominent presence reassured and inspired. His composure and personal leadership allowed his Army of the Tennessee to triumph in the battle that decided Vicksburg's fate.

The battle was arguably the decisive encounter of the war and men on both sides acted as if they recognized this. Diarists North and South comment about the absence of normal prebattle shirking. Men and officers literally rose from their sickbeds to participate. Indicative of the compelling sense of duty is the fact that at least three one-armed veterans charged with their comrades of the Fifth Missouri when Cockrell advanced on the Crossroads. Veteran leaders such as Confederate Colonel Riley marveled at how soldiers suffering from one or more wounds refused to go to the rear and instead continued to fight. In this war, when soldiers fired off their ammunition, they routinely judged that they had done their duty and could honorably withdraw to replenish ammunition. On Champion Hill, Hovey's and Bowen's soldiers alike maintained the fight after depleting their cartridge boxes. On Logan's front, when the Twentieth Ohio ran out of ammunition the men fixed bayonets and stood their ground awaiting the next onslaught.

On May 16, 1863, about three-quarters of a million soldiers served nationwide in the combined Union and Confederate armies.[77] This large batch distilled to the blood of twenty-nine thousand men—Union soldiers belonging to Hovey, Logan, and Crocker; Confederate soldiers in the divisions of Stevenson and Bowen—who risked their lives' essence to fight the battle of Champion Hill.

In his official report General Hovey paid tribute with words that apply equally to blue and gray: "I cannot think of this bloody hill without sadness and pride. Sadness for the great loss of my true and gallant men; pride for the heroic bravery they displayed."[78]

THE BOMBARDMENT OF THE CITY OF VICKSBURG.

When Farragut's fleet appeared at Vicksburg in May 1862, only six hastily constructed blufftop and water batteries defended the city. Vicksburg lay vulnerable to a coup de main had an adequate land force accompanied Farragut. A previously unpublished drawing that appeared in a Confederate newspaper shows Farragut's June 28 bombardment of Vicksburg. (Courtesy Old Court House Museum Collection, Vicksburg, Miss.)

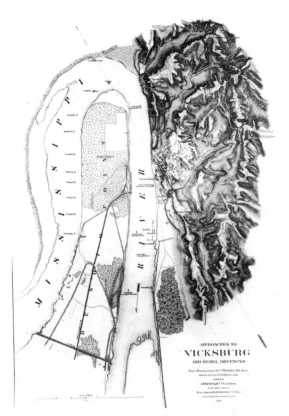

Geography made Vicksburg a naturally formidable position. Following Farragut's repulse, Confederate engineers sited heavy artillery that dominated the sharp river bend leading to the city. (Author's collection)

The river batteries included smoothbores ranging in size up to the nine 10-inch Columbiads, and rifled pieces of varying calibers up to a 7.44-inch Blakely. (Author's collection)

When Secretary of the Navy Welles sent Admiral David D. Porter to lead the
Mississippi Squadron against Vicksburg, Welles observed that the river naval
service "requires great energy, great activity, abundant resources. Porter is full of
each." (National Archives)

Armed with thirteen heavy cannon, armored with 2.5 inches of plate, the iron-clad *Cairo* was one of the original "Pook Turtles." (Library of Congress)

The business end of the *Cairo* at her display berth at Vicksburg National Military Park. (Author's collection)

The news that he had been elected president and commander in chief of the Confederacy found Jefferson Davis at his plantation some twenty miles down-stream from Vicksburg. (Author's collection)

Like Davis, President Abraham Lincoln had personal knowledge of Vicksburg's geography. Unlike Davis, Lincoln possessed an acute appreciation of Vicksburg's strategic importance. (National Archives)

Because of his presumed experience fighting against the Federal navy, Davis selected John C. Pemberton to defend Vicksburg. (Library of Congress)

Events proved that slow-firing Confederate artillery had trouble hitting enemy vessels, such as the *Indianola* shown here, on the mist- and smoke-shrouded river. (Library of Congress)

Major General Ulysses S. Grant assumed command of the Vicksburg expedition
at a time of deep Federal despondency. When a chaplain met with Grant during
Vicksburg's siege, he found the general changed since the campaign's start, his
brow more deeply etched. Otherwise, he remained the same unassuming, modest man, dressed "in an old brown line duster surmounted by an old slouch hat;
his trousers showed holes worn by the boot-straps, where they had rubbed
against the saddle." (Library of Congress)

Porter's April 16 run past Vicksburg was crucial to Grant's strategy. Porter pronounced the details of this 1883 painting of that action perfect and hung it in his library. (Library of Congress)

Grant entrusted Illinois politician Major General John A. McClernand with directing his flank march through Louisiana. McClernand was popular among his troops and detested by Grant, Sherman, and Porter. Porter wrote that McClernand was incompetent, "no soldier, and has the confidence of no one, unless it may be two or three of his staff." (National Archives)

Grant orchestrated a series of diversions to mask his crossing of the Mississippi River, one of which was Grierson's raid. Here, the "triumphal procession" of Grierson's cavalry through Baton Rouge. (Library of Congress)

Westerners of the Eighth Wisconsin, Army of the Tennessee, with their war eagle "Old Abe." (National Archives)

Fighting in wooded terrain characterized Civil War battles and imposed difficult tactical problems. A surging Confederate battle line approaches Logan's division at the Battle of Raymond. *(Harper's Weekly)*

Major General James B. McPherson, who commanded the Seventeenth Corps at Champion Hill, was a Grant favorite. Charles Dana described him as "one of the best officers we had. He was but thirty-two years old at the time and a very handsome, gallant-looking man, with a rather dark complexion, dark eyes, and a most cordial manner. . . . He was a man without any pretensions." (National Archives)

McGinnis's Brigade storms the rebel batteries atop Champion Hill. *(Harper's Weekly)*

The Federal assault on Champion Hill. Although this sketch exaggerates the troop density of the charging column, it captures the ferocity of the combat. *(Harper's Weekly)*

The Plantation Road provided lateral communication for Pemberton's army at Champion Hill. Note the battlefield's typical close terrain. (Author's collection)

Bowen's division emerges from the tree line at the base of Champion Hill and becomes the target of a powerful concentration of Federal fieldpieces. *(Harper's Weekly)*

The one-armed Major General William W. Loring, posed here in the dress uniform and captured sash that he probably wore at Champion Hill, disliked Pemberton and failed to support him in a reasonable manner at Champion Hill. (Courtesy of the Museum of the Confederacy, Richmond, Va.)

The Big Black River, where Irish Mike Lawler broke the Confederate bridge-head in an amazing three-minute charge. (Author's collection)

A valiant standard-bearer plants the colors on the Confederate works during the May 22 charge, one of the two assaults Grant ordered during the war that he always regretted. (Library of Congress)

The well-designed Confederate lines followed an irregular ridge top shown here at the skyline. (National Archives)

The failed assault forced the Army of the Tennessee to engage in a formal siege. Gunners serve their place from behind a protective woven mantelet while marksmen shoot through firing ports beneath the sandbags. (National Archives)

Lieutenant General Joseph E. Johnston took charge of the main effort to relieve Vicksburg. (National Archives)

In the minds of many Army of the Tennessee veterans, the Battle of Milliken's Bend settled the issue of whether a black soldier would fight. (The Metropolitan Museum of Art, New York, Gift of Charles Stewart Smith, 1884)

Soldiers of the Forty-fifth Illinois occupy roofed shelters on the reverse slope facing away from Vicksburg, where they are safe from most Confederate fire. The defenders did not share such relative luxury. (Library of Congress)

The Union men dug approaches right up to the Confederate works. The marker in the photo's middle shows the head of the sap while the high ground just beyond is the parapet of a rebel position. (Author's collection)

In an effort to speed progress, miners belonging to Logan's division tunnel beneath the Third Louisiana Redan, atop which flies the rebel flag. A grenade explodes at the tunnel's entrance. *(Harper's Weekly)*

The mine of June 25 detonates. *(Harper's Weekly)*

A bitter, close-range combat takes place in the crater as a Union soldier tries to return a Confederate grenade. *(Harper's Weekly)*

This photo, taken from a Confederate fort, exhibits the inexorable Union approach as shown by the markers paralleling the road. The two light-colored blocks in the foreground show the Federal position, just yards from the Confederate works, when Pemberton surrendered. (Author's collection)

Grant (left) and Pemberton discuss surrender terms. *(Harper's Weekly)*

When dedicating the Ohio markers at Vicksburg in 1906, a veteran said: "The tramp of the watchful pickets is no longer heard and the sentinel has left his post. The guns are stacked and the swords are rusting in their scabbards. The battle flags no longer lead the legions to battle; the faded uniforms are folded away with a benediction and the men that fell in that sanguinary conflict, sleep peacefully on every battlefield in their green tents, whose doors never outward swing." (Library of Congress)

9

"A Perilous and Ludicrous Charge"

"The affair of Big Black bridge was one which an ex-Confederate participant naturally dislikes to record."

> —Major Samuel Lockett, 1887 ("The Defense of Vicksburg," in *Battles & Leaders*, vol. 3)

THE MORNING OF MAY 17 found General Pemberton's army clinging to a fortified bridgehead on the east bank of the Big Black River. He knew that this was perilous business, but believed he had to hold the bridgehead as a haven for Loring's missing division. Pemberton's last contact with Loring had been via aide-de-camp John Taylor. The previous afternoon Taylor had found Loring on Carter Stevenson's left flank, at which time Loring had said that he would move to cover the army's withdrawal. So Pemberton kept faith by defending the bridgehead. Late on the sixteenth, Pemberton personally had instructed his most dependable divisional commander, John Bowen, to defend the bridgehead until Loring appeared. Pemberton placed his trust in Bowen's division's proven fighting ability and in a line of earthworks.

The Confederate position was indeed a formidable one. A mile of earthworks extended across a neck of land formed by a loop in the river. With flanks secured on the river, the position could only be approached frontally. A stagnant, waist-deep bayou served like a moat to cover much of this front. Rebel pioneers had felled trees and brush to create additional obstacles. Bowen had about five thousand men to defend the position. They included fresh infantry from the Vicksburg garrison, namely Brigadier General John

Vaughn's brigade and the fourth Mississippi regiment from Brigadier General William Baldwin's brigade. Vaughn's Tennessee soldiers defended the middle with Green's brigade on their left and Cockrell's men on their right. Eighteen fieldpieces poked their muzzles over the breastworks. However, vexing staff problems continued. Someone sent the battery horses west over the river so the guns were immobile. This blunder left the gunners and their supporting infantry feeling like they had been set up as a rearguard sacrifice.

A young woman living at a nearby plantation awoke on the morning of May 17 to find the yard "thronged with tired, hungry soldiers, all with the same words upon their lips: 'We are sold by General Pemberton.'"[1] The pervasive feeling of betrayal grew during the morning as Grant's army closed up against the bridgehead. The defenders knew they were heavily outnumbered and that safety lay across the two bridges spanning the river to their rear, and that a three-quarter-mile distance across open ground separated them from the bridges. Quite simply, the Confederate fighting men felt like they were in a position where they ought never to have been placed. The army commander was oblivious to this widely held sentiment.

Although Pemberton believed that the Yankees would soon appear, either his distaste for battle command or his confidence in Bowen was such that he remained at Bovina early on May 17. He sent a message to General Johnston describing the May 14 council of war and his own tortuous logic that had led him to advance over the Big Black in search of Grant's line of supply, and reported his defeat at Bakers Creek. He told Johnston that he had withdrawn with heavy losses to the Big Black Bridge but doubted his ability to hold the river line. If compelled to retreat, Pemberton explained that he would have to abandon the high ground northeast of Vicksburg and retire within Vicksburg's fortifications. Pemberton concluded that he had about sixty days' provisions and "respectfully await your instructions."[2]

Pemberton's comment regarding Johnston's instructions was rather brazen considering that he was disregarding Johnston's orders. Even at this stage of the campaign, there remained an open corridor which Pemberton could have used to join Johnston. Pemberton knew that Grant's army was around Edwards Station and Johnston was somewhere north of Jackson near Canton. Two good highways ran northeast from Vicksburg around Grant's right flank and toward Canton. If Pemberton committed his army to a march along this corridor, it would have risked an attack by Grant against his right flank. But the Big Black River screened his flank nearly all of the way to Canton. There were only two places where Grant's army could have crossed the Big Black to intercept the march, and the roads over which Grant would have to pass to do this were poor. Pemberton never considered such a course of action. His decision to retire within Vicksburg's perimeter again shows that he considered his overweening duty, his sacred trust, to be the literal defense of Vicksburg by positioning his army behind the city's fortifications.

Curiously, at about the same time that Pemberton had to weigh instructions from his commanding officer, his Federal counterpart was confronting a similar situation. While Grant observed his army's deployment in front of the Confederate bridgehead, a hard-riding courier delivered a message from Grant's old nemesis, Henry Halleck. Dated May 11, it contained the suggestion that Grant and General Banks cooperate against either Port Hudson or Vicksburg. As Grant recalled, he told the flabbergasted courier that Halleck's orders were out of date and that he intended to ignore them.[3] As he shoved the message into his pocket the distinctive sounds of Union soldiers cheering washed over his ears. Focusing his binoculars, Grant saw one of his subordinates, General Lawler, apparently in the process of trying to break the Confederate line.

The chain of events leading up to Lawler's assault began at 3:30 A.M., when General McClernand had Osterhaus's and Carr's divisions march toward the Big Black River. Two hours later they contacted the Confederate position and stopped to throw out skirmishers and deploy. As Federal artillery began a desultory bombardment, Lawler's brigade took position on the army's right. Lawler gazed across four hundred to six hundred yards of cleared field to see what appeared to be a well-built line of rifle pits and trenches. He received instructions from Carr to advance his brigade cautiously and probe the Confederate left. In peacetime Irish Mike Lawler was a fat, friendly Illinois farmer. He had served in the Mexican War and had become, according to James Wilson, "a remarkable volunteer tactician."[4] In addition to acquiring combat experience, Lawler had, over time, also gained considerable weight. He found that he could not make a sword belt encircle his waist with any degree of comfort and so wore his sword suspended by a shoulder strap. On the morning of May 17, the Mississippi sun was so oppressive that he had stripped to his shirtsleeves. Thus he presented a rather comical image as he directed his brigade's advance.

His soldiers worked forward to near where the Confederate left butted up against the river. Here was a strip of uncultivated land choked with trees and underbrush that provided shelter from hostile fire. During a several-hour lull, punctuated by the exchange of largely ineffectual skirmish and

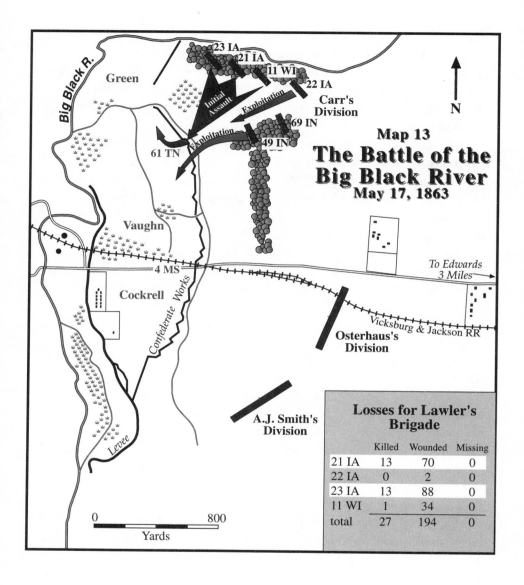

Map 13
The Battle of the Big Black River
May 17, 1863

Losses for Lawler's Brigade			
	Killed	Wounded	Missing
21 IA	13	70	0
22 IA	0	2	0
23 IA	13	88	0
11 WI	1	34	0
total	27	194	0

artillery fire, Colonel William Kinsman of the Twenty-third Iowa had a chance to study the Confederate line up close. Kinsman believed he detected a flaw. Whereas a tangle of felled trees covered most of the rebel front, the colonel found a streambed where apparently the recent heavy rains had washed away all obstructions. A narrow column four abreast could use this as a sheltered approach to the enemy works. Kinsman proposed to

Lawler that he be allowed to lead an immediate bayonet charge. Lawler liked the idea but considered a single regiment inadequate. Consequently, he arranged an assault column with Kinsman's Twenty-third Iowa and the Twenty-first Iowa in the lead, while the Eleventh Wisconsin provided close support and the Twenty-second Iowa took position behind the column as a general reserve. Lawler also asked the colonels of two nearby Indiana regiments to advance a skirmish line to divert Confederate attention away from his own preparations. Lawler's cherished maxim was that of an Irish brawler: "If you see a head, hit it!" About 9 A.M., Lawler led his brigade forward to do just that. But he had also arranged his assault with fine tactical dexterity. Lawler deployed his regiments in column by battalion, willingly sacrificing firepower to gain speed, agility, and mass. The ensuing charge amazed everyone.

The Union column advanced on the Confederate works at an oblique angle. This allowed the Missouri infantry manning some rifle pits on the far left of the trench line to fire a volley into the column's exposed right flank. Colonel Kinsman fell with a dangerous wound, struggled to his feet and staggered a few paces forward while waving his men on, and then fell a second time with a mortal wound. The regimental color-bearer went down with a bad wound. A nearby corporal grasped the colors and ran forward into a small, wooded swamp that was sheltered from the enfilade fire. Even a civilian regimental sutler participated in the Twenty-third Iowa's charge and paid for his bravery with his life. After Kinsman went down, Lieutenant Colonel Samuel Glasgow took command and led the Iowa soldiers through the swamp and over the enemy earthworks. Having breached the line, the Iowa soldiers delivered a devastating enfilade fire up and down the trench that sent the defenders reeling while a lieutenant wrested the flag of the Sixty-first Tennessee from its color-bearer.

Simultaneously, Lawler's other regiments had rushed across more open ground. As they charged, the Twenty-first Iowa's Colonel Samuel Merrill received a serious wound. Undaunted, this regiment and the Eleventh Wisconsin reached the bayou just in front of the rebel works, fired a volley, and, with Lawler joining right in with them, plunged into the water. They waded across, gave a cheer, and charged over the earthworks. It was this cheer that attracted Grant's attention. An eyewitness who saw much of the war claimed that "it was at the same time the most perilous and ludicrous charge I witnessed during the war."[5] In a mere three minutes, at a cost of 14 killed and 185 wounded, Lawler's brigade shattered Pemberton's fortified bridgehead.

The defenders whom Lawler first contacted belonged to General Vaughn's brigade. They were men who hailed from East Tennessee—a region of poor, non-slave-owning farmers with strong Union sentiments—and who had been forcibly conscripted into Confederate service. Their hearts were not in this fight and they broke badly. Meanwhile, Lawler's tactical control was equal to his soldiers' audacity. Three regiments quickly advanced to exploit the breach. Sergeant William Kendall led the Forty-ninth Indiana over the works and thereby earned the Congressional Medal of Honor. Along with the Sixty-ninth Indiana, the Forty-ninth turned to the left to roll up the Confederate line. Simultaneously, the Twenty-second Iowa wheeled right to pin the rebels manning the extreme left flank against the river. Here, normally stalwart troops belonging to Green's brigade occupied the breastworks. When they realized that Lawler had penetrated the line to their right they joined the stampede to the bridges. Many did not make it. Trapped against the river, Colonel Elijah Gates—the officer who yesterday had shaken hands with the magnolia blossom–wielding Cockrell before beginning their charge—and some ninety of his Missourians surrendered to the Eleventh Wisconsin.

The center of the Confederate position quickly unraveled as Indiana regiments worked their way south along the ditches. Colonel Cockrell's men occupied the trenches from the railroad south. Hearing the noise of heavy musketry on his left, Cockrell mounted the parapet to see the Tennessee men fleeing to the rear. He shouted out orders to retreat immediately. As the Missourians took their first steps, the adjacent regiment to their left, the Fourth Mississippi, collapsed from the Indiana soldiers' flank attack. Colonel Riley led his First Missouri across the rear of the adjacent regiment to try to stem the tide. He failed to check the Federal surge. A Missouri officer mounted the parapet to "see through my glass the place where a Mississippi regiment had been stationed, swarming with blue-coats . . . We had been flanked . . . and no alternative remained but to get away from there as fast as possible."[6] Tactical control within Cockrell's brigade was disintegrating. When Riley ordered his regiment to retreat, it left the nearby Sixth Missouri in trouble. That regiment tried to fall back, but the sight of the advancing Union host caused it to rout. To Cockrell's disgust, most of his brigade joined the rout. At least one gunner of the Third Missouri artillery retained his composure. Since the absence of the battery horses meant there was no way to drive the guns to the bridge, he carried his rammer as he ran in order to prevent his enemies from operating his abandoned cannon. His conduct was exceptional. Indicative of the pervasive demoralization among the defenders of the bridgehead is the casualty list for Bowen's superb division: 1 officer and 2 men killed; 9 wounded; 46 officers and 427 men missing.[7]

From the high bluffs on the west side of the Big Black, the engineer who had designed the fortified bridgehead, Major Samuel Lockett, watched the scene unfold with horror. Earlier in the day he had sensed the army's low spirits and received permission from Pemberton to prepare incendiary material to fire the bridges in the event of disaster. Lockett waited while mobs of soldiers thronged over the bridges. He saw the nearby water full of fearful men swimming the river in their haste to escape. When it seemed everyone was safely across, he torched a barrel of turpentine and with the help of a lieutenant tipped it over. The fire quickly spread to piles of turpentine-soaked cotton and fence rails to engulf the bridge in flames. In like fashion, demolition parties burned the other bridge. A soldier of the Sixth Missouri recalls, "Not being much of a runner, I did not get to the bridge until it was a mass of flames; but being a good swimmer, I swung my boots about my neck, plunged in, and made the other side."[8] From a Confederate viewpoint, the Big Black had been a debacle without redemption. The army naturally blamed Pemberton, but it also focused on the defender's conduct. Staff officer Taylor confided to his diary, "Our troops shamefully abandoned the trenches."[9]

After completing his demolition work, Lockett rode west to encounter Pemberton, who had hurriedly returned from Bovina upon learning about the collapse of his bridgehead. While the survivors were streaming past him, the lieutenant general pondered what to do. Earlier he had brought up Lee's Alabama brigade and a fresh brigade from the Vicksburg garrison to occupy the high ground west of the river. He briefly considered supplementing these units with his entire army to make a stand behind the Big Black. But given the large number of stragglers and the absence of Loring's division, he doubted that he had adequate forces to prevent being outflanked. In that event, he would again confront his recurring fear, namely that Grant's army would cut in behind him and capture Vicksburg. At 10 A.M. he gave the order to retreat and personally hastened back to the Hill City, as he later reported, "to reorganize the depressed and discomfited troops."[10] He retired in company with chief engineer Lockett. Glumly, Pemberton reflected, "Just thirty years ago I began my military career by receiving my appointment to a cadetship at the U.S. Military Academy, and to-day—the same date—that career is ended in disaster and disgrace."[11]

The mood was far different on the east side of the Big Black. After his charge, Lawler encountered General Leggett, who was marching with Logan's men toward the sounds of the combat. Lawler told Leggett to let his men rest. Leggett asked, "Did you get any of them?" Lawler growled a response, "Whole acres of them, whole acres of them."[12] The men who overheard this exchange began to cheer. As word spread, the cheer was taken up successively, rolling back along the entire column. Lawler's conduct also impressed Grant, who later said, "When it comes to just plain hard fighting I would rather trust Old Mike Lawler than any of them."[13]

All Union casualties from the engagement at the Big Black River occurred in McClernand's corps: 39 killed, 237 wounded, and 3 missing.[14] The Federal harvest from the field included eighteen field guns, 1,751 prisoners, and five battle flags.[15] Grant rewarded Colonel Kinsman's gallant Twenty-third Iowa with the agreeable duty of escorting the prisoners back north.

WHILE GRANT'S MAIN BODY closed in on Pemberton's bridgehead, Sherman's corps headed for an upstream ford to outflank this position. The men marched through Bolton, where they liberated several wounded men who had been captured during Sherman's ill-fated assault against Chickasaw Bluffs the previous December. It was another hot day, with thirst afflicting corps commander and private alike. Just beyond Bolton, General Sherman rode up to a farmyard where some of his men were drawing water from a well. Sherman stopped to get a drink. He saw a book on the ground and asked a soldier to hand it up to him. It was a copy of the Constitution of the United States. On the title page was the owner's name: Jefferson Davis. The Confederate president's possessions had been moved from his nearby home to this plantation for safekeeping.

Sherman's corps reached the Big Black around 10 A.M. Pickets exchanged fire across the swollen river until an Illinois battery arrived and began to shell the opposite bank. So demoralized were the rebels that they hoisted a white flag, and then crossed over to the eastern bank in skiffs to surrender. Sherman's corps had the army's only pontoons. With the opposition eliminated, men went to work laying a bridge. By 8 P.M. it was ready. The Thirteenth Illinois crossed it, marched two miles, and bivouacked for the night. Its camp marked the farthest advance toward Vicksburg that day.

The other two Federal corps likewise did not manage to mount a pursuit on May 17. Lacking pontoons, McPherson's corps, which Grant ordered to cross the river north of the former Confederate bridgehead in order to avoid a traffic bottleneck, had to improvise. At one of its two bridging sites, McPherson's pioneers worked on both banks to fell two huge trees. Soldiers joined them in midstream and covered them with planking. It was a serviceable, if shaky, footbridge. To help at the second site, Grant again "committed" his aide Colonel Wilson. This time Wilson could not employ his experienced pioneers. The speed of the advance had left them somewhere far to the rear. Lacking timber and tools, Wilson set the tired infantry to hacking apart a nearby cotton warehouse with their axes. Lacking rope, the colonel employed horse picketing lines and artillery prolonges. Having no pontoons, Wilson had the men build thirty-five-foot-long timber cribs, fill them with cotton bales, and float them out into the water to support the bridge decking. Shortly before dawn the structure was ready. Everyone gasped a bit when the big twenty-pounder Parrotts rolled onto the bridge, but it proved amply buoyant. While infantry filed across the twin log-based footbridge, the corps artillery and trains passed safely atop the cotton bridge.

On the battlefield itself, the Federal troops spent the afternoon collecting abandoned Confederate equipment and resting. Engineers did not commence building a bridge until darkness concealed them from enemy marksmen hidden on the bluffs across the river. They did not finish their work until the next morning. At that point, General A. J. Smith's division crossed and "marched very slowly" toward Vicksburg.[16]

The time-consuming passage of the Big Black indicates that the Army of the Tennessee was weary. In seventeen days it had accomplished prodigies. Its achievements since crossing the Mississippi had been Napoleonic in sweep. The army had marched more than two hundred miles, fought and won five battles, inflicted more than 8,000 casualties, captured sixty-six artillery pieces, and separated Pemberton's army from outside help and driven it inside Vicksburg's fortifications. During this time it lost 4,337 men.[17]

A darker Napoleonic feature of the campaign was the swath of destruction the army left in its wake. Some of this stemmed from legitimate need, some of it was wanton. Among those who encouraged this latter behavior was Illinois governor Richard Yates. Speaking to some Illinois troops, he had recalled the Louisiana Purchase and said that the government had paid $10 million—it had actually cost closer to $27 million, but after all Yates was a politician—and *"by heaven we will redeem it, or make it one vast burying-ground."*[18] A young woman who watched the army enter Clinton reported that

stables were torn down, smoke-houses invaded and emptied of all their bacon and hams; chicken-houses were depopulated, vehicles of all kinds
were taken or destroyed, barrels of sugar or molasses were emptied—the
sugar carried off, while the molasses ran in streams in the yard . . . The
dry-goods stores were broken into, the beautiful goods given to Negroes
or destroyed.[19]

The soldiers called it living off the land. For the civilians it was ruin.

ON THE EVENING OF MAY 16, General Johnston received a message from
Pemberton, written that morning, announcing Pemberton's intention to
countermarch to unite with him. There had been an ominous postscript—
"Heavy skirmishing is now going on in my front"—but Johnston took comfort in the fact that Pemberton was finally following his advice.[20] Accordingly, the next morning, while Pemberton's bridgehead collapsed, Johnston
marched his rested men fifteen or so miles toward Edwards Station and the
expected rendezvous. As the troops settled down, another courier arrived to
convey the disastrous intelligence of the defeat at Bakers Creek. Johnston
focused on Pemberton's phrase regarding the likelihood that he would
abandon the high ground northeast of Vicksburg at Haynes' Bluff while
withdrawing into the Vicksburg perimeter. Johnston immediately appreciated that the evacuation of Haynes' Bluff would allow Grant to reestablish
contact with the Federal fleet and thus gain a secure supply line. He sent
a return messenger speeding to Pemberton:

> If Haynes' Bluff is untenable, Vicksburg is of no value, and cannot be held.
> If, therefore, you are invested in Vicksburg, you must ultimately surren-
> der. Under such circumstances, instead of losing both troops and place, we
> must, if possible, save the troops. If it is not too late, evacuate Vicksburg
> and its dependencies, and march to the northeast.[21]

Meanwhile, as the crisis on the Mississippi unfolded, in faraway Richmond, President Jefferson Davis contemplated two plans to retrieve the situation. He hoped that enough reinforcements had reached Johnston so that
the general could intervene decisively. There was one other alternative.
General Robert E. Lee had recently won a smashing victory at Chancellorsville. He had accomplished this while a sizable portion of his army under
Lieutenant General James Longstreet was absent. Given that the shaken
Army of the Potomac would require time to prepare a new offensive, it was
quite possible that Lee could hold his ground while sending Longstreet

west. It was a strategic decision of immense consequence; accordingly, Davis summoned his most trusted general to the capital.

Lee arrived in Richmond on May 15, the day Grant turned his army west to attack Vicksburg from the rear. Ever since Chancellorsville—a battle people were already beginning to call "Lee's masterpiece"—Lee had been clamoring for reinforcements. To Lee, any battle that merely repulsed the enemy was devoid of strategic significance. To convert victory into strategic triumph he needed more men. Instead, to his annoyance, for the past week he had been exchanging telegrams with the War Department regarding the possibility of sending men west. Lee firmly opposed the idea, bluntly saying "it becomes a question between Virginia and the Mississippi."[22] Lee believed that a detachment from his army might not arrive in time to alter the situation, that its absence would jeopardize Richmond's safety, and that the whole scheme was unnecessary because the terrible Mississippi summer climate would soon force Grant to withdraw.

Lee had actually acquired this odd notion that the North's most tenacious general would give up because of the summer's heat from the president. Back in April, Davis had delivered a message to the "People of the Confederate States." While reviewing the progress of the war, he highlighted Confederate successes around Vicksburg. "Within a few weeks," Davis said, the rivers would begin to lower and render them impassable to the Union fleet "and the increasing heat of summer will . . . compel their baffled and defeated forces" to abandon further expeditions against the Mississippi River Valley.[23] Lee surely reasoned that since Davis made his home near Vicksburg, he knew of what he spoke.

During his talks with Davis and at a subsequent cabinet meeting, Lee argued against sending his veterans west. Yet he acknowledged that something drastic had to be done and therefore proposed a second invasion of the North. It might or might not relieve the pressure in the West, but in the past Lincoln had shown a special sensitivity to threats to his capital by summoning troops to its defense. Moreover, there was the chance that a victory gained north of the Potomac would actually lead to Washington's fall and foreign intervention. Davis and his cabinet reflected upon all of this and upon the fact that since Lee had taken command in Virginia he had never lost a battle. With one exception, they endorsed his plan.

That exception was Postmaster General John Reagan, who believed Lee was badly mistaken. A self-made lawyer and politician from Texas, the forceful Reagan had overcome enormous obstacles to create a postal service that accomplished something that had neither been done before nor would be done again. Instead of operating at a deficit, Reagan's postal service made a clear profit. While this hardly qualified him to comment on matters of high strategy, Reagan was unique among cabinet members in that he was the only one to hail from the far side of the Mississippi. This gave him a special knowledge of the consequences of losing control of the river and contact with the resource-rich Trans-Mississippi. Reagan thought the loss of Vicksburg would be a fatal blow to the Confederacy.

He proposed a sham campaign across the Potomac full of noisy preparation and loose talk about capturing Washington. Aided by this deception, Lee would go on the defensive and send Longstreet's corps to operate against Grant. By the time Lincoln realized that an invasion of the North was a bluff, it would be too late. When cabinet members argued that Lee's proposed invasion would force Grant to retreat, Reagan countered that Grant was committed; he would either capture Vicksburg or be destroyed in the effort.[24]

Lee's plan or Reagan's? The Cabinet, after a day of long deliberation, voted five to one in favor of Lee. Distraught, unable to sleep, Reagan arose at dawn to ask the president to call another meeting to reconsider. Davis obliged. After all, he shared the Texan's special concern for this, his home region. After further talk, the cabinet voted again, and again it was five to one. Lee would invade Pennsylvania. As for affairs in Mississippi, Lee offered counsel regarding Johnston's proper strategy. His advice was utterly characteristic of the man. He said that Johnston should attack the Yankees at the first opportunity and before Grant had a chance to consolidate his position.

After Lee returned to his army, Davis received news of Bakers Creek. In response he telegraphed Pemberton: "I made every effort to reinforce you promptly, which I am aggrieved was not successful. Hope that Genl. Johnston will soon join you with enough force to break up the investment and defeat the enemy."[25] On that hope, and on the expectation that the invincible Lee would triumph again, the Confederate commander in chief based his faith.

One hundred miles to the north an anxious Abraham Lincoln, still reeling from the disaster at Chancellorsville, tried to follow Grant's campaign as best he could. He relied upon a garrison commander in Virginia, who had access to the Richmond papers, for news about Grant's whereabouts. Although Lincoln did not know this, his telegraphed requests for information about Grant failed for the reason that the Richmond press was equally ignorant. Finally, Lincoln learned from the Richmond papers dated May 20 and 21 that Grant had beaten Pemberton at Champion Hill. Confirmation came on May 23 when a telegraph operator in Memphis forwarded a report from Lieutenant Colonel John A. Rawlins that provided the first official news of Grant's doings since crossing the Mississippi on April 30.

Lincoln lacked Jefferson Davis's West Point education. Yet he comprehended better than did Davis what was taking place on the Mississippi. Lincoln wrote to a friend, "Whether Gen. Grant shall or shall not consummate the capture of Vicksburg, his campaign . . . is one of the most brilliant in the world."[26]

10

Assault

... like marching men to their graves in line of battle ...

—War diary of Harvey M. Trimble, Ninety-third
Illinois, May 22, 1863

MAY 17 HAD WITNESSED SCENES of near panic as the Confederate field army returned to Vicksburg. An officer described how there were "waggons at the gallop—men rushing madly along with citizens half crazy and women frantic."[1] Demoralized soldiers scattered along the roads leading to the city. They cursed Pemberton for their fate and many declared they would "desert rather than serve under him again."[2] More than a few officers and men loudly proclaimed their conviction that General Pemberton had intentionally betrayed the army.

Following the debacle on the Big Black, Major Lockett hurried back to Vicksburg to prepare for the coming onslaught. Lockett had graduated second in his West Point class of 1859. Traditionally the cream of the class entered the Corps of Engineers, and so it had been with the young Alabama officer. He put his training to the test in September 1862 when he laid out Vicksburg's land fortifications. These extended over an eight-mile arc from Fort Hill on the bluffs, a half-mile above the city, to South Fort, three miles below. An irregular network of hills and ridges lay inland from the river. Lockett's fortifications took advantage of this natural line of defense. The key sectors were where six roads and one rail line entered Vicksburg. Nine strong earthen forts protected these roads. All except one featured exterior moatlike ditches six to ten feet deep and ten to eighteen feet wide. Linking them were trenches and rifle pits buttressed by smaller earthworks. The trees in front had been felled to create a clear line of fire. Workers had weaved their branches together and, in conjunction with telegraph wire and sharpened stakes, had created an abatis, the forerunner of modern barbed wire.

As formidable as these works could become, when Lockett examined them on May 17 and 18 he saw great weaknesses. Months of disuse and a winter of heavy rain had eroded many sections, filled in obstacles, and collapsed earthen walls. Lockett set the soldiers of Smith's and Forney's divisions—the soldiers of the garrison who had not participated in the recent series of field battles—to repair the fortifications. Lockett well knew that military history clearly showed that to endure a siege, the defender required adequate provisions. In order to prevent the enemy's breaching batteries and trenches from approaching too near, the defender needed artillery. In order to repair damage, the garrison had to have shovels. Although Pemberton had been contemplating the prospect of a siege since mid-February, he had failed to ensure that his men had all these necessities. There were only five hundred shovels to be shared among thousands, so the repair work went slowly.

While Lockett supervised the rebuilding of the fortifications, Pemberton ordered Haynes' Bluff evacuated. It quickly became apparent that if the army lacked shovels it did not lack artillery. From the bluff came six-pounder fieldpieces and heavy thirty-pounder Parrotts to choke the road leading to Vicksburg. A major feared that his convoy would be captured by the oncoming enemy. But in the event, he had time to send his wagons back to load some of the corn—corn delivered from the Yazoo River delta but that had not been hauled to Vicksburg—and carry it into the city. When probing Federal cavalry eventually interfered, the major reluctantly had to leave a huge supply of "collected breadstuff and horse-feed" to the enemy.[3]

About noon on the eighteenth, Pemberton joined Lockett to inspect the defenses. He still worried about Loring's whereabouts, but had begun to recover his confidence. No military man could help but note the natural strength of the position. Then his spirit was challenged again upon receipt of Johnston's dispatch ordering the evacuation of Vicksburg "if it is not too late."[4] Even while Pemberton considered this communication, a message arrived from General Bowen that again raised the ugly question about Pemberton's Northern birth. The hard-fighting Bowen was badly discouraged following consecutive days of defeat and retreat.[5] His men were in worse shape. Bowen reported that wild camp rumors were circulating that Pemberton had arranged treacherously to hand over Vicksburg to Grant. Bowen recommended that Pemberton convene a council of war and then issue a general order proclaiming his determination to neither evacuate nor surrender, but to defend the city "to the bitter end."[6]

Here was a pretty stew. Yesterday Pemberton had seen his men break before a Union assault at the Big Black and give up a position he judged readily defensible. He doubted their willingness to fight. Now, hard on the heels of an order to evacuate the city came a serious challenge to his Southern loyalty, a challenge that apparently could only be met by pledging to remain. Pemberton convened a council of war and expressed his strong inclination to ignore Johnston. Just eleven days ago his president had restated the importance of holding Vicksburg. He knew that he also possessed the secretary of war's overt endorsement to accept investment.[7] Whereas the council of war before the battle of Bakers Creek had featured divided opinion among his top generals, this time it was different. Pemberton wrote that the council's "opinion was unanimously expressed that it was impossible to withdraw the army from this position with such morale and material as to be of further service to the Confederacy."

His president's wishes, the considered opinion of his subordinates, Bowen's warning about the army's morale, and his own desire to prove his loyalty despite his Northern birth all pointed in one direction. Pemberton had no doubt what to do: "I have decided to hold Vicksburg as long as possible," he wrote Johnston, "with the firm hope that the Government may yet be able to assist me in keeping this obstruction to the enemy's free navigation of the Mississippi River. I still conceive it to be the most important point in the Confederacy."[8]

Pemberton knew that eventually a besieging force must triumph unless attacked from the outside. Given that he had been unwilling to engage Grant with his own field army, it is difficult to understand on what basis he expected Johnston, whom he knew had a mere six thousand men, to accomplish much. Blind to the illogic of his strategy, Pemberton henceforth relied on Johnston to save Vicksburg. Others wondered if Johnston's army was irrelevant. Recalling the Big Black, a Tennessee soldier wrote, "the feeling was general that they would run over our entrenchments" as soon as the Yankees tried.[9]

AT DAWN ON MAY 18 the Army of the Tennessee renewed its march on Vicksburg. By early afternoon Sherman's corps was within four miles of the

Hill City and had occupied the road linking Vicksburg with the Confederate fortifications on the Yazoo River. While Sherman sent patrols to probe toward the city, Grant arrived to explain his plans. All three corps would advance until contacting the enemy: McClernand on the left, McPherson in the center, and Sherman on the right. In addition, Sherman was to seize Haynes' Bluff so the army would again be tied to the navy and the umbilical cord of the Mississippi River.

By day's end Federal pickets were trading shots with enemy skirmishers at several points along the Vicksburg perimeter. General Sherman reached the high ground north of Vicksburg that overlooked the ground where he had delivered his failed assault five months ago. He was elated. Not only could he now erase the ghosts of his December debacle, he could see the future—and it was bright. He told Grant that until now he had been uncertain if Grant's strategy was sound. The reestablishment of contact with the navy brought the maneuver portion of the campaign to a close. Regardless of what happened next, Sherman concluded that the occupation of Haynes' Bluff marked "the end of one of the greatest campaigns in history."[10]

As the Union soldiers prepared to sleep that night they were in fine spirits. When one officer lay down on his blanket a bullet struck the ground within an inch of his ear. He proposed to his sleep mate that they relocate. His comrade replied, "Lie still and go to sleep and you won't hear 'em strike." The officer tried, but several more bullets came near. He finally moved and later explained, "I'm no coward, but I didn't want to be accidently killed without knowing something about it."[11]

A COOL MORNING BREEZE fragrant with the perfume of flowers and shrubs swept over the Army of the Tennessee's campsites on May 19. Serenaded by the sounds of sweetly singing birds, the men rose to prepare meager breakfasts. They were proud of what they had accomplished. Only the fortress of Vicksburg remained. After Champion Hill and the Big Black, few doubted that this, too, would be theirs soon. A Wisconsin lieutenant wrote in his diary, "It is evident the day cannot pass without a battle, for our forces are now investing Vicksburg and are determined to possess it before night if possible."[12] Grant's own confidence was manifest in the simple assault order he issued. Special Order No. 134 stated: "Army corps commanders will push forward carefully, and gain as close position as possible to the enemy's works until 2 P.M. At that hour they will fire three volleys of artillery from all the pieces in position. This will be the signal for a general charge of all the corps along the whole line."[13]

There were several problems with this order. First, couriers carried it away from army headquarters shortly after 11:16 A.M. This meant that by the time the corps commanders received it and relayed their own instructions down the chain of command, there were less than two hours for the tactical commanders, the officers who would conduct the assault, to make preparations. It was insufficient time to identify weak points or to arrange reserves to exploit any breakthroughs. This inability was in keeping with the general sense of the attack: it was not subtle; instead, it was a great bull rush. By attacking with little preparation, the soldiers would have to advance along the most obvious lines of approach, which presumably were guarded by the heaviest fortifications and the most men. By attacking all along the line there was no concentration of force against a few selected targets. But recent events seemed to indicate that the rebels would not fight anyway, so no senior officer seriously worried about any of this.

The men who were to make the assault had a different view. Among the skeptics was an Illinois captain who cautiously scouted the enemy lines. He saw "three strong bastioned forts on the right, center and left on high grounds within a line of entrenchments and stockades . . . It required but a brief inspection to satisfy me that more than likely we wouldn't go into town that day."[14] Many of the assault troops shared his opinion. Behind their start lines they handed over their valuables, along with final instructions should they not return, to the fortunate few who, because of sickness or special duty, would not accompany the charge.

During the morning, Federal sharpshooters worked their way forward and opened fire. They found that they held a significant advantage over their foes. The Confederate trench line followed the high ground. If a rebel rifleman wanted to shoot accurately at targets in the ravines below, he became silhouetted against the skyline. The artillerists, operating behind open embrasures, were even more vulnerable. Union marksmen got so close to one fort that they kept a loaded artillery piece from being fired for over four hours.

Pemberton had about twenty-one thousand effectives to defend Vicksburg. He deployed them sensibly. Many of the units in General Stevenson's division had not fought well at Champion Hill. Pemberton assigned them to defend almost four miles of trenches running from the railroad to South Fort on the Mississippi River. Because of the direction of Grant's approach, this was likely to be a quiet sector. If a threat developed along Stevenson's front, it was likely to occur close to the railroad. Accordingly, the brigade that had performed the best at Champion Hill, General Lee's Alabamians, defended this sector. General Forney's untarnished division defended the center while General Martin Smith's mostly fresh division occupied the left. Since this division included Vaughn's suspect East Tennesseans, they—along with various stragglers from Loring's division—were stationed in close reserve in a sector of such great natural strength that they were unlikely to be called upon. Pemberton retained Bowen's division in reserve in a fire brigade capacity, ready to rush to squelch any Yankee breakthrough.

At 2 P.M. the Union artillery fired three salvos to signal the start of the assault. Because Grant's orders had not been received until too close to the start time, most units had to cross about a half-mile of rugged ground just to arrive within charging distance of the earthworks. During their approach they endured a fierce artillery barrage. Their final run in was an uphill struggle through man-made obstacles. As these obstacles slowed the attackers, the defenders mounted their firing steps and began shooting. Wherever possible, they had gathered additional weapons to increase their firepower. The soldiers in a Texas outfit had five additional smoothbore muskets charged with buck and ball to supplement their Springfield rifled muskets. The Confederate wall of fire made it quickly apparent that the defenders were not going to be stampeded by the mere sight of a charging blue wave. Near the Jackson Road a Confederate officer encountered an old soldier shot through both cheeks, bleeding profusely, and carrying a shotgun that had been shattered by an enemy bullet. The major consoled him about his wound and asked him where he was going. "He replied that he was going to get another gun."[15]

The Army of the Tennessee included only one battalion of U.S. infantry. Its men were determined to maintain the reputation of the U.S. Regular Army and their experience typified what took place on May 19. Their objective was the Stockade Redan, one of two fortifications guarding the point where the Graveyard Road entered the Vicksburg perimeter. The attackers did not know it, but just before 2 P.M., Pemberton had learned of Sherman's buildup along this sector and ordered Colonel Cockrell to move up from reserve. Four of Cockrell's Missouri regiments had just entered the trenches when the assault came. A regular sergeant depicted the scene:

> Our brave boys moved over the hill at the double quick through a most deadly cross fire of grape, canister shot and shell . . . Our comrades were now falling around us at every step, some killed instantly, others having an arm or a leg shot off, and wounds of all descriptions. As we were crossing

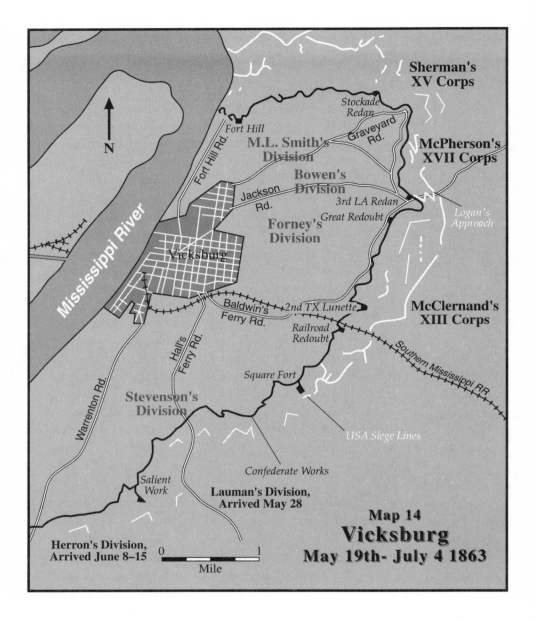

Map 14
Vicksburg
May 19th- July 4 1863

a deep ravine we received a most terrible cross fire, the balls coming like a dense hail storm.[16]

The battalion's commander fell mortally wounded. Color Sergeant James Brown died with a shot through his head. Another regular seized the flag and he, too, went down. Five standard-bearers fell dead or wounded.

Fifty-five bullets holed their flag. The survivors advanced to within twenty-five to fifty yards of the Stockade Redan and could go no further. As they took shelter behind stumps and fallen trees they watched Captain Charles Ewing carry the colors to the exterior slope of the redan and plant it in the ground. A bullet chipped the staff and removed part of one of Ewing's fingers. Ten men had joined Ewing in his gallant dash. They lay huddled in the redan's ditch as fire from their own batteries and from friendly infantry passed overhead. Charles Smart saw

> a Confederate musket held in a vertical position behind the redan. Resting my musket on the fence at full cock and pointed at the Confederate gun, I picked up a piece of a limb of a tree . . . and threw it at the musket, striking it fair and square. As it did so, the man holding the musket raised up in full sight, when I pressed the trigger of my Springfield. The Confederate threw up both hands, falling backwards.[17]

The men trapped in the ditch remained there until nightfall, when they retired to rejoin their battalion. The regular battalion lost 43 percent of its men during the attack. Calling its performance "unequaled in the Army," Sherman authorized it to stitch the honor "First at Vicksburg" onto its colors.[18]

The assault failed everywhere. A Confederate gunner looked out and saw a battlefield "blue with the Yankee dead and wounded."[19] Afterwards, it was easy to see that it had been a hastily arranged, poorly supervised affair. Apparently Generals McPherson and McClernand had decided that their corps had done enough during the campaign and left it up to Sherman to carry the day. Sherman's corps suffered three-quarters of the Federal losses. By Civil War standards, these losses had not been heavy: 157 killed, 777 wounded, and 8 missing. Confederate battle losses totaled perhaps 200.[20]

During the assault of the nineteenth, the defenders cheered every time they repelled a Union charge. A Vicksburg citizen observed that the repulse of Grant's charges "began the moral reconstruction of our army. Men who had been gloomy, depressed, and distrustful now cheerfully and bravely looked the future in the face."[21]

HAVING TRIED TO RUSH the city and failed, Grant set to preparing a more methodical approach. For the navy, meanwhile, it was payback time. The elimination of the heavy Confederate batteries at Haynes' and Snyder's bluffs opened the Yazoo River. Admiral Porter ordered a task force to steam up river and attack Yazoo City. It was here that Isaac Brown had completed the *Arkansas*. Rumor had it that additional rebel ironclads were in varying states of completion. Porter wanted them destroyed.

The rumors were true. Under Brown's energetic leadership, Yazoo City had become, by Southern standards, a significant naval yard. Workers at its five saw and planing mills and at the machine, carpenter, and blacksmith shops had labored to complete an *Arkansas*-style ram named the *Republic*. She was already sheathed with railroad iron and men were hard at work attaching a ram. A second gunboat had been completed except for her armor, while the most formidable of all, a giant boat, 310 feet long and designed to carry armor four and one-half inches thick, was on the stocks. However, once Haynes' Bluff fell, Yazoo City lay defenseless. When the Federal ships approached, Brown ordered the yard and its vessels burned to avoid capture. U.S. Navy landing teams destroyed everything Brown had overlooked, including boilers intended for the Confederate fleet at Mobile. Later raids cleared the Yazoo River tributaries. For the navy it was another success, overshadowed at the time because of what was taking place at Vicksburg itself, but one that helped ensure the security of Grant's lifeline on the Mississippi.

At Vicksburg, reconnaissance on May 20 and 21 confirmed what the failed assault of May 19 indicated. Vicksburg would be a tough nut to crack. While riding on an inspection tour on May 21, Grant also received a reminder regarding his soldiers' condition. As the westerners closed in upon the Hill City, their minds were more focused on their stomachs than on the glittering strategic ramifications of their recent campaign. Since severing communications with Grand Gulf, the army had been subsisting on lean rations. One officer recalls offering an enlisted man $5 for a piece of corn bread and being refused. As Grant passed by, a soldier saw him, reflected upon his empty belly, and said "Hardtack." Other soldiers overheard him, looked up to recognize Grant, and took up the call. Soon scores of soldiers were chanting "Hardtack! Hardtack!" as loudly as they could. Besides being a comment on their current hunger, the chant also symbolized western irreverence, even for their commanding general.

Grant reined in, explained to the men that very soon indeed a road to the landing on the Yazoo River would be complete, steamboats would arrive, and then the army would again have access to the North's bounty. The men laughed and cheered and ate heartily that night when supply wagons delivered the promised provender. Probably Grant was still smiling when years later he recalled in his memoirs that "the bread and coffee were highly appreciated."[22]

Grant faced the choice of beginning siege operations or ordering a second attempt to storm the city. He had to weigh several factors. First, by definition, a siege was a time-consuming affair. While his army lay pinned in the siege lines, Confederate forces elsewhere would have free play. In particular, Grant worried that Johnston could receive substantial reinforcements. Vicksburg might then become a trap for his army as it lay caught between Pemberton and Johnston. By nature Grant was more prone to consider what he could do to his foe than the reverse. If he could quickly capture Vicksburg, he could drive east and secure the entire state of Mississippi and points beyond.[23] In Grant's mind the prospects of immediate success outweighed the unknown hazards of besieging Vicksburg. Later he would claim that his army virtually demanded an assault, that he knew that they would not settle down to the tedium of a siege unless it was shown to be absolutely necessary. This bit of misleading hogwash reveals how guilty Grant felt over what was about to occur.

During the day of May 21, Federal artillery methodically bombarded enemy fortifications. Fourteen guns, including two mighty thirty-pounder Parrotts which oxen and mules had managed to drag along in the army's wake, pulverized the Third Louisiana Redan and scored a direct hit on a particularly annoying twenty-pounder Parrott. The Confederates discovered that Vicksburg's loess soil was easy to dig but provided an inadequate shield. At the Second Texas Lunette, Union artillery knocked out two three-inch rifled guns. Elsewhere, some clever rebel tactics contributed to the impression that the Union artillery was dominating the field. Brigadier General Louis Hébert noticed that McPherson's artillery was concentrating its fire against his artillery. Anxious about one of his prized Parrott rifles, he instructed its crew to wait until a round struck near the gun's embrasure and then pull the piece back to fool the Federals into thinking they had knocked it out. Dutifully, when the counterbattery barrage opened and a near miss covered the embrasure with dust, the gunners obeyed Hébert's instructions. The Federal gunners, believing they had dismounted the Parrott, shifted fire to a new target.[24]

Grant's assault order for May 22 called for a simultaneous attack by all three corps. To ensure that everyone began at the same time, he summoned his generals to his headquarters, where they synchronized their timepieces with his own. This marked the first time in military history that this had ever been done. Grant's instructions emphasized the use of skirmishers and artillery to suppress the defenders' fire. He had also observed the difficulty experienced on May 19 when regimental lines tried to advance through the belt of Confederate obstructions. Accordingly, he ordered his infantry to charge in narrow "columns of platoons," a much more compact, handy formation.[25] He hoped that these assault columns could rapidly weave their way between obstacles and overrun the rebel fortifications before they suffered crippling casualties.

Grant's subordinates did several things to enhance the likelihood of success. General Sherman judged that lack of artillery preparation and the long approach march had contributed to his May 19 failure at the Stockade Redan. Accordingly, he set his men to building artillery emplacements and to improving the roads so that the assault troops could advance quickly. On McPherson's front, gunners dragged their pieces to within three hundred yards of the Confederate earthworks so they could provide close-range fire support. General McClernand, recalling General Hovey's fine use of artillery at both Port Gibson and Champion Hill, ordered him to supervise a twenty-two-gun massed battery which he hoped would eliminate much of the opposition. Finally, all along the line Union sharpshooters had had two days to acquire a feel for the ground. They located good firing positions from where they could support the assault columns by shooting down the Confederate artillerists.

According to plan, at dawn on May 22 the Federal bombardment began. The veteran gunners enjoyed surprising success. Hovey's massed battery knocked out three cannon in the Railroad Redoubt, one in the Second Texas Lunette, and a powerful twenty-four-pounder siege gun positioned to enfilade any assault against the lunette. Blue-clad marksmen also enjoyed partial success at suppressing the rebel artillery. Some gray-clad gunners reported that they could not "put their hands up to prick the cartridge after a cannon is loaded without getting it pierced with a ball."[26]

During the bombardment, the assault troops assembled. As a waiting soldier wrote, the task before them appeared ominous:

> A long line of high, rugged, irregular bluffs, clearly cut against the sky, crowned with cannon which peered ominously from embrasures to the right and left as far as the eye could see. Lines of heavy rifle-pits, surmounted with head logs, ran along the bluffs, connecting fort with fort . . . The approaches to this position were frightful.[27]

Colonel Boomer, who had fought so skillfully at Champion Hill, believed that an assault was a terrible mistake. Unwilling to assume the responsibility for issuing attack orders, he took his regimental officers to division headquarters so they could personally receive orders from someone else. Major Gustavus Lightfoot, an officer who had anglicized his name from Leichtfuss, began handing out his cigars to fellow officers of the Twelfth Missouri. Someone said, "Major, don't give them all away. You may need them yourself before we get back to camp." Lightfoot replied, "Oh, take them; I will have no further use for cigars; this is my last smoke!"[28]

From medieval times through the Napoleonic Wars, a handful of volunteers, known as the forlorn hope, would lead assaults against fortresses. Their task was to remove obstacles, fill in ditches, and raise scaling ladders. So it was on May 22. Staff officers circulated among Sherman's troops and said that those who volunteered for the forlorn hope would receive a sixty-day furlough. The veterans knew that they had to survive first and few liked the odds. While under fire they would have to carry planks to span the ditches and drag ladders with ropes so men could then climb the enemy parapet. As grim as the prospects were, volunteers dutifully filled the ranks of the forlorn hope. Generals Grant and Sherman took station behind some large trees and trained their field glasses on the storming parties as they moved up to the start line. Then they, like scores of other Federal officers, glanced at their timepieces. It was 10 A.M.

The waiting Confederates had endured some four hours of unceasing artillery and sharpshooter fire. When the firing stopped, an appalling silence filled the field. "Suddenly," recalled a Confederate general, "there seemed to spring almost from the bowels of the earth, dense masses of Federal troops, in numerous columns of attack, and with loud cheers and huzzahs, they rushed forward, at the run."[29] Led by six sword-wielding officers, a 150-man forlorn hope carried their planks and ladders along the Graveyard Road.[30] As they climbed out of a deep depression the Confederates sighted them. Because this was such an obvious point to attack, there were numerous defenders here. A double rank leveled their muskets and fired a volley. It destroyed the head of the column and sent the rear ranks searching for cover. Of the men in the forlorn hope, 19 were killed and 34 wounded. The terrible fire erased all thoughts of performing plank-laying and ladder-positioning duties. A handful of men led by Private Howell Trogden advanced with single-minded determination to reach the ditch in front of the Stockade Redan. Trogden had received a new flag from his brigade commander with instructions to place it on the enemy's ramparts. The private had answered he "would do so or die." He struggled through the ditch and redeemed his pledge by planting the flag on the redan's exterior slope.[31] But it was a futile gesture when the assault regiments trailing the forlorn hope quickly went to ground upon confronting enemy fire.

Elsewhere on Sherman's front, Brigadier General James Tuttle's division depended on a success on the Graveyard Road, the adjacent sector, in order to have a realistic chance. When that failed to occur, Tuttle's men remained at their start line. The officer commanding Sherman's other division, Major General Frederick Steele, failed to have his assault brigades in position by the designated hour and his division likewise did not charge. Thus, during the morning, Sherman's corps-sized assault was reduced to the abortive advance of the forlorn hope and a supporting brigade.

On McPherson's front, the troops charged with greater determination. Logan's division, with Logan himself stripping to shirtsleeves to help crew an artillery piece, advanced with characteristic élan. In spite of all preparations, as soon as the blue tide surged forward it encountered overwhelming resistance. An officer in the Eleventh Illinois explained that "the front companies advanced to the crest of the hill and were fairly swept off their feet by the most deadly, concentrated cross and enfilading fire, we were ever under."[32] Taking frightful losses, the soldiers kept advancing. Hostile fire killed Colonel James Dollins of the Eighty-first Illinois, an officer who had been with Grant since Belmont, and hit two-thirds of the regiment's officers.

Leading the way were the color-bearers. As always, they were the special target of numerous foemen. Whenever one went down, someone else seized the colors and carried on. The charging color-bearers braved all fire to arrive at the ditches just in front of the earthworks only to confront a steep, earthen wall. Men who were to bring the scaling ladders found the task impossible, so all the color-bearers could do was plant their flags on the forward slopes of the parapets. They served as beacons, attracting brave men to the storm. The act of planting their flags just beneath the enemy's muskets and cannons required tremendous courage. Only a handful of color-bearers survived such exertion. Among many, six men died while planting the Irish-style, emerald green flag of the Seventh Missouri on the parapet of the Great Redoubt.

General John Stevenson's men, who had shone at Champion Hill, continued to build on their fine fighting record. They surged forward to the ditches below the Confederate parapet, but in the absence of ladders they could accomplish nothing. The defenders above remained sheltered behind the parapets. They raised their rifles over their heads and fired blindly into the huddled assault troops. An Ohio officer recalled that when he and his men sat with their backs pressed hard against the Confederate side of the ditch the bullets just missed. McPherson later reported that his men simply could not climb the steep exterior face of the Confederate fortifications. His men had passed through withering fire to confront an impassable obstacle.

The fiercest morning assault occurred on McClernand's front, where General Lawler's brigade attacked the Railroad Redoubt. This fortification guarded the place where the railroad emerged from a deep cut to enter the Vicksburg perimeter. It was a particularly steep-sided earthwork with a deep ditch to protect the front and a line of rifle pits in the rear. Lawler's brigade charged with the same impetuosity it had exhibited at the Big Black. To an Alabama soldier inside the redoubt it appeared as if a long line of indigo had sprung up from the bowels of the earth. Shaking off losses, Lawler's brigade ran toward the fort. Gallant Lieutenant Colonel Cornelius Dunlap of the Twenty-first Iowa, although still lame from a wound suffered at Port Gibson, went forward to join his men's charge.

The color-bearer of the Twenty-second Iowa planted his staff on the redoubt's exterior slope. Two intrepid sergeants, Joseph Griffith and Nicholas Messenger, led a dozen men scrambling up the steep slope and through a gun embrasure. A brief and fierce hand-to-hand struggle took place and the Iowa soldiers drove the defenders from the redoubt. They maintained a toehold inside the fort while most of the regiment huddled in the ditch outside. Supporting units tried to clear adjacent rifle pits. The brave color-bearer of the Seventy-seventh Illinois managed to carry his flag to the ditch fronting the redoubt and plant it alongside the flag of the Twenty-second Iowa. A standoff ensued, with both attackers and defenders afraid to show themselves. Realizing his charge had run out of impetus, Lawler dispatched a courier to McClernand to ask for reinforcements. Meanwhile, Colonel William Stone of the Twenty-second Iowa and lame Colonel Dunlap of the Twenty-first Iowa met at the top of the earthwork to survey the situation and try to reignite the advance. They immediately paid for their recklessness when a bullet in the skull killed Dunlap and Stone went down with a serious arm wound. Although stunned by a wound himself, inside the redoubt the nineteen-year-old Sergeant Griffith recovered to capture a Confederate lieutenant and twelve men. He escorted them back to Union lines. The next day Grant would promote Griffith to lieutenant and shortly thereafter appoint him to West Point, where he became known as "Grant's cadet."

While Lawler's men were suffering the heaviest losses experienced by any brigade, a few hundred yards to the north Benton's brigade assaulted the Second Texas Lunette. As the bluecoats charged, some men shouted "Vicksburg or hell!" The Texans mounted their firing steps and began shooting the assault formations to tatters. A twelve-pounder ravaged their ranks with canister. Some fifty Indiana men reached the six-foot-deep ditch in front of the lunette. They confronted a steep climb and here, as elsewhere, the men carrying scaling ladders had been unable to wade through the intense fire to keep up. The color-bearer of the Eighteenth Indiana planted his flag on the exterior slope and the men took shelter in the ditch. Captain P. H. White, along with some of his gunners of the Chicago Mercantile Battery and infantrymen of the Twenty-third Wisconsin, dragged a six-pounder artillery piece up to the lunette's embrasure and fired canister into the fortification. It killed or wounded the Arkansas artillerists who were about to fire their own cannon. The Texans tried to block the opening with a cotton bale. The attackers set it on fire and White's gun opened fire anew. Exhibiting incredible tenacity, both sides held firm and continued the fight on opposite sides of the earthworks.

Seeing the futility in uselessly dashing themselves against the Second Texas Lunette, Benton's other three regiments probed for a softer spot south of the fort. Color-bearer Thomas Higgens of the Ninety-ninth Illinois set the pace by running for a low-lying set of rifle pits. Higgens emerged from the wreckage of his regiment's battle line to carry his banner forward. Numerous defenders fired at him at point-blank range only to see him "stumbling over the bodies of his fallen comrades" and still advancing. Higgens survived because of his foe's surpassing admiration for his courage. "Don't shoot at that brave man again," went up the cry. "Come on Yank, Come on."[33] Higgens climbed to the top of the work to see numerous bayonets pointed at his chest. A Texas captain shouted for his men to give way and let him down. The Texans pulled Higgens over the breastworks and wrung his hands in congratulations for his bravery. The captain ruefully admitted that he had never known his men to shoot at a man so close and miss him. Thirty-five years later Higgens received the Congressional Medal of Honor.

Lawler's limited penetration of the Railroad Redoubt was the greatest success anywhere along the lines. His three regiments lost 54 killed, 285 wounded, and 29 missing.[34] Elsewhere, within the first thirty minutes, the assault stalled completely. As one defender wrote, "No troops in the world could stand such a fire."[35] The most intrepid units had planted their flags on the exterior slopes of three Confederate forts: at the Stockade Redan; the Great Redoubt; and the Second Texas Lunette. In the ditch fronting the Second Texas Lunette a considerable Federal force clung to the ground, unable to go either forward or back. About thirty Union troops had penetrated the Railroad Redoubt, but there was no way to reinforce this partial success. Moreover, the tactical Confederate commander at this redoubt, General Lee, had recognized a weakness in the design of the line and had ordered a second set of fortifications built eighty to one hundred yards behind the redoubt. In this second line the Confederates still held firm.

The fighting should have ended at this juncture. However, a hard-spurring courier delivered to Grant a handwritten message from McClernand claiming a considerable success: "We have part possession of two forts, and the Stars and Stripes are floating over them."[36] The Illinois politician wanted McPherson and Sherman to press their attacks to support his pending breakthrough. Sherman happened to be present when Grant received this missive. Grant flatly told his friend, "I don't believe a word of it." His utterance shocked Sherman. Sherman could be a pedantic, form-loving, bureaucratic regular army officer of the old school when he so chose. Unfortunately for the volunteers of the Army of the Tennessee, he did so choose at this moment. Sherman argued that McClernand's note "was official and must be credited."[37]

Reluctantly Grant acceded. Around 2:15 P.M. soldiers belonging to Sherman's and McPherson's corps charged again. Any surprise, and whatever benefit the Union artillery barrage had provided for the first assault, were absent this time. The result was simple slaughter. A Mississippi soldier described how the Federals "continued to advance steadily in face of the leaden storm, brave forms dropping at every step, the line gradually thinning, wavering and quivering like the folds of a stricken monster, but pressing ever forward till it struck our works, when like a wave striking the beach, it went to pieces and disappeared."[38]

Brigadier General Thomas Ransom was one of the Union army's comers, an officer whom McPherson and Grant had identified as worthy of higher command. Ransom charged with four regimental columns. A soldier in the Thirty-eighth Mississippi described what took place:

> They came on as rapidly as the fallen timber would permit, and in perfect order. We waited in silence until the first line had advanced within easy rifle range, when a murderous fire was opened from the breastworks. We had a few pieces of artillery which ploughed their ranks with destructive

effect. Still they never faltered, but came bravely on . . . As they came down the hill one could seem them plunging headlong to the front, and as they rushed up the slope to our works they invariably fell backwards, as the death shot greet them. And yet the survivors never wavered. Some of them fell within a few yards of our works. If any of the first line escaped, I did not see them. They came into the very jaws of death and died.[39]

The colonel of the Eleventh Illinois shouted, "Now men, charge with a will!" and fell mortally wounded. Another colonel went down. Ransom and his staff took charge and urged the men forward. At one point Ransom grabbed the flag of the Ninety-fifth Illinois and shouted "Forward men! We must and will go into that fort!" Inspired, color-bearers belonging to all four of Ransom's assault columns planted their staffs near the Confederate works. The Fourteenth Wisconsin managed to advance to within just a few yards of the Confederate rifle pits before faltering. "No matter where we might appear," remembered a survivor, "the rebels from their works, would have a cross fire upon us."

Ransom's men clung to their position for ten minutes or so, but the general saw that it was useless. He climbed onto a stump and spoke to his soldiers:

Men of the Second Brigade! We cannot maintain this position. You must retire to the cover of that ravine, one regiment at a time, and in order. Move slowly. The first man who runs or goes beyond the ravine shall be shot on the spot. I will stand here and see how you do it.

The regiments dutifully withdrew in succession, each providing covering fire for the next. So fierce was the Confederate fire that a captain *crawled* toward Ransom to beg him to take shelter. "Silence," snarled Ransom in reply.[40] A total of 364 of Ransom's men were casualties from this charge, the second highest brigade total for the day.

While the Fifteenth and Seventeenth Corps renewed their assaults, on McClernand's front very little changed. McClernand had committed most of his available force during the morning, and so there were few men left to renew the effort in the afternoon. Accordingly, near the Railroad Redoubt, the aggressive General Lee asked for volunteers to recapture the post. The Iowa defenders repulsed the first attempt. Lee committed two companies of tough Texans belonging to Waul's Texas Legion. Lieutenant Colonel Pettus, the governor's brother, who had originally commanded the redoubt's defense, received permission to lead this thirty-five-man counterattack. Pettus grabbed a musket and told the Texans that he would show them that an Alabamian would go as far as any of them. Three other Alabama soldiers joined the assault column. Lee, who saw much of this war in both the East and West, later wrote that he never witnessed a more gallant deed than this counterattack by Waul's Legion.[41] So exhausted were the bluecoats that only three attackers received wounds during the ensuing bayonet charge that recaptured the redoubt. The attackers captured the surviving Federals along with a lieutenant colonel and a set of colors. After the successful charge, Pettus commented that he was an Alabamian by birth but that henceforth "he was going to be a Texan by adoption."[42]

The recapture of the Railroad Redoubt eliminated the only penetration of the Confederate line. At the Second Texas Lunette Federal soldiers continued to pour lethal fire through the embrasures. "The middle of the fort," reported Texas Colonel Ashbel Smith, was swept within 2 feet of the ground." Smith shouted, "Volunteers to clear that embrasure!" and four soldiers responded.[43] The valiant four moved to within five paces of the Union soldiers and fired. They cleared the embrasure but one Texan fell dead and another received a mortal wound to the head. More Texans approached the embrasure and hurled lit shells into the ditch below. Here and elsewhere, the bravest Federal soldiers, the ones who had charged the furthest, lay trapped beneath the parapets. Pinned down, they continued to take losses until merciful darkness came and permitted them to struggle back to their start line. Among those who did not return was the cigar-smoking Major Lightfoot and Colonel Boomer. They, along with thirty-five other officers, died during the assault.

Grant's corps commanders had badly let down both him and the army. McPherson was the least blameworthy, but even he failed to mount a truly coordinated assault. Individual brigades valiantly stormed forward, but had to endure terrible enfilade fire because adjacent brigades failed to provide support. Sherman did not have all his assault troops in position by the 10 A.M. start time. He then committed only the "forlorn hope" and two trailing regiments during the morning, and in the afternoon so botched affairs that his three serious attacks went forward at three different times. This permitted the defenders to recover after each charge and shift reserves to meet the next onslaught. Well might some of Sherman's men see in the failed assault of May 22 a repetition of the Chickasaw Bayou. They attributed it to Sherman's "hot headed" ambition—an erroneous explanation; Sherman was simply a poor tactician and throughout the war displayed an inability to fathom assault tactics—and complained that the folks back home did not appreciate what a poor commander he was.[44] McClernand had spread his three divisions along such an extended front that he lacked reserves to exploit possible successes. Then he grossly exaggerated his initial success, thereby prompting Grant to launch the costly afternoon charge.

Likewise, many other senior officers had been culpably negligent. The whole point of the May 22 assault was to profit from experience. Leaders had to realize that flinging troops against well-sited earthworks was bound to fail. The men who reached the ditches found that they literally could not clamber up the outside walls of the key rebel forts. The scaling ladders built for this purpose were not available when the men needed them. Because they could not climb the face of the Confederate forts, the bravest Federal soldiers died in the ditches outside of the forts' walls. Throughout history, the effort to breach an enemy fortification has required a sophisticated mix of concentrated firepower, careful preparation, and valor. The soldiers of the Army of the Tennessee provided the last ingredient. Their superior officers demonstrated their lack of professional training by failing to provide the balance of the mix.

Their failure embittered some of the men who had conducted the attack. Lieutenant Henry Kircher of the Twelfth Missouri wrote in his diary: "It made tears come to my eyes, as I was urging my brave company forward and seeing them drop one after the other likes flies from the first frost. Oh! may I never witness such a sight again . . . may this be the last fit of insanity that our commanders ever have."[45] A captain in the Fourth Iowa called it "a useless expenditure of life . . . but it has satisfied our generals that the enemy's works cannot be taken by storm."[46]

Grant's army had displayed prodigies of valor. Indicative of this were the awards of the Congressional Medal of Honor over the ensuing years. Ninety-eight men, including seventy-eight in the forlorn hope, received the medal. During the May 22 assault the army suffered 3,199 casualties, perhaps half of whom were hit as a result of the renewed effort prompted by McClernand's false claim of success.[47] McClernand's perfidy infuriated Colonel Rawlins. At headquarters that evening he ordered the record book opened and an officer to "charge a thousand lives to the ———— McClernand."[48]

Across the lines, about thirteen thousand Confederates had been actively engaged. After May 22, a Tennessee soldier expressed the widely held conviction that "we can hold our ground" until relieved.[49] Although outnumbered three to one, the defenders had inflicted losses at a ratio of six to one, having suffered only about five hundred losses themselves. Their success was a tribute to Lockett's engineering skills. Neither Grant nor any other Civil War general yet appreciated that the doomed May 19 and 22 assaults marked an epochal shift in the nature of warfare. Soldiers manning well-sited earthworks could hold off two, three, five, and occasionally ten times their numbers. For the next three-quarters of a century—until the advent of German blitzkrieg tactics at the beginning of World War II—the defense held an overwhelming advantage.

As bad as May 22 was from the Federal viewpoint—postwar tabulation would rank it as the fourth costliest Union assault of the war, superseded only by Fredericksburg, Cold Harbor, and the Petersburg Crater—Grant's stubborn refusal to acknowledge defeat greatly increased suffering. Following the army's return to its start line, hundreds of wounded remained in the shot-torn no-man's-land between the lines. Their cries were clearly audible to appalled soldiers, both blue and gray. Two days later a surgeon reported "patients still being brought in from field . . . some dreadfully fly blown when brought in."[50] Grant would not request a truce to care for his wounded. He was far from aloof and well understood soldier experience. When it rained, he told his headquarters guard to take the fly off his tent to erect a shelter. He was a man who berated anyone he saw abusing a dumb animal, someone who did not eat meat until it had been cooked past any hint of pinkness, a general who abhorred riding over a field of recent heavy combat. Yet for three days he tolerated the cries of his tormented soldiers, their blood loss–induced thirst made worse by their seventy-two-hour exposure to the Mississippi sun, in apparent belief that a request for a truce would admit weakness. His was abominable conduct, to be repeated once more in Virginia the next year.

Finally, on the morning of May 25, Pemberton, "in the name of humanity," proposed a cessation of hostilities to remove the few survivors and bury the bloated dead. During the ensuing truce soldiers met between the lines and conversed. Given an opportunity to have a long talk with their opponents, more than a few soldiers discovered that if the settlement of the war was left to the enlisted men of both sides, they would all soon go home.

Although Grant never explained his callous disregard for his wounded, he was quick to shift blame when reporting to higher authority. With characteristic understatement when explaining a setback, he reported to Halleck that "our troops were not repulsed from any point, but simply failed to enter the works of the enemy." He estimated his losses at fifteen hundred and explained that much of this loss stemmed from the fact that McClernand had "misled" him and was "entirely unfit" for corps command.[51] In a letter to his father Grant concluded, "I did my best, however, and looking back can see no blunder committed."[52] Only when writing in the glow of victory years later did Grant acknowledge that the May 22 assault was a mistake.[53]

If blame shifting and a certain lack of candor when reporting failure were part of Grant's makeup, a tenacious refusal to become discouraged was equally present. His fixed determination took root throughout the army. As one veteran recounted, "Every soldier knew that, as we had intrenched before Vicksburg, we would stay there until the city had surrendered."[54] After May 22, Grant concluded that the Confederate citadel could only be taken by a siege, but that it must inevitably fall unless the enemy sent a large relieving force. Naked valor had failed. The spade would be the key to capturing Vicksburg.

11

Siege

[W]e have the rebels in a pretty tight place. they are completely surrounded and if we cant make them surrender any other way we can starve them out.

    —James K. Newton, Fourteenth Wisconsin, May 24, 1863
    (Stephen E. Ambrose, ed., "A Wisconsin Boy at Vicksburg:
    The Letters of James K. Newton," *Journal of Mississippi
    History* 23, no. 1)

THROUGHOUT MILITARY HISTORY, whenever an army found its foe behind fortifications, it also found its options for capturing the citadel reduced to a limited handful: traitors within could open the gates; the fortress could be stormed; assault troops could dig their way up to the enemy lines; the walls could be breached; they could be undermined; or the garrison could be starved. Although Pemberton had some concern about treachery—a warehouse fire that consumed some provisions was thought to be the work of a Union sympathizer, though it probably was not—there were neither gates nor secret passages to permit the possibility of betrayal. The assaults of May 19 and 22 had proven to everyone's satisfaction that Lockett's fortifications could not be overrun. Beginning the day after the failed second assault, the Army of the Tennessee simultaneously employed all remaining siege methods.

If it became a matter of who wielded a shovel best, the advantage lay with Grant's people. Indicative of the material disparity between North and South is the quantity of entrenching tools available. Major Lockett had access to five hundred shovels and picks when he needed to repair quickly the works preceding the first assault. On the morning of May 23, the soldiers in two of Sherman's brigades alone drew double this number from the corps quartermaster. All along the Federal line soldiers dug furiously. Before they were done they would burrow through twelve miles of Mississippi dirt. Their trenches served two purposes: a defensive function to keep the rebels shut inside of their perimeter; and an offensive one to permit safe passage to the very front of the Confederate works. The special lexicon of a siege called such offensive trenches saps, ditches dug outwardly from the attacker's siege line toward the enemy's line. At the head of the saps, soldiers placed a shield—usually a large, wicker basket–like mesh filled with dirt—called a sap roller.

To locate saps properly required a good appreciation for terrain. Otherwise, the men doing the digging would be too vulnerable to hostile fire. Traditionally, sieges have been the special province of the engineer. The challenge for the besiegers was that in the entire army there were only four engineer officers. Grant ordered that all West Point graduates—who had been obliged to study military engineering—be drafted to lend a hand with supervising siege operations. For most of the siege there were only five West Pointers besides Grant himself, and short, fat Bob Macfeeley, the army's chief commissary officer, begged off, explaining that there was nothing in engineering that he was good for unless he would do for a sap-roller!

Because of the lack of professional skill, there was naturally considerable trial and error. Grant's westerners applied the same improvisational energy to siege work that they had devoted to bridge building and acquired a real aptitude for the specialized work. Men who had never built a battery constructed eighty-nine of them. Soldiers unacquainted with the terms sap roller, gabion, and fascine fabricated them from pork barrels, grapevines, and cane, respectively. When the navy offered heavy artillery tubes, soldiers built gun carriages. Their skills amazed the handful of professional engineers.

Sapping operations focused on the roads leading to Vicksburg, since they naturally followed the lay of the land and offered the easiest access to the city. During the course of the siege, the westerners dug thirteen approaches toward the Confederate works. Day after day the sap heads inexorably advanced. Progress would have been far more difficult except for a decision made by General Pemberton. On May 21 Pemberton prohibited skirmish fire and artillery dueling. He demanded that his gunners strictly husband their ammunition so there would be an adequate supply whenever an infantry assault occurred. To help eke out supplies, rebel ordnance officers collected unexploded Parrott shells and had them sent to a Vicksburg foundry to be recapped so they could be fired from the defender's guns. Still, the Confederate inability to return fire allowed Grant's men to sap vigorously and to construct breaching batteries at near point-blank range from the Confederate works. During the siege, Federal engineers attributed the silence of the enemy artillery to a lack of ammunition. Yet the Union army would capture forty thousand rounds of artillery ammunition inside Vicksburg. As Grant's chief engineers commented, "A small portion of this, judiciously used, would have rendered our approach much slower."[1]

In contrast, Pemberton did base the prohibition on skirmish fire on true shortage. Whereas there was ample small arms ammunition, there was a serious lack of percussion caps. These caps exploded upon being struck by a musket's hammer and ignited the powder in the cartridge. Vicksburg's depots had more than 1 million cartridges without caps. Given that the lieutenant general had long anticipated a siege, that caps were not in short supply throughout the Confederacy, and that they were not bulky items to store, this lack is inexplicable. As early as May 20 Pemberton became aware of the critical cap shortage. He asked Johnston to send couriers to hand carry caps to the fortress.

During the ensuing weeks, intrepid men, and a handful of women, tried every means to smuggle caps into the city. They employed watertight boxes attached to the bottom of a skiff or concealed themselves and their precious cargo in hollowed-out logs. They floated past Porter's naval patrols to deliver as many as eighteen thousand caps during a single trip. An ex-slave carried dispatches from the Trans-Mississippi along with several well-corked canteens packed with caps. He would cross above Vicksburg, and then drift with a log down to the city. Others wrapped bandoliers filled with caps around their bodies and used local guides to infiltrate the siege lines. Soldiers in the Forty-fifth Illinois allowed one glib, ten-year-old boy to pass through their lines and enter the city to visit an ill relative. A few nights later, a picket heard strange sounds from a marshy section of the line. Stealthily the pickets surrounded the place and bagged a handful of adult couriers laden with percussion caps. At their head was their guide, the same ten-year-old boy.

Whereas Union rifle fire along the picket line seldom ceased—the noise of constant sharpshooter fire reminded one soldier of the sounds of carpenters shingling a house—the defenders, constrained by the shortage of caps, could do little but endure. Some of the more inventive practiced deception.

One day Federal pickets fired for over an hour at a very active rebel who kept hopping up and down from behind a line of sandbags while taunting constantly, "Try again, will you, Mr. Yankee?" Finally the defender tired of his game. He stood on the parapet in full view to show the marksmen that they had been "cheaply sold." They had been shooting at a stuffed suit of old clothes mounted on a pole.[2]

The besiegers took advantage of the lack of return fire to bombard savagely both the Confederate fortifications and the city itself. Initially, the Federals lacked proper siege artillery, having only one battery of six thirty-pounder Parrotts. Whereas the well-stocked eastern armies could summon a prodigious amount of siege artillery, there was none available in the West. Accordingly, the army improvised. Men took logs of the hardest wood, bored them out to fit six- or twelve-pounder shells, wrapped the tube with reinforcing iron bands, and blasted away with these "trench mortars." Since their field guns did not have the hitting power of a siege gun, they compensated by positioning them at point-blank range. Some gunners dismantled a pair of twelve-pounders, carried them through the approach trenches, and reassembled them in a trench one hundred yards from the Great Redoubt. Some Illinois gunners had a daily detail to carry a James rifle right up to the skirmish line.

Over time, gunners positioned heavy artillery captured from the Confederates and turned them against their former owners. Eventually, Union artillerists sited some 220 guns to fire at Vicksburg. Indicative of the bombardment's intensity is the total of 13,498 rounds fired by four batteries in Logan's division.[3] During one bombardment the chief of artillery in Jacob Lauman's division offered a prize of a field glass to the gunner who made the best shot. The artilleryman who fired a ball that toppled a Confederate flagstaff protruding from a Confederate fort received the prize. Such deadly fire caused a relentless trickle of casualties that slowly deflated the garrison's morale. As early as May 28 a Louisiana captain wrote in his journal, "Denton Struck on the Knee by a piece of Shell—Who else today?"[4]

ON MAY 27, the Confederate waterfront batteries provided a morale-boosting demonstration for soldier and civilian alike. General Sherman had asked for naval assistance against the batteries securing Pemberton's far left flank. Admiral Porter sent the ironclad *Cincinnati*, commanded by his nephew Lieutenant Commander George Bache, to bombard the batteries. The result again proved that a duel between ironclads and well-sited, land-based

heavy artillery was an unequal contest. The *Cincinnati* had barely taken position when a shot penetrated her iron shield and sliced down through her
hull. Water poured in while shot after shot plunged through hay, wood, and
iron into her bowels. The *Cincinnati* was close to sinking when one blow
killed her helmsman. Bache took the wheel and turned her into the bank.
He managed to land the wounded, but the vessel proved unmanageable in
the current. It drifted helplessly while the pummeling continued. After
twenty-five sailors had been killed or wounded and another fifteen drowned,
the *Cincinnati* sank on a shoal. Quartermaster Frank Bois, who had coolly
served as signal officer throughout the engagement, braved all fire to nail
her flag to the stump of the forestaff so she could go down with her colors
still flying. Bois, along with five other sailors, earned the Congressional
Medal of Honor this day.

So perished another of the original Pook Turtles. But Porter believed
his ships were made for fighting and fighting involved risks. He dismissed
the *Cincinnati*'s loss as a hazard of war, remarking that he was willing to lose
all his boats if it could do any good.[5]

During the maneuvers preceding Champion Hill, Pemberton had
feared a direct, waterborne strike against Vicksburg. To resist this threat, he
had left two divisions in the city. The sinking of the *Cincinnati* showed how
unnecessary this reduction in his field army had been.

When he had first visited Vicksburg back in 1862, Admiral Porter had
complained that his "gunboats can't crawl up those hills." Once the siege
started, Porter did the next best thing by taking heavy guns out of his vessels, hauling them ashore, and emplacing them in batteries to pummel the
Confederate works. During the course of the siege, thirteen shore-based
naval guns fired 4,500 rounds. In addition, sailors built three scows to carry
a nine-inch, a ten-inch, and a one-hundred-pounder rifle and position them
within a mile of the city. From these stationary platforms they controlled
Vicksburg's waterfront. From the river, giant mortars rained 7,000 shells on
the city.

Most garrison soldiers did not particularly mind the mortar fire. Mortars
were wildly inaccurate and their shells lacked effective fragmentation. Soldiers joked that they "were good for digging cisterns."[6] For the civilians it
was something else. The indiscriminate mortar fire was a terror weapon
pure and simple. One round exploded in the city hospital, killing eight and
wounding fourteen. One surgeon, buried and maimed beneath the rubble,
managed to tie off his severed arteries to avoid bleeding to death until his
colleagues managed to amputate his leg.

THE TWENTY-SIXTH LOUISIANA DURING THE SIEGE

May 19 (first Federal assault)

Private   Killed—gunshot wound in the head

Captain   Killed—gunshot wound in the left breast

Colonel   Wounded—fracture of the right leg

Lieutenant   Killed—gunshot wound in the left breast

Private   Wounded

Private   Wounded severely—gunshot wound through the jaws

Private   Wounded severely—gunshot wound in the head

Corporal   Wounded severely—gunshot wound in the shoulder

Private   Wounded

Private   Wounded

May 20

Lieutenant   Gunshot wound in the arm

Private   Killed

May 21

Private   Wounded severely—in the head

Private   Wounded in the arm

Sergeant   Wounded severely—in the back

Private   Contusion of the foot

May 22 (second Federal assault)

Lieutenant   Killed

Private   Killed

Private   Killed

Private   Killed

Private   Killed

Private   Gunshot wound in the scalp

Private   Killed

Private   Wounded severely—gunshot wound in the right breast

Private   Wound on chin and left shoulder

May 23

Private   Wounded in left arm, and arm amputated

Private   Wounded severely in the heel by the shell

Sergeant   Gunshot wound in the arm

May 24

Private   Head shot off

May 26

Private   Gunshot wound in the thigh

May 29

Private   Killed

Private   Leg fractured by a shell and amputated

Private   Leg broken by a shot-torn tree limb

Private   Wounded in the wrist by a shell

Private   Wounded in the scalp by a shell

Corporal   Arm broken by a shell

Private   Wounded in the foot by a shell

June 5

Private   Wounded mortally in the head by a shell

Private   Gunshot wound in left shoulder of which he died

Lieutenant   Gunshot wound in the back

Private   Serious gunshot wound in the head

Private   Wounded

June 7

Private   Wounded

Private   Wounded

June 9

Private Mortally wounded
Private Wounded
Private Wounded

June 10

Private Seriously wounded
Private Wounded

June 11

Private Killed
Private Wounded

June 12

Private Killed
Private Wounded
Private Killed

June 13

Private Killed
Private Wounded

June 14

Private Killed

June 16

Private Disabled by concussion
Private Killed

June 18

Private Killed
Sergeant Wounded

June 19

Private Mortally wounded

June 21

Major Killed

June 23

Private Wounded

June 24

Private Wounded
Private Wounded
Private Wounded

June 25 (Logan's mine)

Sergeant Wounded
Private Mortally wounded
Private Wounded
Private Wounded
Private Wounded
Private Seriously wounded and died
of the wound
Lieutenant Wounded
Private Severely wounded
Private Mortally wounded

June 26

Private Severely wounded

June 27

Lieutenant Wounded and foot
amputated
Private Wounded

June 28

Private Mortally wounded
Private Wounded
Private Wounded
Private Wounded
Private Head shot off
Private Wounded

July

Private Died in the service
Private Died in the service

A frontline soldier visiting the hospitals encountered the intermittent naval shell fire raining down on the city. Although he recognized that these shells were less lethal than his daily life in the trenches, it still unnerved him. But the ladies' perfect "indifference" to the shelling and their routine heroism as they went about their duties with "no hesitation, no shrinking, no bravado," rallied him.[7] Gunner Hugh Moss reported that "the women here, altho exposed to much danger, encourage the soldiers in their daily duty" and contributed by cooking and tending to the wounded.[8] The behavior of Vicksburg's citizens was much the same as that of urban dwellers who endured aerial bombardment during World War II. Horrific as it might be, it did not break their spirits.

Confederate soldiers labored nightly to repair the damage done by Union artillery. They were amazingly successful. The artillery fire could and did destroy the raised parapets. But the only effect was to force the defenders to dig deeper. Experience proved that deeply dug trenches were invulnerable to the era's direct-fire, line-of-sight artillery. A rebel wrote, "A ditch is almost perfect protection against a shell fired across it," providing one sits on the side closest to the artillery.[9] The shell's forward momentum sent most of its fragments away from the infantry pressed against the trench's forward wall. Enfilade fire was far more dangerous. One large Federal artillery piece located a mere three hundred yards from the Confederate works partially enfiladed some trench line near the Jackson Road. A defender remembered how he and his comrades built a traverse during the night and "every morning the enemy would begin to batter down this protection, knocking off the top, foot by foot, and often in the evening the shells would be rushing down the ditch very close above our heads."[10] Nonetheless, by June 12 one of Pemberton's aides observed that rather than being closer to reduction, the city's defenses were stronger than ever.

IN CONTRAST TO PEMBERTON, the Union army commander appeared regularly along his siege lines to inspect progress. "Often during those long hot days of June," wrote a veteran, "I saw General Grant . . . worming his quiet way through and along our trenches . . . None but those who personally knew him would have recognized in that stubby form, with its dusty blue blouse, the great General."[11] Among those who did not recognize Grant was a woman living behind Union lines. From her porch she saw Grant ride up smoking his ubiquitous cigar. "Soldier, give me a cigar." "With pleasure, madam," replied Grant. Rawlins, who probably disapproved of women smoking anyway, spoiled the scene: "Madam, allow me to make you acquainted with General Grant." The poor woman turned pale, dropped her cigar, and fled.[12]

Grant also could show up unexpectedly at the soldiers' campfires. Men in the Eighth Illinois recalled that he spoke familiarly with them and with less reserve than a junior officer. Over time, Grant grew restless with the tedious pace of operations. Having worked exceptionally hard all spring, and with no active operations under way, he decided to relax. On June 6 he evaded the vigilant Rawlins and went on a tour of inspection by boat up the Yazoo River. The trip's nominal purpose was to investigate Joe Johnston's movements around Yazoo City. However, Grant's correspondence indicates that he did not find the threat particularly alarming, and because he did not, he apparently began to drink while aboard the steamer. Ulysses S. Grant was a man who held his liquor badly. Aboard the steamboat, reporter Sylvanus Cadwallader claims, he saw him become "stupid in speech and staggering in gait." In fact, whether Cadwallader was actually present or merely gathered his story from camp gossip is unclear. Charles Dana, who was certainly present, discreetly wrote that Grant was "ill and went to bed"—so sick that when news came that the rebels had made it unsafe to continue, Grant was unable to decide what to do. Grant also had the ability to binge and awake the following morning unaffected. He appeared at breakfast "fresh as a rose," although he was unaware of where the steamer had docked.[13]

The episode has remained clouded in controversy. Had news of a drinking binge, real or otherwise, reached either authorities in Washington or the public, the consequences could have been devastating for Grant's career. Instead, a remarkable conspiracy of silence involving Cadwallader, Dana, and a handful of men on Grant's staff successfully concealed the incident. Most importantly, John Rawlins, with iron hand, continued to limit his chief's access to alcohol, and Grant himself never allowed his weakness for drink to put his army's welfare at risk.

Alcohol was a general's prerogative. Grant's soldiers seldom had access to it. Although they rotated between service at the front and relaxation at shaded camps in the rear—a break the beleaguered defenders did not experience; they were so thin on the ground that they remained in the ditches around the clock—many shared their leader's restlessness. The army had young men and out of boredom they sometimes did foolish things. One day some soldiers in the Forty-second Ohio dared one another to run up to the rebel works. A fellow ran forward, grabbed a clod of dirt from top of the parapet, and returned with his trophy. Not to be outdone, a comrade tried the same stunt and was shot. More typically, those with excess energy went sharpshooting.

All Union soldiers on picket duty had orders to fire a designated number of rounds each day. They made life miserable for the defenders who, because of the acute shortage of percussion caps, seldom returned the fire. The rebel works featured firing ports that in theory gave the defender near perfect protection. Instead, they proved lethal. Situated along the skyline, the firing ports made easy targets. Sharpshooters fired against the ports until they had the correct range. They then lashed their rifles securely in position to hold the range. When a shadow darkened the port, the sharpshooters squeezed their triggers. A defender observed, "To use one of these ports meant instant death."[14] Because they were often shooting uphill against silhouetted targets, Federal sharpshooters inflicted an unprecedented number of wounds to the head. In addition, remembered a defender, sharpshooters erected fortifications to protect themselves "at strategic points which commanded a view of our entire lines, and woe to the man or beast that dared to come in range . . . It simply meant death."[15] Among many for whom it meant death was Bowen's respected subordinate, General Green, hit by a sharpshooter behind his right ear.

Sharpshooting seemed to have a strange appeal for many. "The curious thing about it," noted James Wilson, "was that no one seemed to feel any more compunction in taking a good shot at an unknown enemy than at a deer."[16] One day the chaplain of the 116th Illinois deliberately fired five shots, "each time at a head which was incautiously exposed."[17] Such zeal was not limited to Union men. Whenever General Stephen Lee's secretary found he had little office work to perform, he went to the trenches to sharpshoot. Many rebel marksmen worked in teams, with one man raising a handkerchief or piece of cloth to make a Federal soldier raise his head and thus offer a target for his comrade. A soldier described gazing at the Confederate works: "Not a foe was in sight. But somehow from among those innocent looking sand-bags before us the smoke would curl and the minee would come, and woe to the unprotected head. Our casualties were not many, but they were continuous."[18]

Sharpshooting also attracted the stone-cold killers. Private Lorain Ruggles of the Twentieth Ohio received permission to operate as an independent sharpshooter. He would return to camp to boast of his exploits. One day he appeared quite dejected, saying, "Colonel, I aint had no kind of luck to-day. I haint killed a feller."[19] Grant rewarded Ruggles with a fine Henry rifle for his marksmanship. Among the best marksmen in Grant's army was Lieutenant Colonel William Strong. Although sharpshooting was not the expected duty for a colonel, Strong became annoyed at the ability of a rebel cannon crew to slow down his men's progress as they sapped their way forward. Taking a rifle in hand and two soldiers to load additional weapons for him, Strong found a vantage point from which he silenced the enemy cannon. He then saw a rebel sharpshooter crawling into position. Strong carefully placed his hat in an exposed position nearby and waited for his man. Crack went the rebel's rifle and a hole appeared in the colonel's hat. But the rebel had briefly shown himself to make his shot and Strong's return fire killed him. Strong continued his sharpshooting over the ensuing days and had the satisfaction of learning from an enemy deserter that he had hit seventeen Confederates, causing the defenders to call this portion of their lines the "Dead Hole."

Occasionally killing became quite personal. A sharpshooter in the Fourteenth Wisconsin picked up a ball that had struck just at his feet and remarked that the "rebs" would regret throwing their shot around in such a fashion. That afternoon he returned to the rifle pits and loaded his gun with the same ball. He patiently waited until he had a good chance and then fired. He saw his target drop and described himself content "that he had at least wounded a 'Reb' with one of their own bullets."[20]

BY MID-JUNE, the Federal approach trenches were very close to the Confederate works. In places a mere eight-foot-thick bank separated the lines. Just to let the rebels know "that we were there," wrote an Illinois soldier, "we tossed over a few clods and chunks, and thinking that they might be hungry, we tossed over a bone with a very little meat on it."[21] The aroused Confederates responded by tossing back a brickbat. Along the lines, both sides also rediscovered the use of hand grenades. The idea of lobbing explosive by hand had been around for some time. In Europe during the 1700s entire elite infantry formations, styled grenadiers, had been formed for this purpose. At Vicksburg the attackers hurled Ketchum grenades, egg-shaped, one-pound iron shells filled with powder and with a primitive, spring-mounted percussion rod on the front and a feathered rudder at the opposite end for aerial stability. A Michigan gunner recollected how "some smarty suggested that an artillery officer" supervise this work, and, "as I was the first one there, I was the one ordered and I made the remark that it was a piece of damn foolishness."[22] He was threatened with arrest and replied that arrest was preferable to hand grenade service.

Lacking manufactured grenades, the defenders filled glass bottles with powder and balls and inserted fuses in the ends. Brigadier General Francis A. Shoup organized his artillerists into a "hand grenade and thunder barrel corps," the latter being gunpowder-filled barrels with short fuses that men sent rolling toward nearby sap heads. Major Lockett, who rather enjoyed such work, personally lit the fuse on one thunder barrel full of 125 pounds of powder and watched with satisfaction when it exploded to send "fragments of sap-rollers, gabions, and pieces of timber" into the air while hopefully burning and smothering the Yankee sappers.[23]

Not only did the rival lines' close proximity permit grenade tossing, it also allowed fraternization. Soldiers manning the rifle pits could overhear their opponents talking. One night a rebel voice called out to ask if there were any Missouri men in the Union lines. Receiving an affirmative answer, the voice asked, "Is Tom Jones there?"

"He is. Is that you Jim?"

It was. The brothers met and Jim handed Tom a roll of greenbacks to send to the folks at home.[24]

On another sector, after officers posted their pickets, they agreed not to exchange fire. The officers then shared a dram and cigars. At dawn the pickets withdrew and firing resumed. At one point a Confederate officer complained that the Yanks were placing their pickets practically on his parapets. The Union officer replied that that was what they had come to do. The rebel had to acknowledge his point, so they arranged a picket truce with the pickets virtually facing one another. If the officers were not so obliging, the men managed things themselves. Detailing someone to watch for prowling officers, they would sit together and pass the night in chat and banter. Often bands would serenade with Northern tunes answered by "Dixie" and "Bonnie Blue Flag."

While the rank and file alternated between striving to kill one another and sitting down to swap tales, Grant's senior general published a "Congratulatory Order" in a Memphis newspaper. General McClernand's article was characteristically boastful of his own accomplishments and critical of everyone else. It was provocative, but could have been overlooked except that its comments about General Sherman made that officer hopping mad. Sherman fired off a letter to Rawlins that complained vehemently of this "monstrous falsehood."[25] Back on May 22, when McClernand had lethally

misrepresented the progress of his assault, Grant had come close to relieving him. Mulling it over, he had decided that the cause would be better
served if he waited until after Vicksburg fell. This time, he seized upon the
article as a technical breach of War Department regulations and dismissed
the Illinois politician-general.

McClernand had done much to promote the Vicksburg campaign. His
inability to be in on the kill infuriated him. He tried to explain that the article was an honest error in that a staff officer had failed to secure prior permission from Grant before publishing. He failed to dissuade Grant. Mc-
Clernand tried complaining directly to Lincoln in a one-line telegram: "I
have been relieved for an omission of my adjutant. Hear me."[26] The president had no time to become involved in the quarrel. The affair puzzled the
Thirteenth Corps soldiers. Most genuinely liked McClernand and no one
knew anything about his replacement, Major General Edward Ord. For the
rank and file, McClernand's dismissal represented a mysterious loss of a
popular officer.

THE OPENING OF WATER COMMUNICATIONS northward had brought an
influx of military supplies and, over time, reinforcements to the besieging
army. It also brought hordes of civilians. Sanitary and Christian Commission
agents came with immense stores of provisions, clothing, and hospital supplies. Family members and patriotic citizens sent parcels loaded with the
comforts of home. The famed concert singers the Lombard Brothers came
from Chicago to entertain the troops with their renditions of patriotic and
sentimental songs. Politicians flocked around the campsites of their soldier-
constituents to dispense praise and hand out gifts from the grateful people
back home. It was far different for the besieged. Constant service in the
ditches while living on reduced rations was slowly wearing them out.

Confederate soldiers were too familiar with hunger. Even before Grant
had crossed the Mississippi, they often went hungry. The beef was so bad
many refused to eat it. Corn was eaten as fast as it was brought. Before becoming besieged, hungry men entertained one another with memories of
sumptuous meals eaten in the past, reciting the menu from biscuit and butter to turkey and ham, through to puddings, pies, and cake. Finally one soldier interjected, "Oh, hush, boys; a fellow might as well have no belly as
for all the good it does him here!"[27] It was worse once the siege began.

As early as May 26, soldiers noted that their rations were getting
scarce.[28] On June 10 a man received a meal ration of one-quarter pound of

bacon and one-third pound of cornmeal. Eight days later the cornmeal gave out and rice and peas substituted. Pemberton had accepted a siege knowing that his commissary had less than a month's worth of full meat and bread rations. By reducing the ration he certainly could eke out supplies for a good while longer. One way to supplement the food supply was to draw upon stored rice and peas. The commissary had stockpiled a prodigious amount of these foodstuffs, a supply judged to constitute more than 250 days' worth of rations.[29] But somebody had blundered. The amount of rice was not large, and rice made neither a popular nor nutritious ration for men accustomed to bread and meat. More importantly, no one could figure out how to make the pea ration edible. Cooks found that pea meal loaves, intended to replace bread made with flour, had the amazing characteristic of turning rock hard on the outside while remaining raw on the inside.

One night some Southern pickets asked the bluecoats what they had to eat. They replied, "Beef, good bread, molasses, coffee, etc." and they asked what the rebs had. "Some wag replied that we had 'hot biscuit, young lamb, butter, coffee, cake etc.' when a Yank yelled back, 'and pea meal.' Then we all roared."[30]

Many of the support troops in the rear, particularly those fortunate enough to be near the river, ate reasonably well. A Louisiana artillery officer attributed his good health to his consumption of sassafras tea and fresh fish caught nightly by his servants. Those with good connections fared even better. Lieutenant William Drennan took up quarters with a fellow commissary officer "who is really a clever old man. As long as anything is in the city, he will have some—and that too of the best kind. We have good beef, mutton sometimes, ham, flour, rice flour, rice, mollasses etc."[31] Sloppy Confederate staff work that had contributed to the disasters at Bakers Creek and the Big Black also punished the men in the trenches during the siege. Brigade and divisional adjutants failed to scrutinize provision returns. Consequently, rations were issued to thousands who were not on the reports, allowing the unscrupulous to stockpile and hoard. Although Pemberton issued orders requiring the name of every man for whom rations were drawn, somehow the issue was never satisfactorily resolved.

So Pemberton steadily reduced rations. A lieutenant in the Fourth Mississippi reported his daily ration to consist of a small wheat, pea, or rice biscuit, bread, and a square-inch piece of meat. This quarter-ration amounted to 14.5 ounces of food per day, a portion of which was the nearly indigestible pea meal. Wild parsley, boiled without meat or salt, yielded a very thin soup. As the bacon and beef gave out in late June, the army began slaughtering its mules. The army's artillery horses and mules had long since cropped the grass bare and were themselves starving. Mexican teamsters in Waul's Legion worked at drying and jerking the mule meat to render it into something akin to beef jerky. While the mules lasted, unseasoned mule and then rodents provided a meat ration.[32] General Stephen Lee's staff offered to procure for him something better. Lee said he would eat what his men ate. Everyone was eating manfully when the general excused himself. He returned and said, "Well gentlemen, you may have all my share; for while it tastes better than the beef we've had, yet the longer I chew it the larger it gets, and I just had to get rid of it."[33] By mid-June, with the rival trenches close enough so men could talk in a normal conversational tone, defenders began to josh with the bluecoats that Pemberton was to be superseded in a few days by General Starvation.

Whereas the federal troops had access to forest shade and cool springs—and where there were no springs they dug wells—the defenders had neither. Although the sun was debilitating—a Tennessee soldier observed that "the endurance of our men is taxed to the utter-most, they having to lie under a burning sun all day motionless"—the water was deadly.[34] Most of it came from the Mississippi. During the safety of night, men collected muddy, warm river water and hauled it in unclean barrels for the soldiers in the trenches. Inevitably, the poor food and bad water caused assorted gut maladies and sent many to the hospital. By mid-June the defenders were so few that six-foot intervals separated one rifleman from the next. Artillerists who had lost their cannons, including the gunners of the Botetourt Artillery, received brand new Enfields fresh from their case and served as infantry. A Confederate soldier related how the defenders inexorably wore down: "Day by day some friend or comrade died, and 'who next?' was on every man's lips and in every man's heart, only to be answered by the thud of a bullet or the crash of a shell. The mental strain became awful under such conditions."[35]

The strain intensified on June 25, when General Logan tried to storm the city.

THE JACKSON ROAD climbed a razorback ridge up to the Confederate-held heights and then continued into the city. The key fortification guarding the road was the Third Louisiana Redan. The former chief surveyor of Cincinnati, Captain Andrew Hickenlooper, had scouted the redan up close during the May 25 truce arranged to bury the dead. Digging an approach along the road would be difficult, but Hickenlooper judged it could be done. Under his supervision, at daybreak the next morning, a working party from Logan's division broke ground. Initially they made rapid progress. The soil dug easily and there was little resistance from the enemy line four hundred yards away. The sappers' startling advance awakened the gunners of the Appeal Arkansas Artillery, who manned a three-inch rifle inside the redan. On the twenty-eighth they opened fire against the approach, only to receive a smothering return bombardment. During this combat the notable Union artillerist, Captain De Golyer, received a mortal wound from a rebel sharpshooter.

By June 3 the eight-foot-wide, seven-foot-deep approach trench reached a commanding knoll 130 yards east of the redan which Hickenlooper had selected for the construction of a breaching battery. His workers spent two days building a formidable, eight-foot-thick earthwork named Battery Hickenlooper, and then continued digging toward the objective. At the direction of one of the army's most famed sharpshooters, Lieutenant Henry Foster, known as "Coonskin" for the raccoon fur cap he wore, some Indiana soldiers built a wooden tower near the battery. From atop Coonskin's tower, Foster and fellow sharpshooters dominated the sharpshooter combat and thus allowed the diggers to work in relative safety. By June 16 they were within 25 yards of the redan's exterior slope. They dug two lines of rifle pits which branched off from the approach trench. Any defender who tried to shoot at the workers was silhouetted against the skyline and presented a prime target for the riflemen in the pits below. Five days later the sappers were just outside the redan, at which point the Louisiana defenders hurled a barrage of grenades and artillery shells that made further work impossible.

Hickenlooper called for volunteers to tunnel underneath the redan. Thirty-six strong, experienced, former coal miners worked in shifts around the clock to dig a forty-five-foot-long tunnel. The miners could plainly hear the jar of the rebels' picks when they began digging a countermine, but undaunted, the Union men carried on. For the defenders, the experience was unnerving: "So long as they were working we felt pretty safe, but it was rather uncanny . . . not knowing at what moment they might fire their mines."[36] It reduced to a question of "who is going to be the smarter and blow up the other first."[37] The Confederate countermine failed to locate Hickenlooper's mine. The western miners dug three galleries stemming off the main tunnel, filled them with 2,200 pounds of gunpowder, laid parallel strands of navy safety fuse to ensure ignition should one fuse fail, and on June 25 announced all was ready.

Grant spent the morning coordinating efforts to capitalize on the mine's explosion. He arranged a series of diversions to occupy Confederate attention on other sectors and prepared an artillery bombardment to interdict the movement of enemy reserves. Coonskin Foster and one hundred picked sharpshooters manned the rifle pits just outside the redan. General McPherson selected Mortimer Leggett's brigade to spearhead the assault as soon as the mine exploded. The assault column, led by the Forty-fifth Illinois, packed four abreast in the approach trench. Exhibiting the kind of frontline leadership the army expected, Captain Hickenlooper and eleven other soldiers served as a forlorn hope, crouching a mere twenty-five yards in front of the redan. Grant joined McPherson and Logan at Battery Hickenlooper and waited for the blast.

It was a hot airless day. Dust lay thick. The Illinois soldiers in the forlorn hope noticed the birds flying overhead while they waited. It became terribly quiet. At 3:30 P.M. the mine detonated: "The huge fort, guns, caissons, and Rebel troops inside the curtain were lifted up high into the air; a glimmer, and then a gleam of light—a flash—a trembling of the ground beneath our feet, and great clouds of dense black smoke puffed up from the crater of the mine, like jets from a geyser!"[38] Before the smoke cleared, cheering Illinois soldiers entered the crater.

The Confederates had anticipated the blast. Major Lockett had a traverse dug across the open rear of the V-shaped redan. Brigadier General Louis Hébert had withdrawn his Louisiana men to this trench before the mine exploded. The only people in the redan were six brave Mississippi soldiers who were continuing work on the countermine. They were never seen again.

The forlorn hope cleared the rubble from the approach trench and pressed on to the crater. It appeared to them like an immense ditch. As they entered, they saw, to their horror, Lockett's intact traverse. A solid row of rifles held high in hand appeared above the crater rim. The rebels began shooting down the assault party. Lieutenant Colonel Melancthon Smith of the Forty-fifth, sword in hand, fell mortally wounded. Color-bearer Sergeant Henry Taylor ran through the fire to plant his banner at the base of the traverse, but returned when he saw no one was following. They had either fallen to hostile fire or gone to ground. A soldier wrote, "I yet remember the peculiar sensation that came over me as I lay hugging that bank of earth, first looking at the mass struggling for egress and then the splendid display of arms just over the works. I wondered where the ball or balls would hit me and whether it would be instantly over with me when they rose to discharge those guns."[39]

About eighty to one hundred men could simultaneously occupy the crater. Colonel Jasper Maltby divided them into teams, positioning one to provide fire support with rifle and grenade, while the other tried to crawl up the traverse. When this failed, Maltby had one team fire while the other loaded. They worked their weapons so fast that the rifles overheated and fouled within thirty minutes. Maltby substituted two fresh companies to continue the fight. Meanwhile, Hickenlooper and his pioneers brought prefabricated, loopholed head logs to protect the riflemen. It proved a mistake. At point-blank range, Arkansas gunners fired their three-inch rifles into the logs. Deadly wooden splinters scattered through the crater. Among the wounded was Colonel Maltby. The Louisiana defenders followed this up with a barrage of grenades and lit shells. The Union gunners back in Battery Hickenlooper could clearly hear groans and shrieks coming from the crater. General Logan exclaimed, "My God! They are killing my bravest men in that hole."[40]

The soldiers to the rear could see the trenches overlooking the crater filling with rebels as the assault stalled. Among them was the Sixth Missouri, part of Pemberton's mobile reserve. When Colonel Cockrell had heard the detonation and seen the rising smoke plume, he had ordered the regiment forward. Well-liked, brave Colonel Eugene Erwin, a grandson of Henry Clay, had risen from his sickbed that morning to rejoin his regiment. He led the Sixth to the crater, climbed the parapet, raised his sword, and shouted, "Foward, boys, don't let the Louisianans go further than you do."[41] Two bullets immediately lacerated his body and he fell dead. Seeing him die, the Missouri soldiers decided that they had best remain behind the parapet and try to evict the Yankees with bullet, grenade, and shell.

The westerners tried to maintain the fight as best they could. A private managed to return some twenty Confederate grenades before he fell with a mortal wound when one exploded in his hand. Fearing that the rebels were about to sortie, Captain Stewart Tresilian ran back to the battery, seized three ten-pounder shells, cut the fuses to five seconds, returned to the crater, and tossed them over the rim into the Confederate works. The ensuing explosions dampened rebel ardor. From his nearby vantage point, Grant said that if Leggett's brigade could hold the crater through the night, the balance of McPherson's corps could clear a series of nearby rifle pits and thus pave for the way for a decisive breakthrough along the Jackson Road. He also ordered Hickenlooper to dig artillery emplacements at the crater so guns could breach the traverse.

So hour after hour, Federal regiments shuttled into the crater and kept fighting. The Union soldiers named the crater the "Death Hole." "When men, in order to hold their position, are compelled to stop short fused shells and return them to the enemy, they show a courage sublime," recalled an Illinois soldier.[42] During a typical thirty-minute span, the Union men returned six lit shells, knowing full well that to mishandle them meant sure death. Logan's chief of artillery, Major Charles Stolbrand, remained there most of the night. He was an inspiration, tearing the fuses from cartridge boxes that the rebels hurled into the pit, throwing live grenades back at the enemy, stomping on smoldering shell fuses. Bullets pierced his clothing, grazing his skin. Face, hands, and hair were powder-burnt. Federal soldiers fought for twenty-five and one-half hours inside the crater. When it became clear that a battery position could not be built at the crater and there was no chance for a breakthrough, Grant ordered the attack stopped.

The combat at the crater was the siege of Vicksburg in miniature. Officers and men on both sides exhibited ingenuity, tenacity, and surpassing bravery. After the failure, the siege's progress slowed. According to Charles Dana,

> Several things conspired to produce inactivity and a sort of listlessness among the various commands—the heat of the weather, the unexpected length of the siege, the endurance of the defense, the absence of any thorough organization of the engineer department, and, above all, the well-grounded general belief of our officers and men that the town must presently fall through starvation without any special effort or sacrifice.[43]

So oppressive was the heat that the staff surgeon, Doctor E. D. Kittoe, whose people had served in India, prescribed curries and red pepper for the messes that could obtain them. Maintaining the morale of a besieging army is not easy. Soldiers grow bored amid the tedium and danger. The Army of the Tennessee maintained high spirits, saying that "they are going to Vicksburg sure, if it takes all summer to go there."[44]

Back home, Northern people eagerly followed Grant's progress through the pages of their newspapers. Even the eastern press that so heavily focused on the Army of the Potomac gave Grant's campaign favorable attention. The June 6 edition of *Harper's Weekly* offered numerous illustrations of the campaign and published a portrait of Grant. The fact that it looked not

at all like the general was less important than the accompanying words calling him "the hero of the day." The following week *Harper's* featured the
Army of the Tennessee on its front page. Thereafter, the slow pace of siege
operations caused the eastern papers to lose interest. Moreover, Lee was on
the move north again and during the following month his maneuvers mes-
merized the East Coast.

Inside Vicksburg, the garrison hungered for information from the outside almost as much as they were starved for food. Every time a courier
infiltrated Grant's lines, dripping Mississippi mud and carrying precious
percussion caps, wild rumors spread: Lee was already on Arlington Heights
overlooking the Yankee capital; Price had captured Helena; Smith was at
Milliken's Bend. Such was the lack of outside contact, that even the best
informed did not know what to believe. Soldiers and civilians alike invested
all faith in Joe Johnston. Surely he would come to relieve them.

12

"Come Joe! Come Quickly!"

We thought we would jump off the cars, and start immediately for the relief of Vicksburg.

> —John S. Jackman, First Kentucky Brigade, June 3, 1863
> (William C. Davis, ed., *Diary of a Confederate Soldier:
> John S. Jackman of the Orphan Brigade*)

THE MORNING OF MAY 19 found General Joseph E. Johnston thirty-
seven miles northeast of Vicksburg. He presumed that Pemberton had
evacuated the city until he received a message announcing that the lieutenant general had withdrawn into Vicksburg's perimeter. Undoubtedly disgusted, there was nothing Johnston could do except reply, "Hold out."[1]
Johnston immediately ordered the commander of the Port Hudson garrison,
Major General Frank Gardner, to evacuate that post and join him at Jackson.[2] Unlike Pemberton, Gardner did not confront a fast-approaching Federal army when he received this order. Like Pemberton, he chose to ignore
it and actually had the audacity to request reinforcements. Exasperated,
Johnston sent a second order telling Gardner not to allow himself to become
trapped in Port Hudson. This message was too late. On May 23, Banks's
army invested Port Hudson and thereby prevented Gardner's force of more
than seven thousand men from participating in active field operations.

Johnston's opening strategy to prevent Grant from capturing Vicksburg
had been to employ cavalry to raid the rail lines in Grant's rear. The presence of Confederate cavalry in northern Alabama and in Tennessee, plus
the activities of numerous guerrilla bands—some of them under the lead-

ership of partisan chiefs every bit as skilled as the more famous rebels back east—tied down 40 percent of Grant's men. But when he took the balance to capture Haynes' and Snyder's Bluffs and base his supply line on the Mississippi River, he foiled Johnston's strategy. Johnston ruefully remarked to a visiting British tourist that Grant had displayed more energy than he had expected. His second plan was to concede the river but preserve Confederate manpower. Pemberton's and Gardner's stubbornness thwarted this scheme. Back in January, Johnston had predicted the likelihood that Grant could invest Vicksburg and that the Confederates outside would be too few to relieve the city, but that "it would be necessary to try."[3] So he adopted a third strategy by retiring his small army to Canton, on the railroad north of Jackson, where he hoped to assemble a relieving army. Shortly thereafter he received the first of what would become a long chain of letters from Pemberton urging the speedy relief of Vicksburg.

If Confederate troops were to join Johnston, they would have to travel along a delapidated rail system. After 1861, the entire Confederacy failed to produce a single new rail. Motive power declined as essential equipment—boiler flues, chilled tires, and the like—could not be maintained or replaced. Wrecks became far more common. Skilled laborers served in the ranks instead of remaining on their jobs. The best way to husband scarce resources was found to be to reduce train speed. The transfer of Stevenson's division from the Army of Tennessee to Vicksburg in December 1862 took a circuitous three weeks. By the spring of 1863, the run from Mobile to Meridian, the route by which eastern reinforcements would have to travel, took 50 percent longer than it had when war began. Yet in spite of all obstacles, if every resource was bent to the objective, it could be done.[4]

No man worried more deeply about this prospect than President Lincoln. His anxiety increased when it became apparent that Johnston was collecting forces from Tennessee. With Bragg weakened, it seemed apparent that Rosecrans should advance. On May 28 Lincoln telegraphed Rosecrans: "I am very anxious that you do your utmost, short of rashness, to keep Bragg from getting off to help Johnston against Grant."[5] To the president's enormous frustration, Rosecrans balked at any idea of a forward move. Although possessing a significant numerical superiority, he held the curious idea that he was better off advancing after Vicksburg had fallen than before.

On June 2, Lincoln communicated directly with Grant for the first time in 1863. In sharp contrast to the hectoring style he employed with the Army of the Potomac generals, his three-sentence message contained no advice or criticism. It merely inquired about Banks's whereabouts and intentions. For the rest of the siege, the president read the *Richmond Sentinel* and other Southern papers to follow Grant's progress. The problem of relying upon such sources was they exaggerated Confederate success while minimizing Union progress. Furthermore, in keeping with the press of the day, they tended to report the wildest rumor as fact. Thus Lincoln became alarmed to learn that Kirby Smith had crossed the Mississippi and entered the battle for the two fortresses east of the river; that during one failed assault Sherman had been wounded; that at Port Hudson, General Banks had an arm shot off. None of this was true. So Lincoln read, worried, and left it up to Grant to arrange matters satisfactorily.

On the same day that Lincoln wrote to Grant, General Robert E. Lee wrote his president a letter in which he, too, discussed developments in Mississippi. Through the end of May the news from Vicksburg had not particularly alarmed Lee. A South Carolina soldier noted on the first day of June that "Dr Jones of this brigade heard Genl Lee say yesterday that he apprehended no danger from that quarter [Vicksburg] whatever, that the Yankees were exactly where he would wish them."[6] Then Lee learned that Johnston had failed to impede Grant's march on Vicksburg and that Grant appeared to be concentrating his army on the Yazoo River while maintaining a line around Pemberton. With this news in mind, Lee informed Davis that he was "well aware of the difficulties pressing upon all parts of the country." As had been the case so often in the past, strategy seemed reduced to "a mere choice of difficulties." But Lee did not despair. Perhaps Grant's march to Haynes' Bluff meant that the Union army was about to board transports and abandon the campaign. If not, Lee hoped that Johnston could "demolish Grant" and that Kirby Smith could occupy Helena.[7] In any event, Lee intended to carry on with his invasion of the North, an invasion he felt certain would relieve pressure against the Confederate citadel on the Mississippi.

When the Confederate high command examined the strategic chessboard, it focused on operations west of the Mississippi. From its vantage point it seemed that there were large forces who were accomplishing nothing important. When General Kirby Smith assumed command of the Trans-Mississippi, both the secretary of war and the president had impressed upon him the importance of helping defend the lower Mississippi River. Yet once Smith crossed the river, he did little to comply. When Grant marched his army down the Louisiana shore opposite Vicksburg, he entered Smith's domain. But at this time Smith was beset by Banks's invasion of the Red River Valley. The Trans-Mississippi suffered from great shortages of war material. Banks's thrust represented a strike at the heart of what logistical base did exist and consequently Smith attended to it while ignoring Grant.

Smith took some pleasure in the belief that Banks's march west took him out of play for the pending campaign for the Mississippi. On the day of battle at Champion Hill, he predicted to a subordinate that "the decisive battle of the West must soon be fought near Vicksburg" and its outcome would greatly influence the fate of the Trans-Mississippi.[8] As a piece of acute strategic prognostication, this was much. But he had done little to influence the calculus for the decisive battle. At the end of the day, he was another parochial commander more concerned about defending his own base than addressing the greater strategic peril.

Once Banks retreated east to invest Port Hudson, Smith finally turned his attention to Vicksburg. Again he delivered an acute, if overdue, strategic analysis: the fate of the Mississippi River Valley and of the Trans-Mississippi Department depended upon the outcome of the struggle for Vicksburg. Every other objective should stand second to mobilizing strength for a strike at Grant's presumed line of communications on the river's Louisiana shore.[9] The man he turned to to execute this design was Major General Richard Taylor.

As the son of Zachary Taylor, Dick Taylor had fight in his blood. He had learned his trade while serving under Stonewall Jackson. However, he deeply doubted the wisdom of marching his small force to Vicksburg's aid. He had traveled along the route his army would have to follow and knew that a seven-mile-long, narrow peninsula jutted into the Mississippi opposite Vicksburg. Here his force would be on waterlogged ground dominated by the U.S. Navy in flank and rear. Instead, he wanted to threaten New Orleans to force Banks to give up his siege of Port Hudson, thereby freeing its garrison to join Johnston who, in turn, could then relieve Vicksburg. His scheme fell on deaf ears. Accordingly, with full conviction that the effort was futile, he marched toward Vicksburg. During his war service, Taylor accomplished great things with scanty forces through energy and intelligence. He did not exhibit these qualities during the Vicksburg campaign.

In the first week of June he arrived on the Mississippi's west bank with about three thousand men. He divided them to conduct simultaneous nocturnal assaults against Milliken's Bend, Young's Point, and Lake Providence. His effort proved little beyond the fact that in this war, black men serving in the Northern ranks would fight.

IN NOVEMBER 1862, Halleck had authorized Grant to employ refugee slaves as teamsters and laborers. Grant, in turn, appointed Chaplain John Eaton to supervise their camps. He told Eaton that they could relieve white soldiers of many support chores and thus put more rifles in the fighting ranks. The women could serve in camp kitchens and as hospital nurses. But Grant's vision went beyond this. He added that once the Negro as an independent laborer—for he was not yet a freedman—could "do these things well, it would be very easy to put a musket in his hand and make a soldier of him, and if he fought well, eventually to put the ballot in his hand and make him a citizen."[10] His army, as Lorenzo Thomas had found, had decidedly mixed feelings about all of this. The administration had heard rumors that many of Grant's officers did not welcome the idea of enlisting blacks. Such attitudes were intolerable to the government. Halleck informed Grant that he must use his "official and personal influence to remove prejudices on this subject." Halleck elaborated, "The character of the war has very much changed." There was no hope of reconciliation; the Union must either conquer or be conquered. Lincoln had decided that one way to conquer was to utilize blacks. As soldiers, it was the duty of both Halleck and Grant to "cheerfully and faithfully carry out that policy." Halleck concluded that whether it was a good or bad policy could "only be determined by a fair trial."[11] With this letter Halleck had commendably reinforced the American notion of civilian supremacy over the military. When the Confederates attacked Grant's depots at Young's Point and Milliken's Bend on June 7, the "trial" Halleck predicted was at hand.

The major fight took place at Milliken's Bend. Here, about 1,500 Texans attacked 1,061 bluecoats. The defenders had the advantage of a good defensive position composing several lines of thick hedgerows and ditches. But the black men serving in six Louisiana and Mississippi infantry regiments were new to war and poorly armed. The assault took them by surprise. Inexorably, the Texans pushed them back to the riverbank, where they sheltered behind a levee. Texans scaled the levee screaming "No quarter for the officers, kill the damned abolitionists, spare the niggers."[12] This, coupled with the sight of a black flag featuring a skull and crossbones, the traditional symbol of no quarter, struck terror into the hearts of many white officers, who fled for the boats. Most of the blacks remained, and they, along with soldiers of the Twenty-third Iowa—the regiment that had spearheaded the penetration of the Big Black defenses—engaged in an ugly brawl with bayonets and clubbed muskets. Slowly the Texans were gaining the upper hand when the U.S. Navy intervened.

At 3:15 A.M., an army officer hailed the *Choctaw,* which was stationed just offshore, to report the rebel attack. The *Choctaw* opened fire with her one-hundred-pounder rifle and nine-inch gun. Once the rebel infantry drove the defenders behind the levee it was impossible for the *Choctaw* to see targets over the high banks, but it was equally impossible for the rebels to brave the naval fire and close with the defending infantry. A stalemate ensued, during which time many of the Texans broke ranks to loot the Union camp. Sometime after 8:30 A.M. the local Confederate commander spotted the approach of another gunboat and ordered a withdrawal. The Texans lost 44 killed, 131 wounded, and 10 missing during this action while inflicting 652 casualties, including 266 missing. Indicative of the defender's bravery were the casualties suffered by the Ninth Louisiana (African Descent). It lost 43 killed, 106 wounded, and only 1 man missing, the highest single-day casualties sustained by any Union regiment during the campaign.[13]

Even among Union soldiers who retained strong prejudice, the idea that black bodies and not their own would be stopping bullets had appeal. When news of the battle spread among Grant's troops besieging Vicksburg, one Iowa captain wrote his wife, "Good of the darkies! I wish there were more of them in the army."[14] An Iowa sergeant agreed. He wrote in his diary, "Who says that the negro will not fight? I say he will fight! Arm the negroes and let them fight for their liberty!"[15] Charles Dana wrote that "the bravery of the blacks in the battle at Milliken's Bend completely revolutionized the sentiment of the army . . . I heard prominent officers who formerly in private had sneered at the idea of negroes fighting express themselves after that as heartily in favor of it."[16]

Indicative of Confederate attitudes about fighting against blacks were the comments of a woman who wrote in her diary: "It is hard to believe that Southern soldiers—and Texans at that—have been whipped by a mongrel crew of white and black Yankees. There must be some mistake."[17] Taylor, in his official report, wrote that "a very large number of the negroes were killed and wounded, and, unfortunately, some 50, with 2 of their white officers, captured."[18]

The other two prongs of Taylor's attack accomplished little. The commander of the attack against Young's Point called it off when he spotted two tinclad gunboats and a hospital boat patrolling offshore and three Illinois regiments marching out of camp to defend their lines. The strike force directed against Lake Providence never even completed their approach march before its commander decided the whole thing was impossible. Taylor considered his duty done, and ordered a general retreat.

Johnston would try once more to have the Confederates across the river intervene to save Vicksburg. Late in June he wrote to Kirby Smith, "Our only hope of saving Vicksburg now depends on the operations of your troops."[19] He proposed that Smith could somehow float reinforcements and drive cattle across the river into Vicksburg. When Smith inquired of General John Walker, the man on the spot, if this could be done, Walker counted noses—he had about 4,200 men—looked at the topography opposite Vicksburg—and judged the task "utterly impracticable."[20]

Meanwhile, General Theophilus Holmes, a Robert E. Lee discard from back east, commanded the only other force west of the river that could do something to help Vicksburg. Accurately informed that his Federal opponent had been weakened in order to reinforce Grant, Holmes asked Kirby Smith if he might capitalize by marching to retake Helena, Arkansas. Ignoring his own recommendations three weeks earlier to concentrate everything for the defense of the Mississippi, Smith approved the plan. In mid-June Holmes began his march on the Arkansas capital and thus effectively removed his army from any influence on the Vicksburg campaign.

On July 4, Holmes attacked Helena with 7,646 men.[21] These were men who might more profitably have been used against Grant at an earlier date. Alternatively, if they were to make a diversion in support of Pemberton, the attack had to occur much sooner. But poor communications—a dispatch from Richmond recommending the Helena diversion took twenty days to arrive on Kirby Smith's desk—thwarted any possible benefit Pemberton might have derived from an attack on Helena.

Before the battle began, Holmes had told his subordinates, "This is my fight. If I succeed, I want the glory; and if I fail, I am willing to bear the odium." In the event, a savage Confederate infantry assault carried a key Federal battery, but as the battle hung in the balance naval gunfire tipped the scales. Nearly a third of the attacking infantry were casualties. The assault accomplished nothing for the Confederacy. Confederate valor did demonstrate that gray-coated attackers could perish before defended breastworks at about the same six-to-one ratio that Grant's men endured during their May 22 assault.[22]

Had there been close cooperation and coordination of the Confederate forces on both sides of the Mississippi, there is every likelihood that Grant's march through Louisiana would have amounted to yet another failure. Louisiana's waterlogged terrain was little different from the Yazoo Delta region. In the delta small Confederate forces successfully thwarted several major Union thrusts by obstructing river channels and siting small fortifications at key points. An active Confederate force could have done the same along the western shore of the Mississippi River. Instead, during most of April, McClernand's corps—facing virtually no opposition—had built a sixty-three-mile-long road featuring numerous bridges, causeways, and long stretches of corduroy road. Because of Davis's mistaken notion to divide command responsibility at the river, during April the Trans-Mississippi generals had attended to threats directed at the heart of their own empires instead of paying attention to what was happening at Vicksburg.

If an April intervention in Louisiana required some Confederate foresight, the same cannot be said of what had taken place the following month. During early May Grant's campaign depended upon his Louisiana lifeline. While one Federal brigade defended the vital supply depots at Milliken's Bend and Young's Point, only two other brigades protected the road south. It lay vulnerable to a determined strike by even a relatively small force. But soldiers from the Trans-Mississippi did not attempt to intervene until Pemberton's army was already under siege. By then it was too late.

EAST OF THE RIVER, reinforcements rapidly swelled Johnston's force until it became a formidable army. On May 20 two brigades came from Chattanooga. Shortly thereafter, a brigade from the Port Hudson garrison, dispatched before General Gardner became besieged, and Loring's wandering division—minus its transport and artillery—joined Johnston. Although still suffering from near-crippling illness, President Davis was fully alive to the necessity to reinforce Johnston. On May 22 he telegraphed General Bragg: "The vital issue of holding the Missi. at Vicksburg is dependent on the success of Genl. Johnston in an attack on the investing force."[23] Davis asked Bragg to send any reinforcements he could spare. To his great credit, and as he had done throughout this war, Bragg immediately complied, sending John C. Breckinridge's infantry and W. H. Jackson's cavalry division. Richmond authorities also managed to pry loose from General Beauregard another brigade commanded by Brigadier General Nathan "Shanks" Evans, the officer whose whiskey-inspired leadership had helped greatly to win the First Battle of Manassas but whose fondness for alcohol had kept him from further promotion.

By June 3 Johnston had received all of the reinforcements he could expect. His army totaled nearly thirty-one thousand men with seventy-eight pieces of artillery. Johnston and Pemberton combined outnumbered Grant. The South had strained every nerve to provide this force and Johnston still deemed it inadequate. On June 5 he telegraphed the secretary of war that the disparity in numbers was so great "that the relief of Vicksburg is beginning to appear impossible to me."[24] At this moment of crisis Johnston and Davis fell to quarreling about how many men Johnston actually possessed. The Mississippi Valley was in grave peril and neither man could tolerate the least hint that it was their fault. Accordingly, Davis set out to prove that he was making every effort to save Vicksburg while Johnston labored to provide evidence why it could not be done.

The debate proved time-consuming and profitless. Regardless of numbers, Davis knew that Johnston had to act. Davis told Johnston, "We cannot hope for numerical equality and time will probably increase the disparity."[25] This, too, failed to move Johnston. Johnston had already told Davis that he was too late, that he lacked transport to move, and then disputed the number of reinforcements he had received. His conduct was all too familiar to Davis, yet to whom could he turn? His only underemployed senior leader was Beauregard, whom he detested. Nonetheless, he should have relieved Johnston and sent an aggressive major general to replace him. Instead, the overstressed and ill Confederate commander in chief sent Johnston increasingly anxious inquiries about his plans and then waited for him to act.

At his time of greatest opportunity, the first week in June, Johnston believed that his lack of supplies prevented him from operating for more than four days away from the railroad and that his lack of artillery and transport nearly forbid movement at all. In truth, the reinforcements from the East had brought neither artillery nor wagons. The local stock of horses and mules had been much reduced by previous requisitions. But an energetic commander could have achieved much. After all, Grant's march to Jackson had found sufficient draft animals and food, and the area east and north of Jackson was untouched. Pondering alternatives, he judged that if he were to march on Port Hudson to free Gardner, he would expose the state capital and cause the loss of Mississippi. He apparently never considered a thrust to the north. Grant had stripped men from his own logistical base area to support his siege. The Confederate railroads operated well enough for Johnston to move rapidly to northern Mississippi and attack Memphis. The weakened Union garrisons of western Tennessee might not have withstood the superior Confederate force. Confederate control of Memphis would have severed Grant's connections with his northern supply depots.

If he marched neither south nor north, all that remained was west toward Vicksburg. While hesitating to choose this strategy because he believed he lacked manpower, Johnston had to know that henceforth, however fast his army gained strength, it could not match the pace of a Federal buildup. Throughout the war Confederate field commanders habitually entered battle while outnumbered. An aggressive commander, a Lee or Bragg, would have welcomed the near parity that Johnston enjoyed in early June and would have attacked. But such was not Johnston's way. He focused on his army's deficiencies and overlooked compelling national need as well as strategic opportunity.

Joe Johnston had the soldier's touch. Whether in Mississippi in 1863 or the following year in northern Georgia, his mere presence prompted defeated and discouraged soldiers to regain confidence. Initially his soldiers believed he would lead them to Vicksburg's relief. "We are confident of success," wrote a Texas sergeant.[26] Over time, as the army failed to move, soldiers fretted and began to lose this confidence. Camp life became monotonous, to be endured against the backdrop of distant cannonading as Grant tightened his vice on the beleaguered city.

AS JEFFERSON DAVIS HAD PREDICTED, the North overmatched Johnston's buildup. Grant drew strength from his own Sixteenth Corps, which was guarding the railroads in western Tennessee. The Department of Missouri lent a fine fighting division commanded by Major General Francis Herron, a veteran of Prairie Grove, a first-rate officer and a consummate dandy in his patent leather boots and a clean white pocket handkerchief. Herron arrived on June 8 to be followed by Major General John Parke's Ninth Corps, which came from the Department of Ohio and arrived on June 14. Grant received about 27,000 reinforcements between the end of May and mid-June, raising his total strength to 77,000. He used them to complete his siege lines around Vicksburg and assigned 34,000 to his most trusted lieutenant, Sherman, with the mission to prevent Johnston from interfering with the siege. Grant respected Johnston's generalship and believed this formidable foe had between 30,000 and 40,000 men. In his mind Sherman's performance was key to the successful completion of the siege.

The Romans had perfected the art of siege warfare. They would encircle the objective with one line of works while building a second, outward-facing line to defend against relief attempts. Grant instructed Sherman to do the same. Sherman used his men to defend a line extending from Haynes' Bluff to the Vicksburg and Jackson railroad bridge over the Big Black River. In addition, Grant sent overland expeditions to raid areas from where Johnston drew supplies. To deprive Johnston's army of subsistence in case he chose to advance along the Southern Railroad, Union soldiers stripped the adjacent area of food, forage, and livestock. The navy contributed by conducting another successful raid up the Yazoo River. Besides burning military installations and capturing supplies, the navy either destroyed or caused the Confederates to burn eight irreplaceable steamboats. Planters in the Yazoo River Delta had loyally responded to Richmond's call to substitute grains for cotton and had produced towering stands of corn and wheat. The lack of steamboats made it impossible to move these grains to Johnston's army.

Rather than defend the Big Black, which in the summer drought was easily fordable, Sherman opted to defend the high ground behind the river where the roads to Vicksburg converged. On June 22 it appeared that Johnston would test these defenses. Grant received what he thought was reliable intelligence that during the next forty-eight hours Johnston would begin to march. Grant suspected that there would be simultaneous attacks by Pemberton and by the Confederate forces across the Mississippi. He telegraphed alert orders to all his commands and notified Porter about the threat. Summoning Sherman to his headquarters, he explained that if absolutely necessary he was even prepared to lift the siege in order to "whip" Johnston.[27]

The intelligence proved faulty. Still, it served as good practice and allowed Sherman to perfect his countermeasures. By June 27 Sherman had thoroughly explored the ground and had concluded, "If Johnston comes I think he will have a pretty hard time to reach Vicksburg."[28] Grant concurred. Later, when an excited courier arrived to report that Johnston was on his way with thirty thousand men, Grant replied, "No, we are the only fellows who want to get in there. The rebels who are now in want to get out, and those who are out want to stay out." Grant dismissed the rumor with the comment that if Old Joe gained Vicksburg it would give the Union "30,000 more prisoners than we now have."[29]

ON MAY 29, day twelve of the siege, Pemberton received a four-day-old message from Johnston. It promised a relief attempt as soon as Breckinridge's division arrived from Bragg. For Pemberton, this marked the high point of the siege. He had willingly allowed himself to be penned up inside of Vicksburg in the hopes that Johnston would come to his rescue and this communication indicated that his hopes would be fulfilled. Pemberton did not know that on the day he read this encouraging communication, Johnston was penning a very different message. It stated: "I am too weak to save Vicksburg. Can do no more than attempt to save you and your garrison. It will be impossible to extricate you unless you co-operate and we make mutually supporting movements. Communicate your plans and suggestions, if possible."[30] Carrying messages to Vicksburg was hazardous, uncertain business. The courier conveying this message required two weeks before delivering it to Pemberton on the night of June 13. With time slipping away as the garrison's food supply dwindled, Pemberton's next two communications described his difficult plight but failed to address Johnston's request to "communicate plans."

In Richmond, Secretary of War Seddon sensed pending disaster. In an effort to prod Johnston to try something, the secretary employed every artifice when composing his telegrams. Seddon tried flattery. He cajoled. He appealed to Johnston's patriotism. Finally, on June 16 he told Johnston that "Vicksburg must not be lost without a desperate struggle. At all events, you must hazard attack."[31] Johnston's response was to dispatch another courier to Pemberton carrying the same message he had written on May 29.

Three days later Pemberton sent another dispatch describing the garrison's enfeebled state—by now his men had been in the trenches for thirty-four days—and asking, "What aid am I to expect from you?"[32] Pemberton also gave the courier verbal instructions that finally answered Johnston's query about what route to use to relieve the city. Additional messages from Johnston dashed Pemberton's hopes. The best Pemberton could expect was help to extricate his army while conceding Vicksburg to his foe. Pemberton proposed that Johnston create a diversion north of the Vicksburg-Jackson railroad. Pemberton would then attempt a night breakout to the south through a sector he believed was the weakest link in Grant's lines.[33] Pemberton was right when he identified the weakest sector in the Union line. He did not know that his opponent had carefully balanced his own dispositions after weighing Federal strength and the influence of roads and rivers. Grant judged that if Pemberton indeed broke out toward Warrenton, he would enter a cul-de-sac formed by the Mississippi and Big Black rivers. Grant would then pursue, pin the Confederate army against these barriers, and destroy it.

Pemberton's attempted breakout hinged, of course, upon Johnston. On June 23 he received an encouraging communication from that general: "I will have the means of moving toward the enemy in a day or two, and will try to make a diversion in your favor."[34] This was the last message Pemberton received from Johnston. Johnston's announcement on July 3 that he had finally begun to move was intercepted by Grant's men. Pemberton did not read it until after Vicksburg fell.

As Johnston's quartermasters laboriously gathered the wagons, horses, and mules deemed necessary to support the advance, somehow no one could fabricate a mobile pontoon bridge. Johnston believed that such a bridge was indispensable because without it the army could not cross the Big Black River. This was a questionable assessment, given that Sherman judged it so shallow with so many crossing points that it was indefensible. The first pontoon bridge proved a failure and so laborers spent additional time constructing a second. At last, on June 28, Johnston ordered a move toward Vicksburg. But the entire effort unfolded as if there was ample time. Not until July 1 did the army really get under way. The weather was horribly hot. Soldiers fell by the roadside, stricken from sunstroke. On July 2, sergeants kicked awake the drowsy soldiers and by 3 A.M. they were heading for the Big Black. Six hours later they went into camp at Bolton Station, which was hardly a vigorous advance. The next day, "contrary to general expectations," no march orders were issued and the men spent the day resting in camp.[35]

What the men in the ranks did not know was that when the army's advance guard butted up against Sherman's imposing-appearing position behind the Big Black, their commanding general reverted to the engineer officer he once had been. Instead of pressing on, Johnston ordered an extensive reconnaissance of the Federal line. Had Johnston shown intelligent anticipation, had his heart truly been in this march, such scouting could have been performed weeks earlier. On July 3 elements of the army formed in hollow square to listen to Johnston explain his intentions. He announced that they would indeed attack the enemy and relieve Vicksburg. Yet the halt continued through July 4 and gave one private a chance to compare this former national holiday with his current position: "No one would imagine that this is the anniversary we used to celebrate with so much pleasure and noise; the importance of the contest we are now engaged in caused the importance of former success to pale into insignificance; for of what avail is the Declaration of 1776 to us if we are now to be enslaved by the minions of Lincoln."[36]

Meanwhile, from the west came an ominous sound of silence. The cannonading, which Johnston's men had heard for more than forty days, had stopped.

13

"A Hard Stroke for the Confederacy"

I doubt if the soldiers of Lee and of Jackson ever entered into a battle with a thought of defeat; I doubt if the soldiers of Pemberton ever entered into one with a hope of success.

—J. H. Jones, Thirty-eighth Mississippi, 1903 (J. H. Jones, "The Rank and File at Vicksburg," *Publications of the Mississippi Historical Society*)

At 3 P.M. ON JULY 1, Pemberton's army had endured a demonstration of what lay in store for them if their officers decided to defend to the last ditch. After the June 25 mine and assault against the Third Louisiana Redan, General McPherson ordered a new mine to be dug. The men of the Sixth Missouri who occupied the defenses overlooking the crater could hear Captain Hickenlooper's miners at work. Still, two Missouri soldiers stood two-hour shifts at a forward guard post, a position that everyone knew would be buried when another mine exploded. Even while the guards gazed toward the enemy trench, a mere six paces in front of their own works, an overseer and eight slaves were busy countermining in an effort to locate the Union mine. Suddenly firing from the Federal line died down, prompting a Missouri lieutenant to say, "I wouldn't be surprised if this whole hill is blown to hell in less than ten minutes."[1]

The explosion came shortly thereafter when eighteen hundred pounds of powder ignited and literally blew some of the defenders into the sky. All but one of the underground working party disappeared in a permanent tomb caused by the blast. The two unlucky guards at the forward post perished as well. The explosion caught Colonel Cockrell outside the redan. The blast blew his uniform jacket off and lifted him into the air. Shaken and badly bruised, Cockrell ran to his reserve, a regiment which he had once commanded, and screamed, "Forward my brave, old Second Missouri, and prepare to die!" As the Missourians advanced toward the breach they passed stretcher bearers carrying victims "whose faces and hands presented a charred, blackened and swollen appearance."[2] They formed up behind the crater to receive the expected assault. Here they stood exposed to a terrible bombardment for two hours. Improvised trench mortars lobbed shells that rarely failed to kill or maim one or two men. A Missouri rebel described how siege artillery pounded his position, the large shells literally bursting in the defenders' faces, "killing and disabling the men, and almost covering us with earth."[3] The survivors rose up, shook themselves off, and closed ranks. The bluecoats chose not to follow up the explosion with a charge. At nightfall, still fearing a Union attack, Lieutenant Colonel Pembroke Senteny of the Second Missouri reconnoitered the opposing line. A sharpshooter killed this highly respected officer with a shot to the head. During the bloody day of July 1, the Sixth Missouri lost eight killed and forty-eight wounded; the Second had its colonel and three men killed along with thirty-five wounded; the Fifth suffered similarly. In forty-eight hours, shelling from the three wooden trench mortars alone killed twenty-one and wounded seventy-two Confederates.[4]

The Federal mine and bombardment subtracted about 10 percent of the fast-dwindling Missouri brigade. That night Generals Bowen and Pemberton, the latter looking careworn and anxious, inspected the repair work behind the crater. They knew that Grant's army was digging additional mines. They did not know that in fact seven were nearly complete. As the July 1 explosion proved, the Confederate works were literally a powder keg waiting to explode.

On the morning of June 30, Grant had summoned his generals to discuss whether or not to storm the city. They wanted to let starvation take its course and Grant had concurred. But he was growing restive. The day after the mine exploded, Grant told Charles Dana that if the enemy did not give up by July 6, he would storm Vicksburg.[5]

Inside the city, on July 2, Pemberton summoned his division and brigade commanders to a council of war. He laid out all of his correspondence from Johnston and then invited discussion about what to do. Conversation focused on the possibility of a breakout somewhere along the lines, but there was no real enthusiasm for this notion. As young General Shoup related, no one "thought there was any tolerable probability of success."[6] Exposure and malnutrition had taken too heavy a toll. A survivor remembered how the weakened soldiers "staggered like drunken men when they walked."[7]

July 3 dawned with the promise of another hot, sultry day. At 10 A.M. a white flag appeared from the Confederate lines and the firing stopped. Three riders, led by General Bowen—selected because he had once been Grant's neighbor—rode out to deliver a letter from Pemberton to Grant in which Pemberton proposed an armistice and the appointment of commissioners to determine the conditions under which Vicksburg would surrender. Grant rejected this proposal—the only terms he would offer were unconditional surrender—but agreed to meet Pemberton that afternoon.

As the day progressed a bank of dark, brooding clouds gathered to the west, giving promise of a storm. Not a breath of air stirred. White flags, planted along the rival picket lines to indicate a truce, hung limp to their staffs. At the appointed time Grant and some other officers rode through the Union entrenchments to within easy pistol-shot distance of the rebel entrenchments. They dismounted near a large oak tree. Here Grant waited, and then waited some more. He was not a spiteful man. He had once sympathetically described Pemberton as "a northern man who had got into bad company."[8] Twenty minutes passed before there was a commotion among the nearby Confederate pickets. John Pemberton emerged, followed by an aide, several orderlies, and General Bowen.

The Confederates halted thirty feet from Grant and dismounted. Grant took several steps toward Pemberton and stopped. Pemberton took several steps toward Grant, and halted. Although they had known one another as young officers in Mexico, neither acknowledged the other. Grant believed that the defeated party should speak first. Pemberton refused to play his role. An embarrassing silence ensued. At last Pemberton's aide made the introductions and the two generals shook hands. In an insolent and overbearing manner, Pemberton asked what terms of capitulation Grant proposed. Grant replied that the terms were as stated in the morning exchange of letters. Overwrought, Pemberton said in an excited manner, "If this is all you have to offer, the conference may as well terminate, and hostilities be at once resumed."

"Very well," said Grant, "I am quite content to have it so."[9] Grant turned and called for his horse. At this point brave General Bowen performed his last service for the Confederacy by interceding and suggesting that the opposing subordinates talk the thing over while the commanding generals withdrew.

A Confederate officer observed the encounter: "General Grant wore a full beard cropped short, and I could see that it was sprinkled with gray. General Pemberton's was long and flowing, and he pulled it nervously during the entire interview. General Grant had a cigar in his mouth, but he was not smoking it, and appeared calm and solid."[10] While Grant and Pemberton tried to make small talk, Bowen and McPherson tried to arrange a surrender. There were too many sticking points, prickly issues of honor and substantive details as well. The meeting ended with the agreement that by 10 P.M. Grant would state his surrender terms.

An uneasy truce persisted through the evening while Pemberton and his senior officers awaited Grant's proposal. Suddenly there was clattering of hooves and a panting Signal Corps officer appeared. He had just decoded a message between Grant and Porter. It said that Grant would accept the garrison's parole in lieu of a surrender and transportation to Northern prisons. This was a far cry from unconditional surrender and very welcome news.[11] What had transpired was that Grant's subordinates had prevailed upon him to change his position. They argued that to tie up all available transportation to ship the garrison north would seriously impede further operations. Grant agreed. So General Pemberton's stubbornness earlier in the day earned his cause a small victory. When the receipt of Grant's formal terms confirmed the decoded message, Pemberton spoke to his officers: "Gentlemen, I have done what I could."[12] He put to a vote the question of whether to accept the terms. Everyone except Generals Baldwin and Lee—who wanted to hold on in hopes that Johnston would finally come—voted to accept.

Pemberton endorsed the council's consensus, while observing that it would be far better for him personally to die at the head of the army in a desperate breakout attempt rather than surrender and endure "the obloquy which I know will be heaped upon me."[13] Some of that criticism would come from the uncomfortable fact that the surrender would take place on the national independence day. For many Confederates this seemed proof that Pennsylvania-born Pemberton had betrayed them. In his after-action report, Pemberton would explain that he chose July 4 on the basis that he could get better terms. Regardless, it did not sit well with the embittered rank and file.

Early the next morning the Union soldiers fired off salutes with blank cartridges in honor of the national holiday. Then soldiers on both sides took seats on the parapets in full view of one another and waited to learn what the generals had decided. Around 10 A.M., a Stars and Stripes rose above a Confederate fort. Stretching away from this fort came a succession of white flags appearing above the Confederate works. As each fort raised a white flag, cheering broke out from the Union lines opposite them. They had struggled for forty-seven days to obtain these bastions and now they had surrendered. The Confederates marched out of their ditches to stack arms, remove their equipment, and lay down their colors. So close were the rival lines at many places that when the defenders emerged to stack their arms in front of their works, they placed them in the most forward Union trenches. There simply was no intervening ground.

A soldier in the Seventeenth Louisiana recalled that July 4 featured a "peculiar, deathlike silence." His regiment was in reserve and did not know about the surrender. A courier arrived and the order came to "Fall in." The regiment marched toward the fortifications to see cheering bluecoats pouring over the trenches. "Look! Captain, look! Why don't you order the boys to fire?" screamed a soldier. With tears in his eyes, and great emotion in his voice, the captain explained, "We are surrendered."[14]

GRANT AND HIS STAFF rode through the Confederate lines to meet once more with Pemberton. As poorly as Pemberton had behaved on the previous day, on this climactic occasion he behaved worse. There was no one to receive Grant as he climbed the porch where awaited Pemberton and his staff. The Confederates saluted Grant, and then sat down. There were no spare chairs for Grant and for an embarrassing long while no one offered Grant a seat. The general asked if he might have a drink of water because the day was exceedingly warm. The Confederates gestured inside, but no one helped him find his way. Grant groped his way through to the kitchen, where a black servant gave him a cup of cold water. Throughout it all Pemberton behaved in a hostile, sullen manner.

Back in January of 1861, an Illinois congressman had delivered a speech responding to Southern pretensions that they would hold the Mississippi River and thereby inflict terrible economic punishment upon the midwestern states. "The men of the northwest would hew their way to the Gulf of Mexico with their swords," pledged Representative John Logan.[15] On July 4, Logan's division received the honor of marching into Vicksburg to serve as the Union garrison. Leading the way was the gallant Lead Mine Regiment, the Forty-fifth Illinois. As it entered the city it passed through the defeated troops and judged them a "hard looking set."[16]

Meanwhile, Grant and his staff departed from the interview with Pemberton to join his men inside the city. Citizens thronged the pitted and torn streets and scowled at the Union officers as they rode past houses and public buildings riddled from foundation to roof. Even the shade trees showed scars from the bombardment. Grant arrived at the Vicksburg courthouse to join Logan and watch while the Forty-fifth's colonel called his regiment to attention. An officer ascended the cupola, lowered the Confederate colors, and raised the regiment's battle-torn flag atop the Confederate citadel.[17]

At noon Admiral Porter's flag-steamer, the *Black Hawk*, led a procession of gunboats, rams, and transports toward the Vicksburg levee to share in the celebration. Nattily attired in white pants and blue jackets, the *Black Hawk*'s crew commenced firing salutes just as it reached the front of the city. Grant arrived at the levee and rode up the gangplank of Porter's flag-steamer. Dismounting, the general shook hands with the naval officer to whom he owed so much. Porter opened his wine locker to toast the celebration. Amid general conviviality Porter noticed that Grant sat alone and remained quiet as if nothing of importance had occurred. Years later Porter retained a vivid image of the scene. He said of Grant, "No one, to see him sitting there with that calm exterior amid all the jollity . . . would ever have taken him for the great general who had accomplished one of the most stupendous military feats on record."[18]

In contrast, the admiral exulted in victory: "Let those laugh who win. I won in spite of many obstacles, and enjoyed my victory immensely."[19] Porter found time amid the celebration to pen a report to Washington in which he eloquently praised the army's perseverance and ability: "If ever an army was entitled to the gratitude of a nation, it is the Army of the Tennessee and its gallant leaders."[20]

Some of the Union soldiers thoroughly enjoyed their July 4 celebration. In the camp of the Sixty-eighth Ohio the "boys drank beer" and a general sent his compliments and a barrel of whiskey.[21] Among the surrendered troops, individual acts of defiance were not uncommon. Soldiers broke their Enfield rifles rather than hand them over to the enemy. They went to great lengths to avoid surrendering their battle flags. The recently widowed wife of Colonel Erwin of the Sixth Missouri sewed the regiment's flag inside her petticoat in order to smuggle it through Union lines. The brigade chaplain took the flag of Guibor's Battery to a local businessman so he could conceal it in a store. Before departing the city, Mrs. Mary Bowen hid two colors in the ambulance carrying her sick husband. For the next eighty-two years, until two months after V-E Day, the city of Vicksburg would refuse to celebrate the July 4 national holiday.

As had been the case throughout the campaign, there were numerous acts of compassion and decency between the rival armies. Grant ordered his commissary made available to the hungry Confederates. Federal medical personnel entered the city to help care for sick and wounded rebels. A hard-fighting Missouri soldier related that he "was treated very well by the Federals" all the time he remained in Vicksburg.[22]

Throughout military history a siege usually features far heavier losses among those outside the fortress who are trying to gain entrance than among the defenders. Such was not the case at Vicksburg. During the forty-seven-day siege, incomplete returns place Confederate losses at 805 killed, 1,938 wounded, and 129 missing. In contrast, after the May 22 assault, Federal losses were 104 killed, 419 wounded, and 7 missing, a total less than one-fourth that of the defenders. Pemberton surrendered 29,491 men. Seven-hundred nine of them refused to sign paroles, preferring the perils of Northern prisons to further service as a soldier.[23] As soon as the paroles were properly signed for the balance, the able-bodied Confederates departed the city. Nineteen-year-old artillerist Hugh Moss wrote:

> I stopped and looked back at the crestfallen city of Vicksburg . . . and thought of how many months we had nobly held the place against all the efforts of the Yankee nation, and bore privations and hardships of all kinds—tears rose to my eyes and my very heart swelled with emotion—being a prisoner did not in the least affect me, but the loss of the place, which was such a great downfall to the Confederacy . . . caused me much pain.[24]

ONE OF THE REASONS Grant had accepted a surrender which gave paroles to the defeated foe was that he believed despondent soldiers would be unlikely to fight again and that they would spread demoralization throughout the Confederacy. What transpired gave credence to his thinking. Pemberton wanted to keep his army intact and ready for renewed service once they were exchanged. Instead, as soon as they exited the Vicksburg perimeter, many of the Louisiana troops belonging to Baldwin's brigade broke ranks, refused to continue, and headed for their homes west of the river. They were not alone. Never had these Confederate soldiers been so discouraged.

Even the survivors of the elite Missouri brigade—a unit that had lost at least half its men during the campaign—were dispirited. A Missouri private wrote to his wife: "I hope we will not have to fight anymore. God speed the time when peace shall be made."[25]

With his army disintegrating around him as it marched east, Pemberton decided he had to bow to the inevitable and give his men a thirty-day furlough. President Davis disagreed. Stunned by the twin disasters of Gettysburg and Vicksburg, he believed that every man must now stand firm. He ordered Pemberton to shorten the length of the furloughs and call for the men to make another sacrifice for the cause. Pemberton tried to comply by granting varying lengths of furloughs based on how far a soldier had to travel to reach home. He intended for every soldier, except his poor Missouri troops, who could not get home at all, to have ten days at home.

Furlough or not, the former defenders of Vicksburg voted with their feet. They had been away for a long time and suffered much. Now they went home. Soon Confederate commanders in areas all around Vicksburg were complaining about shirkers, deserters, and men absent without leave. At one typical Mississippi rail station, soldiers swarmed the cars. The situation got so out of hand that Pemberton issued orders for the depot guards to fire on them if they refused to leave the trains.[26] Here was a reward indeed for prior heroic sacrifice. By August 8, a mere 1,154 men had reported to the designated assembly point. Over the coming weeks many returned. Many others did not. There were not enough captured Union men to exchange for the recent vast haul of prisoners made on the Mississippi. Lee's bag of nearly 6,000 Army of the Potomac men at Chancellorsville provided the South with the largest tradable stockpile. The general officers who surrendered at Vicksburg received quick exchange for the Chancellorsville prisoners. For the rank and file, exchange occurred as slots became available. Providentially for future rebel hopes, somehow the Confederate staff managed to lose the official parole roles. This made it much easier to get the men back in the ranks in time for the 1864 campaign.

Another reason many did not return to the army was the continuing effects of privation and disease suffered during the siege. At the time of surrender, fifty-seven hundred Confederate soldiers were in Vicksburg's hospitals. Scores of men who had been weakened by the long siege succumbed during the weeks after the surrender. On July 13, gallant John Bowen died of dysentery. Louisiana Captain Gabriel M. Killgore had battled poor health since the early spring of 1863. He was too sick to accompany his regiment in the field but served in the ditches during the siege. He entered the hospital after the surrender. On July 16 he noted in his journal that "he could scarcely breathe from obstructed respiration." The next day he felt "better than usual." On July 18 he had "a stroke of partial paralysis." His July 20 entry, describing the prospects for returning home, was to be his last. Seven days later, on his way home to his wife and two-year-old daughter, Killgore died.[27] On into 1864 men continued to die from diseases contracted during the siege of Vicksburg.

The fall of Vicksburg also had repercussions for Johnston's army and for the Port Hudson garrison. Upon learning of Vicksburg's surrender, Johnston ordered his army back to Jackson. The news cast a gloom over most of the troops. On the early morning of July 9, General Sherman appeared before Jackson with a formidable force. Although Joe Johnston had long known Vicksburg to be doomed, and well appreciated that Jackson would become a Union target once Vicksburg fell, somehow he had neglected to prepare. So, judging that Jackson's entrenchments were "very badly located and constructed," seven days later he issued orders to evacuate Jackson.[28] At midnight the soldiers moved through Jackson and across a pontoon bridge, the same pontoons that had been prepared so laboriously to support the march to relieve Vicksburg. Under the eyes of Johnston himself the veteran Orphan Brigade covered the retreat. Johnston admired the Kentuckians conduct and told them so. As a Kentucky soldier noted, the brigade "has covered so many retreats, the boys know just how such things have to be done."[29] One of Johnston's men observed, "The men are very low spirited and have been ever since they heard of the fall of Vicksburg . . . Desertions are frequent."[30] Heavy desertions continued into August.

Also lost by the evacuation of Jackson was a priceless fleet of Confederate rolling stock which lay trapped on the western side of the Pearl River. Grant's May 14 visit to the city had caused the destruction of the railroad bridge across the Pearl. Had Johnston rebuilt the bridge, this rolling stock could have returned to Confederate service.[31] But throughout his service in this war, Johnston had displayed a consistent disregard of Confederate resources. In 1861, he had unnecessarily retreated from Harper's Ferry when much of the arsenal remained still available for salvage. The following year he had hastily retired from the Centreville position, an abandonment that condemned vast quantities of supplies to the torch.[32] His subsequent retreat before McClellan in the Peninsula surprised the War Department and forced the evacuation of Norfolk before its irreplaceable naval equipment and machinery could be evacuated.[33] The retreat from Jackson was simply more of the same.

On July 7 the besieging Union forces at Port Hudson learned of Vicksburg's surrender. A Federal officer recounted, "Then a mighty hurrah ran around Port Hudson, like the prophetic uproar of ramshorns around Jericho.

" 'What are you yelling about?' an Alabamian called to us from across the ravine.

" 'Vicksburg has gone up!' a score of voices shouted.

" 'Hell!' "[34]

Two days later General Gardner surrendered this final Confederate stronghold on the Mississippi River and received paroles for his nearly six-thousand-man garrison.

In its effort to hold Port Hudson and Vicksburg during the three-month period beginning with the May 1 Battle of Port Gibson and ending with the July 26 evacuation of Jackson, the Confederacy lost 47,625 officers and men killed, wounded, missing, or captured. This figure does not include losses from sickness, discharge, or desertion.[35] The Army of the Tennessee lost 10,484 casualties while capturing 241 artillery pieces; Banks's army suffered 4,362 casualties and captured 51 artillery pieces at Port Hudson.[36] The casualties suffered by the Confederacy neither include ancillary subtractions, such as the nearly 5,000 total lost at Post of Arkansas, nor does the artillery total include captures by the U.S. Navy. In sum, in a campaign without precedent during this war, an offensive force suffered fewer than one-third of the more than 47,000 losses it inflicted. Such was Grant's genius.

ON JULY 7, as Union soldiers in the trenches outside of Port Hudson bayed their victory hosannas to friend and foe alike, about 1,100 miles to the east a one-sentence telegram arrived in Washington. Addressed to the secretary of the navy—and to Welles' immense satisfaction, it arrived before any message from the army—it brought news from Admiral Porter: "Sir: I have the honor to inform you that Vicksburg has surrendered to the U.S. forces on this 4th of July."[37] Welles conveyed it to Lincoln and described the president's reaction: ". . . his countenance beaming with joy; he caught my hand, and, throwing his arm around me, exclaimed . . . 'I cannot, in words, tell you my joy over this result. It is great, Mr. Welles, it is great!' "

Happily the president signed Porter's permanent commission as rear admiral, dating it from July 4. To the rank-conscious, this was a splendid reward. In characteristic fashion, Lincoln immediately tried to use a western success as a goad for his eastern generals. He believed if General George Meade could follow up his victory at Gettysburg by substantially damaging

Lee's army, the rebellion would be finished. But Meade was not Grant, and Lee was not Pemberton. To Lincoln's enormous frustration, the Army of Northern Virginia returned to its namesake state unmolested by Meade.

Later in July, Chaplain Eaton, fresh from Vicksburg, met with Lincoln and was immediately subjected to a barrage of questions about the man whom the president now called his "fighting General." It seemed to Eaton that Lincoln was doing all in his power to "measure the personal character" of his western generals. Having listened to Eaton's accounts, the president asked if either Grant or Eaton had heard of the recent "raid" in Washington? Eaton had not.

"Well," said Mr. Lincoln, "you know a raid in Washington is different from what you military men mean . . . with us it is an attack by our friends in Congress seeking to influence a change in policy." Recently, Lincoln continued, a party of congressmen had protested to Lincoln that Grant must be relieved of command because he drank too much. "I then began to ask them if they knew what he drank, what brand of whiskey he used, telling them most seriously that I wished they would find out." They conferred and concluded that they could not tell what brand he consumed. The president concluded, "I urged them to ascertain and let me know, for if it made fighting generals like Grant, I should like to have some of it for distribution."[38]

On July 13 Lincoln wrote to his "fighting General." To date they had never met. While Lincoln could and did make keen judgments about his generals based upon their correspondence, this was not the case with Grant. As the president explained to another general, "Grant is a copious worker, and fighter, but a very meagre writer, or telegrapher."[39] Lincoln's communication to Grant was a curiously candid note of appreciation. After providing "grateful acknowledgment" for Grant's "almost inestimable service," Lincoln analyzed Grant's campaign. He hinted that Grant had been slow to arrive at his ultimately successful strategy of a downstream crossing. Lincoln elaborated, "I never had any faith, except a general hope that you knew better than I," in the various schemes to approach Vicksburg from above. He added that back in May, he believed that once over the river Grant should have marched to join Banks at Port Hudson and that Grant's drive on Jackson was a mistake. The president did not mention that during the critical second week in May he had worried, How could the army possibly be fed? and worse, How could the nation endure if Grant lost it entirely? He had been unable to sleep, such was his anxiety. Lincoln concluded, "I now wish to make the personal acknowledgment that you were right, and I was wrong."[40]

When Grant, that "meagre writer," did not reply to this letter Lincoln worried that he had perhaps been a bit meager with his compliments and a bit blunt with his analysis. Almost a month passed until Lincoln, in his next letter, tried to inquire casually if Grant had received his earlier communication. What Lincoln really wanted to know was Grant's reaction to his letter. Instead, all Grant said in his response was that the July 13 letter was "duly received."[41] That said, Grant passed on to a discussion of future strategy.

Grant's reply must have made Lincoln shake his head in bemused puzzlement. The president had a great ability to plumb the minds of his subordinates and understand what motivated them. This ability to find a responsive chord and strike it was one of the key's to Lincoln's leadership. Literal and businesslike, without pretense, Grant thwarted this approach. He was simply unlike Lincoln's other generals. Back in March, Lincoln and Halleck had dreamed up a crude bribe to inspire their principal field army commanders. Halleck announced that there was a vacant major generalcy in the regular army and the first general who won "an important and decisive victory" would earn this promotion.[42] A grateful government gave it to Grant. Characteristically, Grant in turn asked that Sherman and McPherson receive promotion to brigadier general in the regular army.

THE DAY THAT LINCOLN PENNED his first letter to Grant, President Davis wrote a letter of an altogether different tone: "We are now in the darkest hour of our political existence."[43] Midsummer 1863 found the tide of war turning against the Confederacy. The men Bragg sent to relieve Vicksburg had sufficiently weakened his army so as to encourage Rosecrans to advance. In nine days of exceptional maneuver, Rosecrans drove Bragg from Tennessee. On the day Vicksburg surrendered, Bragg's army retreated into Chattanooga. Lee, Pemberton, Holmes, and Bragg, the commanders of the South's four major field armies, had all been defeated.

But it was Vicksburg and Gettysburg that captured public attention. At the time, most Southerners considered Vicksburg far more significant.[44] In part, it was a matter of perspective. Lee's soldiers emphasized their success during Gettysburg's first two days and their ability to conduct an orderly return to Virginia. Civilians largely shared this view. At worst, Gettysburg had been a drawn battle. In contrast, everyone recognized the disaster on the Mississippi.

Typical was Georgia governor Joseph Brown. Omitting any mention of Gettysburg, on July 17 he urged his people not to despair over "the late serious disasters to our arms" in Mississippi and Tennessee.[45] Edmund Ruffin, the venerable fire-eater who had touched off the first gun aimed at Fort Sumter, likewise labeled the loss of the Mississippi a disaster. Looking at the map, Southerners saw the country cut in half. Looking to the future, many despaired. A Confederate congressman wrote, "The disastrous movement of Lee into Pennsylvania and the fall of Vicksburg, the latter especially, will end in the ruin of the South . . . the failure of the Government to re-enforce Vicksburg . . . has so broken down the hopes of our people that even the little strength yet remaining can only be exerted in despair."[46] South Carolina infantryman Tally Simpson had marched with Lee's army to Gettysburg and back. Upon hearing of Vicksburg's fall, he wrote home to call it a "hard stroke for the Confederacy." Upon further reflection, he elaborated: "The fall of Vicksburg has caused me to lose confidence in something or somebody."[47]

Whereas eastern Confederate soldiers invested hope in Lee, the westerners had no such lodestar. Tennessee major Flavel Barber contrasted the elation of victory one year before with the situation following Vicksburg's fall: "We still have courage and resolution left but we are fighting more because we know our cause to be just than because we are sanguine of success."[48] A Texas sergeant serving in Johnston's army expressed much greater despondency: "I have little hope of the future."[49]

Lee remained uncomprehending about what had taken place on the Mississippi. Once his army limped safely home from its slaughter in Pennsylvania, he assessed affairs in the West. He wrote to Davis that the wisest course now was "to select some point on the Mississippi and fortify it strongly."[50] He elaborated that a small garrison with adequate provisions could hold such works against the type of attack Grant had mounted against Vicksburg. Where such a fort could be built given Federal control of both banks of the river, Lee omitted to mention. How such a fort could restore the severed link to the Trans-Mississippi he did not say.

Federal control of the Mississippi separated the Confederacy into two sections. Union patrols along the river interdicted almost all communication between East and West. "Thenceforth," wrote Sherman, the Confederates "could not cross it save by stealth."[51] Illustrative of this fact was the experience of a small group of rebel volunteers who escorted an officer who was trying to travel to Louisiana. This officer had the important duty of carrying 1.5 million Confederate dollars in back pay and 30,000 rounds of ammunition to the Third Louisiana regiment, which had been paroled and re-formed after Vicksburg's surrender. In spite of traveling with an experienced blockade runner, the party spent nearly a month in the Mississippi swamps dodging gunboats and Federal patrols before venturing across the river.[52] In Sherman's words, the complete isolation of West from East rendered military affairs on the west bank "unimportant."[53]

Jefferson Davis knew that this war was a test of wills. Harking back to the days of the American Revolution, he found hope in the rebels' ability to persevere in the face of setback and defeat. In August he told Lee that the Southern people seemed to have quickly recovered from their depression over defeat in the West and were again exhibiting "that fortitude . . . needful to secure ultimate success."[54] A Virginia captain spoke for Davis, Lee, and the soldiers of the Army of Northern Virginia when he wrote his wife that "by God's grace we will soon strike the enemy such a blow, that his hopes of subjugation will be as far off as before the fall of Vicksburg."[55]

If that blow were to be struck, it would be performed by hungry soldiers. An extremely rainy Virginia summer of 1863 ruined the wheat crop. The loss of the Mississippi Valley eliminated the accumulation of molasses and sugar which heretofore had been mixed with other foods and used as a substitute.[56] In Dalton, Georgia, the winter camp of the Army of Tennessee in 1863–1864, a veteran of the campaigning around Vicksburg wrote that the food was the worst yet.

The loss of access to the Trans-Mississippi, along with other Confederate setbacks, drove Richmond officials to ever more draconian measures to procure food for the armies. Government agents bought cattle, hogs, and corn at controlled prices far below the market prices. Furthermore, they used a debased currency to make these purchases. Not surprisingly, planters tried to avoid selling to the government by hiding their produce, declaring they merely had enough for their own use, or, where possible, taking it across Federal lines where they could be paid in greenbacks or gold. In turn, the Confederate government resorted to impressment. Not even conscription caused so much discontent and outright resentment. "This practice," observed General Taylor, "alienates the affections of the people, debauches the troops, and ultimately destroys its own capacity to produce results."[57]

The loss of the Trans-Mississippi's "hogs and hominy" forced the Confederacy to substitute food for war munitions aboard its blockade runners. This measure proved inadequate. During the winter of 1864–1865, Lee's army barely endured on a diet of imported meat from Nassau in the Bahamas. The enervating effects of low-quality "Nausea bacon," as the soldiers called it, substantially reduced army mobility. So bad had the situation become that by the beginning of 1865, the *Southern Cultivator* opined that every possible means must be used to encourage food production: "This war cannot be kept up without food."[58]

Back in 1862, Grant and Sherman's plan had been to hold the Mississippi River and leave the interior alone except for occasional raids against the railroads. Sherman had believed that "we could make ourselves so busy that our descent would be dreaded the whole length of the river."[59] Following the fall of Vicksburg, this is what transpired, and the Mississippi Valley became a lawless region. Whereas earlier in the war Southern women had shamed the reluctant to join the army, now that the government had proven unable to keep the enemy at bay, public spirit changed. There remained numerous men of conscription age, but they were finding it ever easier to shelter themselves among a sympathetic population and avoid service. The fringe areas of Confederate control were increasingly overrun with stragglers and deserters, while the state troops assigned to round them up were proving unwilling to force their neighbors back into the ranks. Ironically, Confederate cavalry and provost patrols began using dogs that had been trained to chase escaped slaves to hunt down draft dodgers and deserters. A Louisiana soldier home on leave in November 1863 found the locals carrying on a very active, but illicit, cotton trade with Union-occupied Baton Rouge. Women always carried the cotton, since guards would let them pass. The local Confederate cavalry took regular bribes to allow the trade to continue and earned the name "cotton tollers." Open theft by formed Confederate units was so common that it caused the soldier to lament, "Nearly everybody seemed to have lost all sense of right and wrong."[60]

THE CAPTURE OF VICKSBURG also had an immediate impact upon the morale of the Army of the Tennessee. It had never known defeat and Vicksburg seemed to crown its achievements. Consequently, the army fell into an understandable complacency. They had labored hard and risked much. Officers sought home leave, and men obtained furloughs and discharges whenever possible. The ranks thinned, with many regiments becoming mere skeletons. The Federal and state governments seemed loath to enforce the politically unpopular draft to replenish their ranks. The war on the

Mississippi was at a natural lull, but it threatened to become a strategic drift, like the one that had occurred after the capture of Corinth the previous year.

Grant pondered higher strategy and concluded that the key port of Mobile, Alabama, should be the next target. The navy could convey him to the Alabama coast, from where he could campaign against the soft underbelly of the Confederacy. Assistant Secretary of the Navy Gustavus Fox saw the merit of attacking Mobile while "all rebeldom is in an infernal panic."[61] He felt unable to issue any orders until he learned what the army intended. Grant's notion also tempted the commander in chief. However, Secretary of State William H. Seward strongly urged the view that something had to be done on the Texas coast. Seward feared that France's recent meddling in Mexico might extend to Texas.[62] It was important, in spite of an ongoing civil war, to show France that the Monroe Doctrine still stood. In addition, British and French merchants were openly flouting the blockade by establishing regular steamer routes to the Mexican port of Matamoros, just across the Rio Grande from Texas. Here hundreds of vessels exchanged war supplies for cotton while enjoying the perfect safety of "neutral" waters. These factors persuaded Lincoln that it was more important to reestablish national authority in west Texas than to prepare an expedition to Mobile.[63]

Grant's Mobile scheme showed real strategic imagination. He requested permission to embark upon it three times until regretfully giving it up at the end of September. Then and thereafter he believed it a missed opportunity to deal "the enemy a heavy blow."[64] Grant best revealed his own dissatisfaction with his Vicksburg campaign in a letter to his father written in mid-June. At that time he was confident that the city's fall was a mere matter of time. But, he wrote, "The fall of Vicksburg now will only result in the opening of the Mississippi River and demoralization of the enemy. I intended more from it."[65]

While the Army of the Tennessee dispersed to areas of secondary strategic importance, and Grant himself languished, the Mississippi River opened to commercial traffic. On July 16 the riverboat *Imperial* completed a voyage from St. Louis to New Orleans carrying a cargo of Midwest produce and six hundred longhorn cattle captured at Natchez; the cattle had been intended to feed rebel forces east of the Mississippi. It remained a hazardous trip, with frequent ambushes from bushwhackers along both banks. Not until December 1863 did the first boatload of sugar and molasses arrive in Louisville from New Orleans. The opening of the Mississippi did not have the impact many had imagined. During the time the river

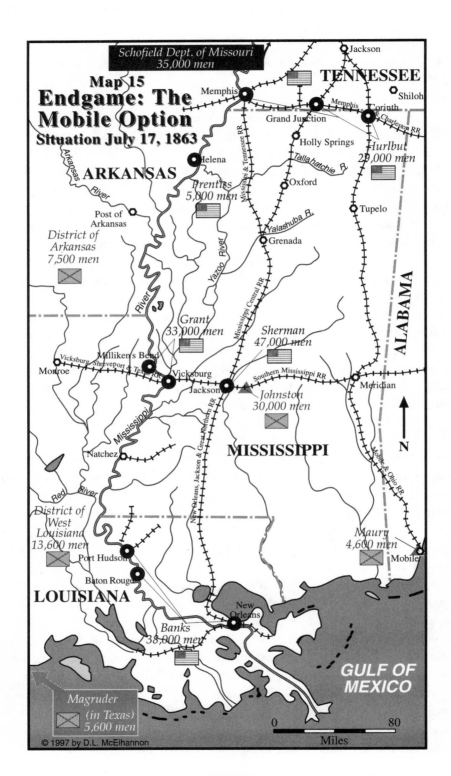

Map 15
Endgame: The Mobile Option
Situation July 17, 1863

Schofield Dept. of Missouri
35,000 men

Jackson

TENNESSEE

Memphis

Shiloh

Memphis & Charleston RR

Corinth

Grand Junction

Holly Springs

Hurlbut
29,000 men

ARKANSAS

Helena

Tallahatchie R.

Prentiss
5,000 men

Oxford

Tupelo

Post of
Arkansas

Yalashuba R.

Grenada

District of
Arkansas
7,500 men

ALABAMA

Grant
33,000 men

Sherman
47,000 men

Milliken's Bend

Vicksburg, Shreveport & Texas RR

Monroe

Vicksburg

Southern Mississippi RR

Meridian

Jackson

Johnston
30,000 men

Natchez

MISSISSIPPI

N

District of
West
Louisiana
13,600 men

Maury
4,600 men

Port Hudson

Mobile

Baton Rouge

LOUISIANA

New
Orleans

Banks
38,000 men

Magruder
(in Texas)
5,600 men

GULF OF
MEXICO

© 1997 by D.L. McElhannon

0   80
Miles

308

was closed, midwestern merchants had found that the rail lines heading east, or a combination of rail to Chicago and water transport on the Great Lakes, provided a most satisfactory route to carry foodstuffs and goods to the great cities on the Atlantic seaboard and on to Europe. Indeed, in comparison with 1860, 1864 saw a 70 percent reduction in the cargo departing from New Orleans. The people, north and south, who inhabited what once had been boomtown river ports found out after the war that the nation's business had passed them by. The substitution of west-to-east transportation for north-to-south transportation down the Mississippi River was one factor that frustrated Southern political leaders who had hoped that the old Northwest would not support Lincoln's war.

MEANWHILE, Jefferson Davis appreciated too late some of what Grant had done. He complained to confidants that Grant, with one army, had been allowed to defeat separate Confederate forces at Port Hudson, Vicksburg, and Jackson. He did not comprehend that his own order to Pemberton regarding the necessity of holding the two river fortresses had contributed to this. Instead, he blamed Johnston. It helped that Johnston wrote a report that absolved himself of all blame and that this report hinged upon some narrowly constructed legalisms. Johnston's claims were like a red flag before a bull. Davis zealously set to work to rebut Johnston. If there was anything at which Jeff Davis excelled it was this, debating language's fine meaning. He had his War Department assemble all of Johnston's communications since that general took command in the West. Davis combed the documents, which ranged from November 1862 to the time Vicksburg lay besieged, and then delivered a point-by-point refutation.[66] It was petty, it was worse than unnecessary, and Davis could not help himself.[67]

In mid-August, John Pemberton learned that a court of inquiry would be held to investigate Vicksburg's fall. He rejoiced at the news.[68] Having lost the battle of bullets, he hoped to retrieve his reputation via a paper war. In contrast, the prospects of an inquiry alarmed Joe Johnston. Glibly, he asked Richmond to postpone it, since his own pressing duties would prevent his attendance. The War Department slapped him down, curtly responding that he would be temporarily relieved of command in order to participate.[69] The court began to assemble evidence until September 8, when the War Department suspended its assembly until further notice. The Chickamauga campaign—the South's last try to win this war by offensive action—was under way, and its importance superseded all else, except in the minds of Pemberton and Johnston.

After Vicksburg's surrender, one of Pemberton's staff officers had published some articles in a Mobile newspaper that blamed defeat on the lack of heavy guns to control the Mississippi and on the lack of cavalry. Moreover, he wrote, Pemberton had engaged at Bakers Creek "under protest, against his own judgment, and in obedience to positive orders."[70] Even though the Chickamauga campaign was in full progress at this point, the article was a slur Johnston could not ignore. He complained to Richmond, formally accused the article's author of "publishing a false statement," and demanded an official investigation.[71] Again he was ignored.

One thing all Confederates agreed upon was that Vicksburg had fallen for lack of food. On this issue, too, blame casting abounded. Just as the fighting generals refought the campaign of men and cannon, so those officers charged with provisioning the army refought it using numbers of bushels of corn and pounds of hog meat. One thing became clear from this exercise. A rich agricultural region surrounded Vicksburg. Before Porter's gunboats ran the batteries, there were ample stores of food on both sides of the river, much of it assembled at depots up and down the rivers of western Louisiana and Texas and along the Mississippi itself. What was lacking was the means to transport it to the armies. The lack of railroads west of the Mississippi meant that supplies had to move by water—and there were too few steamboats assigned this duty. Once Porter controlled the river, steamer traffic from west to east ceased entirely.

In addition, Vicksburg's chief commissary agent, W. H. Johnson, had found his work greatly hampered by hostile, competing bureaucracies. Not until March 10 did he reach an understanding with Vicksburg's military authorities. On that date, General Carter Stevenson told him that he regarded Vicksburg's fate a matter of supply. Johnson renewed his search for supplies and found that his predecessor had arranged for them to be sent to western Louisiana. He hastened to ship them east aboard steamers that crossed the Mississippi and entered the Big Black River to unload. And here a tremendous number of supplies sat until they were destroyed to be kept out of Grant's hands. Additional food rotted on the Vicksburg wharves because of a lack of storage facilities.[72]

In the absence of food from the Trans-Mississippi, Vicksburg still enjoyed access to the very productive plantations of the Yazoo River Delta, which grew a large corn surplus. It was a roadless region, so the transport of supplies depended upon light draft boats. They carried the grain to above Haynes' Bluff, and then wagons hauled the grain over eleven miles of road to Vicksburg. Four factors had interfered with this supply line: The planters were not terribly keen to do business with the Confederate commissary; there was a lack of suitable watercraft; Porter's forays into the delta; and the need to retain supplies to support Confederate efforts to oppose Grant's drives from above the city. When Grant began his campaign below Vicksburg, there was not enough time to assemble the supplies before Pemberton fell back to the city. The Confederates abandoned a vast amount of foodstuffs at Haynes' Bluff.[73] Lastly, Vicksburg could draw upon central Mississippi for supplies via the railroad. However, the heavy army demand upon the railroad to move men and munitions relegated foodstuffs to a low priority.

So, while bountiful supplies existed, moving them to Vicksburg had presented enormous problems.[74] Nothing could have restored access to the Trans-Mississippi once the Federal navy assumed its choke hold on the Red River. But Vicksburg's other two sources of supply should have been adequate. As one Confederate officer concluded, "In the commissary department there has been a great want of foresight and energy. The troops at Port Hudson and Vicksburg should never have been reduced to short rations. These strongholds, by proper management, could have easily been provisioned for six or twelve months."[75]

Then there was the issue of Vicksburg's heavy artillery. The citadel's raison d'être was to stop Federal ships from steaming past. "If we had only had enough of heavy guns to sink every boat that tried to pass," wrote a soldier early in the siege, "we would not be beleaguered now."[76] Then and thereafter, Pemberton's apologists tried to excuse him on the grounds that the artillery failed. Was its failure exceptional? In the spring of 1862, the Confederate fortification at Island Number Ten, which sheltered some 140 guns of all types, had been unable to stop Federal ironclads from steaming down the Mississippi. Likewise, Farragut had conned his fleet upstream from the Mississippi's mouth past the forts guarding New Orleans, which had some 75 to 80 guns that could bear on the river. The tactical lesson was that determined vessels could run the batteries. These events occurred before Pemberton arrived to take command of Vicksburg, and he, as well as other Confederate strategists, had the opportunity to profit from the experience.

For the remainder of the war the duel between ships and land-based artillery centered on the handful of ports the South still controlled. Major Edward Manigault wrote a detailed diary describing his experiences conducting portions of the artillery defense of Charleston. It sheds light on the problems Vicksburg's river gunners confronted. Manigault commanded a heavy artillery battalion. By virtue of its location and symbolic importance,

Charleston received first call on weapons and equipment, and Manigault's battalion benefited. Yet his diary is a catalogue of failed fuses, faulty friction tubes, improperly manufactured shells, and inaccurate guns. After one embarrassing failure, Manigault conducted extensive firing practice on an artillery range. He had erected a 40-foot-long, 7-foot-high target 700 yards from the guns and had his four officers estimate the range out of earshot of one another. Their estimates were 650, 700, 800, and 900 yards. In a similar exercise with the target set at 1,158 yards, two officers estimated the distance to be 1,000 yards and one estimated 850. Proper fusing depended upon accurate range estimation. Under ideal daylight conditions with a fixed target—not Vicksburg's mist and smoke-filled murk with a moving enemy returning the fire—these officers had difficulty correctly estimating the range.

The performance of their thirty-pounder Parrott rifles and eight-inch siege howitzers was far worse. The first day of practice, out of eight shots, only one fragment of one shell struck the target and another fragment grazed it. Other shells burst short or long, with the first graze of solid shot landing anywhere from 79 to 168 yards off target. Sixteen shots fired by a different battery five days later saw one clean hit and the fragment of one other shell strike the target. A third trial with a more skilled battery crew managed five hits out of ten shots. With the target set at 1,158 yards on two separate days, one fragment of one of twenty-two rounds hit the target and another landed 42 yards short and ricocheted through the target. The balance missed, with many rounds apparently wobbling in flight, losing their sabots prematurely, or failing to burst.[77] In sum, these dismal results suggest that the inability of Confederate artillerists on the Mississippi to prevent Federal warships from running the guns was due to inadequate technical means.

However, consider what might have taken place had the *Arkansas* remained at Vicksburg instead of meeting her untimely demise during an unnecessary mission to Baton Rouge. In conjunction with the land-based artillery, she might have blocked the river. Furthermore, her presence might have allowed the completion of additional ironclads at Yazoo City. This required the correct employment of slender Confederate resources and remains a tantalizing "what if?" scenario.

PEMBERTON'S DISASTER did not lessen Davis's faith in this man. The president sought a corps command for Pemberton in Bragg's army. He told

Bragg that he still considered him among the ablest of generals. Bragg had to reply that no one in his army would serve under him. A sixty-year-old chaplain who served with the First Missouri Cavalry explained that Pemberton was universally regarded as incompetent and possibly a traitor. He pleaded with the president "to relieve us of these drones and pigmies" that heretofore had led the western armies.[78] A Mississippi congressman was more restrained. He declined to pass judgment on Pemberton's competence but shared the chaplain's conclusion. He informed Davis that because everyone had entirely lost confidence in Pemberton, that general's usefulness was "utterly destroyed."[79]

The unemployed and unemployable lieutenant general circulated in Richmond hoping for an assignment. In May of 1864, as his old foes Grant and Sherman launched their invasions of Virginia and Georgia, respectively, and the outmanned South battled desperately for survival, Pemberton swallowed his pride and took the patriotic step of resigning his general's commission. He found a place as a lieutenant colonel of artillery and served in that capacity for the remainder of the war. In the spring of 1865, Davis assured him, "I thought and still think that you did right to risk an army for the purpose of keeping command of even a section of the Mississippi."[80]

It is hard to share Davis's assessment. In 1863, once Porter's fleet ran the batteries, Vicksburg had failed in its purpose and Pemberton's duty changed. His inability to fathom Grant's intentions is incredible. Many of his officers and some of his soldiers appreciated the implications of Porter's success.[81] Particularly after Grant landed at Bruinsburg, Pemberton's new duty was not to hold Vicksburg but either to defeat Grant or to safely evacuate his army. He required a flexible mind capable of rising above the letter of his instructions. Frederick the Great reputedly said, "It is no disgrace to be defeated; it is a disgrace to be surprised." Pemberton's career ended in befitting disgrace.

Writing one year after the war, a Southern journalist, Edwin Pollard, described Pemberton as "one of those men whose idea of war began with a bureau of clothing and equipment, and ended with a field-day or dress-parade."[82] From 1863 on, soldiers argued about the surrender and whether Pemberton had been disloyal. Writing in 1894, one of Kirby Smith's officers stated that he had no doubt that Pemberton "sold out" Vicksburg. This conspiracy buff saw Pemberton's negotiations with Grant as closing "the deal by fixing the price and day of surrender." To prove his point he added, "General Pemberton was a poor man before, but after the war, without any apparent effort on his part, he turned up in Philadelphia . . . and lived like a nabob."[83] Like the city itself, Vicksburg's veterans had long memories. A Missouri veteran attending a Confederate reunion in Little Rock in 1928 reported that people at that gathering made the charge that Pemberton had sold Vicksburg and its garrison for $100,000.

Other judgments from Vicksburg veterans were less harsh. One officer observed that Pemberton's major flaw was his inability to get along with his subordinates. One of Pemberton's former brigade commanders was even more sympathetic: "Gen. Pemberton was as gallant and as loyal a man to the cause he was sworn to support as Gen. Lee himself. He was not a great general, but he had a hard place to fill."[84]

If there was an officer with whom Pemberton could feel sympathy, he was among the ranks of his foes. Like Pemberton, John McClernand found himself unemployed, with his reputation tarnished, and no prospects for a new command. McClernand had powerful political friends and they urged Lincoln to intervene on his behalf. Although Lincoln considered McClernand a friend, appreciated his contributions to Grant's victories, and fully realized the value of having a Democrat in the front ranks of the war, he could see no clear way to intervene. Any intervention would risk profoundly displeasing Grant, and this was a risk Lincoln refused to take. When McClernand received Lincoln's reply that there was no command available, he, like Pemberton, sought retribution through a court of inquiry. Lincoln declined to authorize it, citing the same reasons that prevented a court from convening to hear Pemberton's case: the Chickamauga campaign was under way and officers could not be spared to sit at a court of inquiry. Thwarted in his efforts to defend himself against "the proscription and calumnies" of Grant, in the first month of 1864 McClernand recognized the inevitable and resigned his commission as major general.[85] So ended the military career of a distinguished patriot. Had he possessed more self-control he would have emerged from the war as one of its real heroes.

Instead, the nation celebrated the achievements of Grant and Sherman and the U.S. Navy. In Lincoln's homey words, "Uncle Sam's Web-feet" had made their tracks at "all the watery margins" on "the rapid river . . . up the narrow muddy bayou, and wherever the ground was a little damp."[86] While the campaign hardly featured the seamless cooperation that Grant, Sherman, and Porter described in their memoirs, it had been a notable combined-services achievement. Grant and Porter had overcome traditional army-navy rivalry in pursuit of the national good. They shared a dogged persistence toward the main objective that triumphed in spite of inevitable friction. Confederate general Stephen Lee put it well in his postwar reflections when he wrote that the work of the western navy "was as decisive" as were "the mighty Union armies."[87]

Many Americans who rose to high command displayed physical courage both during the Mexican War and the Civil War. Grant and Johnston belong to this group, although it is unclear whether Pemberton does. Some Civil War generals could shine while implementing orders from a superior. Far fewer possessed moral courage—a willingness to make and implement decisions—in an environment of rumor and uncertainty. Grant exhibited moral courage in full measure. In contrast, his two opponents—Pemberton and Johnston—shrank from responsibility because decision making might involve committing error; displays of initiative opened the door to failure.

As a junior officer in the Mexican War, Grant served under General Zach Taylor. Grant was an impressionable twenty-four-year-old and came to admire Taylor's calm ability to face danger or responsibility, to exhibit moral courage. Grant learned much from Taylor and wrote of him in his memoirs, "General Taylor was not an officer to trouble the administration much with his demands, but was inclined to do the best he could with the means given him."[88] This, of course, also perfectly describes Grant. Success did not change Grant, the son of a tanner. When some Illinois politicians visited him at Vicksburg, they asked about his political views. Grant replied, "There is one subject with which I am perfectly acquainted, and if you like to talk about that, I am your man."

"What is that, General?"

"Tanning leather," Grant answered.[89]

ON AUGUST 26, 1863, Abraham Lincoln sat at his writing desk in the Executive Mansion to draft a reply to an invitation to attend a mass meeting in Springfield, Illinois. It would be most agreeable, he reflected, to return home to visit old friends. However, the continuing crushing press of business forbade it. Although the meeting involved men who labeled themselves as unconditionally for the Union, Lincoln knew this was not so. Many of the attendees were dissatisfied with his leadership on the ground that he had not sought some compromise with the South in order to restore peace. It was to them Lincoln wrote:

> You desire peace; and you blame me that we do not have it. But how can we attain it? There are but three conceivable ways. First, to suppress the rebellion by force of arms. This I am trying to do. Are you for it? . . . If you are not for it, a second way is, to give up the Union. I am against this.

Are you for it? If you are, you should say so plainly. If you are not for force, nor yet for dissolution, there only remains some imaginable compromise.

The president did not believe that any compromise was possible. The strength of the rebellion lay in its armies. They dominated the country and the people within their range of control and prevented any significant Southern peace movement from arising. Even so, Lincoln asked, suppose Northern and Southern peace people proclaimed a compromise that embraced a restoration of the Union; "in what way can that compromise be used to keep Lee's army out of Pennsylvania?" The president concluded that until the rebel armies were defeated, there could be no peace.

He then turned to the second major source of displeasure with his leadership: "To be plain, you are dissatisfied with me about the negro. Quite likely there is a difference of opinion between you and myself upon that subject. I certainly wish that all men could be free, while I suppose you do not." But he explained that he had adopted no measure solely for the purpose of freeing the slaves. Rather, the Emancipation Proclamation was a tool carefully crafted to promote the war and thus restore the Union. "You say you will not fight to free negroes. Some of them seem willing to fight for you; but, no matter. Fight you, then, exclusively to save the Union. I issued the proclamation on purpose to aid you in saving the Union." Lincoln continued: "I thought that whatever negroes can be got to do as soldiers, leaves just so much less for white soldiers to do, in saving the Union. Does it appear otherwise to you?" But the black man, like the white, had to have reasons to stake his life in battle. The promise of freedom in the Emancipation Proclamation provided that reason.

The president finished his letter with an overview of the state of the war. He was a moody man, but the successes of the summer of 1863 had caused his spirits to rise. Because of Grant's victory at Vicksburg, "the signs look better. The Father of Waters again goes unvexed to the sea." Because of Grant's victory, peace did not seem so distant. "I hope it will come soon, and come to stay; and so come as to be worth the keeping in all future times. It will then have been proved that, among free men, there can be no successful appeal from the ballot to the bullet."[90]

Many soldiers echoed Lincoln's conclusion that there could and should be no peace until the rebels were defeated. A Democratic colonel who served at the siege wrote about his hometown friends who were becoming ever more stridently antiwar, and said, "If the Democrats are not in favor of whipping these Aristocratic Rebels until they consider they are whipped, I am not with the democrats."[91] Likewise, General Sherman believed that talk about armistice or peace before the Union armies completed the subjugation of the South was wrongheaded. He concluded that "the section of thirty-pounder Parrott rifles now drilling before my tent is a more convincing argument" than any peace initiative. War alone could decide the issue. The only question for the people of the North to resolve was "Can we whip the South?"[92]

For all Union people living west of the Appalachian Mountains, Vicksburg was a tremendous victory. It elated Union morale and deflated Southern spirit. Pemberton's surrender reduced the Confederacy to only one remaining major army in the West. Yet, less than two months after Vicksburg, Lincoln would have to issue another call for three hundred thousand more soldiers because disaster had occurred. The Confederate response to defeat on the Mississippi and in Pennsylvania would be a tremendous counterstroke in the middle, in northern Georgia along the banks of Chickamauga Creek. Uniting men from Johnston's command in Mississippi and from Lee's command in Virginia with the Army of the Tennessee, Jefferson Davis assembled sufficient force to send Rosecrans reeling back to Chattanooga. Here the Federal soldiers were besieged and, much like the Confederate defenders of Vicksburg, lived on short rations while their horses died from starvation. It would be up to U. S. Grant to rescue them.

From Vicksburg, reporter and headquarters confidant Sylvanus Cadwallader anticipated some of this when he wrote on August 1 that many people hoped that Vicksburg's capture marked the near end of the war: "People wait anxiously to see the practical results so long predicted . . . To me nothing is plainer than that a majority of the people will be seriously disappointed. The war will still go on."[93] Few would have believed that it would go on for two more terrible years.

Troops Present for the Vicksburg Campaign: May 1, 1863

Union Forces

Army of the Tennessee: Maj. Gen. Ulysses S. Grant, Commanding
    Escort: 4th Illinois Cavalry, Co. A
    Engineers: 1st Battalion, Engineer Regiment of the West

Thirteenth Corps: Maj. Gen. John A. McClernand
    Escort: 3rd Illinois Cavalry, Co. L
    Pioneers: Kentucky Infantry (Independent Co.)

Ninth Division: Brig. Gen. Peter J. Osterhaus
    First Brigade: Brig. Gen. Theophilus T. Garrard
    118th Illinois
    49th Indiana
    69th Indiana
    7th Kentucky
    120th Ohio
    Second Brigade: Col. Lionel A. Sheldon
    54th Indiana
    22nd Kentucky
    16th Ohio
    42nd Ohio
    114th Ohio
    Artillery: Capt. Jacob T. Foster
    Michigan Light, 7th Battery
    Wisconsin Light, 1st Battery

Tenth Division: Brig. Gen. Andrew J. Smith
        Escort: 4th Indiana Cavalry, Co. C
  First Brigade: Brig. Gen. Stephen G. Burbridge
    16th Indiana
    60th Indiana
    67th Indiana
    83rd Ohio
    96th Ohio
    23rd Wisconsin
  Second Brigade: Col. William J. Landram
    77th Illinois
    97th Illinois
    108th Illinois
    130th Illinois
    19th Kentucky
    48th Ohio
      Artillery
    Illinois Light, Chicago Mercantile Battery
    Ohio Light, 17th Battery

Twelfth Division: Brig. Gen. Alvin P. Hovey
        Escort: 1st Indiana Cavalry, Co. C
  First Brigade: Brig. Gen. George F. McGinnis
    11th Indiana
    24th Indiana
    34th Indiana
    46th Indiana
    29th Wisconsin
  Second Brigade: Col. James R. Slack
    47th Indiana
    24th Iowa
    28th Iowa
    56th Ohio
      Artillery
    2nd Illinois Light, Battery A
    1st Missouri Light, Battery A
    Ohio Light, 2nd Battery
    Ohio Light, 16th Battery

Fourteenth Division: Brig. Gen. Eugene A. Carr
        Escort: 3rd Illinois Cavalry, Co. G
  First Brigade: Brig. Gen. William P. Benton
     33rd Illinois
     99th Illinois
     8th Indiana
     18th Indiana
     1st U.S. (siege guns)
  Second Brigade: Col. William M. Stone (Brig. Gen. Michael
      K. Lawler)
     21st Iowa
     22nd Iowa
     23rd Iowa
     11th Wisconsin
  Artillery
     Iowa Light, 1st Battery
     Indiana Light, 1st Battery
  Cavalry
     2nd Illinois (five companies)
     3rd Illinois (three companies)
     6th Missouri (seven companies)

Fifteenth Corps: Maj. Gen. William T. Sherman
        Escort: 4th Iowa Cavalry

First Division: Maj. Gen. Frederick Steele
  First Brigade: Col. Francis H. Manter
     13th Illinois
     27th Missouri
     29th Missouri
     30th Missouri
     31st Missouri
     32nd Missouri
  Second Brigade: Col. Charles R. Woods
     25th Iowa
     31st Iowa
     3rd Missouri
     12th Missouri

17th Missouri
76th Ohio
Third Brigade: Brig. Gen. John M. Thayer
4th Iowa
9th Iowa
26th Iowa
30th Iowa
Artillery
Iowa Light, 1st Battery
2nd Missouri Light, Battery F
Ohio Light, 4th Battery
Cavalry
Kane County (Illinois) Independent Co.
3rd Illinois, Co. D

Second Division: Maj. Gen. Frank P. Blair
First Brigade: Col. Giles A. Smith
113th Illinois
116th Illinois
6th Missouri
8th Missouri
13th U.S.
Second Brigade: Col. Thomas Kilby Smith
55th Illinois
127th Illinois
83rd Indiana
54th Ohio
57th Ohio
Third Brigade: Brig. Gen. Hugh Ewing
30th Ohio
37th Ohio
47th Ohio
4th West Virginia
Artillery
1st Illinois Light, Batteries A, B, H
Ohio Light, 8th Battery
Cavalry
Thielemann's (Illinois) Battalion, Cos. A and B
10th Missouri, Co. C

Third Division: Brig. Gen. James M. Tuttle
  First Brigade: Brig. Gen. Ralph P. Buckland
     114th Illinois
     93rd Indiana
     72nd Ohio
     95th Ohio
  Second Brigade: Brig. Gen. Joseph A. Mower
     47th Illinois
     5th Minnesota
     11th Missouri
     8th Wisconsin
  Third Brigade: Brig. Gen. Charles L. Matthies
     8th Iowa
     12th Iowa
     35th Iowa
  Artillery: Capt. Nelson T. Spoor
     1st Illinois Light, Battery E
     Iowa Light, 2nd Battery

Seventeenth Corps: Maj. Gen. James B. McPherson
     Escort: 4th Co. Ohio Cavalry

Third Division: Maj. Gen. John A. Logan
     Escort: 2nd Illinois Cavalry, Co. A
  First Brigade: Brig. Gen. John E. Smith
     20th Illinois
     31st Illinois
     45th Illinois
     124th Illinois
     23rd Indiana
  Second Brigade: Brig. Gen. Mortimer D. Leggett
     30th Illinois
     20th Ohio
     68th Ohio
     78th Ohio
  Third Brigade: Brig. Gen. John D. Stevenson
     8th Illinois
     81st Illinois
     7th Missouri

32nd Ohio
Artillery: Maj. Charles J. Stolbrand
  1st Illinois Light, Battery D
  2nd Illinois Light, Batteries G and L
  Michigan Light, 8th Battery
  Ohio Light, 3rd Battery

Sixth Division: Brig. Gen. John McArthur
        Escort: 11th Illinois Cavalry, Co. G
  First Brigade: Brig. Gen. Hugh T. Reid
    1st Kansas
    16th Wisconsin
  Second Brigade: Brig. Gen. Thomas E. G. Ransom
    11th Illinois
    72nd Illinois
    95th Illinois
    14th Wisconsin
    17th Wisconsin
  Third Brigade: Col. William Hall
    11th Iowa
    13th Iowa
    15th Iowa
    16th Iowa
  Artillery: Maj. Thomas D. Maurice
    2nd Illinois Light, Battery F
    Minnesota Light, 1st Battery
    1st Missouri Light, Battery C
    Ohio Light, 10th Battery

Seventh Division: Brig. Gen. Isaac F. Quinby; Brig. Gen. Marcellus
  M. Crocker
        Escort: 4th Missouri Cavalry, Co. F
  First Brigade: Col. John B. Sanborn
    48th Indiana
    59th Indiana
    4th Minnesota
    18th Wisconsin
  Second Brigade: Col. Samuel A. Holmes
    56th Illinois

17th Iowa
10th Missouri
24th Missouri
80th Ohio
Third Brigade: Col. George B. Boomer
93rd Illinois
5th Iowa
10th Iowa
26th Missouri
Artillery: Capt. Frank C. Sands; Capt. Henry Dillon
1st Missouri Light, Battery M
Ohio Light, 11th Battery
Wisconsin Light, 6th and 12th Batteries

Confederate Forces

Lt. Gen. John C. Pemberton commanding

Bowen's Division: Brig. Gen. John S. Bowen
First Brigade: Col. Francis M. Cockrell
1st & 4th Missouri
2nd Missouri
3rd Missouri
5th Missouri
6th Missouri
Wade's Missouri Battery
Landis's Missouri Battery
Guibor's Missouri Battery
Second Brigade: Brig. Gen. Martin E. Green
15th Arkansas
19th Arkansas
20th Arkansas
21st Arkansas
12th Arkansas Sharpshooter Battalion
1st Arkansas Cavalry Battalion (dismounted)
1st Missouri Cavalry (dismounted)
3rd Missouri Cavalry (dismounted)
Lowe's Missouri Battery
3rd Missouri Battery

Forney's Division: Maj. Gen. John H. Forney
  Hébert's Brigade: Brig. Gen. Louis Hébert
    3rd Louisiana
    21st Louisiana
    36th Mississippi
    37th Mississippi
    38th Mississippi
    43rd Mississippi
    7th Mississippi Infantry Battalion
    2nd Alabama Artillery Battalion, Co. C
    Appeal Arkansas Artillery
  Moore's Brigade: Brig. Gen. John C. Moore
    37th Alabama
    40th Alabama
    42nd Alabama
    35th Mississippi
    40th Mississippi
    2nd Texas
    Pointe Coupee Artillery, Co. B
    1st Mississippi Light Artillery, Batteries A, C, D, E, G, I

Loring's Division: Maj. Gen. William W. Loring
  First Brigade: Brig. Gen. Lloyd Tilghman
    1st Confederate Battalion
    6th Mississippi
    23rd Mississippi
    26th Mississippi
    14th Mississippi Artillery, Co. C
    1st Mississippi Light Artillery, Co. G
  Second Brigade: Brig. Gen. Abraham Buford
    27th Alabama
    35th Alabama
    54th Alabama
    55th Alabama
    9th Arkansas
    3rd Kentucky
    7th Kentucky
    12th Louisiana
    Pointe Coupee Artillery, Cos. A and G

Third Brigade: Brig. Gen. Winfield S. Featherston
    3rd Mississippi
    22nd Mississippi
    31st Mississippi
    33rd Mississippi
    1st Mississippi Sharpshooter Battalion
    1st Mississippi Light Artillery, Co. D

Smith's Division: Maj. Gen. Martin L. Smith
  First Brigade: Brig. Gen. William E. Baldwin
    17th Louisiana
    31st Louisiana
    4th Mississippi
    46th Mississippi
    Tobin's Tennessee Artillery
  Third Brigade: Brig. Gen. Francis A. Shoup
    26th Louisiana
    27th Louisiana
    28th Louisiana
    McNally's Arkansas Battery
  Vaughn's Brigade: Brig. Gen. John C. Vaughn
    60th Tennessee
    61st Tennessee
    62nd Tennessee

Stevenson's Division: Maj. Gen. Carter L. Stevenson
  First Brigade: Brig. Gen. Seth M. Barton
    40th Georgia
    41st Georgia
    42nd Georgia
    43rd Georgia
    52nd Georgia
    Cherokee Georgia Artillery
  Second Brigade: Brig. Gen. Stephen D. Lee
    20th Alabama
    23rd Alabama
    30th Alabama
    31st Alabama
    46th Alabama

Waddell's Alabama Battery
Third Brigade: Brig. Gen. Alfred Cumming
  34th Georgia
  36th Georgia
  39th Georgia
  56th Georgia
  57th Georgia
Fourth Brigade: Col. Alexander W. Reynolds
  3rd Tennessee (provisional army)
  31st Tennessee
  43rd Tennessee
  59th Tennessee
  3rd Maryland Artillery
Waul's Texas Legion
Cavalry
  Wirt Adams's Mississippi Cavalry
  20th Mississippi Mounted Infantry

Notes

━━ Prologue ━━

Manuscript and published sources cited in the Notes appear in full at their first use in each chapter; subsequent citations in that chapter are shortened. Several often used sources are designated only by shortened titles (and, where applicable, by volume and/or part numbers or state affiliations as well): these include *War of the Rebellion: Official Records of the Union and Confederate Armies* (shortened to *Official Records*); *Official Records of the Union and Confederate Navies in the War of the Rebellion* (shortened to *Official Records . . . Navy*); *Battles and Leaders of the Civil War* (shortened to *Battles and Leaders*); and the various publications of the state chapters of the Military Order of the Loyal Legion of the United States (abbreviated as MOLLUS Papers). All sources appear in full in the Bibliography.

1. David D. Porter, *Incidents and Anecdotes of the Civil War* (New York: D. Appleton & Co., 1886), 95–96.

2. L. Moody Simms Jr., ed., "A Louisiana Engineer at the Siege of Vicksburg: Letters of Henry Ginder," *Louisiana History* 8, no. 4 (Fall 1967): 377.

3. J. F. C. Fuller, *The Generalship of Ulysses S. Grant* (London: John Murray, 1929), 157.

4. George Dewey, *Autobiography of George Dewey: Admiral of the Navy* (New York: Charles Scribner's Sons, 1913), 73.

5. S. H. M. Byers, "Some Recollections of Grant," in *The Annals of the War* (Philadelphia: Times Publishing Co., 1879), 342.

6. Grant to Banks, May 10, 1863, *Official Records*, vol. 24, pt. 3:288.

━━ 1. Battles on the River ━━

1. This occurred from Hampton Roads (the sortie of the *Virginia*) to Galveston Bay (the capture of the *Harriet Lane*) inclusive, and would happen twice more (the sortie of the *Arkansas* and the destruction of the *Indianola*) during the Vicksburg campaign.

2. Eliot Callender, "What a Boy Saw on the Mississippi," in MOLLUS Papers— Illinois, 1: 52.

3. Edwin C. Bearss, *Hardluck Ironclad: The Sinking and Salvage of the Cairo* (Baton Rouge: Louisiana State University Press, 1966), 72.

4. Detailed report of Colonel Ellet, commanding Ram Fleet, June 11, 1862, in *Official Records . . . Navy*, 23:133.

5. H. Allen Gosnell, *Guns on the Western Waters: The Story of River Gunboats in the Civil War* (Baton Rouge: Louisiana State University Press, 1949), 20.

6. David Donald, ed., *Inside Lincoln's Cabinet: The Civil War Diaries of Salmon P. Chase* (New York: Longmans, Green & Co., 1954), 107.

7. The March 28, 1814, action between the *Essex* and the British vessels *Phoebe* and *Cherub*. Out of a 255-man crew, the *Essex* suffered 58 killed, 66 wounded, and 31 missing, an astonishingly high percentage.

8. For an examination of this point see Rowena Reed, *Combined Operations in the Civil War* (Annapolis, Md.: Naval Institute Press, 1978), 199.

9. David Martin, *The Vicksburg Campaign: April 1862–July 1863* (Conshohocken, Pa.: Combined Books, 1990), 39.

10. Report of Fleet Surgeon, June 28, 1862, in *Official Records . . . Navy*, 18:620.

11. S. B. Coleman, "A July Morning with the Rebel Ram 'Arkansas,'" MOLLUS Papers—Michigan, 1: 319.

12. Alfred Thayer Mahan, *The Gulf and Inland Waters* (New York: Charles Scribner's Sons, 1883), 100.

13. Coleman, "A July Morning with the Rebel Ram 'Arkansas,'" 317–319.

14. Isaac N. Brown, "The Confederate Gun-Boat 'Arkansas,'" *Battles and Leaders*, 3:575.

15. George W. Gift, "The Story of the Arkansas," part 3, *Southern Historical Society Papers* 12, no. 4 (April 1884):166.

16. Mahan, *The Gulf and Inland Waters,* 101.

17. Brown, "The Confederate Gun-Boat 'Arkansas,'" 3:576.

18. Ibid.

19. George W. Gift, "The Story of the Arkansas," part 2, *Southern Historical Society Papers* 12, no. 3 (March 1884):118.

20. Ibid., 117.

21. Albert T. Goodloe, *Confederate Echoes* (Nashville, Tenn.: M. E. Church, 1907), 250.

22. Clement Sulivane, "The Arkansas at Vicksburg in 1862," *Confederate Veteran*, 30, no. 11 (November 1917):490.

23. L. S. Flatau, "A Great Naval Battle," *Confederate Veteran* 25, no. 10 (October 1917):459.

24. Shelby Foote, *The Civil War: A Narrative*, vol. 1 (New York: Random House, 1963), 555.

25. Sulivane, "The Arkansas at Vicksburg in 1862," 491.

—— 2. Fates Intermingled ——

1. John C. Pemberton, *Pemberton: Defender of Vicksburg* (Chapel Hill: University of North Carolina Press, 1942), 24.

2. Michael B. Ballard, *Pemberton: A Biography* (Jackson: University Press of Mississippi, 1991), 58.

3. Cited in ibid., 104.

4. Davis to Pickens, August 5, 1862, in Dunbar Rowland, ed., *Jefferson Davis Constitutionalist: His Letters, Papers and Speeches*, vol. 5 (Jackson: Mississippi Department of Archives and History, 1923), 311.

5. Davis to Pickens, August 16, 1862, *Official Records*, 14:597–98. Also in Rowland, *Jefferson Davis Constitutionalist*, 5:319.

6. Davis to Pettus, September 30, 1862, *Official Records*, vol. 17, pt. 2:716.

7. For Pemberton's formal notification, see Randolph to Pemberton, October 14, 1862, ibid., 727–28. Regarding unity of action, see Davis to Phelan, October 11, 1862, ibid., 726–27.

8. See Randolph to Pemberton, September 30, 1862, ibid., 716–17.

9. Phelan to Davis, December 9, 1862, ibid., 788–789.

10. Bell Irvin Wiley, ed., *"This Infernal War": The Confederate Letters of Sgt. Edwin H. Fay* (Austin: University of Texas Press, 1958), 179.

11. Waddy to Cuney, November 20, 1862, *Official Records*, vol. 17, pt. 2:755; and Reed to Smith, December 23, 1862, ibid., 802. Pemberton's initial intent was ambiguous and confused the commissary officers. His staff sorted it out. Pemberton wanted rations for a 10,000-man field force plus a 7,500-man garrison.

12. Lucius W. Barber, *Army Memoirs of Lucius W. Barber* (Chicago: J. M. W. Jones Stationery & Printing Co., 1894), 91.

13. Alexander G. Downing, *Downing's Civil War Diary* (Des Moines: Historical Department of Iowa, 1916), 93.

14. Ira Blanchard, *I Marched with Sherman: Civil War Memoirs of the Twentieth Illinois Volunteer Infantry* (San Francisco: J. D. Huff & Co., 1992), 82.

15. Earl J. Hess, ed., *A German in the Yankee Fatherland: The Civil War Letters of Henry A. Kircher* (Kent, Ohio: Kent State University Press, 1983), 76.

16. Barber, *Army Memoirs*, 89.

17. Special Field Orders, No. 1, November 7, 1862, *Official Records*, vol. 17, pt. 2:326. Special Field Order No. 6 also addresses looting. See ibid., 349–50.

18. Bruce Catton, *Grant Moves South* (Boston: Little, Brown, 1960), 336.

19. Henry Halleck to Ulysses S. Grant, November 15, 1862, *Official Records*, vol. 17, pt. 1:470.

20. David D. Porter, *Incidents and Anecdotes of the Civil War* (New York: D. Appleton & Co., 1886), 123. For Lincoln's character assessment of McClernand, see David Donald, ed., *Inside Lincoln's Cabinet: The Civil War Diaries of Salmon P. Chase* (New York: Longmans, Green & Co., 1954), 161.

21. See Halleck to Grant, December 5, 1862, *Official Records*, vol. 17, pt. 1:473.

22. Ulysses S. Grant to Mary Grant, December 15, 1862, in Jesse Grant Cramer, ed., *Letters of Ulysses S. Grant to His Father and His Youngest Sister, 1857–1878* (New York: G. P. Putnam's Sons, 1912), 96.

23. For Sherman's understanding of his mission, see Sherman to Porter, December 8, 1862, *Official Records*, vol. 17, pt. 2:392.

24. A. F. Brown, "Van Dorn's Operations in Northern Mississippi," *Southern Historical Society Papers* 5, no. 4 (October 1878): 157.

25. Report of Colonel Robert C. Murphy, December 20, 1862, *Official Records*, vol. 17, pt. 1:508–509. A cavalry officer's report censures "the drunkenness or inefficiency of commanding officers." See Report of Major John J. Mudd, December 27, 1862, ibid., 513.

26. Brown, "Van Dorn's Operations in Northern Mississippi," 157.

27. John Eaton, *Grant, Lincoln and the Freedmen: Reminiscences of the Civil War* (New York: Longmans, Green, & Co., 1907), 26.

28. Grant to Loomis, December 23, 1862, *Official Records*, vol. 17, pt. 2:469.

29. William Tecumseh Sherman, *Memoirs of General W. T. Sherman* (New York: Library of America, 1990), 353.

30. Ulysses S. Grant, *Personal Memoirs* (New York: Da Capo Press, 1982), 226.

31. Porter to Fox, August 5, 1862, in Gustavus V. Fox, *Confidential Correspondence of Gustavus V. Fox, Assistant Secretary of the Navy*, vol. 2 (New York: De Vinne Press, 1919), 127.

32. Gideon Welles, *Diary of Gideon Welles*, vol. 1 (Boston: Houghton Mifflin Co., 1911), 157–158.

33. For a good depiction of service aboard the tinclads, see George W. Brown, "Service in the Mississippi Squadron, and Its Connection with the Siege and Capture of Vicksburg," MOLLUS Papers—New York, 1:303–13.

34. General Order No. 9, October 20, 1862, *Official Records . . . Navy*, 23:425.

35. Thomas O. Selfridge, *Memoirs of Thomas O. Selfridge, Jr.* (New York: G. P. Putnam's Sons, 1924), 116.

36. John C. Wideman, whose research unraveled the mechanics of how the torpedoes operated, provides an easy-to-understand sketch of how the torpedoes sunk the *Cairo* in his *The Sinking of the USS Cairo* (Jackson: University Press of Mississippi, 1993), 52–53.

37. Edwin C. Bearss, *Hardluck Ironclad: The Sinking and Salvage of the Cairo* (Baton Rouge: Louisiana State University Press, 1966), 99.

38. Ibid., 101.

39. Porter to Welles, December 27, 1862, *Official Records . . . Navy*, 23:580.

40. Brown, Isaac N. "Confederate Torpedoes in the Yazoo," *Battles & Leaders*, 3:580.

41. Stephen G. Burbridge's brigade landed on December 25 and burned a bridge and trestle and tore up some track. However, high water had already severed the rail line.

42. This marvelous tale, related by both telegraph operators and confirmed by Stephen D. Lee, is in Lee's "Details of Important Work by Two Confederate Telegraph Operators, Christmas Eve, 1862, Which Prevented the Almost Complete Surprise of the Confederate Army at Vicksburg," *Publications of the Mississippi Historical Society* 8 (1904): 54.

43. George W. Morgan, "The Assault on Chickasaw Bluffs," *Battles & Leaders*, 3:467.

44. Hess, *A German in the Yankee Fatherland*, 47.

45. For Union losses, see Return of Casualties, *Official Records*, vol. 17, pt. 1:625. For Confederate losses, see Return of Casualties, ibid., 671.

46. Recall that at Fredericksburg, Lee did not order field fortifications to be erected until after Ambrose Burnside's assault.

47. Hess, *A German in the Yankee Fatherland*, 48.

48. Florence Cox, ed., *Kiss Josey For Me!* (Santa Ana, Calif.: Friis-Pioneer Press, 1974), 116.

49. Editor, "Concerning the Siege of Vicksburg," *Confederate Veteran* 2, no. 10 (October 1894): 295.

50. Flavel C. Barber, *Holding the Line: The Third Tennessee Infantry, 1861–1864* (Kent, Ohio: Kent State University Press, 1994), 89.

51. William T. Sherman to John Sherman, January 6, 1863, in Rachel Sherman Thorndike, ed., *The Sherman Letters* (New York: Charles Scribner's Sons, 1894), 180.

52. Porter, *Incidents and Anecdotes*, 129.

53. See Grant to McPherson, January 8, 1863, *Official Records*, vol. 17, pt. 2:545. For Halleck's order, see Halleck to Grant, January 7, 1863, ibid., 542.

54. See Davis to Holmes, October 21, 1862, in Rowland, *Jefferson Davis Constitutionalist*, vol. 5:356–57.

55. Special Orders, No. 275, November 24, 1862, *Official Records*, vol. 17 pt. 2:757–58.

56. For a good example of Davis's deference, see Davis to Holmes, December 21, 1862, in Rowland, *Jefferson Davis Constitutionalist*, vol. 5:386–88.

57. Joseph E. Johnston, *Narrative of Military Operations* (New York: D. Appleton & Co., 1874), 152.

58. Ibid., 153.

59. Samuel Carter III, *The Final Fortress: The Campaign for Vicksburg, 1862–1863* (New York: St. Martin's Press, 1980), 97. Carter quotes the *Vicksburg Whig*.

60. Johnston's relevant correspondence is provided in Johnston, *Narrative of Military Operations*, 495–497.

61. Johnston to Davis, January 2, 1863, in ibid., 495.

62. Johnston to Davis, January 7, 1863, *Official Records*, vol. 20, pt. 2:488.

63. In fact the numbers were about 40,000, 25,000, and 11,000, with another 8,000 serving in garrison for Sherman and several thousand garrisoning New Orleans.

64. Johnston to Cooper, January 2, 1863, in Johnston, *Narrative of Military Operations*, 498–499; and Johnston to Davis, January 2, 1863, *Official Records*, vol. 17, pt. 2:823.

65. Davis to Seddon, December 23, 1862, *Official Records*, vol. 17 pt. 2:802.

66. Pemberton to Davis, March 15, 1863, *Official Records*, vol. 24, pt. 3:670.

67. Frank L. Byrne and Jean Powers Soman, *Your True Marcus: The Civil War Letters of a Jewish Colonel* (Kent, Ohio: Kent State University Press, 1985), 220.

68. Charles A. Dana, *Recollections of the Civil War* (New York: D. Appleton & Co., 1898), 59.

69. Total losses were 1,061. See Return of Casualties in the Union Forces Engaged at Post of Arkansas, *Official Records*, vol. 17, pt. 1:719.

70. R. R. Garland, "Report of Colonel R. R. Garland, April 1, 1863," *Southern Historical Society Papers* 22 (1894): 12.

71. Hess, *A German in the Yankee Fatherland*, 56.

72. McClernand to Lincoln, January 16, 1863, *Official Records*, vol. 17, pt. 2:566.

73. Halleck to Grant, January 12, 1863, *Official Records*, vol. 17, pt. 2:555.

74. Grant to Halleck, January 11, 1863, *Official Records*, vol. 17, pt. 2:553.

75. William T. Sherman to John Sherman, January 6, 1863, Thorndike, *Sherman Letters*, 180.

—— 3. Ebb Tide ——

1. Frank L. Byrne and Jean Powers Soman, *Your True Marcus: The Civil War Letters of a Jewish Colonel* (Kent, Ohio: Kent State University Press, 1985), 238.

2. Carlos W. Colby, "Bullets, Hardtack and Mud: A Soldier's View of the Vicksburg Campaign," *Journal of the West* 4, no. 2 (April 1965): 140 (diary entry of January 29, 1863).

3. "News of the Day: The Operations Against Vicksburgh," *New York Times*, January 12, 1863, 4.

4. Ulysses S. Grant, *Personal Memoirs* (New York: Da Capo Press, 1982), 231.

5. Grant to Halleck, January 18, 1863, *Official Records*, vol. 17, pt. 2:573. Because of what was to come, this is a particularly important communication. Sherman had previously told Grant that somehow Vicksburg should be approached from the rear. See Sherman to Grant, January 17, 1863, ibid., 571.

6. Luke R. Roberts to Cassea M. Roberts, April 17, 1863, Luke R. Roberts Papers, Thirtieth Alabama Infantry, Harrisburg Civil War Roundtable Collection, U.S. Army Military History Institute (MHI), Carlisle, Pa.

7. Colonel Giles A. Smith's report of March 28 is reprinted in William Tecumseh Sherman, *Memoirs of General W. T. Sherman* (New York: Library of America, 1990), 335–37.

8. Ibid., 334.

9. W. C. Michael, "How the Mississippi Was Opened," MOLLUS Papers—Nebraska, 1:48.

10. William L. B. Jenney, "Personal Recollections of Vicksburg," MOLLUS Papers—Illinois, 3:256.

11. E. Cort Williams, "The Cruise of the 'Black Terror,' " MOLLUS Papers—Ohio 3:165.

12. McClernand to Yates, March 15, 1863, John A. McClernand Letters, Reavis Collection, Chicago Historical Society.

13. Gideon Welles, *Diary of Gideon Welles*, vol. 1 (Boston: Houghton Mifflin Co., 1911), 249. The entry date is dated March 17, 1863.

14. *New York Times*, March 12, 1863, 8; *New York Times*, March 28, 1863, 1.

15. Dan Bauer, "Who Knows the Truth About the Big Bender?" *Civil War Times Illustrated* 27, no. 8 (December 1988): 40.

16. Alexander Abrams claims to have seen them tumbling out of the hall as he went to work at dawn. See Abrams, *A Full and Detailed History of the Siege of Vicksburg* (Atlanta: Intelligencer Steam Power Presses, 1863), 16.

17. Richard Taylor, *Destruction and Reconstruction* (1879; reprint, New York: Longmans, Green & Co., 1955), 146.

18. John Carson, "Capture of the Indianola," *Confederate Veteran* 32, no. 10 (October 1924): 380–83.

19. The exact details of this violent, nocturnal encounter are difficult to ascertain. The reports on both sides differ from one another and are internally inconsistent with regard to how many blows were delivered in what order. The best account is Brent's February 25, 1862, letter to Major E. Surget, which is reproduced in the *Southern Historical Society Papers* 1, no. 2 (February 1876): 94–99.

20. Lawrence L. Hewitt, *Port Hudson: Confederate Bastion on the Mississippi* (Baton Rouge: Louisiana State University Press, 1987), 77.

21. George Dewey, *Autobiography of George Dewey: Admiral of the Navy* (New York: Charles Scribner's Sons, 1913), 88.

22. Ibid., 92-101.

23. Porter to Welles, March 26, 1863, *Official Records . . . Navy*, 24:479.

24. Report of Colonel Charles R. Ellet, March 25, 1863, *Official Records . . . Navy*, 20:19–20.

25. Report of Lieutenant Colonel John Ellet, March 25, 1863, ibid., 21. For a Confederate view of this action, see Moss's entry of March 25 in ibid., 20–21.

26. Earl J. Hess, ed., *A German in the Yankee Fatherland: The Civil War Letters of Henry A. Kircher* (Kent, Ohio: Kent State University Press, 1983), 62.

27. Grant to Banks, March 22, 1863, *Official Records . . . Navy*, 20:9.

28. See Farragut to Porter, March 22, 1863, ibid., 12.

29. Porter to Farragut, March 26, 1863, ibid., 29. Porter said much the same thing in a letter to Farragut written four days earlier. For Grant's appreciation, see Grant to Farragut, March 26, 1863, ibid., 27.

30. For these two very important communications, see Grant to Porter, March 29, 1863, *Official Records*, vol. 24, pt. 3:152; and Porter to Grant, March 29, 1863, ibid., 152.

31. Grant to Porter, April 2, 1863, ibid., 168.

32. Pemberton to Davis, March 15, 1863, ibid., 669–70; and Pemberton to Davis, April 4, 1863, *Official Records . . . Navy*, 20:88.

33. Pemberton to Johnston, March 14, 1863, *Official Records*, vol. 24, pt. 3:669.

34. Reed to Seddon, May 7, 1863, MSS1 R8386a 39, Virginia Historical Society, Richmond, Va.

35. Abrams, *A Full and Detailed History of the Siege of Vicksburg*, 9.

—— 4. The Hazardous Enterprise ——

1. This problem was manifest throughout the war for Federal generals. Hattaway and Jones calculate that in January 1863 about one-third of all Union forces were on guard duty. See Herman Hattaway and Archer Jones, *How the North Won* (Urbana: University of Illinois Press, 1983), 357.

2. Grant to Halleck, April 21, 1863, *Official Records*, vol. 24, pt. 1:31.

3. Paul H. Hass, ed., "The Vicksburg Diary of Henry Clay Warmoth," part 1, *Journal of Mississippi History* 31, no. 4 (November 1969): 338.

4. Manning F. Force, "Personal Recollections of the Vicksburg Campaign," MOLLUS Papers—Ohio, 1:296; and William A. Russ Jr., ed., "The Vicksburg Campaign as Viewed by an Indiana soldier," *Journal of Mississippi History* 19, no. 4 (October 1957): 266.

5. Charles H. Lutz to A. Lutz, April 11, 1863, Civil War Miscellaneous Collection, MHI, Carlisle, Pa.

6. Lincoln to Hurlbut, March 20, 1863, in Roy P. Basler, ed., *The Collected Works of Abraham Lincoln*, vol. 6 (New Brunswick, N.J.: Rutgers University Press, 1953), 142. The editor notes that his message should probably be dated March 25.

7. Gustavus V. Fox to David Farragut, April 2, 1863, *Official Records . . . Navy*, 20:44.

8. James Harrison Wilson, *Under the Old Flag*, 2 vols. (New York: D. Appleton & Co., 1912), 1:134.

9. Ibid., 137.

10. Charles A. Dana, *Recollections of the Civil War* (New York: D. Appleton & Co., 1898), 61.

11. Earl J. Hess, ed., *A German in the Yankee Fatherland: The Civil War Letters of Henry A. Kircher* (Kent, Ohio: Kent State University Press, 1983), 94.

12. George Dodd Carrington diary, April 11, 1863, Chicago Historical Society.

13. Frank L. Byrne and Jean Powers Soman, *Your True Marcus: The Civil War Letters of a Jewish Colonel* (Kent, Ohio: Kent State University Press, 1985), 243.

14. Hass, "The Vicksburg Diary of Henry Clay Warmoth," part 1, 347.

15. Mary Ann Anderson, ed., *The Civil War Diary of Allen Morgan Geer* (New York: Cosmos Press, 1977), 89. The entry is dated April 10.

16. Thomas to Stanton, April 12, 1863, *Official Records*, vol. 24, pt. 3:187.

17. Davis to senators and representatives from Arkansas, March 30, 1863, in Dunbar Rowland, ed., *Jefferson Davis Constitutionalist: His Letters, Papers and Speeches*, vol. 5 (Jackson: Mississippi Department of Archives and History, 1923), 462.

18. Davis to Flanagin, April 3, 1863, in ibid., 5:466.

19. Davis to Pemberton, March 16, 1863, in ibid., 5:447.

20. Davis to Brooks, April 2, 1863, in ibid., 5:464.

21. Pemberton to Cooper, April 11, 1863, *Official Records*, vol. 24, pt. 3:733.

22. Pemberton to Cooper, April 9, 1863, ibid., 730.

23. Cockrell to Hutchinson, April 12, 1863, ibid., 736.

24. Pemberton to Johnston, April 12, 1863, ibid., 738.

25. David D. Porter to Gustavus V. Fox, April 25, 1863, in Gustavus V. Fox, *Confidential Correspondence of Gustavus V. Fox, Assistant Secretary of the Navy*, 2 vols. (New York: De Vinne Press, 1919), 2:176.

26. "Galway," "The Siege of Vicksburgh," *New York Times*, April 16, 1863, 1.

27. David D. Porter, *Incidents and Anecdotes of the Civil War* (New York: D. Appleton & Co., 1886), 175.

28. For Porter's doubts, see Porter to Fox, April 25, 1863, in Fox, *Confidential Correspondence*, 2:172.

29. The Confederate commander, Colonel Edward Higgens, describes thirty-seven heavy pieces, but three of them are usually rated as fieldpieces. See Edwin C. Bearss, *The Campaign for Vicksburg*, 3 vols. (Dayton, Ohio: Morningside House, 1986), 2:64.

30. Henry Walke, *Naval Scenes and Reminiscences of the Civil War in the United States* (New York: F. R. Reed & Co., 1877), 355.

31. J. T. Hogane, "Reminiscences of the Siege of Vicksburg," part 1, *Southern Historical Society Papers* 11, nos. 4–5 (April–May 1883): 224.

32. James K. Worthington to Elizabeth Worthington, April 23, 1863, James K. Worthington letters, Civil War Times Illustrated Collection, MHI, Carlisle, Pa.

33. Porter, *Incidents and Anecdotes*, 177.

34. Report of Fleet Surgeon, April 17, 1863, *Official Records . . . Navy*, 24:564. The killed pilot and three wounded aboard the *General Price* must be added to the surgeon's list.

35. Pemberton to Chalmers, April 18, 1863, *Official Records*, vol. 24, pt. 3:765.

36. A. Hugh Moss, *The Diary of A. Hugh Moss* (New York: Scribner Press, 1948), 21. The entry is dated April 17.

37. Lee to Davis, April 27, 1863, *Official Records*, vol. 25, pt. 2:752–53.

38. McClernand to Grant, April 19, 1863, *Official Records*, vol. 24, pt. 3:207. McClernand said much the same thing the previous day as well.

39. Carrington diary, April 22, 1863.

40. Ira Blanchard, *I Marched with Sherman: Civil War Memoirs of the Twentieth Illinois Volunteer Infantry* (San Francisco: J. D. Huff & Co., 1992), 82.

41. William T. Sherman to Ellen Sherman, April 23, 1863, in M. A. Howe, ed., *Home Letters of General Sherman* (New York: Charles Scribner's Sons, 1909), 253.

42. Flavel C. Barber, *Holding the Line: The Third Tennessee Infantry, 1861–1864*, ed. Robert Ferrell (Kent, Ohio: Kent State University Press, 1994), 112.

43. Benjamin Franklin Stevenson, *Letters from the Army* (Cincinnati: Robert Clarke & Co., 1886), 215.

44. William T. Sherman to John Sherman, April 26, 1863, in Rachel Sherman Thorndike, ed., *The Sherman Letters* (New York: Charles Scribner's Sons, 1894), 201.

45. Ulysses S. Grant, *Personal Memoirs* (New York: Da Capo Press, 1982), 127.

46. Eldridge Smith to Lyman Smith, June 25, 1863, Perry R. Smith letters, Civil War Times Illustrated Collection, MHI, Carlisle, Pa.

47. Bowen to Memminger, April 27, 1863, *Official Records*, vol. 24, pt. 3:792.

48. Cited in D. Alexander Brown, *Grierson's Raid* (Urbana: University of Illinois Press, 1962), 223.

49. Ibid., 25.

50. W. A. Campbell, "Humors of the March," *Confederate Veteran* 1, no. 7 (July 1893): 216.

51. Brown, *Grierson's Raid*, 108.

52. See Pemberton to Johnston, April 29, 1863, *Official Records*, vol. 24, pt. 3:802.

53. Edward Fontaine diary, April 23,1863, cited in John K. Bettersworth, ed., *Mississippi in the Confederacy As They Saw It* (Baton Rouge: Louisiana State University Press, 1961), 112.

54. Grant, *Personal Memoirs*, 256–57.

55. Brown, *Grierson's Raid*, 223.

56. Ibid., 150.

57. Porter to Welles, April 24, 1863, *Official Records . . . Navy*, 24:607.

58. Porter to Fox, April 25, 1863, in Fox, *Confidential Correspondence*, 2:175.

59. General Order of Acting Rear Admiral Porter, May 2, 1863, *Official Records . . . Navy*, 24:626.

60. Porter to Welles, April 29, 1863, ibid., 610, sets the losses aboard the *Benton*, *Pittsburgh*, and *Tuscumbia* at twenty-four killed, fifty-six wounded. However, a count taken from the individual ship reports yields the numbers stated in the text.

61. Paul H. Hass, ed., "The Vicksburg Diary of Henry Clay Warmoth," part 2, *Journal of Mississippi History* 32, no. 1 (February 1979): 63; and Report of John Cronan, Acting Carpenter, April 30, 1863, *Official Records . . . Navy,* 24:622.

62. Captured letter of Alfred Mitchell, April 30, 1863, *Official Records . . . Navy,* 24:629.

63. Pemberton to Bowen, April 28, 1863, *Official Records,* vol. 24, pt. 3:797.

64. Bowen to Pemberton, April 28, 1863, ibid., 797.

65. According to Charles E. Hooker, on April 1, Pemberton's effective total was 48,829, with a total enrolled force of more than 72,000. See Hooker, *Confederate Military History Extended Edition, Volume 9, Mississippi* (Wilmington, N.C.: Broadfoot Publishing Co., 1987), 127–32.

66. Pemberton to Johnston, December 5, 1862, *Official Records,* vol. 17, pt. 2:784.

67. Pemberton to Stevenson, April 28, 1863, *Official Records,* vol. 24, pt. 3:800.

68. William L. B. Jenney, "Personal Recollections of Vicksburg," MOLLUS Papers—Illinois, 3:258.

69. Sherman to Grant, April 28, 1863, *Official Records,* vol. 24, pt. 3:243.

70. Grant, *Personal Memoirs,* 252.

71. William T. Sherman to Ellen Sherman, April 29, 1863, in Howe, *Home Letters,* 258.

____ 5.   The Battle of Port Gibson ____

1. Grant to Halleck, May 3, 1863, *Official Records,* vol. 24, pt. 1:32.

2. Lewis B. Jessup diary, May 1, 1863, Regimental Files, Twenty-fourth Indiana, Vicksburg National Military Park (VNMP), Vicksburg, Miss.

3. Report of Colonel Isham W. Garrott, May 1863, *Official Records,* vol. 24, pt. 1:679; and William Milner Kelly, "A History of the Thirtieth Alabama Volunteers," *Alabama Historical Quarterly* 9, no. 1 (Spring 1947):135.

4. Jerald H. Markham, *The Botetourt Artillery* (Lynchburg, Va.: H. E. Howard, Inc., 1986), 33.

5. William Candace Thompson, "From Shiloh to Port Gibson," *Civil War Times Illustrated* 3, no. 6 (October 1964): 23.

6. Edwin C. Bearss, *The Campaign for Vicksburg,* 3 vols. (Dayton, Ohio: Morningside House, 1986), 2:385.

7. Thompson, "From Shiloh to Port Gibson," 24.

8. Report of Colonel James R. Slack, May 5, 1863, *Official Records,* vol. 24, pt. 1:611.

9. R. S. Bevier, "Incidents and Personal Sketches of the Missouri First and Second Confederate Brigades," in appendix to Osborn H. Oldroyd, *A Soldier's Story of the Siege of Vicksburg* (Springfield, Ill.: n.p., 1885), 161.

10. R. S. Bevier, *History of the First and Second Missouri Confederate Brigades, 1861–1865* (St. Louis: Bryan, Brand & Co., 1879), 180.

11. Details of this action provided by Ira Blanchard, *I Marched with Sherman: Civil War Memoirs of the Twentieth Illinois Volunteer Infantry* (San Francisco: J. D. Huff & Co., 1992), 85–86.

12. James E. Payne, "Missouri Troops in the Vicksburg Campaign," *Confederate Veteran* 36, no. 8 (August 1928): 303.

13. Grant to Halleck, May 3, 1863, *Official Records*, vol. 24, pt. 1:33.

14. Bevier writes that his Fifth Missouri lost more than 100 out of the 350 who began the battle. See Bevier, "Incidents and Personal Sketches," 162.

15. Paul H. Hass, ed., "The Vicksburg Diary of Henry Clay Warmoth," part 2, *Journal of Mississippi History* 32, no. 1 (February 1979): 68.

16. Richard L. Howard, *History of the 124th Regiment, Illinois Infantry Volunteers* (Springfield, Ill.: H. W. Rokker, 1880), 79.

17. Thompson, "From Shiloh to Port Gibson," 23.

18. Bowen to Pemberton and Pemberton to Bowen, May 1, 1863, *Official Records*, vol. 24, pt. 1:660–61.

19. Pemberton to Davis, May 1, 1863, *Official Records*, vol. 24, pt. 3:807.

20. John C. Francis to Cassea Roberts, May 9, 1863, Luke R. Roberts Papers, Harrisburg Civil War Roundtable Collection, MHI, Carlisle, Pa.

21. S. H. M. Byers, "Some Recollections of Grant," in *Annals of the War Written by Leading Participants North and South* (1879; reprint, Edison, N.J.: Blue & Grey Press, 1996), 342.

22. Johnston to Pemberton, May 1, 1863, *Official Records*, vol. 24, pt. 3:808.

23. Pemberton to Commanding Officer or Quartermaster, Edwards Depot, May 2, 1863, ibid., 815. Pemberton told the Edwards Depot commander to forward the instructions to Loring or Brigadier General Lloyd Tilghman.

24. See Pemberton to Pettus, May 3, 1863, ibid., 826.

25. Thompson to Stevenson, May 4, 1863, ibid., 830.

26. William L. Ritter, "Sketch of the Third Maryland Artillery," part 2, *Southern Historical Society Papers* 10, nos. 8–9 (August–September 1883):397.

27. Grant to Bingham, April 30, 1863, *Official Records*, vol. 24, pt. 3:248; Grant to Sullivan, May 3, 1863, 268; and Grant to Sherman, May 3, 1863, ibid., 268.

28. Davis to Pemberton, May 7, 1863, ibid., 842.

29. Pemberton to Gardner, May 8, 1863, ibid., 845.

___ 6. Blitzkrieg through Mississippi ___

1. "General Grant expects to discover in what manner the enemy intend to fight, and will then make new combinations accordingly." Sherman to Blair, May 9, 1863, *Official Records*, vol. 24, pt. 3:286.

2. George Dodd Carrington diary, May 4, 1863, Chicago Historical Society.

3. John V. Boucher to Polly Boucher, May 6, 1863, Boucher Family Papers, Civil War Miscellaneous Collection, U.S. Military History Institute (MHI), Carlisle, Pa.

4. David D. Porter, *Incidents and Anecdotes of the Civil War* (New York: D. Appleton & Co., 1886), 186. Fred Grant told the same story at an army reunion in 1905.

5. Ira Blanchard, *I Marched with Sherman: Civil War Memoirs of the Twentieth Illinois Volunteer Infantry* (San Francisco: J. D. Huff & Co., 1992), 87.

6. Osborn H. Oldroyd, *A Soldier's Story of the Siege of Vicksburg* (Springfield, Ill.: n.p., 1885), 22.

7. Historian Edwin Bearss uncovered this important piece of revisionist history. See Edwin C. Bearss, *The Campaign for Vicksburg*, 3 vols. (Dayton, Ohio: Morningside House, 1986), 2:461–70, 480–81. Regarding provisions, as early as May 9 McPherson was reporting that food was scarce. For an example, see McPherson to McArthur, May 9, 1863, *Official Records*, vol. 24, pt. 3:287.

8. Loring to Memminger, May 9, 1863, *Official Records*, vol. 24, pt. 3:849.

9. Stafford to Loring and Stevenson, May 10, 1863, ibid., 852.

10. Pemberton to Theo. Johnston, May 11, 1863, ibid., 858.

11. Pemberton's perceptions, which are key to what took place, are in Pemberton to Davis, May 12, 1863, ibid., 859.

12. Pemberton to Gregg, May 12, 1863, ibid., 862.

13. Grant to Banks, May 10, 1863, ibid., 288.

14. Grant to McPherson, May 11, 1863, ibid., 297.

15. Gregg's instructions are in Pemberton to Gregg, May 11, 1863, ibid., 855–56.

16. Henry O. Dwight, "A Soldier's Story: The Affair on the Raymond Road," *New York Tribune*, November 21, 1886, 11.

17. Flavel C. Barber, *Holding the Line: The Third Tennessee Infantry, 1861–1864* ed. Robert Ferrell (Kent, Ohio: Kent State University Press; 1994), 120.

18. Manning F. Force, "Personal Recollections of the Vicksburg Campaign," MOLLUS Papers—Ohio, 1:299.

19. Blanchard, *I Marched with Sherman*, 88.

20. Dwight, "A Soldier's Story," 11.

21. Mary Ann Anderson, ed., *The Civil War Diary of Allen Morgan Geer* (New York: Cosmos Press, 1977), 99.

22. Letter of an Anonymous Yankee, Sixty-eighth Ohio Infantry Regiment, Vicksburg Campaign, May 26, 1863, Civil War Times Illustrated Collection, MHI, Carlisle, Pa.

23. Bearss, *The Campaign for Vicksburg*, 2:498.

24. Blanchard, *I Marched with Sherman*, 89.

25. Howard Stevens, letter, May 31, 1863, Gregory A. Cocco Collection, Harrisburg Civil War Roundtable Collection, MHI, Carlisle, Pa.

26. Seddon to Beauregard, May 2, 1863, and Beauregard to Seddon, May 3, 1863, *Official Records*, 14:923–924.

27. Johnston to Pemberton, May 13, 1863, *Official Records*, vol. 24, pt. 3:870.

28. Johnston to Seddon, May 13, 1863, *Official Records*, vol. 24, pt. 1:215.

29. Taylor to Loring, May 13, 1863, *Official Records*, vol. 24, pt. 3:873.

30. Report of Colonel John B. Sanborn, May 25, 1863, *Official Records*, vol. 24, pt. 1:729.

31. Henry S. Keene diary, May 14, 1863, Regimental Files, Sixth Wisconsin Battery, Vicksburg National Military Park (VNMP), Vicksburg, Miss.

32. Miriam Poole, ed., " 'No Rest for the Wicked': Henry Seaman's Vicksburg Diary," *Civil War Times Illustrated* 22, no. 5 (September 1983): 23.

33. Pemberton to Johnston, May 14, 1863, *Official Records*, vol. 24, pt. 3:877.

34. John C. Taylor diary, May 13, 1863, Harry Baylor Taylor Papers, Special Collections, Alderman Library, University of Virginia, Charlottesville, Va. See MS 9965A,

box 1, file "Military Dispatches and Orders, 1863, June 5–November 3." In his diary Taylor, who was Pemberton's aide, confuses events on May 13 and 14.

35. Joseph E. Johnston, *Narrative of Military Operations* (New York: D. Appleton & Co., 1874), 181.

36. Johnston to Pemberton, May 15, 1863, *Official Records,* vol. 24, pt. 3:882.

37. Taylor diary, May 15, 1863. See MS 9965A, box 1, file "Military Dispatches and Orders, 1863, June 5–November 3."

38. William A. Drennan, letter to his wife, May 30, 1863, Drennan Papers Mississippi Department of Archives and History, Jackson, Miss. Drennan was a lieutenant on Featherston's staff.

39. Calvin Smith, "'We Can Hold Our Ground': Calvin Smith's diary," *Civil War Times Illustrated* 24, no. 2 (April 1985): 28.

40. Cumming to Lee, November 3, 1899, folder 15, vol. 12, record group 12, Mississippi Department of Archives and History, Jackson, Miss. This is a more candid account than Cumming's report in the *Official Records.* Vicksburg National Military Park has a copy. Hereafter cited as Cumming to Lee, November 3, 1899, Mississippi Archives.

____ 7. To the Crossroads ____

1. Cumming to Lee, November 3, 1899, Mississippi Archives.

2. William A. Drennan, letter to his wife, May 30, 1863, Drennan Papers, Mississippi Department of Archives and History, Jackson, Miss..

3. Ibid.

4. McClernand to Blair, May 15, 1863, *Official Records,* vol. 24, pt. 3:313.

5. McClernand to Hovey, May 16, 1863, ibid., 316.

6. John C. Taylor Diary, May 16, 1863, Harry Baylor Taylor Papers, Special Collections, Alderman Library, University of Virginia, Charlottesville, Va. See MS 9965A, box 1, file "Military Dispatches and Orders, 1863 June 5–November 3."

7. Report of Major General Carter L. Stevenson, July 29, 1863, *Official Records,* vol. 24, pt. 2:94.

8. John B. Sanborn, *The Crisis at Champion's Hill: The Decisive Battle of the Civil War* (St. Paul, Minn.: n.p., 1903), 10.

9. Charles A. Dana, *Recollections of the Civil War* (New York: D. Appleton & Co., 1899), 64.

10. Vicksburg National Military Park historian Terrence Winschel notes in a letter to the author that he doubts if Pemberton was informed about the buildup of Union strength against his left flank.

11. Osborn H. Oldroyd, *A Soldier's Story of the Siege of Vicksburg* (Springfield, Ill.: n.p., 1885), 25.

12. T. J. Williams, "The Battle of Champion's Hill," MOLLUS Papers—Ohio, 5:205.

13. For an example, see C. J. Durham diary, May 16, 1863, Regimental Files, Eleventh Indiana, Vicksburg National Military Park (VNMP), Vicksburg, Miss.

14. Report of John C. Taylor, July 29, 1863, *Official Records,* vol. 24, pt. 2:122.

15. John Stevenson's Seventh Missouri was in the rear guarding the wagons.

16. Drennan letter, May 30, 1863, Drennan Papers.

17. Jerald H. Markham, *The Botetourt Artillery* (Lynchburg, Va.: H. E. Howard, 1986), 38.

18. Cumming to Lee, November 3, 1899, Mississippi Archives.

19. Charles R. Longley, "Champion's Hill," MOLLUS Papers—Iowa, 1:212–213.

20. Williams, "The Battle of Champion's Hill," 206.

21. Israel M. Ritter diary, May 16, 1863, Civil War Miscellaneous Collection, U.S. Army Military History Institute (MHI), Carlisle, Pa.

22. Manning F. Force, "Personal Recollections of the Vicksburg Campaign," MOLLUS Papers—Ohio, 1:302.

23. W. S. Morris, et. al., *Thirty-First Regiment Illinois Volunteers* (Herrin, Ill.: Crossfire Press, 1991), 64.

24. Ibid., 64–65.

25. Drennan letter, May 30, 1863, Drennan Papers.

26. Ira Blanchard, *I Marched with Sherman: Civil War Memoirs of the Twentieth Illinois Volunteer Infantry* (San Francisco: J. D. Huff & Co., 1992), 92.

27. E. Z. Hays, ed., *History of the Thirty-Second Regiment, Ohio Veteran Volunteer Infantry* (Columbus, Ohio: Cort & Evans, 1896),43.

28. Ibid., 43.

29. For details of this action, see Editor, "The Brave and True Capt. S. J. Ridley," *Confederate Veteran* 2, no. 11 (November 1894):343; see also Charles E. Bassett to W. T. Rigby, July 14, 1902, Regimental Files, 124th Illinois, VNMP.

30. W. O. Connor to F. G. Obenchain, February 23, 1904, attached to Connor to Rigby, February 24, 1904, Regimental Files, Cherokee Artillery, VNMP.

31. Richard L. Howard, *History of the 124th Regiment, Illinois Infantry Volunteers* (Springfield, Ill.: H. W. Rokker, 1880), 96.

32. Bassett to Rigby, July 14, 1902, Regimental Files, 124th Illinois, VNMP; Howard, *History of the 124th Regiment, Illinois Infantry Volunteers*, 97, tells much the same story.

33. Connor to Obenchain, February 23, 1904, Regimental Files, Cherokee Artillery, VNMP.

34. Hays, *History of the Thirty-Second Regiment, Ohio Veteran Infantry*, 45.

35. Blanchard, *I Marched with Sherman*, 93.

36. Bassett to Rigby, July 14, 1902, Regimental Files, 124th Illinois, VNMP.

37. Ulysses S. Grant, "The Vicksburg Campaign," in *Battles & Leaders*, 3:511.

—— 8. The Hill of Death ——

1. Statements of Confederate staff officers, August 20, 1863, *Official Records*, vol. 24, pt. 2:121.

2. William A. Drennan, letter to his wife, May 30, 1863, Drennan Papers, Mississippi Department of Archives and History, Jackson, Miss.

3. Phillip Thomas Tucker, *The South's Finest: The First Missouri Confederate Brigade from Pea Ridge to Vicksburg* (Shippensburg, Pa.: White Mane Publishing, 1993), 162.

4. Memoirs, undated, William A. Ruyle papers, Fifth Missouri, Harrisburg Civil War Roundtable Collection, U.S. Military History Institute (MHI), Carlisle, Pa.

5. Report of Col. Amos Riley, July 1, 1863, Regimental Files, First Missouri, Vicksburg National Military Park (VNMP), Vicksburg, Miss.

6. Reports of Colonel Elijah Gates, August 1, 1863, *Official Records*, vol. 24, pt. 2:119.

7. T. J. Williams, "The Battle of Champion's Hill," MOLLUS Papers—Ohio, 5:207.

8. James E. Payne, "Missouri Troops in the Vicksburg Campaign," *Confederate Veteran* 36, no. 9 (September 1928):341.

9. Israel M. Ritter diary, May 16, 1863, Civil War Miscellaneous Collection, MHI, Carlisle, Pa.

10. Williams, "The Battle of Champion's Hill," 207–9.

11. A. H. Reynolds, "Vivid Experiences at Champion Hill, Miss.," *Confederate Veteran* 28, no. 1 (January 1910):21.

12. Memoirs, undated, Ruyle papers, Fifth Missouri, Harrisburg Civil War Roundtable Collection, MHI.

13. Lewis B. Jessup diary, May 16, 1863, Regimental Files, Twenty-fourth Indiana, VNMP.

14. Ibid.

15. Reports of Brigadier General George F. McGinnis, May 19, 1863, *Official Records*, vol. 24, pt. 2:50.

16. Tucker, *The South's Finest*, 165–66.

17. S. H. M. Byers, "Some Recollections of Grant," in *Annals of the War Written by Leading Participants North and South* (1879; reprint, Edison, N.J.: Blue & Grey Press, 1996), 345–346.

18. Lewis B. Jessup diary, May 16, 1863, Regimental Files, Twenty-fourth Indiana, VNMP.

19. Drennan letter, May 30, 1863, Drennan Papers.

20. Statement of Jacob Thompson, July 21, 1863, *Official Records*, vol. 24, pt. 2:126.

21. Reports of Lieutenant General John C. Pemberton, August 2, 1863, *Official Records*, vol. 24, pt. 1:264.

22. Byers, "Some Recollections of Grant," 346.

23. Harvey M. Trimble diary, May 15, 1863, Regimental Files, Ninety-third Illinois, VNMP.

24. Report of Colonel Holden Putnam, May 25, 1863, *Official Records*, vol. 24, pt. 2:66.

25. Harvey M. Trimble, ed., *History of the Ninety-Third Regiment Illinois Volunteer Infantry* (Chicago: Blakely Printing Co., 1898), 30.

26. S. H. M. Byers, "How Men Feel in Battle: Recollections of a Private at Champion Hills," *Annals of Iowa* 2, no. 6 (July 1896):443.

27. Henry G. Hicks, "The Campaign and Capture of Vicksburg," MOLLUS Papers—Minnesota 6:100.

28. Report of Lieutenant Colonel Ezekiel Sampson, Fifth Iowa, May 25, 1863, *Official Records*, vol. 24, pt. 2:315.

29. Reports of Colonel Elijah Gates, August 1, 1863, ibid., 119.

30. Byers, "How Men Feel in Battle," 445.

31. Because the massed artillery helped stem the tide, there are some competing claims regarding who deserves credit. Sanborn clearly attributes the formation of the gun

line to Grant. See John B. Sanborn, *The Crisis at Champion's Hill: The Decisive Battle of the Civil War* (St. Paul, Minn.: n.p., 1903), 13.

32. Sanborn, *The Crisis at Champion's Hill*, 14.

33. Henry S. Keene diary, May 16, 1863, Regimental Files, Sixth Wisconsin Battery, VNMP.

34. Payne, "Missouri Troops in the Vicksburg Campaign," 341.

35. T. B. Sproul, letter to editor, *Confederate Veteran* 2, no. 7, (July 1894):199.

36. Stephen D. Lee, "The Campaign of Vicksburg, Mississippi, in 1863—from April 12 to and Including the Battle of Champion Hills, or Bakers Creek, May 16, 1863," *Publications of the Mississippi Historical Society* 3 (1900):48.

37. Napoléon actually said: "The issue of a battle is the result of a single instant, a single thought. The adversaries come into each other's presence with various combinations; they mingle, they fight for a length of time; the decisive moment appears; a psychological spark makes the decision; and a few reserve troops are enough to carry it out." Quoted in J. Christopher Herold, *The Mind of Napoleon* (New York: Columbia University Press, 1955), 222–23.

38. Williams, "The Battle of Champion's Hill," 210.

39. Report of Lieutenant Joseph Strong, May 30, 1863, *Official Records*, vol. 24, pt. 2:59.

40. Reynolds, "Vivid Experiences at Champion Hill, Miss.," 21.

41. Ibid.

42. Osborn H. Oldroyd, *A Soldier's Story of the Siege of Vicksburg* (Springfield, Ill.: n.p., 1885), 23.

43. Joseph Orville Jackson, ed., *"Some of the Boys . . . :" The Civil War Letters of Isaac Jackson, 1862–1865* (Carbondale: Southern Illinois University Press, 1960), 94.

44. Reports of Major General John A. McClernand, June 17, 1863, *Official Records*, vol. 24, pt. 1:150.

45. Report of Brigadier General Peter J. Osterhaus, May 26, 1863, *Official Records*, vol. 24, pt. 2:13.

46. Pemberton reports, August 2, 1863, *Official Records*, vol. 24, pt. 1:264.

47. Report of Colonel Thomas M. Scott, May 28, 1863, *Official Records*, vol. 24, pt. 2:89.

48. McClernand reports, June 17, 1863, *Official Records*, vol. 24, pt. 1:150.

49. Osterhaus report, May 26, 1863, *Official Records*, vol. 24, pt. 2:15.

50. Report of Colonel Edward Goodwin, May 28, 1863, ibid., 88.

51. Pemberton reports, August 2, 1863, *Official Records*, vol. 24, pt. 1:264–65.

52. Statements of Confederate staff officers, August 20, 1863, *Official Records*, vol. 24, pt. 2:121.

53. Winfield S. Featherston's report says, "We had a guide, who carried us the nearest way." Ibid., 91.

54. Reports of Major General William Loring, August 28, 1863, ibid., 76.

55. McClernand's order of May 16, 1863, *Official Records*, vol. 24, pt. 3:318.

56. E. T. Eggleston, "Scenes Where General Tilghman Was Killed," *Confederate Veteran* 1, no. 10 (October 1893): 296.

57. J. G. Spencer to Frank H. Foote, September 18, 1910, Regimental Files, First Mississippi Light Artillery, VNMP.

58. Ibid.

59. D. M. Matthews, "A Reminiscence of Champion Hill," *Confederate Veteran* 21, no. 5 (May 1913): 208.

60. Reynolds, "Vivid Experiences at Champion Hill," 22.

61. J. G. Spencer to Frank H. Foote, September 18, 1910, Regimental Files, First Mississippi Light Artillery, VNMP.

62. T. A. Manahan, letter to editor, *Confederate Veteran* 2, no. 8 (August 1894):227. Another of Loring's men writes, "Orders were given to fall back to Vicksburg, but Loring swore he would not take his men to Vicksburg, and he didn't." In Matthews, "A Reminiscence of Champion Hill," 208.

63. Drennan letter, May 30, 1863, Drennan Papers.

64. James Dinkins, "Witticisms of Soldiers," *Confederate Veteran* 3, no. 9 (September 1895):270–71.

65. Byers, "Some Recollections of Grant," 346.

66. *History of the Forty-Sixth Regiment, Indiana Volunteer Infantry* (Logansport, Ind.: Wilson, Humphreys & Co., 1888), 62.

67. Eugene B. Harrison diary, May 16, 1863, Sixty-eighth Ohio, Civil War Miscellaneous Collection, MHI, Carlisle, Pa.

68. C. J. Durham diary, May 17, 1863, Regimental Files, Eleventh Indiana, VNMP.

69. Lewis B. Jessup diary, May 16, 1863, Regimental Files, Twenty-fourth Indiana, VNMP.

70. *History of the Forty-Sixth Regiment, Indiana Volunteer Infantry*, 63.

71. Adam Shower, letter, May 18, 1863, in James Fogle letters, Regimental Files, Eleventh Indiana, VNMP.

72. Federal losses are derived from the Return of Casualties, *Official Records*, vol. 24, pt. 2:7–10.

73. McGinnis reports, May 19, 1863, ibid., 51.

74. Edwin C. Bearss, *The Campaign for Vicksburg*, 3 vols. (Dayton, Ohio: Morningside House, 1986), 2:642.

75. John A. Leavy journal, May 16, 1863, Letters and Diaries Files, VNMP.

76. Sanborn, *The Crisis at Champion's Hill*, 28.

77. The breakdown was 444,300 Union, 297,000 Confederate. These figures are based on map 92 in U.S. Military Academy, *The West Point Atlas of American Wars*, vol. 1 (New York: Frederick A. Praeger Publishers, 1959).

78. Reports of Brigadier General Alvin P. Hovey, May 25, 1863, *Official Records*, vol. 24, pt. 2:44.

____ 9. "A Perilous and Ludicrous Charge" ____

1. Lida Lord Reed, "A Woman's Experience During the Siege of Vicksburg," *Century* 61, no. 6 (April 1901):922.

2. Pemberton's letter is partially reproduced in Report of General Joseph E. Johnston, December 24, 1863, *Official Records*, vol. 24, pt. 1:241.

3. In his *Memoirs*, p. 274, Grant confuses the presence of a staff officer delivering a message from Banks with Halleck's May 11 communication. For a discussion of this,

see: Williams, Kenneth P., *Lincoln Finds a General* (New York: Macmillan, 1956), 4:367, 382. What is notable is that Grant knew that the administration wanted him to unite with Banks before tackling Vicksburg and that he chose an alternative strategy.

4. James Harrison Wilson, *Under the Old Flag*, 2 vols. (New York: D. Appleton & Co., 1912), 1:177.

5. Sylvanus Cadwallader, *Three Years with Grant* (Lincoln: University of Nebraska Press, 1996), 83.

6. R. S. Bevier, "Incidents and Personal Sketches of the Missouri First and Second Confederate Brigades," in appendix to Osborn H. Oldroyd, *A Soldier's Story of the Siege of Vicksburg* (Springfield, Ill.: n.p., 1885), 165.

7. Reports of Colonel Elijah Gates, August 15, 1863, *Official Records*, vol. 24, pt. 2:120.

8. James Synnamon, "A Veteran with Many Wounds," *Confederate Veteran* 21, no. 12 (December 1913):582.

9. John C. Taylor diary, May 17, 1863, Harry Baylor Taylor Papers, Special Collections, Alderman Library, University of Virginia, Charlottesville, Va. See MS 9965A, box 1, file "Military Dispatches and Orders, 1863 June 5–November 3."

10. Reports of Lieutenant General John C. Pemberton, August 2, 1863, *Official Records*, vol. 24, pt. 1:269.

11. Samuel H. Lockett, "The Defense of Vicksburg," in *Battles & Leaders*, 3:488.

12. W. S. Morris, et al., *Thirty-First Regiment Illinois Volunteers* (Herrin, Ill.: Crossfire Press, 1991), 66.

13. Wilson, *Under the Old Flag*, 1:178.

14. Return of Casualties, *Official Records*, vol. 24, pt. 2:130.

15. Reports of Brigadier General Eugene A. Carr, May 31, 1863, *Official Records*, vol. 24, pt. 1:617.

16. Joseph Orville Jackson, ed., *"Some of the Boys . . . ": The Civil War Letters of Isaac Jackson, 1862–1865* (Carbondale: Southern Illinois University Press, 1960), 96.

17. These totals are the sums of the previously reported battles. Recall that Confederate returns are incomplete for Port Gibson, Champion Hill, and the Big Black. Francis Vinton Greene, *The Mississippi* (Wilmington, N.C.: Broadfoot Publishing Co., 1989), 170, provides an even greater disparity in relative losses.

18. Ira Blanchard, *I Marched with Sherman: Civil War Memoirs of the Twentieth Illinois Volunteer Infantry* (San Francisco: J. D. Huff & Co., 1992), 82.

19. John Eaton, *Grant, Lincoln and the Freedmen: Reminiscences of the Civil War* (New York: Longmans, Green, & Co., 1907), 79–80.

20. Johnston, report, December 24, 1863, *Official Records*, vol. 24, pt. 1:241.

21. Johnston to Pemberton, May 17, 1863, *Official Records*, vol. 24, pt. 3:888.

22. Lee to Seddon, May 10, 1863, *Official Records*, vol. 25, pt. 2:790.

23. Jefferson Davis to the People of the Confederate States, April 10, 1863, in Dunbar Rowland, ed., *Jefferson Davis Constitutionalist: His Letters, Papers and Speeches*, vol. 5 (Jackson: Mississippi Department of Archives and History, 1923), 471.

24. Reagan's account of this is in John H. Reagan, *Memoirs: With Special Reference to Secession and the Civil War* (New York: Neale Publishing Co., 1906), 150–53.

25. Davis to Pemberton, May 23, 1863 in Rowland, *Jefferson Davis Constitutionalist*, 5:494.

26. Lincoln to Arnold, May 26, 1863, in Roy P. Basler, ed., *The Collected Works of Abraham Lincoln*, vol. 6 (New Brunswick, N.J.: Rutgers University Press, 1953), 230.

____ 10. Assault ____

1. William A. Drennan, letter to his wife, May 30, 1863, Drennan Papers, Mississippi Department of Archives and History, Jackson, Miss.

2. Alexander Abrams, *A Full and Detailed History of the Siege of Vicksburg* (Atlanta: Intelligencer Steam Power Presses, 1863), 29.

3. J. T. Hogane, "Reminiscences of the Siege of Vicksburg," part 1, *Southern Historical Society Papers* 11, nos. 4–5 (April–May 1883):226.

4. Johnston to Pemberton, May 17, 1863, *Official Records*, vol. 24, pt. 3:888.

5. Editor, "Vicksburg: Some New History in the Experience of Gen. Francis A. Shoup," *Confederate Veteran* 2, no. 6 (June 1894):172. Shoup particularly mentions Bowen's despair.

6. Bowen to Pemberton, May 18, 1863, *Official Records*, vol. 24, pt. 3:890.

7. Back in March, Secretary of War Seddon had told Pemberton to stockpile food at Vicksburg in case of a siege. See Seddon to Pemberton, March 12, 1863, ibid., 664.

8. Pemberton to Johnston, May 18, 1863, ibid., 890. For Pemberton's mid-February correspondence, see Pemberton to Davis, February 17, 1863, ibid., 632.

9. George C. Osborn, ed., "A Tennessean at the Siege of Vicksburg: The Diary of Samuel Alexander Ramsey Swan, May–July 1863," *Tennessee Historical Quarterly* 14, no. 4 (December 1955):357.

10. Ulysses S. Grant, *Personal Memoirs* (New York: Da Capo Press, 1982), 276. Fred Grant also recalls that this conversation took place on the eighteenth.

11. J. J. Kellogg, *The Vicksburg Campaign and Reminiscences* (Washington, Iowa: Evening Journal, 1913), 25.

12. Henry S. Keene diary, May 19, 1863, Regimental Files, Sixth Wisconsin Battery, Vicksburg National Military Park (VNMP), Vicksburg, Miss.

13. Special Order No. 134, May 19, 1863, *Official Records*, vol. 24, pt. 3:329.

14. Kellogg, *The Vicksburg Campaign*, 27.

15. J. T. Hogane, "Reminiscences of the Siege of Vicksburg," part 2, *Southern Historical Society Papers* 11, no. 7 (July 1883):293.

16. William W. Gardner to Levi Fuller, May 25, 1863, Regimental Files, Thirteenth U.S. Infantry, VNMP.

17. Charles H. Smart, "Personal Recollections of Vicksburg, May 1863," Regimental Files, Thirteenth U.S. Infantry, VNMP.

18. Edwin C. Bearss, *The Campaign for Vicksburg*, 3 vols. (Dayton, Ohio: Morningside House, 1986), 3:763.

19. A. Hugh Moss, *The Diary of A. Hugh Moss* (New York: Scribner Press, 1948), 25. The entry is dated May 19.

20. Return of Casualties, *Official Records*, vol. 24, pt. 2:159; Bearss, *The Campaign for Vicksburg*, 3:773.

21. Lida Lord Reed, "A Woman's Experience During the Siege of Vicksburg," *Century* 61, no. 6 (April 1901):923.

22. Grant, *Personal Memoirs*, 277.

23. Grant's ambitions are explained in his June 15, 1863, letter to his father. See Jesse Grant Cramer, ed., *Letters of Ulysses S. Grant to His Father and His Youngest Sister, 1857–1878* (New York: G. P. Putnam's Sons, 1912), 99.

24. Abrams, *A Full and Detailed History of the Siege of Vicksburg*, 31.

25. General Field Orders, May 21, 1863, *Official Records*, vol. 24, pt. 3:333–34.

26. Moss, *Diary*, 27; the entry is dated May 22. Abrams also attests to the effectiveness of the Federal marksmen; see *A Full and Detailed History of the Siege of Vicksburg*, 33.

27. William E. Strong, "The Campaign Against Vicksburg," MOLLUS Papers—Illinois, 2:328–329.

28. Bearss, *The Campaign for Vicksburg*, 3:843.

29. Stephen D. Lee, "The Siege of Vicksburg," *Publications of the Mississippi Historical Society* 3 (1900):60.

30. Bearss, in *The Campaign for Vicksburg*, 3:816 n. 8, says four officers; but Blair, in *Official Records*, vol. 24, pt. 2:257, says six officers.

31. Bearss, *The Campaign for Vicksburg*, 3:816.

32. George Dodd Carrington diary, May 22, 1863, Chicago Historical Society, Chicago, Ill.

33. David Martin, *The Vicksburg Campaign: April 1862–July 1863* (Conshohocken, Pa.: Combined Books, 1990), 126.

34. Return of Casualties, *Official Records*, vol. 24, pt. 2:161.

35. Lee, "The Siege of Vicksburg," 60.

36. McClernand to Grant, May 22, 1863, *Official Records*, vol. 24, pt. 1:172.

37. William Tecumseh Sherman, *Memoirs of General W. T. Sherman* (New York: Library of America, 1990), 352.

38. Simeon R. Martin, "Facts About Co. 'I' of the 46th Mississippi Infantry," Regimental Files, Forty-sixth Mississippi, VNMP.

39. J. H. Jones, "The Rank and File at Vicksburg," *Publications of the Mississippi Historical Society* 7 (1903):20–21.

40. Jim Huffstodt, *Hard Dying Men: The Story of General W. H. L. Wallace, General T. E. G. Ransom, and Their "Old Eleventh" Illinois Infantry in the American Civil War (1861–1865)* (Bowie, Md.: Heritage Books, 1991), 143–45.

41. Benjamin LeBree, ed., *Camp Fires of the Confederacy* (Louisville: Courier-Journal Job Printing Co., 1898), 63.

42. Tom J. Foster, "Reminiscences of Vicksburg," *Confederate Veteran* 2, no. 8 (August 1894):244.

43. Report of Colonel Ashbel Smith, July 10, 1863, *Official Records*, vol. 24, pt. 2:388–389.

44. Miriam Poole, ed., " 'No Rest for the Wicked': Henry Seaman's Vicksburg Diary," *Civil War Times Illustrated* 22, no. 5 (September 1983):26.

45. Earl J. Hess, ed., *A German in the Yankee Fatherland: The Civil War Letters of Henry A. Kircher* (Kent, Ohio: Kent State University Press, 1983), 101.

46. Florence Cox, ed., *Kiss Josey For Me!* (Santa Ana, Calif.: Friis-Pioneer Press, 1974), 155.

47. General Summary of Casualties, *Official Records*, vol. 24, pt. 2:167.

48. William L. B. Jenney, "Personal Recollections of Vicksburg," MOLLUS Papers—Illinois, 3:262.

49. Calvin Smith, " 'We Can Hold Our Ground': Calvin Smith's Diary," *Civil War Times Illustrated* 24, no. 2 (April 1985):30.

50. Eugene B. Harrison diary, May 24, 1863, Sixty-eighth Ohio, Civil War Miscellaneous Collection, U.S. Military History Institute (MHI), Carlisle, Pa.

51. Grant to Halleck, May 24, 1863, *Official Records*, vol. 24, pt. 1:37.

52. Ulysses S. Grant to Jesse Grant, June 15, 1863, in Cramer, *Letters of Ulysses S. Grant*, 99.

53. Grant, *Personal Memoirs*, 444–46.

54. S. H. M. Byers, "Some Recollections of Grant," in *Annals of the War Written by Leading Participants North and South* (1879; reprint, Edison, N.J.: Blue & Grey Press, 1996), 347.

—— 11. Siege ——

1. Reports of . . . Chief Engineers Army of the Tennessee, November 29, 1863, *Official Records*, vol. 24, pt. 2:175.

2. S. H. M. Byers, "Some Recollections of Grant," in *Annals of the War Written by Leading Participants North and South* (1879; reprint, Edison, N.J.: Blue & Grey Press, 1996), 348.

3. Report of Major Charles J. Stolbrand, July 16, 1863, *Official Records*, vol. 24, pt. 2:293.

4. Douglas Maynard, ed., "Vicksburg Diary: The Journal of Gabriel M. Killgore," *Civil War History* 10, no. 1 (March 1964):49.

5. Report of Major General Sherman, June 2, 1863, *Official Records . . . Navy*, 25:56. Also see A. Hugh Moss, *The Diary of A. Hugh Moss* (New York: Scribner Press, 1948), 30, for a description of this action.

6. Joseph Orville Jackson, ed., *"Some of the Boys . . . ": The Civil War Letters of Isaac Jackson, 1862–1865* (Carbondale: Southern Illinois University Press, 1960), 98.

7. J. H. Jones, "The Rank and File at Vicksburg," *Publications of the Mississippi Historical Society* 7 (1903):28. John C. Taylor makes a similar observation in his diary on June 20. See MSS 9965-a, box 1, Harry Baylor Taylor Papers, Special Collections, Alderman Library, University of Virginia, Charlottesville, Va.

8. Moss, *Diary*, 31.

9. Jones, "The Rank and File at Vicksburg," 21.

10. Ibid., 24.

11. J. J. Kellogg, *The Vicksburg Campaign and Reminiscences* (Washington, Iowa: Evening Journal, 1913), 59. Regarding Pemberton, see George C. Osborn, ed., "A Tennessean at the Siege of Vicksburg: The Diary of Samuel Alexander Ramsey Swan, May–July 1863," *Tennessee Historical Quarterly* 14, no. 4 (December 1955):370.

12. Kellogg, *The Vicksburg Campaign*, 36. James Harrison Wilson, *Under the Old Flag*, 2 vols. (New York: D. Appleton & Co., 1912), 1:211–12, tells a similar story.

13. Sylvanus Cadwallader, *Three Years with Grant* (Lincoln: University of Nebraska Press, 1996), 103; Charles Dana, *Recollections of the Civil War* (New York: D. Appleton and

Company, 1898), 83. Modern opposing views are in Brooks Simpson's introduction to Cadwallader and Dan Bauer's *Who Knows the Truth About the Big Bender?* Regarding Cadwallader's inconsistencies, recall he wrote from memory, having lost his papers in the Chicago fire.

14. Jones, "The Rank and File at Vicksburg," 25.

15. John E. Gaskell, "When Vicksburg Was Surrendered," *Confederate Veteran* 35, no. 10 (October 1927):373.

16. Wilson, *Under the Old Flag*, 1:219.

17. Diary of Chaplain N. M. Baker diary, May 28, 1863, Regimental Files, Twenty-fourth Iowa, Vicksburg National Military Park (VNMP), Vicksburg, Miss.

18. Richard L. Howard, "The Vicksburg Campaign," MOLLUS Papers—Maine, 2:36–37.

19. Manning F. Force, "Personal Recollections of the Vicksburg Campaign," MOLLUS Papers—Ohio, 1:308.

20. Stephen E. Ambrose, ed., "A Wisconsin Boy at Vicksburg: The Letters of James K. Newton," *Journal of Mississippi History* 23, no. 1 (January 1961):11.

21. N. M. Baker, diary, June 17, 1863, Regimental Files, Twenty-fourth Iowa, VNMP.

22. Captain M. D. Elliot to William T. Rigby, December 12, 1903, Regimental Files, Eighth Battery, Michigan Light Artillery, VNMP.

23. Report of Operations, July 8, 1863, *Official Records*, vol. 24, pt. 2:408; and Reports of Major Samuel H. Lockett, July 26, 1863, ibid., 334.

24. Kellogg, *The Vicksburg Campaign*, 50–51.

25. Sherman to Rawlins, June 17, 1863, *Official Records*, vol. 24, pt. 1:162.

26. McClernand to Lincoln, June 23, 1863, ibid., 158.

27. James H. M'Neilly, "Humors of Soldier Life," *Confederate Veteran* 1, no. 10 (October 1893): 309.

28. Maynard, "Vicksburg Diary: The Journal of Gabriel M. Killgore," 48.

29. "Statement of Stores on Hand, April 15, 1863, at Vicksburg," Department of Mississippi and East Louisiana Order Book MSS1R 8386 a55, Virginia Historical Society, Richmond, Va. This statement tabulates quantities in terms of daily rations. I have divided by 30,000—close to the total Pemberton surrendered—to derive my figures.

30. Marion B. Richmond, "The Siege of Vicksburg," *Confederate Veteran* 37, no. 4 (April 1929):140.

31. William Drennan diary, May 30–July 4, 1863, Drennan Papers, Mississippi Department of Archives and History, Jackson, Miss.

32. See Editor, "Words of a Veteran About Vicksburg," *Confederate Veteran* 2, no. 10 (October 1894):312.

33. J. D. Harewell, "Why Did He Eat Mule Meat?" *Confederate Veteran* 29, no. 9 (September 1921):357.

34. Osborn, "A Tennessean at the Siege of Vicksburg," 360.

35. Jones, "The Rank and File at Vicksburg," 24.

36. Editor, "Vicksburg: Some New History in the Experience of Gen. Francis A. Shoup," *Confederate Veteran* 2, no. 6 (June 1894):172–74.

37. Taylor diary, June 16, 1863, Harry Baylor Taylor Papers, MSS 9965-a, box 1.

38. William E. Strong, "The Campaign Against Vicksburg," MOLLUS Papers—Illinois 2:340.

39. Jerome B. Darnn, letter, March 13, 1902, Regimental Files, Twentieth Illinois, VNMP. This letter is unaddressed.

40. Earl S. Miers, *The Web of Victory: Grant at Vicksburg* (Baton Rouge: Louisiana State University Press, 1984), 283.

41. Edwin C. Bearss, *The Campaign for Vicksburg*, 3 vols. (Dayton, Ohio: Morningside House, 1986), 3:920.

42. Unsigned letter, February 20, 1903, Regimental Files, Thirtieth Illinois file, VNMP.

43. Charles A. Dana, *Recollections of the Civil War* (New York: D. Appleton & Co., 1898), 93.

44. Jackson, *"Some of the Boys . . . ,"* 108.

___ 12. "Come Joe! Come Quickly!" ___

1. Johnston to Pemberton, May 19, 1863, *Official Records*, vol. 24, pt. 3:892.

2. See Johnston to Gardner, May 19, 1863, *Official Records*, ibid., 896–97.

3. Johnston to Davis, January 2, 1863, *Official Records*, vol. 17, pt. 2:823. Johnston accurately cites this communication in his *Narrative of Military Operations* (New York: D. Appleton & Co., 1874), 495. Regarding Johnston's comment on Grant, see Walter Lord, ed., *The Freemantle Diary* (Boston: Little, Brown, 1954), 98.

4. Recall that in September Longstreet's corps would travel 965 miles by rail in ten days to fight at Chickamauga. For the best discussion of Southern railroad problems, see Robert C. Black, *The Railroads of the Confederacy* (Chapel Hill: University of North Carolina Press, 1952).

5. Lincoln to Rosecrans, May 28, 1863, in Roy P. Basler, ed., *The Collected Works of Abraham Lincoln*, vol. 6 (New Brunswick, N.J.: Rutgers University Press, 1953), 236.

6. Guy R. Everson and Edward H. Simpson Jr., eds., *"Far, Far from Home": The Wartime Letters of Dick and Tally Simpson, Third South Carolina Volunteers* (New York: Oxford University Press, 1994), 237.

7. Lee to Davis, June 2, 1863, copy, Mss2 L515 a72, Virginia Historical Society, Richmond, Va.

8. Smith to Holmes, May 16, 1863, *Official Records*, vol. 22, pt. 2:839–40.

9. See Smith to Taylor, May 20, 1863, *Official Records*, vol. 26, pt. 2:12–13.

10. John Eaton, *Grant, Lincoln and the Freedmen: Reminiscences of the Civil War* (New York: Longmans, Green, & Co., 1907), 15.

11. Halleck to Grant, March 31, 1863, *Official Records*, vol. 24, pt. 3:157.

12. Edwin C. Bearss, *The Campaign for Vicksburg*, 3 vols. (Dayton, Ohio: Morningside House, 1986), 3:1180.

13. Return of Casualties, *Official Records*, vol. 24, pt. 2:470; Reports of Brigadier General Elias S. Dennis, June 16, 1863, ibid., 448; Bearss, *The Campaign for Vicksburg*, 3:1206.

14. Florence Cox, ed., *Kiss Josey For Me!* (Santa Ana, Calif.: Friis-Pioneer Press, 1974), 163.

15. Alexander G. Downing, *Downing's Civil War Diary* (Des Moines: Historical Department of Iowa, 1916), 120. The entry is dated June 7.

16. Charles A. Dana, *Recollections of the Civil War* (New York: D. Appleton & Co., 1898), 86.

17. Kate Stone diary, June 10, 1863, in Bearss, *The Campaign for Vicksburg*, 3:1183 n. 57.

18. Report of Major General Richard Taylor, June 8, 1863, *Official Records*, vol. 24, pt. 2:459.

19. Johnston to Smith, June 26, 1863, *Official Records*, vol. 24, pt. 3:979.

20. Walker to Smith, July 3, 1863, *Official Records*, vol. 22, pt. 2:915–16.

21. Edwin A. Pollard, *The Lost Cause* (New York: E. B. Treat Co., 1866), 397.

22. Holmes states that the Confederates suffered 1,636 losses. Report of Lieutenant General Theophilus H. Holmes, August 14, 1863, *Official Records*, vol. 22, pt. 1:411. Union losses were 239. See Prentiss to Rawlins, July 9, 1863, ibid., 390–91.

23. Davis to Bragg, May 22, 1863 in Dunbar Rowland, ed., *Jefferson Davis Constitutionalist: His Letters, Papers and Speeches*, vol. 5 (Jackson: Mississippi Department of Archives and History, 1923), 492.

24. Johnston to Seddon, June 5, 1863, in Johnston, *Narrative of Military Operations* 508.

25. Davis to Johnston, May 28, 1863, in Rowland, *Jefferson Davis Constitutionalist*, 5:499.

26. Bell Irvin Wiley, ed., *"This Infernal War": The Confederate Letters of Sergeant Edwin H. Fay* (Austin: University of Texas Press, 1958), 282. Among many examples of Johnston's restorative influence, see Flavel C. Barber, *Holding the Line: The Third Tennessee Infantry, 1861–1864*, ed. Robert Ferrell (Kent, Ohio: Kent State University Press, 1994), 122.

27. Grant to Sherman, June 23, 1863, *Official Records*, vol. 24, pt. 3:431.

28. M. A. Howe, ed., *Home Letters of General Sherman* (New York: Charles Scribner's Sons, 1909), 268.

29. Jacob W. Wilkin, "Vicksburg," MOLLUS Papers—Illinois, 4:234.

30. Johnston to Pemberton, May 25 and 29, 1863, *Official Records*, vol. 24, pt. 3:917, 929.

31. Seddon to Johnston, June 16, 1863, in Johnston, *Narrative of Military Operations*, 512.

32. Pemberton to Johnston, June 19, 1863, *Official Records*, vol. 24, pt. 3:967.

33. Pemberton to Johnston, June 21, 1863, ibid., 969.

34. Johnston to Pemberton, June 22, 1863, ibid., 971.

35. Samuel Pasco, *Private Pasco: A Civil War Diary* (Oak Brook, Ill.: McAdams Multigraphics, 1990), 44.

36. Ibid., 44.

——— 13. "A Hard Stroke for the Confederacy" ———

1. Phillip Thomas Tucker, *The South's Finest: The First Missouri Confederate Brigade from Pea Ridge to Vicksburg* (Shippensburg, Pa.: White Mane Publishing, 1993), 200.

2. Ephraim M. Anderson, *Memoirs: Historical and Personal* (Dayton, Ohio: Morningside Bookshop, 1972), 352.

3. Ibid., 353.

4. Report of S. R. Tresilian, August 17, 1863, *Official Records*, vol. 24, pt. 2:208.

5. Charles A. Dana, *Recollections of the Civil War* (New York: D. Appleton & Co., 1898), 94.

6. Editor, "Vicksburg: Some New History in the Experience of Gen. Francis A. Shoup," *Confederate Veteran* 2, no. 6 (June 1894):173.

7. J. H. Jones, "The Rank and File at Vicksburg," *Publications of the Mississippi Historical Society* 7 (1903):29.

8. Bruce Catton, *Grant Moves South* (Boston: Little, Brown, 1960), 460.

9. William E. Strong, "The Campaign Against Vicksburg," MOLLUS Papers—Illinois, 2:345. Strong was an eyewitness to this scene. Pemberton asserts that it was Grant, not Bowen, who suggested that the generals step aside. Pemberton presents his version of the surrender in "Terms of Surrender at Vicksburg—General Pemberton Replies to General Badeau," *Southern Historical Society Papers* 10, nos. 6–9 (August-September 1882):406–15.

10. Jones, "The Rank and File at Vicksburg," 29.

11. See Edward S. Gregory, "Vicksburg During the Siege," in *Annals of the War Written by Leading Participants North and South* (1879; reprint, Edison, N.J.: Blue & Grey Press, 1996), 124

12. John C. Pemberton, *Pemberton: Defender of Vicksburg* (Chapel Hill: University of North Carolina Press, 1942), 231.

13. Samuel H. Lockett, "The Defense of Vicksburg," in *Battles & Leaders*, 3:492.

14. John E. Gaskell, "Surrendered at Vicksburg," *Confederate Veteran* 33, no. 8 (August 1925):286.

15. "Grant's March," *Harper's Weekly* 7, no. 336 (June 6, 1863):362.

16. J. P. Jones, letter to his wife, July 4, 1863, Regimental Files, Forty-fifth Illinois, Vicksburg National Military Park (VNMP), Vicksburg, Miss.

17. Edwin C. Bearss, *The Campaign for Vicksburg*, 3 vols. (Dayton, Ohio: Morningside House, 1986), 3:1294–1295, examines the controversy over which flag was raised.

18. David D. Porter, *Incidents and Anecdotes of the Civil War* (New York: D. Appleton & Co., 1886), 201.

19. Richard S. West Jr., *The Second Admiral: A Life of David Dixon Porter* (New York: Coward-McCann, 1937), 171.

20. Porter to Welles, July 4, 1863, *Official Records . . . Navy*, 25:104.

21. Eugene B. Harrison diary, July 4, 1863, Sixty-eighth Ohio, Civil War Miscellaneous Collection, MHI, Carlisle, Pa.

22. Memoirs, undated, William A. Ruyle, Fifth Missouri, Harrisburg Civil War Roundtable Collection, U.S. Military History Institute (MHI), Carlisle, Pa.

23. Summary of the Casualties, *Official Records*, vol. 24, pt. 2:328; General Summary of Casualties, ibid., 167; Consolidated statement of prisoners of war captured, ibid., 325.

24. A. Hugh Moss, *The Diary of A. Hugh Moss* (New York: Scribner Press, 1948), 47. The entry is dated July 11, 1863.

25. Tucker, *The South's Finest*, 207.

26. Thompson to Forney, July 15, 1863, *Official Records*, vol. 24, pt. 3:1005.

27. Douglas Maynard, ed., "Vicksburg Diary: The Journal of Gabriel M. Killgore," *Civil War History* 10, no. 1 (March 1964):53.

28. Joseph E. Johnston, *Narrative of Military Operations* (New York: D. Appleton & Co., 1874), 205.

29. William C. Davis, ed., *Diary of a Confederate Soldier: John S. Jackman of the Orphan Brigade* (Columbia: University of South Carolina Press, 1990), 80.

30. F. Jay Taylor, ed., *Reluctant Rebel: The Secret Diary of Robert Patrick, 1861–1865* (Baton Rouge: Louisiana State University Press, 1959), 120.

31. For Davis's not unbiased assessment of this, see Dunbar Rowland, ed., *Jefferson Davis Constitutionalist: His Letters, Papers and Speeches*, vol. 6 (Jackson: Mississippi Department of Archives and History, 1923), 498.

32. Fearing a Federal offensive, Johnston withdrew from Centreville, Virginia, about three and one-half miles north of Manassas Junction, on March 9, 1862. So precipitous was the retreat that at the meat-packing plant at Thoroughfare Gap alone, more than a thousand tons of bacon were burned.

33. On Johnston's orders, the Confederates evacuated Norfolk, Virginia, on May 9, 1862. Among the abandoned ordnance were numerous heavy pieces of artillery. Had they been preserved, more heavy guns would have been available to defend Vicksburg.

34. John William DeForest, *A Volunteer's Adventures: A Union Captain's Record of the Civil War* (New Haven, Conn.: Yale University Press, 1946), 145.

35. Joseph Jones, "The Medical History of the Confederate States," *Southern Historical Society Papers* 20 (1892):135.

36. General Summary of Casualties, *Official Records*, vol. 24, pt. 2:167; Return of Casualties, ibid., 550; Richard B. Irwin, "The Capture of Port Hudson," in *Battles & Leaders*, 3:598.

37. Porter to Welles, July 4, 1863, *Official Records . . . Navy*, 25:103.

38. John Eaton, *Grant, Lincoln and the Freedmen: Reminiscences of the Civil War* (New York: Longmans, Green, & Co., 1907), 88–90.

39. Lincoln to Burnside, July 27, 1863, in Roy P. Basler, ed., *The Collected Works of Abraham Lincoln*, vol. 6 (New Brunswick, N.J.: Rutgers University Press, 1953), 350.

40. Lincoln to Grant, July 13, 1863, in Basler, *Collected Works of Abraham Lincoln*, 6:326.

41. Grant to Lincoln, August 23, 1863, in ibid., 6:374 n. 1.

42. Halleck to Grant, March 1, 1863, *Official Records*, vol. 24, pt. 3:75.

43. Davis to E. K. Smith, July 14, 1863, in Rowland, *Jefferson Davis Constitutionalist*, 5:554.

44. For a fine discussion of this, see Gary W. Gallagher, "Lee's Army Has Not Lost Any of Its Prestige," in Gary W. Gallagher, ed., *The Third Day at Gettysburg and Beyond* (Chapel Hill: University of North Carolina Press, 1994).

45. Ibid., 7.

46. Dargan to Seddon, July 24, 1863, *Official Records*, ser. 4, vol. 2:664–65.

47. Guy R. Everson and Edward H. Simpson Jr., eds., *"Far, Far from Home": The Wartime Letters of Dick and Tally Simpson, Third South Carolina Volunteers* (New York: Oxford University Press, 1994), 256–57.

48. Flavel C. Barber, *Holding the Line: The Third Tennessee Infantry, 1861–1864*, ed. Robert Ferrell (Kent, Ohio: Kent State University Press, 1994), 141.

49. Bell Irvin Wiley, ed., *"This Infernal War": The Confederate Letters of Sergeant Edwin H. Fay* (Austin: University of Texas Press, 1958), 290.

50. Lee to Davis, July 16, 1863, in Rowland, *Jefferson Davis Constitutionalist*, 5:567.

51. William Tecumseh Sherman, *Memoirs of General W. T. Sherman* (New York: Library of America, 1990), 370.

52. See Will H. Tunnard, "Running the Mississippi Blockade," *Confederate Veteran* 24, no. 1 (January 1916):27–28.

53. Sherman, *Memoirs*, 370.

54. Davis to Lee, August 11, 1863 in Rowland, *Jefferson Davis Constitutionalist*, 5:588–89.

55. Gallagher, "Lee's Army Has Not Lost Any of Its Prestige," 15.

56. For insight into the dire state of the Confederate Commissary, see the Bureau of Subsistence report of October 18, 1864, MSS1R 8386 a56, Francis Gildart Ruffin Papers, Virginia Historical Society.

57. Taylor to Boggs, January 21, 1864, *Official Records*, vol. 34, pt. 2:902–3.

58. "How shall we feed the army?" *Southern Cultivator* 23, no. 2 (February 1865): 19–20.

59. Sherman to Grant, October 4, 1862, *Official Records*, vol. 17, pt. 2:261.

60. Taylor, *Reluctant Rebel*, 132–33.

61. Fox to Porter, July 16, 1863, in Gustavus V. Fox, *Confidential Correspondence of Gustavus V. Fox, Assistant Secretary of the Navy*, 2 vols. (New York: De Vinne Press, 1919), 2:186. Grant's scheme is in Grant to Halleck, July 18, 1863, *Official Records*, vol. 24, pt. 3:530.

62. Napoleon III wanted to create a French bastion in Mexico to provide a base from which territory in Central and South America could be added to imperial France. By the summer of 1863, more than thirty thousand French troops were in Mexico.

63. Lincoln to Banks, August 5, 1863, and Lincoln to Grant, August 9, 1863, in Basler, *The Collected Works of Abraham Lincoln*, 6:364, 374; and Tyler Dennet, ed., *Lincoln and the Civil War in the Diaries and Letters of John Hay* (New York: Dodd, Mead & Co., 1939), 77. The entry is dated August 9, 1863.

64. Adam Badeau, *Military History of General U. S. Grant*, 3 vols. (New York: D. Appleton & Co., 1885), 1:413.

65. Letter to Jesse Grant, June 15, 1863, in Jesse Grant Cramer, ed., *Letters of Ulysses S. Grant to His Father and His Youngest Sister, 1857–1878* (New York: G. P. Putnam's Sons, 1912), 99.

66. Barksdale to Davis, July 29, 1863, in Rowland, *Jefferson Davis Constitutionalist*, 5:556–63.

67. For Davis's fascinating overview of Johnston's wartime service, see Davis to Phelan, February 18, 1865, in Rowland, *Jefferson Davis Constitutionalist*, 6:491–503.

68. Pemberton to Davis, August 15, 1863, *Official Records*, vol. 24, pt. 3:1057.

69. See Johnston to Cooper, August 17, 1863, and Cooper to Johnston, August 20, 1863, ibid., 1058.

70. Lieutenant General Pemberton—Siege of Vicksburg—Court of Inquiry, ibid., 1063.

71. Johnston to Cooper, September 12, 1863, ibid., 1061.

72. See W. H. Johnson to Northrop, August 10, 1863, ibid., 1051–52.

73. J. T. Hogane, "Reminiscences of the Siege of Vicksburg," part 1, *Southern Historical Society Papers* 11, nos. 4–5 (April–May 1883):226.

74. For a defense of Pemberton on the issue of supplies by his chief of staff, see R. W. Memminger, "The Surrender of Vicksburg—A Defense of General Pemberton," *Southern Historical Society Papers* 12, nos. 7–9 (July–September 1884):352–60.

75. Watson to Cooper, August 4, 1863, *Official Records*, vol. 24, pt. 3:1043–44.

76. George C. Osborn, ed., "A Tennessean at the Siege of Vicksburg: The Diary of Samuel Alexander Ramsey Swan, May–July 1863," *Tennessee Historical Quarterly* 14, no. 4 (December 1955):360. The entry is dated May 28.

77. Warren Ripley, ed., *Siege Train: The Journal of a Confederate Artilleryman in the Defense of Charleston* (Columbia: University of South Carolina Press, 1986), 109, 111–12, 114–16.

78. Kavanaugh to Davis, August 13, 1863, in Rowland, *Jefferson Davis Constitutionalist*, 5:591.

79. Barksdale to Davis, July 29, 1863, in ibid., 581–82.

80. Davis to Pemberton, March 11, 1865, in ibid., 6:203.

81. For yet one more example, see Barber, *Holding the Line*, 112.

82. Edwin A. Pollard, *The Lost Cause* (New York: E. B. Treat Co., 1866), 387.

83. Jesse W. Sparks, "Pemberton's Surrender of Vicksburg," *Confederate Veteran* 2, no. 7 (July 1894):203.

84. Editor, "Vicksburg: Some New History in the Experience of Gen. Francis A. Shoup," 174.

85. McClernand to Lincoln, January 14, 1864, in Basler, *The Collected Works of Abraham Lincoln*, 6:383–84 n. 1.

86. Lincoln to James C. Conkling, August 26, 1863, in ibid., 409–10.

87. Stephen D. Lee, "The Campaign of Generals Grant and Sherman against Vicksburg in December, 1862, and January 1st and 2nd, 1863, Known as the, 'Chickasaw Bayou Campaign,'" *Publications of the Mississippi Historical Society* 4 (1901): 19–20.

88. Ulysses S. Grant, *Personal Memoirs* (New York: Da Capo Press, 1982), 47.

89. J. F. C. Fuller, *The Generalship of Ulysses S. Grant* (London: John Murray, 1929), 421.

90. Lincoln to Conkling, August 26, 1863, in Basler, *The Collected Works of Abraham Lincoln*, 6:406–410.

91. Frank L. Byrne and Jean Powers Soman, *Your True Marcus: The Civil War Letters of a Jewish Colonel* (Kent, Ohio: Kent State University Press, 1985), 269.

92. Sherman, *Memoirs*, 364–66.

93. Sylvanus Cadwallader, *Three Years with Grant* (Lincoln: University of Nebraska Press, 1996), 126.

Bibliography

Students of the Civil War are fortunate in that the conflict featured a happy confluence of a highly literate soldiery and the absence of censorship. Period letters and diaries, particularly when written during a campaign or just after a dramatic event, provide a special window into history. They relate what common participants found important. Few soldiers concerned themselves with battle tactics or grand strategy. Instead, they wrote about their physical experience; a hot, dusty march or another night spent on short rations. Diaries are full of self-satisfied detail about stealing and cooking a pig the day before a battle while afterward they contain only a terse few words about the battle itself. Home letters are often much the same. Most soldiers who have experienced combat up close want to forget the horrors they have seen, do not want to frighten the folks back home, or conclude that there is no possibility for someone who has not been there to comprehend what it was like.

In an interview conducted in 1894, former General Shoup claimed that the Confederates were so disorganized on May 18 that when Sherman appeared before Vicksburg's fortifications, "There was not a man in the trenches or near them, from the Jackson Road to the river on the left." Shoup says Sherman could have waltzed into Vicksburg. Intrigued, I investigated this claim. General Baldwin's after action report in the *Official Records* says that his brigade "had scarcely got in position [between the Jackson Road and the river] when the enemy appeared." The historian must consider the sources' biases and weigh the evidence. Shoup, like virtually all Southerners, wanted to discredit the detested Sherman's generalship. Baldwin, like virtually all officers making official reports, did not want to appear negligent in any way. In this case there was an apparent honest error. Shoup marched outside the works in order to cover some last-minute foraging efforts. When he passed the trenches they were indeed unoccupied. Shortly thereafter Baldwin's men arrived behind Shoup while Sherman's skirmishers appeared to his front. Not knowing that the defenses had been manned, Shoup believed that Sherman had a great opportunity which he failed to take advantage of. This entire incident is simply one small example of what the military historian confronts repeatedly.

A writer seeking to describe military history accurately does so at the risk of committing considerable error. Probably no military leader in history fought more battles than the Emperor Napoléon. He viewed military history with great suspicion, referring to it as "agreed upon fiction." He commented that while many invoke "historical fact," they are often mere words. In the heat of battle it is particularly difficult to ascertain when events actually occurred. The emperor concluded, "if, later on, there is a consensus, this is only because there is no one left to contradict."

Nearly a century later an Illinois soldier, Wilbur Cummings, was gathering material for his own reminiscences of service in Grant's army from Shiloh to Vicksburg and encountered the same problems Napoléon had identified. One of Cummings's old officers who had distinguished himself in numerous battles put it well: "Well, Wilbur, after reading all the histories and articles . . . I am in doubt whether I was there at all." Likewise, sailor S. B. Coleman was aboard the *Tyler* during her encounter with the *Arkansas*. While writing his recollections Coleman noted, "I have read several reports of this fight and it is unnecessary to say that none of them agree."

Emperor Napoléon, Wilbur Cummings's old comrade, and Acting Master Coleman provide a useful caution for both the historian and his readers.

—— Manuscript Sources ——

Chicago Historical Society, Chicago, Illinois
George Dodd Carrington diary (Carrington was a second lieutenant in the Eleventh Illinois)
John A. McClernand Letters, Reavis Collection

Mississippi Department of Archives and History, Jackson, Mississippi
Drennan Papers

U.S. Army Military History Institute, Carlisle, Pennsylvania (MHI)
Civil War Miscellaneous Collection
Boucher Family Papers (John V. Boucher served in the Tenth Missouri)
Eugene B. Harrison diary (Harrison was a surgeon in the Sixty-eighth Ohio)
Edgar R. Kellogg letters
Charles H. Lutz letters (Lutz served in the Eleventh Illinois)
Parks-Towle-Ferguson Family letters
Israel M. Ritter diary (Ritter served in the Twenty-fourth Iowa)
Joseph W. Westbrook Papers (Westbrook served in the Fourth Mississippi)

Civil War Times Illustrated Collection
Vicksburg Campaign: Letter of an Anonymous Yankee of the Sixty-eighth Ohio Regiment
L. B. Claiborne Papers (Claiborne served in the Pointe Coupee Artillery)
Francis A. Dawes diary (Dawes served in the Twenty-fourth Iowa)
Robert M. Dihel letters (Dihel served in the Thirtieth Illinois)
John W. Ford letters (Ford served in the Seventh Kentucky)
Perry R. Smith letters
James K. Worthington letters (Worthington served in the Ninety-ninth Illinois)

Harrisburg Civil War Roundtable Collection
Gregory A. Cocco Collection: Howard Stevens letters (Stevens served in the Twentieth Illinois)
Luke R. Roberts Papers (Roberts served in the Thirtieth Alabama)
William A. Ruyle papers (Ruyle was a sergeant in the Confederate Fifth Missouri)

William T. Sherman Papers

Special Collections, Alderman Library, University of Virginia, Charlottesville, Virginia
Harry Baylor Taylor Papers (The papers of John C. Taylor, one of Pemberton's staff officers, are contained in this collection. Taylor kept some of the draft and original messages sent by Pemberton and received from Johnston during the siege. These are in MSS 9965. Fragments of these messages are not reproduced in the *Official Records* and provide insight into the two generals' thoughts. MSS 9965-a, box 1, has Taylor's siege diary, later annotated in his own hand.)

Vicksburg National Military Park (VNMP), Vicksburg, Mississippi
All documents are in the Regimental Files except the Leavy journal.
Hugh W. Adams letter, Seventh Kentucky (U.S.)
Joseph Baker diary, Forty-second Ohio
N. M. Baker diary, Twenty-fourth Iowa
Charles E. Bassett letter, 124th Illinois
Rob Buchanan letter, Seventh Missouri (U.S.)
W. O. Connor letter, February 23, 1904, Cherokee Artillery (Georgia)
Jerome B. Darnn letter, Twentieth Illinois
C. J. Durham diary, Eleventh Indiana
Captain M. D. Elliot letter, Eighth Battery, Michigan Light Artillery
Thomas D. Fisher diary
James Fogle letters, Eleventh Indiana
William W. Gardner letter, Thirteenth U.S. Infantry
Lewis B. Jessup diary, Twenty-fourth Indiana
J. P. Jones letter, Forty-fifth Illinois
Harry S. Keene diary, Sixth Wisconsin Battery
John A. Leavy journal, Letters and Diaries Files
Jesse M. Lee diary, Fifty-ninth Indiana
Simeon R. Martin memoir, Forty-sixth Mississippi
Elias Moore diary, 114th Ohio
James K. Newton diary, Fourteenth Wisconsin
F. G. Obenchain letters, Botetourt (Virginia) Artillery
Amos Riley report, First Missouri (CSA)
Augustus G. Sinks diary, Forty-sixth Indiana
W. M. Sleeth letter, Seventy-eighth Ohio
Charles H. Smart, Thirteenth U.S. Infantry
J. G. Spencer letter, First Mississippi Light Artillery
W. M. Thomson letter, Fourth Ohio Cavalry

Harvey M. Trimble diary, Ninety-third Illinois
Charles Wood diary, Twenty-ninth Wisconsin

Virginia Historical Society, Richmond, Virginia
  William Benthall Brooks diary
  Department of Mississippi and East Louisiana Order Book
  Robert E. Lee letter to Jefferson Davis, June 2, 1863
  Josiah Staunton Moore Papers
  Francis Gildart Ruffin Papers

—— Published Sources ——

Primary

Abernethy, Byron R., ed. *Private Elisha Stockwell, Jr., Sees the Civil War.* Norman: University of Oklahoma Press, 1958.

Abrams, Alexander. *A Full and Detailed History of the Siege of Vicksburg.* Atlanta: Intelligencer Steam Power Presses, 1863. Abrams worked for the *Vicksburg Whig* during the siege and saw and heard much firsthand. He also was extremely biased and anti-Pemberton.

Ambrose, Stephen E., ed. "A Wisconsin Boy at Vicksburg: The Letters of James K. Newton." *Journal of Mississippi History* 23, no. 1 (January 1961): 1–14.

Anderson, Ephraim M. *Memoirs: Historical and Personal.* Dayton, Ohio: Morningside Bookshop, 1972. A reprint of the recollections of a Missouri rebel. One of the best of the genre.

Anderson, Mary Ann, ed. *The Civil War Diary of Allen Morgan Geer.* New York: Cosmos Press, 1977. Geer served in the Twentieth Illinois.

Annals of the War Written by Leading Participants North and South. 1879. Reprint, Edison, N.J.: Blue & Grey Press, 1996. Originally published in the *Philadelphia Weekly Times.*

Barber, Flavel C. *Holding the Line: The Third Tennessee Infantry, 1861–1864.* Edited by Robert Ferrell. Kent, Ohio: Kent State University Press, 1994.

Barber, Lucius W. *Army Memoirs of Lucius W. Barber.* Chicago: J. M. W. Jones Stationery & Printing Co., 1894. Barber was a corporal in the Fifteenth Illinois.

Basler, Roy P., ed. *The Collected Works of Abraham Lincoln.* Vol. 6. New Brunswick, N.J.: Rutgers University Press, 1953.

Battles and Leaders of the Civil War. 4 vols. Secaucus, N.J.: Castle, n.d.

Baumgartner, Richard A., and Larry M. Strayer, eds. *Ralsa C. Rice: Yankee Tigers: Through the Civil War with the 125th Ohio.* Huntington, W.Va.: Blue Acorn Press, 1992.

Bevier, R. S. *History of the First and Second Missouri Confederate Brigades, 1861–1865.* St. Louis: Bryan, Brand & Co., 1879.

———. "Incidents and Personal Sketches of the Missouri First and Second Confederate Brigades." In appendix to *A Soldier's Story of the Siege of Vicksburg,* by Osborn H. Oldroyd. Springfield, Ill.: n.p., 1885.

Blanchard, Ira. *I Marched with Sherman: Civil War Memoirs of the Twentieth Illinois Volunteer Infantry.* San Francisco: J. D. Huff & Co., 1992.

Brown, Isaac N. "The Confederate Gun-Boat 'Arkansas.'" In *Battles and Leaders of the Civil War.* Vol. 3. Secaucus, N.J.: Castle, n.d.

———. "Confederate Torpedoes in the Yazoo." In *Battles and Leaders of the Civil War.* Vol. 3. Secaucus, N.J.: Castle, n.d.

Byers, S. H. M. "How Men Feel in Battle: Recollections of a Private at Champion Hills." *Annals of Iowa* 2, no. 6 (July 1896): 438–449.

———. "Some Recollections of Grant." In *Annals of the War Written by Leading Participants North and South.* 1879. Reprint, Edison, N.J.: Blue & Grey Press, 1996.

Byrne, Frank L., and Jean Powers Soman. *Your True Marcus: The Civil War Letters of a Jewish Colonel.* Kent, Ohio: Kent State University Press, 1985.

Cadwallader, Sylvanus. *Three Years with Grant.* Lincoln: University of Nebraska Press, 1996.

Cantrell, Oscar A. *The History of the Fifty-sixth Georgia Volunteers.* Atlanta: Intelligencer Steam Power Presses, 1864.

Coffin, Charles Carleton. *The Boys of '61.* Boston: Dana Estes & Co., 1896.

Colby, Carlos W. "Bullets, Hardtack and Mud: A Soldier's View of the Vicksburg Campaign." *Journal of the West* 4, no. 2 (April 1965): 129–168.

Cox, Florence, ed. *Kiss Josey For Me!* Santa Ana, Calif.: Friis-Pioneer Press, 1974. The letters of Captain Henry Ankeny, Fourth Iowa Infantry.

Cramer, Jesse Grant, ed. *Letters of Ulysses S. Grant to His Father and His Youngest Sister, 1857–1878.* New York: G. P. Putnam's Sons, 1912.

Crummer, Wilbur F. *With Grant at Donelson, Shiloh, and Vicksburg.* Oak Park, Ill.: E. C. Crummer and Co., 1915. Crummer served in the Forty-fifth Illinois.

Dana, Charles A. *Recollections of the Civil War.* New York: D. Appleton & Co., 1898.

Davis, Kathleen, ed. *Such Are the Trials: The Civil War Diaries of Jacob Gantz.* Ames: Iowa State University Press, 1991.

Davis, William C., ed. *Diary of a Confederate Soldier: John S. Jackman of the Orphan Brigade.* Columbia: University of South Carolina Press, 1990.

Dawes, Rufus R. *Service With the Sixth Wisconsin Volunteers.* Madison: State Historical Society of Wisconsin, 1962.

Dean, Benjamin D. *Recollections of the Twenty-sixth Missouri Infantry.* Lamar, Mo.: Southwest Missourian Office, 1892.

DeForest, John William. *A Volunteer's Adventures: A Union Captain's Record of the Civil War.* New Haven, Conn.: Yale University Press, 1946. A Connecticut captain's detailed account covering the Port Hudson campaign. A superb resource and fine read.

Dennet, Tyler, ed. *Lincoln and the Civil War in the Diaries and Letters of John Hay.* New York: Dodd, Mead & Co., 1939.

Dewey, George. *Autobiography of George Dewey: Admiral of the Navy.* New York: Charles Scribner's Sons, 1913. The Dewey of Manila Bay who served with Farragut on the Mississippi.

Donald, David, ed. *Inside Lincoln's Cabinet: The Civil War Diaries of Salmon P. Chase.* New York: Longmans, Green & Co., 1954. The administration's eastern focus is abundantly clear in these diaries. Unfortunately, Chase did not keep a diary between October 1862 and August 1863.

Downing, Alexander G. *Downing's Civil War Diary.* Des Moines: Historical Department of Iowa, 1916. Downing was a sergeant in the Eleventh Iowa.

Dwight, Henry O. "A Soldier's Story: The Affair on the Raymond Road." *New York Tribune,* November 21, 1886.

Eaton, John. *Grant, Lincoln and the Freedmen: Reminiscences of the Civil War.* New York: Longmans, Green, & Co., 1907. Eaton supervised the contraband programs in Grant's department and met with him frequently during the campaign.

Everson, Guy R., and Edward H. Simpson Jr., eds. *"Far, Far from Home": The Wartime Letters of Dick and Tally Simpson, Third South Carolina Volunteers.* New York: Oxford University Press, 1994.

Fox, Gustavus V. *Confidential Correspondence of Gustavus V. Fox, Assistant Secretary of the Navy.* 2 vols. New York: De Vinne Press, 1919.

Freeman, Douglas Southall, ed. *Lee's Dispatches to Jefferson Davis.* New York: G. P. Putnam's Sons, 1957.

"Galway." "Our Vicksburgh Correspondence." *New York Times,* March 28, 1863, 1.

———. "The Siege of Vicksburgh." *New York Times,* April 16, 1863, 1.

Gibbon, John. *The Artillerist's Manual.* 1860; rev. 1863. Reprint, Dayton, Ohio: Morningside, 1991.

Goodloe, Albert T. *Confederate Echoes.* Nashville, Tenn.: M. E. Church, 1907.

Grant, Ulysses S. *Personal Memoirs.* New York: Da Capo Press, 1982.

———. "The Vicksburg Campaign." In *Battles and Leaders of the Civil War.* Vol. 3. Secaucus, N.J.: Castle, n.d.

"Grant's March." *Harper's Weekly* 7, no. 336 (June 6, 1863): 362.

Gregory, Edward S. "Vicksburg During the Siege." In *Annals of the War Written by Leading Participants North and South.* 1879. Reprint, Edison, N.J.: Blue & Grey Press, 1996.

Hall, Winchester. *The Story of the Twenty-sixth Louisiana Infantry.* N.p., 1890.

Hass, Paul H., ed. "The Vicksburg Diary of Henry Clay Warmoth." Parts 1 and 2. *Journal of Mississippi History* 31, no. 4 (November 1969): 334–47; 32, no. 1 (February 1979): 60–74.

Hess, Earl J., ed. *A German in the Yankee Fatherland: The Civil War Letters of Henry A. Kircher.* Kent, Ohio: Kent State University Press, 1983. Kircher served in the Twelfth Missouri.

Hewett, Janet B., Bryce A. Suderow, and Noah Andre Trudeau, eds. *Supplement to the Official Records of the Union and Confederate Armies.* Part I—Reports: Vol. 4, no. 4. Wilmington, N.C.: Broadfoot Publishing Company, 1995. Pemberton's unfinished, postwar letter defending his strategy is on pages 307–343.

Howard, Richard L. *History of the 124th Regiment, Illinois Infantry Volunteers.* Springfield, Ill.: H. W. Rokker, 1880.

Howe, M. A., ed. *Home Letters of General Sherman.* New York: Charles Scribner's Sons, 1909.

"How Shall We Feed the Army?" *Southern Cultivator* 23, no. 2 (February 1865): 19–20.

Hunt, Gaillard. *Israel, Elihu and Cadwallader Washburn.* New York: Macmillan, 1925.

Irwin, Richard B. "The Capture of Port Hudson." In *Battles and Leaders of the Civil War.* Vol. 3. Secaucus, N.J.: Castle, n.d.

Jackson, Joseph Orville, ed. *"Some of the Boys . . . ": The Civil War Letters of Isaac Jackson, 1862–1865.* Carbondale: Southern Illinois University Press, 1960. Jackson served in the Eighty-third Ohio.

Johnston, Joseph E. *Narrative of Military Operations.* New York: D. Appleton & Co., 1874.

Jones, J. H. "The Rank and File at Vicksburg." *Publications of the Mississippi Historical Society* 7 (1903): 17–31.

Jones, Jenkin Lloyd. *An Artilleryman's Diary.* Madison: Wisconsin History Commission, 1914. A private's account of service in the Sixth Wisconsin Battery.

Kellogg, J. J. *The Vicksburg Campaign and Reminiscences.* Washington, Iowa: Evening Journal, 1913. An engaging writer, Captain Kellogg served in Company B of the 113th Illinois.

Kimbell, Charles B. *History of Battery "A" First Illinois Light Artillery Volunteers.* Chicago: Cushing Printing Co., 1899.

Kneiper, Pearl Mae, ed. "Letter of a Mississippi Confederate Soldier to His Father-in-Law in Massachusetts." *Journal of Mississippi History* 5, no. 1 (January 1943): 41–44.

LeBree, Benjamin, ed. *Camp Fires of the Confederacy.* Louisville: Courier-Journal Job Printing Co., 1898.

Lee, Stephen D. "The Campaign of Generals Grant and Sherman against Vicksburg in December, 1862, and January 1st and 2nd, 1863, Known as the, 'Chickasaw Bayou Campaign.'" *Publications of the Mississippi Historical Society* 4 (1901): 15–36.

———. "The Campaign of Vicksburg, Mississippi, in 1863—from April 12 to and Including the Battle of Champion Hills, or Baker's Creek, May 16, 1863." *Publications of the Mississippi Historical Society* 3 (1900): 21–53.

———. "Details of Important Work by Two Confederate Telegraph Operators, Christmas Eve, 1862, Which Prevented the Almost Complete Surprise of the Confederate Army at Vicksburg." *Publications of the Mississippi Historical Society* 8 (1904): 51–55.

———. "The Siege of Vicksburg." *Publications of the Mississippi Historical Society* 3 (1900): 55–71.

Lockett, Samuel H. "The Defense of Vicksburg." In *Battles and Leaders of the Civil War.* Vol. 3. Secaucus, N.J.: Castle, n.d.

Long, A. L., ed. *Memoirs of Robert E. Lee.* Secaucus, N.J.: Blue and Grey Press, 1983.

Lord, Walter, ed. *The Freemantle Diary.* Boston: Little, Brown, 1954.

Maynard, Douglas, ed. "Vicksburg Diary: The Journal of Gabriel M. Killgore." *Civil War History* 10, no. 1 (March 1964): 33–53.

Meyers, Augustus. *Ten Years in the Ranks, U.S. Army.* New York: Stirling Press, 1914.

Montgomery, Frank A. *Reminiscences of a Mississippian in Peace and War.* Cincinnati: Robert Clarke Co. Press, 1901. An unreconstructed rebel, Montgomery served in the First Mississippi Cavalry.

Morgan, George W. "The Assault on Chickasaw Bluffs." In *Battles and Leaders of the Civil War.* Vol. 3. Secaucus, N.J.: Castle, n.d.

Moss, A. Hugh. *The Diary of A. Hugh Moss.* New York: Scribner Press, 1948. Moss served in a heavy artillery battery overlooking the Mississippi.

"News of the Day: The Operations Against Vicksburgh." *New York Times,* January 12, 1863, 4.

Newsome, Edmund. *Experience in the War of the Great Rebellion.* Carbondale, Ill.: Edmund Newsome Publisher, 1880. Newsome served in the Eighty-first Illinois.

Official Records of the Union and Confederate Navies in the War of the Rebellion. 30 vols. Washington, D.C.: U.S. Government Printing Office, 1894–1922.

Oldroyd, Osborn H. *A Soldier's Story of the Siege of Vicksburg.* Springfield, Ill.: n.p., 1885. An articulate Ohio sergeant's account.

Ordnance Manual for the Use of Officers of the Confederate States Army. 1863. Reprint, New York: Morningside Bookshop, 1976.

Osborn, George C., ed. "A Tennessean at the Siege of Vicksburg: The Diary of Samuel Alexander Ramsey Swan, May–July 1863." *Tennessee Historical Quarterly* 14, no. 4 (December 1955): 353–72. A fine source, reflecting the fluctuating spirits of the besieged.

Pasco, Samuel. *Private Pasco: A Civil War Dairy.* Oak Brook, Ill.: McAdams Multigraphics, 1990. Pasco was a soldier in the Third Florida Infantry.

Poole, Miriam, ed. " 'No Rest for the Wicked': Henry Seaman's Vicksburg Diary." *Civil War Times Illustrated* 22, no. 5 (September 1983): 18–31.

Porter, David D. *Incidents and Anecdotes of the Civil War.* New York: D. Appleton & Co., 1886.

Porter, Horace. *Campaigning with Grant.* New York: Century Co., 1897.

Quaife, M. M., ed. *Absalom Grimes: Confederate Mail Runner.* New Haven, Conn.: Yale University Press, 1926.

Reagan, John H. *Memoirs: With Special Reference to Secession and the Civil War.* New York: Neale Publishing Co., 1906.

Reed, Lida Lord. "A Woman's Experience During the Siege of Vicksburg." *Century* 61, no. 6 (April 1901): 922–28.

Ripley, Warren, ed. *Siege Train: The Journal of a Confederate Artilleryman in the Defense of Charleston.* Columbia: University of South Carolina Press, 1986. Details of how another Confederate bastion handled the artillery-versus-ship battle.

Roher, Walter A. "Confederate Generals—the View from Below." *Civil War Times Illustrated* 18, no. 4 (July 1979): 10–13.

Roth, Margaret Brobst, ed. *Well Mary: Civil War Letters of a Wisconsin Volunteer.* Madison: University of Wisconsin Press, 1960.

Rowland, Dunbar, ed. *Jefferson Davis Constitutionalist: His Letters, Papers and Speeches.* 10 vols. Jackson: Mississippi Department of Archives and History, 1923.

Russ, William A., Jr., ed. "The Vicksburg Campaign as Viewed by an Indiana Soldier." *Journal of Mississippi History* 19, no. 4 (October 1957): 263–69.

Russell, William Howard. *My Diary North and South.* New York: Harper, 1954.

Sanborn, John B. *The Crisis at Champion's Hill: The Decisive Battle of the Civil War.* St. Paul, Minn.: n.p., 1903.

Sanders, Mary Elizabeth, ed. "Letters of a Confederate soldier, 1862–1863." *Louisiana Historical Quarterly* 29, no. 4 (October 1946): 1229–40.

Selfridge, Thomas O. *Memoirs of Thomas O. Selfridge, Jr.* New York: G. P. Putnam's Sons, 1924. Selfridge commanded the *Cairo.*

Sherman, William Tecumseh. *Memoirs of General W. T. Sherman.* New York: Library of America, 1990.

Simms, L. Moody, Jr., ed. "A Louisiana Engineer at the Siege of Vicksburg: Letters of Henry Ginder." *Louisiana History* 8, no. 4 (Fall 1967): 371–78.

Simon, John Y., ed. *The Papers of Ulysses S. Grant.* 20 vols. Carbondale: Southern Illinois University Press, 1967–1995.

———. *The Personal Memoirs of Julia Dent Grant.* New York: G. P. Putnam's Sons, 1975.

Simon, John Y., and David L. Wilson, eds. *Ulysses S. Grant: Essays, Documents.* Carbondale: Southern Illinois University Press, 1981.

Smith, Calvin. " 'We Can Hold Our Ground': Calvin Smith's Diary." *Civil War Times Illustrated* 24, no. 2 (April 1985):24–31.

Stevenson, Benjamin Franklin. *Letters from the Army.* Cincinnati: Robert Clarke & Co., 1886. Stevenson served in the Union Twenty-second Kentucky.

Stillwell, Leander. *The Story of a Common Soldier of Army Life in the Civil War, 1861–1865.* Erie, Kans.: Franklin Hudson Publishing Co., 1920.

Taylor, F. Jay, ed. *Reluctant Rebel: The Secret Diary of Robert Patrick, 1861–1865.* Baton Rouge: Louisiana State University Press, 1959.

Taylor, Richard. *Destruction and Reconstruction.* 1879. Reprint, New York: Longmans, Green & Co., 1955.

Thompson, William Candace. "From Shiloh to Port Gibson." *Civil War Times Illustrated* 3, no. 6 (October 1964): 20–25.

Thorndike, Rachel Sherman, ed. *The Sherman Letters.* New York: Charles Scribner's Sons, 1894.

Urquhart, Kenneth, ed. *Vicksburg: Southern City Under Siege.* New Orleans: Historic New Orleans Collection, 1980. A Confederate parson's long letter to his wife detailing life inside the besieged city.

Villard, Henry. *Memoirs of Henry Villard.* 2 vols. Boston: Houghton Mifflin Co., 1904.

Walke, Henry. *Naval Scenes and Reminiscences of the Civil War in the United States.* New York: F. R. Reed & Co., 1877. Walke commanded the *Carondelet* in the battle against the *Arkansas.* He had some explaining to do, and devotes many pages accordingly.

War of the Rebellion: Official Records of the Union and Confederate Armies. 128 parts in 70 vols. Washington, D.C.: U.S. Government Printing Office, 1880–1901.

Watson, William. *Letters of a Civil War Surgeon.* West Lafayette, Ind.: Purdue Research Foundation, 1961.

Welles, Gideon. *Diary of Gideon Welles.* Vol. 1 Boston: Houghton Mifflin Co., 1911.

Wiley, Bell Irvin. "The Confederate Letters of Warren G. Magee." *Journal of Mississippi History* 5, no. 4 (October 1943): 204–13.

Wiley, Bell Irvin, ed. *"This Infernal War": The Confederate Letters of Sergeant Edwin H. Fay.* Austin: University of Texas Press, 1958.

Wilson, James Grant, ed. *General Grant's Letters to a Friend, 1861-1880.* New York: T. Y. Crowell & Co., 1897.

Wilson, James Harrison. *Under the Old Flag.* 2 vols. New York: D. Appleton & Co., 1912. Volume 1 provides a fascinating, gossipy account by an intelligent, insufferably vain man who boasts that Grant merely followed his strategy throughout the campaign, don't you know.

W. L. F. "The Siege of Vicksburgh." *New York Times,* March 12, 1863, 8.

Confederate Veteran Articles

Campbell, W. A. "Humors of the March." *Confederate Veteran* 1, no. 7 (July 1893): 216.

Carson, John. "Capture of the Indianola." *Confederate Veteran* 32, no. 10 (October 1924): 380–83.

Dinkins, James. "Witticisms of Soldiers." *Confederate Veteran* 3, no. 9 (September 1895): 270–71.

Editor. "The Brave and True Capt. S. J. Ridley." *Confederate Veteran* 2, no. 11 (November 1894): 343.

———. "Concerning the Siege of Vicksburg." *Confederate Veteran* 2, no. 10 (October 1894): 295.

———. "Vicksburg: Some New History in the Experience of Gen. Francis A. Shoup." *Confederate Veteran* 2, no. 6 (June 1894): 172–74.

———. "Words of a Veteran About Vicksburg." *Confederate Veteran* 2, no. 10 (October 1894): 312.

Eggleston, E. T. "Scenes Where General Tilghman Was Killed." *Confederate Veteran* 1, no. 10 (October 1893): 296.

Flatau, L. S. "A Great Naval Battle." *Confederate Veteran* 25, no. 10 (October 1917): 458–59.

Foster, Tom J. "Reminiscences of Vicksburg." *Confederate Veteran* 2, no. 8 (August 1894): 244.

FWM. "Career and Fate of Gen. Lloyd Tilghman." *Confederate Veteran* 1, no. 9 (January 1893): 274–75.

Gaskell, John E. "Surrendered at Vicksburg." *Confederate Veteran* 33, no. 8 (August 1925): 286.

———. "When Vicksburg Was Surrendered." *Confederate Veteran* 35, no. 10 (October 1927): 372–73.

Harewell, J. D. "Flags Captured at Vicksburg." *Confederate Veteran* 29, no. 2 (February 1921): 64. Harewell was S. D. Lee's secretary.

———. "In and Around Vicksburg." *Confederate Veteran* 30, no. 9 (September 1922): 333–34.

———. "Why Did He Eat Mule Meat?" *Confederate Veteran* 29, no. 9 (September 1921): 357.

Lambert, R. A. "In the Mississippi Campaigns." *Confederate Veteran* 37, no. 8 (August 1929): 292–93.

Manahan, T. A. Letter to editor. *Confederate Veteran* 2, no. 8 (August 1894):227.

Matthews, D. M. "A Reminiscence of Champion Hill." *Confederate Veteran* 21, no. 5 (May 1913): 208.

M'Neilly, James H. "Humors of Soldier Life." *Confederate Veteran* 1, no. 10 (October 1893): 307–10.

———. "Under Fire at Port Hudson." *Confederate Veteran* 27, no. 9 (September 1919): 336–39.

Payne, James E. "General Pemberton and Vicksburg." *Confederate Veteran* 36, no. 7 (July 1928): 247.

———. "Missouri Troops in the Vicksburg Campaign." Parts 1 and 2. *Confederate Veteran* 36, no. 8 (August 1928): 302–303; no. 9, (September 1928): 340–41.

Reynolds, A. H. "Vivid Experiences at Champion Hill, Miss.," *Confederate Veteran* 28, no. 1 (January 1910): 21–22.

Richmond, Marion B. "The Siege of Vicksburg." *Confederate Veteran* 37, no. 4 (April 1929): 139–41.

Ritter, William L. "The Battle of Jackson." *Confederate Veteran* 28, no. 12 (December 1920): 448–49.

Sparks, Jesse W. "Pemberton's Surrender of Vicksburg." *Confederate Veteran* 2, no. 7 (July 1894): 202–3.

Sproul, T.B. Letter to editor. *Confederate Veteran* 2, no. 7 (July 1894): 199.

Sulivane, Clement. "The Arkansas at Vicksburg in 1862." *Confederate Veteran* 30, no. 11 (November 1917): 490–91.

Synnamon, James. "A Veteran with Many Wounds." *Confederate Veteran* 21, no. 12 (December 1913): 582.

Tunnard, Will H. "Running the Mississippi Blockade." *Confederate Veteran* 24, no. 1 (January 1916): 27–28.

Weidemeyer, J. M. "Missourians East of the Mississippi." *Confederate Veteran* 18, no. 11 (November 1910): 502.

MOLLUS PAPERS

Military Order of the Loyal Legion of the United States (MOLLUS) Papers. Reprint, Wilmington, N.C.: Broadfoot Publishing Co., 1991–1995. References are to this edition unless otherwise specified.

Brown, George W. "Service in the Mississippi Squadron, and Its Connection with the Siege and Capture of Vicksburg." New York, vol. 1, 303–13.

Callender, Eliot. "What a Boy Saw on the Mississippi." Illinois, vol. 1, 51–67. Chicago: A. C. McClurg & Co., 1891.

Coleman, S. B. "A July Morning with the Rebel Ram 'Arkansas.'" Michigan, vol. 1, 315–25.

Force, Manning F. "Personal Recollections of the Vicksburg Campaign." Ohio, vol. 1, 293–309.

Furness, William E. "The Negro as a Soldier." Illinois, vol. 2, 457–487. Chicago: A. C. McClurg & Co., 1894.

Grant, Frederick D. "A Boy's Experience at Vicksburg." New York, vol. 3, 86–100. A glimpse of U. S. Grant the father during his greatest campaign.

Hains, Peter C. "An Incident of the Battle of Vicksburg." District of Columbia, vol. 1, 65–71.

Hickenlooper, Andrew. "Our Volunteer Engineers." Ohio, vol. 3, 301–18. Cincinnati: Robert Clarke & Co., 1890.

Hicks, Henry G. "The Campaign and Capture of Vicksburg." Minnesota, vol. 6, 82–107.

Howard, Richard L. "The Vicksburg Campaign." Maine, vol. 2, 28–40.

Jenney, William L. B. "Personal Recollections of Vicksburg." Illinois, vol. 3, 247–65.

Longley, Charles L. "Champion's Hill." Iowa, vol. 1, 208–14.

Meacham, Justin W. "Military and Naval Operations on the Mississippi." Wisconsin, vol. 4, 387–95.

Michael, W. C. "How the Mississippi Was Opened." Nebraska, vol. 1, 34–58.

Strong, William E. "The Campaign Against Vicksburg." Illinois, vol. 2, 313–54. Chicago: A. C. McClurg & Co., 1894. Strong served on McPherson's staff.

Wilkin, Jacob W. "Vicksburg." Illinois, vol. 4, 215–37.

Williams, E. Cort. "The Cruise of the 'Black Terror.'" Ohio, vol. 3, 144–65. Cincinnati: Robert Clarke & Co., 1890.

Williams, T. J. "The Battle of Champion's Hill." Ohio, vol. 5, 204–12.

Southern Historical Society Papers

Brent, Major Joseph L. "Capture of the Indianola." *Southern Historical Society Papers* 1, no. 2 (February 1876): 94–99.

Brown, A. F. "Van Dorn's Operations in Northern Mississippi." *Southern Historical Society Papers* 5, no. 4 (October 1878): 154–61.

Garland, R. R. "Report of Colonel R. R. Garland, April 1, 1863." *Southern Historical Society Papers* 22 (1894): 10–13.

Gift, George W. "The Story of the Arkansas." Parts 1–4. *Southern Historical Society Papers* 12, nos. 1–2 (January–February 1884): 48–54: no. 3 (March 1884): 115–19; no. 4 (April 1884): 163–70; no. 5 (May 1884): 205–12. Gift was a lieutenant aboard the *Arkansas*.

Hogane, J. T. "Reminiscences of the Siege of Vicksburg." Parts 1 and 2. *Southern Historical Society Papers* 11, nos. 4–5 (April–May 1883): 223–27; no. 7 (July 1883): 291–97.

Jones, Joseph. "The Medical History of the Confederate States." *Southern Historical Society Papers* 20 (1892): 109–66.

Memminger, R. W. "The Surrender of Vicksburg—A Defense of General Pemberton." *Southern Historical Society Papers* 12, nos. 7–9 (July–September 1884): 352–60.

Pemberton, John C. "Terms of Surrender at Vicksburg—General Pemberton Replies to General Badeau." *Southern Historical Society Papers* 10, no. 6–9 (August–September 1882): 406–15.

Read, C. W. "Reminiscences of the Confederate States Navy." *Southern Historical Society Papers* 1, no. 5 (May 1876): 331–62.

Ritter, William L. "Sketch of the Third Maryland Artillery." Parts 1 and 2. *Southern Historical Society Papers* 10, no. 7 (July 1883): 328–32; nos. 8–9 (August–September 1883): 392–401.

Secondary

Adams, Michael C. *Our Masters the Rebels: Speculations on Union Military Failure in the East, 1861–1865.* Cambridge, Mass.: Harvard University Press, 1978.

Anders, Leslie. *The Twenty-First Missouri: From Home Guard to Union Regiment.* Westport, Conn.: Greenwood Press, 1975.

Arnold, James R. *The Armies of U. S. Grant.* London: Arms & Armour Press, 1995.

———. *Chickamauga 1863: The River of Death.* London: Osprey Publishing, 1992.

Badeau, Adam. *Military History of General U. S. Grant.* 3 vols. New York: D. Appleton & Co., 1885. Badeau did not join Grant's staff until 1864. His opinions about Vicksburg are interesting, but the "facts" he cites are unreliable.

Ballard, Michael B. *Pemberton: A Biography.* Jackson: University Press of Mississippi, 1991. Unbiased, well-documented.

Bauer, Dan. "Who Knows the Truth About the Big Bender?" *Civil War Times Illustrated* 27, no. 8 (December 1988): 36–43.

Bearss, Edwin C. *The Campaign for Vicksburg.* 3 vols. Dayton, Ohio: Morningside House, 1986.

———. "Grand Gulf's Role in the Civil War." *Civil War History* 5, no. 1 (March 1959): 5–29.

———. *Hardluck Ironclad: The Sinking and Salvage of the Cairo.* Baton Rouge: Louisiana State University Press, 1966.

———. "Sherman's Demonstration Against Snyder's Bluff." *Journal of Mississippi History* 27, no. 2 (May 1965): 168–86.

Bettersworth, John K., ed. *Mississippi in the Confederacy As They Saw It.* Baton Rouge: Louisiana State University Press, 1961.

Black, Robert C. *The Railroads of the Confederacy.* Chapel Hill: University of North Carolina Press, 1952.

Boatner, Mark Mayo, III. *The Civil War Dictionary.* New York: David McKay Co., 1959.

Brown, D. Alexander. *Grierson's Raid.* Urbana: University of Illinois Press, 1962. A well-researched, entertaining, day-by-day account.

Carter, Samuel, III. *The Final Fortress: The Campaign for Vicksburg, 1862–1863.* New York: St. Martin's Press, 1980.

Catton, Bruce. *Grant Moves South.* Boston: Little, Brown, 1960.

———. *Grant Takes Command.* Boston: Little, Brown, 1968.

Coggins, Jack. *Arms and Equipment of the Civil War.* New York: Doubleday & Co., 1962.

Connelly, Thomas Lawrence, and Archer Jones. *The Politics of Command: Factions and Ideas in Confederate Strategy.* Baton Rouge: Louisiana State University Press, 1973.

Coulter, E. Merton. "Commercial Intercourse with the Confederacy in the Mississippi Valley, 1861–1865." *Mississippi Valley Historical Review* 5, no. 4 (March 1919): 377–95.

Daniel, Larry J. "Bruinsburg: Missed Opportunity or Postwar Rhetoric?" *Civil War History* 32, no. 3 (September 1986): 256–67.

Foote, Shelby. *The Civil War: A Narrative.* Vol. 1. New York: Random House, 1963.

Foster, G. Allen. *The Eyes and Ears of the Civil War.* New York: Criterion Books, 1963.

Fox, William F. *Regimental Losses in the American Civil War.* 1898. Reprint, Dayton, Ohio: Morningside House, 1974.

Frank, Joseph Allan, and George A. Reaves. *"Seeing the Elephant": Raw Recruits at the Battle of Shiloh.* New York: Greenwood Press, 1989.

Fuller, J. F. C. *The Generalship of Ulysses S. Grant.* London: John Murray, 1929.

Gallagher, Gary W. "Lee's Army Has Not Lost Any of Its Prestige." In *The Third Day at Gettysburg and Beyond.* Edited by Gary W. Gallagher. Chapel Hill: University of North Carolina Press, 1994.

Gault, W. P. *Ohio at Vicksburg.* Columbus, Ohio: Ohio Vicksburg Battlefield Commission, 1906.

Glover, Edwin A. *Bucktailed Wildcats: A Regiment of Civil War Volunteers*. New York: Thomas Yoseloff, 1960.

Goff, Richard D. *Confederate Supply*. Durham, N.C.: Duke University Press, 1969.

Gosnell, H. Allen. *Guns on the Western Waters: The Story of River Gunboats in the Civil War*. Baton Rouge: Louisiana State University Press, 1949.

Greene, Francis Vinton. *The Mississippi*. 1882. Reprint, Wilmington, N.C.: Broadfoot Publishing Co., 1989. An objective study first published as part of Scribner's *Campaigns of the Civil War* series.

Griffith, Paddy. *Battle Tactics of the Civil War*. New Haven, Conn.: Yale University Press, 1989.

Hagerman, Edward. *The American Civil War and the Origins of Modern Warfare*. Bloomington: Indiana University Press, 1988.

Hattaway, Herman. *General Stephen D. Lee*. Jackson: University Press of Mississippi, 1976.

Hattaway, Herman, and Archer Jones. *How the North Won*. Urbana: University of Illinois Press, 1983. Thought-provoking analysis.

Hays, E. Z., ed. *History of the Thirty-Second Regiment, Ohio Veteran Volunteer Infantry*. Columbus, Ohio: Cort & Evans, 1896.

Herold, J. Christopher. *The Mind of Napoleon*. New York: Columbia University Press, 1955.

Hewitt, Lawrence L. *Port Hudson: Confederate Bastion on the Mississippi*. Baton Rouge: Louisiana State University Press, 1987.

History of the Forty-sixth Regiment, Indiana Volunteer Infantry. Logansport, Ind.: Wilson, Humphreys & Co., 1888.

Hoehling, A. A., ed. *Vicksburg: Forty-seven Days of Siege*. Englewood Cliffs, N.J.: Prentice-Hall, 1969. A nice compilation of firsthand accounts.

Hooker, Charles E. *Confederate Military History Extended Edition, Volume IX, Mississippi*. 1899. Reprint, Wilmington, N.C.: Broadfoot Publishing Co., 1987.

Huffstodt, Jim. *Hard Dying Men: The Story of General W. H. L. Wallace, General T. E. G. Ransom, and Their "Old Eleventh" Illinois Infantry in the American Civil War (1861–1865)*. Bowie, Md.: Heritage Books, 1991.

Jones, Archer. "Tennessee and Mississippi, Joe Johnston's Strategic Problem." *Tennessee Historical Quarterly* 18, no. 2 (June 1959): 134–47.

———. "The Vicksburg Campaign." *Journal of Mississippi History* 29, no. 1 (February 1967): 12–27.

Kelly, William Milner. "A History of the Thirtieth Alabama Volunteers." *Alabama Historical Quarterly* 9, no. 1 (Spring 1947): 115–89.

Lang, George, Raymond L. Collins, and Gerard F. White, eds. *Medal of Honor Recipients, 1863–1994*. New York: Facts on File, 1995. The Medal of Honor was the only military award for valor issued during the war. A total of 1,520 men received it.

Lewis, Lloyd. *Captain Sam Grant*. Boston: Little, Brown, 1950.

Lonn, Ella. *Foreigners in the Confederacy*. Chapel Hill: University of North Carolina Press, 1940.

———. *Foreigners in the Union Army and Navy*. Baton Rouge: Louisiana State University Press, 1951.

Lord, Francis A. *They Fought for the Union*. New York: Bonanza Books, 1960.

Mahan, Alfred Thayer. *The Gulf and Inland Waters*. New York: Charles Scribner's Sons, 1883.

Markham, Jerald H. *The Botetourt Artillery*. Lynchburg, Va.: H. E. Howard, 1986.

Martin, David. *The Vicksburg Campaign: April 1862–July 1863*. Conshohocken, Pa.: Combined Books, 1990.

Mason, F. H. *The Forty-Second Ohio Infantry*. Cleveland: Cobb, Andrew & Co., 1876.

McPherson, James M. *Drawn with the Sword: Reflections on the American Civil War*. New York: Oxford University Press, 1996.

Miers, Earl S. *The Web of Victory: Grant at Vicksburg*. Baton Rouge: Louisiana State University Press, 1984.

Military Analysis of the Civil War: An Anthology by the Editors of Military Affairs. Millwood, N.Y.: KTO Press, 1977.

Morris, W. S., et al. *Thirty-First Regiment Illinois Volunteers*. Herrin, Ill.: Crossfire Press, 1991.

Mullins, Michael A. *The Fremont Rifles: A History of the Thirty-Seventh Illinois Veteran Volunteer Infantry*. Wilmington, N.C.: Broadfoot Publishing Co., 1990.

Oates, Stephen B. *Confederate Cavalry West of the River*. Austin: University of Texas Press, 1961.

Parks, Joseph Howard. *General Edmund Kirby Smith, C.S.A.* Baton Rouge: Louisiana State University Press, 1954.

Pemberton, John C. *Pemberton: Defender of Vicksburg*. Chapel Hill: University of North Carolina Press, 1942. A grandson's defense.

Pollard, Edwin A. *The Lost Cause*. New York: E. B. Treat Co., 1866. Entertaining, highly opinionated "history" written while events were fresh in everyone's memories.

Ramsdell, Charles W. *Behind the Lines in the Southern Confederacy*. Baton Rouge: Louisiana State University Press, 1944. A fine, insightful book.

Reed, Rowena. *Combined Operations in the Civil War*. Annapolis, Md.: Naval Institute Press, 1978. Opinionated and challenging.

Soley, James Russell. "Naval Operations in the Vicksburg Campaign." In *Battles and Leaders of the Civil War*. Vol. 3. Secaucus, N.J.: Castle, n.d.

Starr, Stephen Z. *The Union Cavalry in the Civil War*. 2 vols. Baton Rouge: Louisiana State University Press, 1985.

Still, William N., Jr. *Iron Afloat: The Story of the Confederate Armorclads*. Columbia: University of South Carolina Press, 1985.

Swinton, William. *The Twelve Decisive Battles of the War: A History of the Eastern and Western Campaigns*. New York: Dick & Fitzgerald, 1867.

Trimble, Harvey M., ed. *History of the Ninety-Third Regiment Illinois Volunteer Infantry*. Chicago: Blakely Printing Co., 1898.

Tucker, Phillip Thomas. *The South's Finest: The First Missouri Confederate Brigade from Pea Ridge to Vicksburg*. Shippensburg, Pa.: White Mane Publishing, 1993. Hyperbolic when no exaggeration is needed; some historical inaccuracies, but also some fine manuscript research.

U.S. Military Academy. *The West Point Atlas of American Wars: Volume I, 1689–1900*. New York: Frederick A. Praeger Publishers, 1959.

Warner, Ezra J. *Generals in Gray: Lives of the Confederate Commanders.* Baton Rouge: Louisiana State University Press, 1959.

West, Richard S., Jr. *The Second Admiral: A Life of David Dixon Porter.* New York: Coward-McCann, 1937.

Wideman, John C. *The Sinking of the USS Cairo.* Jackson: University Press of Mississippi, 1993.

Williams, Kenneth P. *Lincoln Finds a General: A Military Study of the Civil War.* Vol. 4. New York: Macmillan, 1956.

Winschel, Terrence J. "Chickasaw Bayou: A Battlefield Guide." Vicksburg National Military Park pamphlet. N.p., n.d.

Wolseley, General Viscount. "An English View of the Civil War, Part V." *North American Review* 149, no. 395 (October 1889): 446–459.

Woodworth, Steven E. *Jefferson Davis and His Generals: The Failure of Confederate Command in the West.* Lawrence: University Press of Kansas, 1990 .

Index

Numbers in *italics* indicate illustrated references.

25786